# THE CAMBRIDGE COMPANION TO
## BRITISH ROMANTICISM

### SECOND EDITION

This new edition of *The Cambridge Companion to British Romanticism* has been fully revised and updated and includes two wholly new essays, one on recent developments in the field and one on the rapidly expanding publishing industry of this period. It also features a comprehensive chronology and a fully up-to-date guide to further reading. For the past decade and more the *Companion* has been a much-admired and widely used account of the phenomenon of British Romanticism that has inspired students to look at Romantic literature from a variety of critical angles and approaches. In this new incarnation, the volume will continue to be a standard guide for students of Romantic literature and its contexts.

STUART CURRAN is Professor Emeritus of English at the University of Pennsylvania.

*A complete list of books in the series is at the back of this book*

# THE CAMBRIDGE COMPANION TO

# BRITISH ROMANTICISM

EDITED BY
STUART CURRAN

CAMBRIDGE
UNIVERSITY PRESS

# CAMBRIDGE
## UNIVERSITY PRESS

University Printing House, Cambridge CB2 8BS, United Kingdom

Cambridge University Press is part of the University of Cambridge.

It furthers the University's mission by disseminating knowledge in the pursuit of education, learning and research at the highest international levels of excellence.

www.cambridge.org
Information on this title: www.cambridge.org/9780521136051

© Cambridge University Press 1993, 2010

First published 1993
Second edition 2010
3rd printing 2013

*A catalogue record for this publication is available from the British Library*

*Library of Congress Cataloguing in Publication data*
The Cambridge companion to British romanticism / edited by Stuart Curran. – 2nd ed.
p.   cm. – (Cambridge companions to literature)
Includes bibliographical references and index.
ISBN 978-0-521-19924-7 – ISBN 978-0-521-13605-1
1. English literature–19th century–History and criticism–Handbooks,
manuals, etc.   2. English literature–18th century–History and criticism–Handbooks,
manuals, etc.   3. Romanticism–Great Britain–Handbooks, manuals, etc.
I. Curran, Stuart.   II. Title.   III. Series.
PR457.C33 2010
820.9ʹ145–dc22        2010014636

ISBN 978-0-521-19924-7 Hardback
ISBN 978-0-521-13605-1 Paperback

# CONTENTS

# ILLUSTRATIONS

# CONTRIBUTORS

STEPHEN C. BEHRENDT, University of Nebraska

MARSHALL BROWN, University of Washington

MARILYN BUTLER, University of Oxford

STUART CURRAN, University of Pennsylvania

P. M. S. DAWSON, University of Manchester

MORRIS EAVES, University of Rochester

JERROLD E. HOGLE, University of Arizona

WILLIAM KEACH, Brown University

GARY KELLY, University of Alberta

PETER THORSLEV, University of California, Los Angeles

The forty years in Great Britain from 1785 to 1825, the period generally construed as the age of Romanticism, saw a crucial transition between an Enlightenment world view and the values of modern, industrial society. So different to a contemporary apprehension are those two cultures that we might resort to Shelley's claims for Dante, as a "bridge thrown over the stream of time, which unites the modern and ancient world," to characterize this age that spanned them. It was a turbulent period at whose center lies the longest experience of warfare – twenty-two years – in modern history, warfare conducted on a world scale. Although the counterrevolutionary and Napoleonic wars were all too real, leaving Europe exhausted and (except for Great Britain) bankrupt, they might stand as well as a metaphor for an age of conflict, stress, and tumult.

There was a day when scholars of the literature of this period sought for safe categories to resolve its instabilities, even when, like Arthur Lovejoy, they had to resort to a patent stretching of terms that would allow for conjoining "Romanticisms" rather than rely on a singular definition for the age. But as the currents of traditional literary criticism and scholarship in recent years have drawn increasing sophistication from new philosophical and historical inquiries, the problem of contemporary definition has been exacerbated – or perhaps rendered obsolete. The convenient labels by which critics sought to untrouble the roiling waters of actuality have grown more and more irrelevant to the true historical situation, or (which is to say much the same thing) they have seemed rather a falsification than an explanation of the nature of the age.

The present volume affords an opportunity not for a consolidation of outmoded categories but for a reassessment, a rethinking, of essential terms. If the aesthetics and history of the time reveal a similar preoccupation with process rather than completion, with skeptical explorations over dogmatic assurances, of multivalent instead with unitary modes of thought, then it follows that a criticism representing the main concerns of the age needs to be conducted along dialectical lines that honor rather than resolve into simple formulas the tensions responsible for its dynamic energies. This volume is a collaborative effort of an international panel of distinguished scholars who have sought to give English-speaking students, whatever their culture or level of training, coherent access to the historical roots, the intellectual ferment, and the cultural range of the Romantic age without sacrificing its diversity and even its salutary contradictions. At the intersection of competing philosophical traditions, of political and class divisions, of emergent gender distinctions, of high and low and sacred and profane cultures, of battles of the books (prose and poetry, fiction and history), and contested claims among the arts, the literature of this age – the incomparable literature of Romanticism – reflects the tensions that attend and often empower its creation. The authors recognize that this book will most often be turned to by students of the six great poets who dominate the modern canon (Blake, Wordsworth, Coleridge, Byron, Shelley, and Keats); but they are also well aware that in recent decades newer voices, novelists and women authors particularly, have increasingly resonated in our classrooms as in our historical perspective. By giving space to those other voices the volume at once testifies to the literary riches of the age and encourages readers to explore them further on their own. In this second edition many essays have been revised to accord with new criticism and scholarship, and we add an introductory essay by Jerrold Hogle that establishes the trajectory of those recent critical shifts in cultural apprehension, as well as another, by Stephen Behrendt, that examines the many and diverse imperatives relating to class, gender, and regional values that drove the vibrant publishing industry in this period.

1749    b. Charlotte Turner, later Smith (May 4)

1752    b. Frances Burney (June 17)

1756    b. William Godwin (March 3)

1757    b. William Blake (November 28)

1758    b. Mary Darby, later Robinson (November 27)

1759    b. Robert Burns (January 25); b. Mary Wollstonecraft (April 27)

1760    George III crowned King of England

1762    b. Helen Maria Williams

1764    b. Ann Ward, later Radcliffe (July 9)

1768    Royal Society founded; b. Maria Edgeworth (January 1)

1770    b. Ludwig van Beethoven (December 16); b. Georg Friedrich Hegel (August 27); b. James Hogg (bap. December 9); b. William Wordsworth (April 7)

1771    b. Walter Scott (August 15)

1772    b. Samuel Taylor Coleridge (October 21); b. David Ricardo (April 19)

1773    Muzio Clementi settles in London; b. Francis Jeffrey (October 23)

1774    b. Robert Southey (August 15)
        Goethe, *The Sorrows of Young Werther*

1775    b. Jane Austen (December 16); b. Charles Lamb (February 10); b. Walter Savage Landor (January 30); b. Matthew G. ("Monk") Lewis (July 9); b. Joseph Mallord William Turner (April 23)

1776    Declaration of Independence of American colonies; b. John Constable (June 11); b. E. T. A. Hoffman (January 24); b. Sydney Owenson, later Lady Morgan (December 25); d. David Hume Adam Smith, *The Wealth of Nations*

1777    b. Thomas Campbell (July 27)

1778    b. Humphrey Davy (December 17); b. William Hazlitt (April 10); d. Jean Jacques Rousseau

1779    b. Thomas Moore (May 28); d. David Garrick

1781    Surrender of General Cornwallis at Yorktown, Virginia; Herschel discovers the planet Uranus
Samuel Johnson, completion of *Lives of the English Poets*
Immanuel Kant, *Critique of Pure Reason*
Thomas Warton, final (third) volume, *A History of English Poetry*

1782    James Watt patents steam engine capable of motive power
Frances Burney, *Cecilia*

1783    William Pitt Prime Minister; Peace of Versailles recognizes independence of the United States; b. Marie Henri Beyle (Stendhal) (January 23); b. Washington Irving (April 3); b. Jane Taylor (September 23)
William Blake, *Poetical Sketches*
Hannah Cowley, *A Bold Stroke for a Husband*
George Crabbe, *The Village*
Catherine Macauley, final (eighth) volume, *A History of England, from the Accession of James I to That of the Brunswick Line*

1784    b. James Henry Leigh Hunt (October 19); d. Samuel Johnson
Charlotte Smith, *Elegiac Sonnets, and Other Essays*

1785    b. Thomas De Quincey (August 15); b. Alessandro Manzoni (March 7); b. Thomas Love Peacock (October 18)
William Cowper, *The Task*

1786    b. Carl Maria von Weber (November 18); d. Frederick the Great
Robert Burns, *Poems, Chiefly in the Scottish Dialect*
Helen Maria Williams, *Poems, in Two Volumes*

1787    Constitution of the United States of America ratified; b. Mary Russell Mitford (December 16)

1788    Mental illness of George III; penal colony founded at Botany Bay, Australia; Warren Hastings, Governor General of India, impeached in the House of Commons; b. George Gordon Byron, later Lord Byron (January 22); d. Thomas Gainsborough
Jeremy Bentham, *An Introduction to the Principles of Morals and Legislation*
Edward Gibbon, final volume of *The Decline and Fall of the Roman Empire*
Immanuel Kant, *Critique of Practical Reason*
Charlotte Smith, *Emmeline, or, The Orphan of the Castle*

1789    Convening of the Three Estates in France; storming of the Bastille (July 14); National Assembly adopts the Declaration of the Rights of Man (August); b. James Fenimore Cooper (September 15)
William Blake, *The Book of Thel, Songs of Innocence*
Erasmus Darwin, *The Loves of the Plants*

Charlotte Smith, *Ethelinde, or The Recluse of the Lake*

1790    b. Alphonse Lamartine (October 21); d. Adam Smith; d. Thomas Warton, Henry James Pye named to succeed him as poet laureate
Edmund Burke, *Reflections on the Revolution in France*
Immanuel Kant, *Critique of Judgement*
Mary Wollstonecraft, *A Vindication of the Rights of Man*

1791    Joseph Priestley's house and library burned by "Church-and-King" mob in Birmingham; Louis XVI, attempting to flee France, is captured; Wordsworth travels to France; Haydn in London at invitation of Johann Peter Salomon (returns 1793–4); b. Michael Faraday (September 22); d. Wolfgang Amadeus Mozart
Anna Laetitia Barbauld, *An Epistle to William Wilberforce*
James Boswell, *Life of Johnson*
Isaac D'Israeli, *Curiosities of Literature*, vol. I
Elizabeth Inchbald, *A Simple Story*
James Mackintosh, *Vindiciæ Gallicæ*
Thomas Paine, *The Rights of Man*, part I
Ann Radcliffe, *The Romance of the Forest*
Charlotte Smith, *Celestina*

1792    Austro-Prussian invasion of France; royal family imprisoned; September Massacres; abolition of French monarchy, France declares itself a republic; British victorious over Tipu Sultan in Mysore, India; b. Percy Bysshe Shelley (August 4); d. Joshua Reynolds
Robert Anderson, *Works of the British Poets* (–1795, 13 volumes)
Thomas Holcroft, *Anna St. Ives*
Mary Robinson, *Vancenza, or, The Dangers of Credulity*
Samuel Rogers, *The Pleasures of Memory*
Charlotte Smith, *Desmond*
Helen Maria Williams, first volumes of *Letters from France*
Mary Wollstonecraft, *A Vindication of the Rights of Woman*

1793    Execution of Louis XVI; England and France declare war; Jean-Paul Marat assassinated; Robespierre becomes director of the Committee of Public Safety, "Terror" in Paris; execution of Marie Antoinette; treason trials against "Jacobins" in Scotland; Lorenzo Da Ponte appointed Poet of King's Opera, London; b. John Clare (July 13); b. Felicia Dorothea Browne (later Hemans) (September 23)
William Blake, *America, Marriage of Heaven and Hell, Visions of the Daughters of Albion*
William Godwin, *An Enquiry Concerning Political Justice*

Hannah More, *Village Politics*
Charlotte Smith, *The Emigrants*, *The Old Manor House*
Dugald Stewart, *Outlines of Moral Philosophy*
William Wordsworth, *Descriptive Sketches*, *An Evening Walk*

1794　Execution of Danton; arrest and execution of Robespierre; forma-
tion of French Directorate; *habeas corpus* suspended in England;
state trials of leaders of London Corresponding Society end in
acquittal; d. Edward Gibbon
William Blake, *The First Book of Urizen, Europe, Songs of Innocence
and of Experience*
Johann　Gottlieb　Fichte,　*Whole　Theory　of　Knowledge*
(*Wissenschaftslehre*)
William Godwin, *Things as They Are, or the Adventures of Caleb
Williams*
Thomas Paine, *The Age of Reason*, part I
William Paley, *Evidences of Christianity*
Ann Radcliffe, *The Mysteries of Udolpho*
Mary Robinson, *Poems*
Charlotte Smith, *The Wanderings of Warwick*, *The Banished Man*

1795　Two Acts, prohibiting seditious meetings and treasonable con-
spiracy; Warren Hastings acquitted; England seizes Dutch posses-
sions – Cape of Good Hope, Ceylon, and Indonesian islands; army
of Napoleon in Italy; b. Thomas Carlyle (December 4); b. John
Keats (October 31); d. James Boswell
William Blake, *The Book of Ahania*, *The Book of Los*, *The Song of
Los*
Hannah More, first *Cheap Repository Tracts*
Thomas Paine, *The Age of Reason*, part II
Charlotte Smith, *Montalbert*

1796　Spain changes allegiance, aligning with France against England;
France threatens invasion; first exhibition of oil paintings by J. M.
W. Turner; d. Robert Burns
*Monthly Magazine* founded
Robert Bage, *Hermsprong*
Edmund Burke, *Letter to a Noble Lord*, *Letters on a Regicide Peace*
Frances Burney, *Camilla*
Samuel Taylor Coleridge, *Poems on Various Subjects*
Mary Hays, *Memoirs of Emma Courtney*
Elizabeth Inchbald, *Nature and Art*
Matthew G. Lewis, *The Monk, a Romance*

Mary Robinson, *Sappho and Phaon: In a Series of Legitimate Sonnets*

Robert Southey, *Joan of Arc*

Charlotte Smith, *Marchmont*

1797 British naval mutinies; Franco-Austrian Treaty of Campo Formio establishes Ligurian and Cisalpine Republics but cedes historic Republic of Venice to Austria; b. Franz Schubert (January 31); d. Edmund Burke; b. Mary Wollstonecraft Godwin (August 30); d. Mary Wollstonecraft (September 10)

*Anti-Jacobin Review* founded

Samuel Taylor Coleridge, *Poems*, second edition

Harriet, with Sophia, Lee, *The Canterbury Tales* (–1805)

Ann Radcliffe, *The Italian*

Mary Robinson, *Walsingham, or, The Pupil of Nature*

Charlotte Smith, *Elegiac Sonnets, and Other Poems*, 2 volumes

Robert Southey, *Poems*, vol. 1

Jane West, *A Gossip's Story*

1798 Wolf Tone rebellion in Ireland put down; France invades Egypt, fleet destroyed by Nelson in Battle of the Nile; b. Giacomo Leopardi (June 29)

Joanna Baillie, *A Series of Plays ... [on] the Passions*, vol. 1

Samuel Taylor Coleridge, *Fears in Solitude ... [with] France, an Ode; and Frost at Midnight*

Maria and Richard Lovell Edgeworth, *Practical Education*

William Godwin, *Memoirs of the Author of A Vindication of the Rights of Woman*; ed. *Posthumous Works by [Mary Wollstonecraft]*

Elizabeth Inchbald (after Kotzebue), *Lovers' Vows*

Walter Savage Landor, *Gebir*

Matthew G. Lewis, *The Castle Spectre*

Thomas Malthus, *Principles of Population*

Mary Robinson, *Thoughts on the Condition of Women, and on the Injustice of Mental Subordination*

Charlotte Smith, *The Young Philosopher*

William Wordsworth and Samuel Taylor Coleridge, *Lyrical Ballads*

1799 Coup d'état of Eighteenth Brumaire, Napoleon becomes First Consul; London Corresponding Society banned; Six Acts against radical activities; publisher Joseph Johnson imprisoned on charge of seditious libel; b. Honoré de Balzac (May 20); b. Eugéne Delacroix (April 26); b. Aleksandr Pushkin (June 6); d. George Washington

Thomas Campbell, *The Pleasures of Hope*

William Godwin, *St. Leon*
Mungo Park, *Travels in the Interior of Africa*
Mary Robinson, *The False Friend, The Natural Daughter*
Anna Seward, *Original Sonnets on Various Subjects*
Robert Southey, *Poems*, vol. II
Jane West, *A Tale of the Times*
(Wordsworth, two-book *Prelude*)

1800    Abortive French landing in Ireland; battles of Alexandria, Hohenlinden, Marengo; Malta seized by Britain; Alessandro Volta produces electrochemical generator; b. Thomas Babington Macaulay (October 25); d. William Cowper; d. Mary Robinson
Robert Bloomfield, *The Farmer's Boy*
Joseph Cottle, *Alfred*
Maria Edgeworth, *Castle Rackrent*
Thomas Moore trans., *Odes of Anacreon*
Mary Robinson, *Lyrical Tales*
William Wordsworth and Samuel Taylor Coleridge, *Lyrical Ballads*, 2 volumes

1801    Act of Union with Ireland (January 1); Pitt government falls over Catholic Emancipation; Henry Addington becomes Prime Minister; Britain annexes Ceylon
Maria Edgeworth, *Belinda, Moral Tales for Young People*
James Hogg, *Scottish Pastorals*
Leigh Hunt, *Juvenilia; or, a Collection of Poems*
Matthew G. Lewis, *Tales of Wonder*
Thomas Moore, *Poems of the Late Thomas Little*
Amelia Opie, *Father and Daughter*
Robert Southey, *Thalaba the Destroyer*

1802    Peace of Amiens (March 25, 1802–May 18, 1803) celebrated with gas lighting in Soho; John Field, "the Irish Chopin," emigrates to Russia; Napoleon named Consul for life; b. Victor Hugo (February 26); b. Letitia Elizabeth Landon (August 14)
William Cobbett's *Weekly Political Register, Edinburgh Review* founded
Sir Humphrey Davy, *Discourse Introductory to a Course of Lectures on Chemistry*
Amelia Opie, *Poems*
Walter Scott, *Minstrelsy of the Scottish Border*, vols. I–II

1803    War resumed with France; British capture Delhi, India; British army adopts Captain Henry Shrapnel's timed bomb filled with shot; Robert Fulton demonstrates working steamship on the Seine, but cannot secure financing; France sells Louisiana Territory to the United States; Irish patriot Robert Emmet executed; b. Hector Berlioz (December 11); d. Vittorio Alfieri
Erasmus Darwin, *The Temple of Nature*
William Hayley, *Life and Posthumous Writings of William Cowper*
Jane Porter, *Thaddeus of Warsaw*

1804    William Pitt returns as Prime Minister; renewed illness of George III; Napoleon crowned hereditary emperor; Britain declares war on Spain; b. Amadine Dupin (George Sand) (July 1); d. Immanuel Kant
Maria Edgeworth, *Popular Tales*, *The Modern Griselda*
Matthew G. Lewis, *The Bravo of Venice*
Amelia Opie, *Adeline Mowbray, or, The Mother and Daughter*

1805    British defeat French fleet at Trafalgar; Nelson dies; France defeats Austria and Russia at Austerlitz; b. Samuel Palmer (January 27); d. Friedrich Schiller
*Eclectic Review* founded
Henry Cary trans., Dante, *Inferno*
William Godwin, *Fleetwood; or The New Man of Feeling*
Walter Scott, *The Lay of the Last Minstrel*
Robert Southey, *Madoc*
Ann and Jane Taylor, with Adelaide O'Keeffe, *Original Poems for Infant Minds*
Mary Tighe, *Psyche; or, The Legend of Love*
(Wordsworth, *The Prelude* completed in manuscript)

1806    d. William Pitt; d. Charles James Fox, leader of Whig minority; coalition ministry of "All the Talents," Grenville as Prime Minister; end of Holy Roman Empire; France defeats Prussia at Jena; first steam-operated textile mill opens in Manchester; b. Elizabeth Barrett (March 6); b. John Stuart Mill (May 2); d. Charlotte Smith
George Gordon, Lord Byron, *Fugitive Pieces*
Elizabeth Inchbald, *The British Theatre* (–1809; 25 volumes)
Thomas Moore, *Epistles, Odes, and Other Poems*
Sydney Owenson, *The Wild Irish Girl*
Mary Robinson, *The Poems*, 3 volumes

1807    Slave trade abolished in British dominions; Lord Grenville resigns over Catholic Emancipation – Duke of Portland succeeds him as Prime Minister; Russia signs Treaty of Tilsit, withdrawing from war with Napoleon; France invades Portugal and Spain
George Gordon, Lord Byron, *Hours of Idleness*, *Poems on Several Occasions*
George Crabbe, *Poems*
Georg Friedrich Hegel, *Phenomenology of Mind*
Thomas Moore, *Irish Melodies* (–1821)
Sydney Owenson, *Lays of an Irish Harp*
Charlotte Smith, *Beachy Head; with Other Poems*
William Sotheby, *Saul*
Germaine de Staël, *Corinne*
Henry Kirke White, *The Remains*, ed. Southey
William Wordsworth, *Poems, in Two Volumes*

1808    Widespread revolt in Spain, Joseph Bonaparte named King; British troops land in Portugal; Convention of Cintra allows French withdrawal; b. Gerard Labrunie (Nerval) (May 22)
Leigh Hunt editor of *The Examiner*
Felicia Dorothea Browne (later Hemans), *Poems*
John Dalton, *A New System of Chemical Philosophy*
Johann Wilhelm von Goethe, *Faust*, part 1
Elizabeth Hamilton, *The Cottagers of Glenburnie*
Hannah More, *Coelebs in Search of a Wife*
Walter Scott, *Marmion; a Tale of Flodden Field*

1809    Death of Sir John Moore in Peninsular War; Arthur Wellesley, Duke of Wellington, Commander-in-Chief of British troops; Napoleon captures Vienna, Peace of Schönbrunn; Perceval as Prime Minister; Covent Garden and Drury Lane theatres burn, are rebuilt; b. Charles Darwin (February 12); b. Alfred Tennyson (August 6); d. Franz Josef Haydn; d. Thomas Holcroft; d. Thomas Paine; d. Anna Seward
*Quarterly Review* founded
Joel Barlow, *The Columbiad* (Philadelphia, 1807)
William Blake, *Milton*
George Gordon, Lord Byron, *English Bards and Scotch Reviewers*
Thomas Campbell, *Gertrude of Wyoming; a Pennsylvanian Tale*
Maria Edgeworth, *Tales of Fashionable Life*, first issue

Margaret Holford, *Wallace; or, the Fight of Falkirk*

1810  Napoleon annexes Holland; deepening recession; George III increasingly incapacitated; b. Frederick Chopin (February 22); b. Elizabeth Gaskell (September 29); b. Robert Schumann (June 8)
Anna Laetitia Barbauld, *The British Novelists*, 50 volumes
Alexander Chalmers, *Works of the British Poets*, 21 volumes
George Crabbe, *The Borough*
Jane Porter, *The Scottish Chiefs*
Samuel Rogers, *The Voyage of Columbus*
Walter Scott, *The Lady of the Lake*
Anna Seward, *Poetical Works*, ed. Scott
Percy Bysshe Shelley, *Original Poetry by Victor and Cazire*, *Posthumous Fragments of Margaret Nicholson*, *Zastrozzi*
Robert Southey, *The Curse of Kehama*
William Wordsworth, *Essay on Epitaphs*

1811  George III declared insane, Prince of Wales installed as Regent; Shelley expelled from Oxford; Luddite antifactory riots in the Midlands; b. Franz Liszt (October 22)
Jane Austen, *Sense and Sensibility*
Mary Brunton, *Self-Control*
David Ricardo, *On the High Price of Bullion*
Percy Bysshe Shelley, *The Necessity of Atheism*

1812  Frame-breaking Bill against Luddites; Prime Minister Perceval assassinated in the House of Commons, replaced by Lord Liverpool; war declared with the United States; Napoleon, invading Russia, driven back with disastrous losses; Sarah Siddons retires from the stage; b. Robert Browning (May 7); b. Charles Dickens (February 7)
Anna Laetitia Barbauld, *Eighteen Hundred and Eleven*
George Gordon, Lord Byron, *Childe Harold's Pilgrimage*, i–ii, *The Curse of Minerva*
Henry Cary trans., Dante, *Purgatory*, *Paradise*
William Combe, *The Tour of Dr. Syntax in Search of the Picturesque*, illustrated by Rowlandson
George Crabbe, *Tales in Verse*
Maria Edgeworth, *Tales of Fashionable Life*, second issue
Felicia Hemans, *Domestic Affections and Other Poems*
James Montgomery, *The World before the Flood*
Horace and James Smith, *Rejected Addresses*
William Tennant, *Anster Fair*

1813    Napoleon in full retreat; Wellington, victorious in Peninsular War, liberates Spain; French driven from Holland, Italy, and Switzerland; Leigh Hunt imprisoned for libel on Prince Regent; Southey appointed poet laureate after Scott turns down post; Wordsworth given sinecure as Distributor of Stamps; b. Giuseppe Verdi (October 10); b. Richard Wagner (May 22)
Jane Austen, *Pride and Prejudice*
George Gordon, Lord Byron, *The Giaour*, *The Bride of Abydos*
Samuel Taylor Coleridge, *Remorse*
Hannah Cowley, *The Works*, 3 volumes
James Hogg, *The Queen's Wake*
Mary Russell Mitford, *Narrative Poems on the Female Character*
Thomas Moore, *Intercepted Letters; or, The Twopenny Post-Bag*
Amelia Opie, *Tales of Real Life*
Robert Owen, *A New View of Society*
Walter Scott, *The Bridal of Triermain*, *Rokeby*
Percy Bysshe Shelley, *Queen Mab*
Germaine de Staël, *On Germany* (*De l'Allemagne*, 1810)

1814    Allied armies invade France; Paris falls; Napoleon abdicates, is exiled to Italian island of Elba; Congress of Vienna (September 1814–June 1815) secures conservative world order; American war ended by Treaty of Ghent; British develop first steam warship; George Stephenson invents first locomotive; Edmund Kean's debut at Covent Garden; b. Mikhail Lermontov (October 15); d. Johann Gottlieb Fichte
*New Monthly Magazine* founded
Jane Austen, *Mansfield Park*
Mary Brunton, *Discipline*
George Gordon, Lord Byron, *The Corsair*, *Lara*
George Daniel, *The Modern Dunciad*
Maria Edgeworth, *Patronage*
Leigh Hunt, *The Feast of the Poets*
Lady Morgan (Sydney Owenson), *O'Donnel: A National Tale*
Thomas Malthus, *Observations on the Effect of the Corn Laws*
Walter Scott, *Waverley*
Robert Southey, *Roderick the Last of the Goths*
William Wordsworth, *The Excursion*

1815    Napoleon escapes Elba, enters France (March); Battle of Waterloo (June); Napoleon exiled to Atlantic island of St. Helena; Louis XVIII installed as King of France; English national debt stands above £850 million; b. Anthony Trollope (April 24)

*Beowulf* published in Copenhagen

George Gordon, Lord Byron, *Hebrew Melodies*

Leigh Hunt, *The Descent of Liberty, a Mask*

August Wilhelm Schlegel, *A Course of Lectures on Dramatic Art and Literature* (1809), trans. John Black

Walter Scott, *Guy Mannering, The Lord of the Isles*

William Wordsworth, *Poems, The White Doe of Rylstone*

1816    Elgin Marbles exhibited, purchased for British Museum; Byron, separated from wife, leaves England; Ugo Foscolo in England; severe economic depression; Spa Fields riot; b. Charlotte Brontë (April 21); d. R. B. Sheridan

Jane Austen, *Emma*

George Gordon, Lord Byron, *Childe Harold's Pilgrimage*, III, *Prisoner of Chillon, Siege of Corinth [and] Parisina*

Samuel Taylor Coleridge, *Christabel; Kubla Khan, a Vision; The Pains of Sleep, The Statesman's Manual*

Felicia Hemans, *The Restoration of the Works of Art to Italy*

Margaret Holford, *Margaret of Anjou*

Leigh Hunt, *The Story of Rimini*

Thomas Love Peacock, *Headlong Hall*

Walter Scott, *The Antiquary, The Black Dwarf, Old Mortality*

Percy Bysshe Shelley, *Alastor, and Other Poems*

Jane Taylor, *Essays in Rhyme, on Morals and Manners*

1817    Suspension of *habeas corpus*; suppression of democratic societies; trial of publisher William Hone; Shelley loses custody suit for children; Byron in Venice; d. Princess Charlotte, sole legitimate child of future George IV and heir to throne; d. Jane Austen; d. Germaine de Staël

*Black Dwarf*, Hone's radical paper, founded; *Blackwood's Edinburgh Magazine* founded

George Gordon, Lord Byron, *The Lament of Tasso, Manfred*

Samuel Taylor Coleridge, *Biographia Literaria, Sybilline Leaves, Zapolya*

Maria Edgeworth, *Harrington, Ormond*

William Godwin, *Mandeville*

William Hazlitt, *Characters of Shakespeare's Plays, The Round Table*

John Keats, *Poems*

James Mill, *The History of British India*

Thomas Moore, *Lalla Rookh*

Lady Morgan, *France*

Thomas Love Peacock, *Melincourt*

Ricardo, *Principles of Political Economy and Taxation*

Percy Bysshe Shelley, *Laon and Cythna* (withdrawn)

Robert Southey, *Wat Tyler* (unauthorized piracy)

1818  Trial and imprisonment of publisher Richard Carlile; the Shelleys leave England for Italy; b. Emily Brontë (July 30); b. Karl Marx (May 5); d. Mary Brunton; d. "Monk" Lewis

Jane Austen, *Northanger Abbey*, *Persuasion*

George Gordon, Lord Byron, *Beppo*, *Childe Harold's Pilgrimage*, IV

Susan Ferrier, *Marriage*

Henry Hallam, *A View of the State of Europe during the Middle Ages*

William Hazlitt, *Lectures on the English Poets*, *A View of the English Stage*

Leigh Hunt, *Foliage*

John Keats, *Endymion*

Henry Hart Milman, *Samor, Lord of the Bright City*

Thomas Moore, *The Fudge Family in Paris*

Lady Morgan, *Florence McCarthy: An Irish Tale*

Thomas Love Peacock, *Rhododaphne: or The Thessalian Spell*

Walter Scott, *Rob Roy*, *The Heart of Midlothian*

Mary Shelley, *Frankenstein; or, The Modern Prometheus*

Percy Bysshe Shelley, *The Revolt of Islam*

1819  Peterloo Massacre; passage of the Six Acts against radical activity, unions; William Parry's arctic expedition; Columbia, Ecuador, and Venezuela declare independence from Spain; b. Alexandrina Victoria, future Queen of England (May 24); b. George Eliot (Mary Ann Evans) (November 22); b. John Ruskin (February 8); d. James Watt

George Gordon, Lord Byron, *Don Juan*, I–II, *Mazeppa*

Barry Cornwall (Bryan Waller Procter), *Dramatic Scenes*

George Crabbe, *Tales of the Hall*

William Hazlitt, *Lectures on the English Comic Writers*

Thomas Love Peacock, *Nightmare Abbey*

Walter Scott, *The Bride of Lammermoor*, *A Legend of Montrose*

Percy Bysshe Shelley, *Rosalind and Helen*

William Wordsworth, *Peter Bell*, *The Waggoner*

1820   Death of George III; accession of Regent as George IV; divorce trial of his consort, Queen Caroline; revolution in Spain; revolt in Naples; "Cato Street conspiracy" to assassinate government ministers discovered; Walter Scott knighted; Sir Humphrey Davy President of Royal Society; b. Florence Nightingale (May 12); d. Sir Joseph Banks

*London Magazine* founded

Elizabeth Barrett, *The Battle of Marathon*

Bernard Barton, *Poems*

William Blake, *Jerusalem: The Emanation of the Giant Albion*

Caroline Bowles (later Southey), *Ellen Fitzarthur*

Thomas Bowdler, *The Family Shakespeare*

Edward Bulwer-Lytton, *Ismael*

John Clare, *Poems Descriptive of Rural Life and Scenery*

Barry Cornwall, *Marcian Colonna and Other Poems*

William Godwin, *Of Population*

William Hazlitt, *Lectures on the Dramatic Literature of the Age of Elizabeth*

John Keats, *Lamia, Isabella, The Eve of St. Agnes, and Other Poems*

John Sheridan Knowles, *Virginius, a Tragedy*

Thomas Malthus, *Principles of Political Economy*

Charles Maturin, *Melmoth the Wanderer*

Thomas Love Peacock, "The Four Ages of Poetry"

Sir Walter Scott, *The Abbot, Ivanhoe, The Monastery*

Mary Shelley, *Matilda* (unpublished)

Percy Bysshe Shelley, *The Cenci, Prometheus Unbound, Swellfoot the Tyrant*

William Wordsworth, *The River Duddon, a Series of Sonnets*

1821   Austria suppresses Neapolitan uprising; Greek War of Independence begins; Bolivia, Chile, Peru, and Uruguay declare independence from Spain; b. Charles Baudelaire (April 9); b. Gustave Flaubert (December 12); d. Napoleon; d. Queen Caroline; d. Elizabeth Inchbald; d. John Keats

*Manchester Guardian* founded

Joanna Baillie, *Metrical Legends of Exalted Characters*

George Gordon, Lord Byron, *Don Juan*, III–V, *Marino Faliero [with] The Prophecy of Dante, Sardanapalus, The Two Foscari, and Cain*

John Clare, *The Village Minstrel*
Thomas De Quincey, *Confessions of an English Opium Eater*
Pierce Egan, *Life in London*
John Gait, *Annals of the Parish*
L. E. L. (Laetitia Landon), *The Fate of Adelaide*
James Mill, *Elements of Political Economy*
Lady Morgan, *Italy*
Sir William Edward Parry, *Journal of a Voyage for the Discovery of a North-West Passage*
Sir Walter Scott, *Kenilworth*
Percy Bysshe Shelley, *Adonais*, *Epipsychidion*, "A Defence of Poetry" (unpublished)
Robert Southey, *A Vision of Judgement*

1822    Suicide of Lord Castlereagh; Canning succeeds him as Foreign Secretary and Tory leader of the House of Commons; d. E. T. A. Hoffmann; d. Percy Bysshe Shelley
*The Liberal* founded (four issues only)
Thomas Lovell Beddoes, *The Bride's Tragedy*
Caroline Bowles, *The Widow's Tale*
George Gordon, Lord Byron, *The Vision of Judgement*
Kenelm Digby, *The Broad Stone of Honour*
Samuel Rogers, *Italy*
Sir Walter Scott, *Haitian Hill*, *The Pirate*, *The Fortunes of Nigel*, *Peveril of the Peak*
Percy Bysshe Shelley, *Hellas*
John Wilson (Christopher North), *Lights and Shadows of Scottish Life*
William Wordsworth, *Ecclesiastical Sketches*

1823    War between France and Spain; Byron in Greece as representative of London Philhellenes; Mary Shelley returns to England; d. Robert Bloomfield; d. Ann Radcliffe; d. David Ricardo
Rudolf Ackermann produces the first of the Annuals, the *Forget-Me-Not*
George Gordon, Lord Byron, *The Age of Bronze*, *Don Juan*, VI–XIV, *The Island*, *Werner*
John Franklin, *Narrative of a Journey to the Polar Sea*
William Hazlitt, *Liber Amoris*
Felicia Hemans, *The Vespers of Palermo*, *The Siege of Valencia; The Last Constantine*
Leigh Hunt, *Ultra-Crepidarius*

Charles Lamb, *Essays of Elia*
Thomas Moore, *Fables for the Holy Alliance*, *The Loves of the Angels*
Sir Walter Scott, *Quentin Durward*
Mary Shelley, *Valperga*

1824    Opening of National Gallery; London Institute inaugurated; Charles X King of France; d. Byron
*Westminster Review* founded
George Gordon, Lord Byron, *The Deformed Transformed*, *Don Juan*, XV–XVI
Thomas Carlyle trans., Goethe's *Wilhelm Meister*
Susan Ferrier, *The Inheritance*
James Hogg, *Private Memoirs and Confessions of a Justified Sinner*
Laetitia Elizabeth Landon, *The Improvisatrice*
Walter Savage Landor, *Imaginary Conversations*, vols. I–II
Mary Russell Mitford, *Our Village* (–1832)
James Morier, *The Adventures of Hajji Baba of Ispahan*
Sir Walter Scott, *St. Ronan's Well*, *Redgauntlet*
Percy Bysshe Shelley, *Posthumous Poems*
Robert Watt, *Bibliotheca Britannica*

1825    Major financial crash; d. Anna Laetitia Barbauld; d. Henry Fuseli
John Milton, *De Doctrina Christiana* first published
Anna Laetitia Barbauld, *Works*
Thomas Carlyle, *Life of Schiller*
Samuel Taylor Coleridge, *Aids to Reflection*
William Hazlitt, *The Spirit of the Age*, *Table Talk*
Felicia Hemans, *The Forest Sanctuary*, *Lays of Many Lands*
James Hogg, *Queen Hynde*
Laetitia Elizabeth Landon, *The Troubadour*
Sir Walter Scott, *The Betrothed*, *The Talisman*
Robert Southey, *A Tale of Paraguay*

1826    Fallout from financial distress includes failure of Scott's publisher, Ballantyne; Liverpool government falls; new elections; George Canning as Prime Minister; d. John Adams; d. Thomas Jefferson; d. Carl Maria von Weber
Burke's *Peerage* first published
Elizabeth Barrett, *An Essay on Mind, with Other Poems*
Benjamin Disraeli, *Vivian Grey* (–1827)

Sir Walter Scott, *Woodstock*
Mary Shelley, *The Last Man*

1827    Greek independence won at Navorino; d. George Canning; Duke of
Wellington as Prime Minister; University of London founded; Scott
acknowledges he is the Great Unknown (the "author of Waverley").
d. Ludwig van Beethoven; d. William Blake; d. Ugo Foscolo;
d. Helen Maria Williams
Edward Bulwer-Lytton, *Falkland*
John Clare, *The Shepherd's Calendar*
Reginald Heber, *Hymns, Written and Adapted to the Weekly Church
Service of the Year*
Sir Walter Scott, *The Chronicles of Canonsgate*
Alfred and Charles Tennyson, *Poems by Two Brothers*

1828    Corporation and Test Acts repealed; d. Franz Schubert
Edward Bulwer-Lytton, *Pelham*
Sir John Franklin, *Journal of a Second Expedition to the Polar Sea*
Felicia Hemans, *Records of Woman*
Leigh Hunt, *Lord Byron and Some of His Contemporaries*
Mary Russell Mitford, *Rienzi*
Sir William Edward Parry, *Narrative of an Attempt to Reach the
North Pole*
Sir Walter Scott, *The Fair Maid of Perth*

1829    Catholic Emancipation; d. Sir Humphrey Davy; d. Friedrich
Schlegel
Thomas Hood, *The Epping Hunt*
Douglas Jerrold, *Black Ey'd Susan*
James Mill, *Analysis of the Human Mind*
Thomas Love Peacock, *The Misfortunes of Elphin*
Sir Walter Scott, *Anne of Geierstein*

1830    Death of George IV; accession of brother, Duke of Clarence, as
William IV; Wellington's government falls; Earl Grey becomes
Prime Minister as head of a Whig government; increasing agitation
for parliamentary reform; revolution in France ends Bourbon mon-
archy; Liverpool to Manchester railway opens; d. William Hazlitt
*Fraser's Magazine*, Hood's *Comic Annual* founded
Edward Bulwer-Lytton, *Paul Clifford*
William Cobbett, *Rural Rides*
Catherine Gore, *Women as They Are, or, The Manners of the Day*
Felicia Hemans, *Songs of the Affections*

Douglas Jerrold, *Sally in Our Alley*
Charles Lyell, *Principles of Geology* (–1833)
Thomas Moore, *Letters and Journals of Lord Byron*
Sir Walter Scott, *Tales of a Grandfather*
Mary Shelley, *The Fortunes of Perkin Warbeck*
Alfred, Lord Tennyson, *Poems Chiefly Lyrical*

# I

JERROLD E. HOGLE

# Romanticism and the "schools" of criticism and theory

For students of English literature from the 1780s through to the mid 1830s, "Romanticism" and the "Romantic period" are not what they used to be – one good reason for a second edition of this volume. To be sure, "Romanticism" as a literary movement or a complex of beliefs and styles of art, and "Romantic" as a descriptor of that type of writing or writer, have long referred to "being like romance":[1] to reworking an aesthetic mode, particularly the European quest-romance of the twelfth through the sixteenth centuries, where imagination, desire, and myth-making heighten what we usually take as perceived "reality" to extend its limits with symbolic suggestions that deepen, expand, or transcend everyday human awareness. Such a relocation of "romance," in fact, was already in progress well before 1780. By then "romantic" as a signifier had already strayed from mainly describing supernatural tales of chivalry, including their expressions of love, parodied in Cervantes's *Don Quixote* (1605–15), to characterize the assertively "natural," but also mythological and idealizing, landscape paintings of Claude Lorrain and Salvator Rosa from the seventeenth century as these came to Britain from southern France and northern Italy (to many, then, the "regions of romance") to become exemplars of grand sublimity within the late eighteenth-century culture of "sensibility" (Eichner, 'Romantic,' p. 5). It has thus seemed proper to connect "Romantic" with William Wordsworth's claim in a revision of his preface to the 1800 edition of the *Lyrical Ballads* – for many the collection that launched British Romanticism – that these poems, whether written by him or Samuel Taylor Coleridge, take "incidents and situations" based in "common life," including a revivified "nature," and "throw over them a certain colouring of imagination, whereby ordinary things" are "presented to the mind in [such] an unusual aspect" that readers can now "trace" in them "the primary laws of our nature ... the manner in which we associate ideas in a state of excitement."[2] This paradoxical "return to nature" that also transfigures its basic impressions to arrive at "what is more integral than nature, within [the] self," therefore became defined by 1970 as "the internalization of quest-romance" in the works of William Blake, Percy Bysshe Shelley, and John Keats, as well as Wordsworth and Coleridge – and even, in a more ironic fashion, George Gordon, Lord Byron – all according to Harold Bloom, one of the most prominent exponents of Romanticism by the 1960s.[3] But after 1970–1, this scheme and other senses of one overall Romantic stance have come to be seriously questioned from many different points of view. For some, these critiques have meant exploding "the Romantic canon" both as a grouping of writers who disagree too much to be a movement and as a category wrongly limited to only six male poets plus a few more within their spheres of influence.[4] For others, there has been so much "over-systemizing and simplifying" of a retrospective construct *called* "Romanticism"[5] that the label has become problematic as a way of describing a cacophonous totality of conflicting voices, ideologies, gender roles, classes, genres, styles, and modes of publication in Britain during the time between the American and French Revolutions and the accession of Queen Victoria.

After all, there have never been steady "grounds" for the ascription of "Romantic" to this whole era in literature or of "Romanticism" to a unified vision shared by many writers. Certainly none of the British authors now given the label called their own work "romantic" with any consistency. True, both Coleridge and William Hazlitt did accept the distinction between the antiquated "classic" and the newly modernized "romantic" styles being advanced in Germany, particularly by Friedrich and A. W. von Schlegel, and echoed in France, especially in Germaine de Staël's *On Germany* (1813).[6] For Hazlitt by 1816, "classical" writing depicts conventionalized objects that bring "universal associations" with them as though they were outside of individual minds, while "romantic" objects gain affective power only from the super-added "ideas with which they are habitually associated" by particular observers and readers (Hazlitt, cited in Whalley, "England," p. 211). Yet even Hazlitt did not apply this label widely to the poets around him, and the idea of any dominant literary movement proved impossible to sustain throughout the early nineteenth century. Though a "Lake School" (from England's Lake District) was identified to include Wordsworth and Coleridge by 1802, the "Cockney School" label scathingly applied to Keats in 1817, by Byron among others (because of Keats's suburban and middle-class status), revealed a cultural arena of competing schemes of poetry, even though Byron and Keats were quite similar in dividing their own uses of "romantic" between picturesque scenes from Continental Europe and states of erotic longing, like a Petrarchan lover's, doomed by the perpetual distance of their objects of desire (pp.194–6). It was not until 1833 that Coleridge was first designated "the founder of the romantic school of poetry" in a more comprehensive sense (p. 234), and that sense was so amorphous that Victorian criticism oscillated for decades between tight restrictions and over-generous vagueness regarding whom and what Romanticism encompassed (pp. 235–57).

Nonetheless, most critics of the twentieth and twenty-first centuries believe that "the Romantic" as both a period and a movement "canonized itself towards the end of [the nineteenth] century" (p. 157). At the same time, the reasons they accept this argument, then disagree on others, stem from a key factor rarely noted in these discussions: nearly all informed crit-ics, past and present, base their labels and judgments not simply on "gen-eral principles" but on theories – their own or those of others – about the "nature" of valuable literature, its relationships with what it claims to represent and the cultural features of its time that helped produce it, its capacity for expressing its author's beliefs and affecting its audience emo-tionally and intellectually, and its ways of using language to make verbal art, including allusive language already loaded with suggestions from much earl-ier or contemporary writing. Even the primary explanations for the different views of Romanticism we have already noted come from these more fun-damental theoretical differences, many of them initiated or modified at the time of the Romantics, who developed their works out of several different philosophical orientations, most of them conflicted and undergoing changes at the time. Such is even more the case with university-based interpretive criticism since the dawn of the twentieth century. As institutions of higher learning have attracted both conservative and revisionary scholars of litera-ture, quasi-"schools" of critical orientation transcending single universities have arisen to promulgate their methods of literary and cultural analysis in publications and classrooms, and their differences are all rooted in particu-lar theoretical assumptions, however much some of these are the products of ideologies (or systems of beliefs) that are troubled by conflicts they only seem to have resolved.

To understand the debates about Romanticism and where they now leave it (if there *is* an "it"), we must therefore expose how the most influential views of what "Romantic" writing is and does, as well as the arguments that call Romanticism into question, come from basic theoretical stances built on interlocking and foundational, if sometimes conflicted, assumptions. Many of these genuinely look back and respond to stances *in* what we call "Romantic" writing, thereby placing Romantic and more current theory in frequent and revealing dialogues with each other. I therefore want to pre-sent an overview here of how the different "schools" of criticism that have done the most important work with Romanticism since the late nineteenth century have redefined and debated the "Romantic" in ways demanded by their different foundations in theory, nearly all of those with Romantic roots – though we should also keep in mind that these "schools" are not entirely separate, that they frequently incorporate parts of one another, and that all the identifiable "schools" reveal disagreements among their various proponents. In this process, I want to argue that any future study of Romanticism, whether it ultimately decides to accept or reject such a label, must be based on an informed understanding of all these differing positions and the theories behind them, as I know to be the case in the essays that follow. It is that understanding that can best help us grasp the full vitality and the lasting cultural importance of all that this revolutionary and multi-faceted period entails in its many instigations of, and its resistances to, what we have come to see as the modern world.

## I The codifications of "old" historicism, "new" criticism, and their confluence

As it turns out, even the solidification of an "English Romantic school" in criticism at the end of the nineteenth century is enabled by a theoretical base with a Romantic ancestry, and that same criticism is ultimately bedeviled by problems inherent in this very base. Beginning in 1878, the British scholar Edward Dowden codifies "the Romantic movement" as the integration of two aging literary schemes: "romance" in need of being "saved and ennobled by the presence and power of truth" and "naturalism" in need of being "saved and ennobled by the presence and power of imagination" (Dowden, cited in Whalley, "England," p. 251). Even so, in seeing the cause of this coalescence as a pervasive and collective way of thinking visible in the "kinship between the literature of [this] epoch and the various other manifestations of the mind of the time," Dowden must finally acknowledge his debt to Hippolyte Taine's influential French *History of English Literature* (1864–69; Dowden, cited in Whalley, "England," pp. 252, 247). Taine employs the model of "mineralogy" tracing "diverse ... crystals" organically back to "simple physical forms" to claim that there "is a system in human sentiments and ideas" at any given period in a nation or region ("the mind of the time") and that "this system has for its motive power" certain "simple spiritual forms ... common to men of one race, age, or country."[7] Hearkening back especially to P. B. Shelley's "the spirit of the age" in *A Defence of Poetry* (1821) – for Shelley an "energetic development" in his era's "national will" of an "accumulation of the power of communicating and receiving intense and impassioned conceptions" (Adams, *Critical Theory*, p. 529) – Taine posits a "disposition" in "all the conceptions of a century" (Taine, cited in Adams, *Critical Theory*, p. 612) that would soon become the overriding *period mentality* in many twentieth-century histories of literary eras. It is this sense of a world view within a time frame that most led to what has more recently been called "old" historicism, and many arguments since Dowden's for a basic "Romantic vision" common to Western writers and artists from about 1790 to 1830 have accepted this "large coherence of thought and practice" as a pervasive reality, though the ingredients of that coherence have differed from critic to critic.[8] All this while, though, the late Victorian grounds of *those* grounds were and remain deeply troubled. Dowden himself questions whether Taine's "mind of the time" helps critics "comprehend ... the individual genius of an artist" who may not conform to a dominant belief-system and whether any *Zeitgeist* (or "spirit of the time") takes sufficient account of "the universal mind of humanity" and what it has produced with ongoing value "not bounded by an epoch nor contained by a race" (Dowden, cited in Whalley, "England," p. 252).

The early twentieth century, while certainly furthering the *Zeitgeist* view of Romanticism, therefore found these questions rising to the surface even in some of its most historical approaches to literature. Faced with questionings of Romanticism's moral and political implications in the wake of World War I and Russia's communist revolution (see Gleckner, *Romanticism,* pp. 26–40), Arthur O. Lovejoy rises to champion Romantic writing in a landmark essay of 1924. But he does so by dividing the realm he defends and urging what his title does, a renewed "Discrimination of Romanticisms" instead of synoptic attempts to establish one "spirit of the age." Lovejoy was then and remains the principal figure who enunciated a form of criticism called "The History of Ideas" that continues to attract interest, at least through its own ongoing journal. This scheme is "old historicist" in accepting the relatively unified effect of several cultural forces at a given time on how previous or rising ideas are redefined from period to period. But it also assumes, in line with the ongoing products of a "universal mind" *and* Dowden's notion of artistic variants within period mentalities, that there are "unit-ideas," such as the Judeo-Christian "Great Chain of Being" that, initially but not only in the Middle Ages, depicts the fundamental hierarchy of the cosmos that the structures of human civilization should duplicate. These "thought-complexes" usually retain their fundamental features as they pass from one era to the next, if they survive at all. They should thus be seen as clearly distinct from each other even if multiple "unit-ideas" all become modified by the *Zeitgeist* of later times or cultural groups (Lovejoy, cited in Gleckner, *Romanticism,* pp. 68–9). For Lovejoy in 1924, too many descriptions of Romanticism have taken "quite distinct thought-complexes" and forced them into one reputed mentality (*ibid.*). Instead Lovejoy advocates distinguishing, to start with, what Dowden sees as flowing together: the "naturalism," including an idealized "primitivism," that descends to Wordsworth and others from articulations of it around 1740 ("nature" as superior to "art") from the use of local symbols as primarily metonyms for suggesting "the entire reach of the human imagination" ("art" as superior to "nature") just as Friedrich Schlegel suggested in Germany and the later Coleridge would argue in his *Biographia Literaria* (1817; Lovejoy, cited in Gleckner, *Romanticism*, pp. 70–7). In fact, Lovejoy's whole approach resembles Coleridge's 1808 thinking about the differences between the "predetermined ... mechanic form" that artists can "impress" on any "material" and the "organic form" that "shapes, as it develops itself, from within" the interpenetration of material perception and imagination (Coleridge, cited in Adams, *Critical Theory*, p. 471). "Mechanic" and "organic" are "thought-complexes," as well as devices, that retain their fundamental natures between the times of, say, Shakespeare and Wordsworth, like Lovejoy's unit-ideas. Yet Coleridge also believes that different times and nations have produced their own distinct manifestations of each, sometimes to the point of obscuring their differences, which now, as with Lovejoy's "units," need to be emphasized anew.

Lovejoy's provocative claims, however, which (as we shall see) some critics have recently echoed, did not expose the fissures in "old" historicism for long, considering how much acceptance there has been, until recently, of the strongest reactions to him. The defense of Romanticism's period unity has been joined after 1924 many times, often in *comparative* literary histories in which unit-ideas carry not just across eras but across national boundaries over the same period of time. Still, the most influential retort to Lovejoy was surely the comparativist, "old" historicist, *and* history-of-ideas argument of the Austrian philologist-critic Rene Wellek in 1949. Wellek is unequivocal: "the major romantic movements" for him in Britain, Germany, and France "form a unity of theories, philosophy, and style, and ... these, in turn, form a coherent group of ideas each of which implicates the other" (Wellek, cited in Gleckner, *Romanticism*, p. 182). In substantial quoted evidence from poets and theorists of all three nations, Wellek finds that, even though individual poets vary in construing the key concepts conservatively or progressively, there is a shared linkage of writing to the "workings and nature of poetic imagination," now more organically defined; essentially "the same conception of nature and its relation to man," who can now "read nature as a symbol of something behind or within [it] not ordinarily perceived"; and "basically the same poetic style, with a use of imagery, symbol, and myth which is clearly distinct from that of eighteenth-century neo-classicism," much as the Schlegels, Coleridge, and Hazlitt claimed (pp. 193–4). Yes, this overall "conception occurs ... only fitfully" in Byron as Wellek reads him (p. 200), and several other writers of this era are even more outside that "dominance of a system of ideas and poetic practices" (p. 205). Wellek's key move, though, is to half agree and half disagree with Lovejoy about ideas themselves. On the one hand, Wellek concurs that shapes of ideas "have their anticipations and survivals" from age to age (p. 205), like a floating "signifier" or mere image as defined by Ferdinand de Saussure.[9] Yet, on the other hand, Wellek maintains that the "system of norms," including "themes" and "philosophies," that fill these vessels, as in Saussurean "signifieds" (or concepts) to which signifiers may point (*ibid.*), can be fundamentally changed, like styles of expression, as one period mentality replaces another (Wellek, cited in Gleckner, *Romanticism*, pp. 182–3). Wellek even intensifies this argument by drifting beyond "old" historicism and the history of ideas, while still affirming both, and invoking his knowledge of Russian formalism and Prague School linguistics from the earlier twentieth century. He concretizes his Romantic "system of norms" in a verbal objectification of the new "themes" and "philosophies" as these fuse in Romantic poems with a distinctive reworking of "conventions" and "styles" (p. 182), so much so that Romantic "content" cannot finally be distinguished from Romantic "form."

By 1949, we should remind ourselves, partly because of Wellek's transmission of his East European influences to America and Britain, literary historicism had come under assault from what was now being called "the new criticism." This "school" of interpretation does not deny the reference of literary signs to other writings or to historical circumstances, but it resists the historicist's dissolving of texts into period (and even authorial) mentalities in favor of affirming the unique mode of any art-object's existence, the internal structure or form, and the aesthetic functions of literary works that all make literature a distinct kind of discourse and literary criticism a discipline focused on an object with its own special nature. Such an orientation, most immediately indebted to the earlier modernist criticism of T. S. Eliot and I. A. Richards, thus insists, indeed, that "in a successful work, form and content cannot be separated" and that "the primary concern of criticism" is "the relation of the various parts to each other in building up" the "whole" of a verbal "object," to quote the Yale new critic Cleanth Brooks in 1951.[10] With these assumptions, new criticism looks back to Coleridge's sense of the achievement of "organic" form by the "symbol," especially as his theory imports from Germany the arguments of F. W. von Schelling and especially Immanuel Kant. For Coleridge in 1816, "a symbol" as opposed to "allegory" (for him "a [mechanic] translation of abstract notions into a picture language") is "characterized ... by the translucence of the eternal [from Kant's 'Ideas' in the mind to mental intimations of God] through and in the temporal [concrete signifiers]" in a way that "partakes of the [greater] reality which it renders intelligible," yet in which the symbol "abides itself as a living part in that unity of which it is the representative" (Coleridge, cited in Adams, *Critical Theory*, p. 476).

In new critical thinking, achieving such a "multaiety in unity" (Coleridge's phrase) must especially involve the focusing of abstract or emotive elements on what T. S. Eliot in 1919 called an "*objective correlative*," a materially verbalized "formula" whereby a complex "emotion" is coalesced in a scheme of concrete words so that the "sensory experience" of the latter can generate the full "emotion" in the reader's psyche (Eliot, cited in Adams, *Critical Theory*, p. 766). By this standard, the new criticism feared at times that much Romantic poetry should not qualify as really fine art. Brooks himself in 1939 sees the major Romanticists, because some apparently want imagination to leap beyond concrete symbols, as frequently unable to achieve "a fusion of image and idea," the key to the "serious irony" of forcing contradictions into an equipoise – in this view the special affect achieved by literature at its best (Brooks, cited in Gleckner, *Romanticism*, p. 144). But another re-defense of Romantic writing came to the rescue again in the 1940s, this one very much in the terms of the new criticism: the "synaesthesia" of sensory and imaginative elements in numerous Romantic poems came to be seen as producing the "irony" of different but "complementary impulses" being activated simultaneously in sensitive readers (R. H. Fogle, cited in Gleckner, *Romanticism*, p. 154). By 1949 Brooks's Yale colleague W. K. Wimsatt affirms that the best "Romantic nature poetry" shows a "solidity of symbol and ... sensory verbal qualities" not "washed out by" any "abstraction," which makes the "imaginative structure" of much Romantic writing a form of the "concrete universal" unique to great art (Wimsatt, cited in Gleckner, *Romanticism*, pp. 219–30). Wellek's argument for content as form the same year, it turns out, makes his claim for a well-codified "Concept of Romanticism" an outcome of the new criticism just as much as a product of period historicism and the history of ideas.

Indeed, the most influential schematization in theory and criticism about the Romantic era through the 1950s and 1960s extended this attempt to synthesize new-critical, old-historical, and history-of-ideas assumptions into one overriding unity. Given its emphasis on literature as a discipline, new criticism readily joined with the history of ideas by the early 1950s to establish the thoroughgoing study of literary theory itself and how its assumptions have changed since ancient times. M. H. Abrams makes Romanticism central to this effort by using *The Mirror and the Lamp* (1953)[11] to show how Romantic theory and poetry, within the *Zeitgeist* of Britain and Germany around 1800, recombine parts of several theories of the European past to replace the neoclassic view of poetry as the "mirror of nature" revealing the *highest* nature concealed from human awareness outside us with the Romantic notion of the "poem as heterocosm," given its life by the "lamp" of imagination, through which the poet organically unites inner associations with concrete perceptions and words in an "act analogous to God's creation of the world," whether any particular poet believes in that deity or not (Abrams, *Mirror*, p. 272). Reinforcements of this coalescence soon followed in abundance, though some steered towards emphasizing the period's mentality and others towards Romantic transformations of previous ideas and aesthetic forms. For Morse Peckham, all Romantic writing comes out of "a shift from conceiving the cosmos as a static mechanism to conceiving it as a dynamic organism," even though there are varying articulations of this paradigm-shift ranging from "radical" (Coleridge's) to "positive" (Wordsworth's) to "negative" (Byron's; Peckham, cited in Gleckner, *Romanticism*, pp. 231–57). For Northrop Frye in 1963, fascinated by age-old myth-patterns as both ideas and sheer forms in part because of C. G. Jung's "collective unconscious" of enduring archetypes, Romanticism is a "historical center of gravity," enabling a relative "uniformity of tone and mood" in texts, in which previous mythic efforts to identify the "human with the non-human" are reworked by and relocated to a "center" of imagination "where inward and outward manifestations of a common motion and spirit are unified" (Frye, cited in Gleckner, pp. 298–313). It is into this period-based yet form-oriented apotheosis of the "Romantic" that Bloom's "internalization of quest-romance" arrives in 1969 to so define the peculiar psychology and journey of the striving speaker in many actual texts of this Romantic revival of myth. Concurrently, though, Abrams reenters the conversation, most impressively with *Natural Supernaturalism* (1971),[12] to make sure that historicist and formalist analyses are entirely balanced and integrated with each other. He completes the drive towards coalescence visible in Wellek by defining the Romantic "spirit of the age" as a direct engagement with the "political, intellectual, and moral circumstances of a period of revolutionary upheaval" whereby a dominant "politics of vision" ("old" historicism) takes verbal shape in a "distinctive complex," like an objective correlative, common to many poems (new criticism) in which "philosophical empiricism," including Kant's reaction to it, is fused with "great poetic forms" rooted in biblical prophecies of salvation (history of ideas). The result is a Romantic literature of "infinite longings … inherent in the human spirit" whereby "militant external action" is transmuted into "an imaginative act" of either unfulfilled desire or potential transcendence well suited to the new-critical equipoise of vibrant and vibrating contraries (Abrams, cited in Gleckner, pp. 314–30).

## II The disruptions of psychoanalysis, deconstruction, and Marxism

Yet even while these orientations developed and combined, there were adjacent ones, with their own Romantic ancestries, rising to prominence in the same decades with the effect at times of helping to reinforce the above conceptions of Romanticism but more often of unsettling their codifications at the level of their most basic assumptions. In arguing for an internalized quest-romance in the late 1960s, for example, Bloom is drawing partly on psychoanalysis in the tradition of Sigmund Freud by focusing on a striving subject who "rises from the id" and struggles to fulfill such preconscious drives in the "nightmare world of the reality-principle" (Bloom, *Romanticism,* pp. 16–19). Bloom, in fact, goes on to extend these assumptions, beginning in *The Anxiety of Influence* (1973),[13] by analyzing how "strong," mainly Romantic poets can achieve a "reaction-formation" and "sublation" (or raising-up from beneath) that allows their deepest questing drives to speak in their verse through and past the limits of precursor-texts written by their "father" figures. However, Bloom is actually a latecomer in finding Freudian psychoanalysis both prefigured in Romantic writing and suited to the interpretation of many Romantic texts as though such works are like dreams as Freud understood them by 1900, sublimations of unconscious "dream-content" half appearing in the more readable "dream-thoughts" learned from education and social interaction (Freud, cited in Rivkin and Ryan, *Literary Theory,* p. 400). Among the responses to Lovejoy proclaiming a deep unity in Romanticism is Mario Praz's 1931 view of the "Romantic agony" that results from the rising and repression of the "*homo sensualis*" foregrounded by the Marquis de Sade during the Romantic period, the "impulse mysterious" of which there are surface symptoms pointing to irrational and pre-conscious depths, as in Coleridge's "Kubla Khan" (written 1797) – "oh that deep romantic chasm" (line 12) – and Mary Shelley's original *Frankenstein* (published 1818) with its gestation of the hero's artificial creature out of the pre-conscious dreams of both the author and Frankenstein himself (see Praz, cited in Gleckner, *Romanticism,* pp. 82–5). In 1936, on another plane, Herbert Read regards the surrealist art of his own time as replaying the "opposition and interaction" in European Romanticism over a century earlier "between the world of objective fact – the sensational and social world of active and economic existence – and the world of subjective fantasy" emerging largely out of the personal *and* collective unconscious (Read, cited in Gleckner, *Romanticism,* p. 103).

Given so much encouragement from Romantic writing itself, which Michel Foucault has seen as helping to begin the modern sense of the human being as a depth of self-obscuring layers unable to consciously represent its whole self to itself,[14] such views have led to numerous psychoanalytic readings of Romantic poems, plays, and novels over the last several decades. In many of them from the 1930s to the 1960s, subjectivity, caught in Freud's Oedipal triangle of subject-mother-father, struggles with its inmost drives to both recover and gain independence from the memory-traces of a lost Mother (such as Wordsworth's "nature") in the face of a repressive super-ego, the internalized voice of the Father that also intones the norms of society (the "world" of "getting and spending"), whether the critic's focus is on the poet's own psychological development, as in the biographical strain in old historicism, or on the figures in the poet's texts, as in the new criticism.[15] Some such readings see the Romantic text as enabling a self-reunification of the divided psyche, or at least its accommodation of itself to the world, as in much new criticism and in Freud's "talking cure" that uses words as the primary avenue to self-understanding and re-socialization. But Freud's assumptions also suggest that the articulation of the self must eventually face the subject's gaping difference from itself, the fundamental disunity between consciousness, with its search for social acceptance, and the unconscious, with its self-concealments behind learned modes of behavior or expression that disguise earlier memory-traces of very primal, sexual, and antisocial drives. Consequently, as the psychoanalytic approach to Romantic texts developed, especially after the mid 1960s, its emphasis shifted primarily to subjectivities in texts that are and remain divided against themselves rather than verbal registers unified by a poetic equipoise among contraries.

This turn, not surprisingly, has coincided with the increased prominence of the French neo-Freudian Jacques Lacan. Influenced by Freud but also by G. W. F. Hegel's Romantic-era dialectic between Spirit and its material "other," the "throwing-forth" of the subject to construct itself without pre-definition in Martin Heidegger's existential phenomenology, and the articulation of the self by many signifiers as they become attached to and detached from signifieds in Saussure's linguistics, Lacan posits the incipient subject, permeated from birth by pre-linguistic signs that are visceral sensations and drives, as being recast as a figure in the social arena, having to fashion an other-from-itself (an "I" in language) *for* others (the gazes of other subjects, among them the gaze of the figure set up as the Father/super-ego). This alienation of the self works to achieve what it lacks after being ejected from the mother: a wholeness of selfhood like the image the child first sees of its full body reflected during what Lacan calls the "mirror stage" (see Lacan, cited in Rivkin and Ryan, *Literary Theory*, pp. 441–61). That quest occurs via a "throwing" of the amorphous self into the public system of signs that subsumes, interprets, and refigures the pre-linguistic nonsense of the body's sensations. The primordially "othered" subject must therefore achieve its self-construction in this alien verbal medium, the vast "Other" of all symbols, that both subjects the "I" to the oversight of the Father's Law (still a superego of social dictates) and defers all arrivals either to the desired whole or back to the mother. Such a deferral keeps occurring in a movement of the self-in-process, ending only in death, across the signifiers of both it and its objects that always incorporate the pre-linguistic "unconscious" (including the erotic and death drives) within the ingredients of the "Other" of myriad signifiers. Given that so many Romantic texts prefigure this casting of the "I" onto a sea of mysterious signs *and* obscure inner drives – Wordsworth's solitary walker, Coleridge's Ancient Mariner, Byron's Childe Harold, P. B. Shelley's "Alastor" Poet, Keats's seeker of his own truth on a Grecian urn, and Mary Shelley's Frankenstein, creature, and Walton the arctic explorer – it is not surprising that this Lacanian "quest-romance" of the alienated subject has become the journey of the "I" in several readings of Romantic writing. A 1986 example is Charles Rzepka's take on Coleridge's "Christabel" (1797–1800). Here the title character both carries through and fails in her quest for sexual identity, deferring her attainment of both sexuality and death, by alienating herself into signs under her Father's gaze that offer a double of her ("Geraldine") as a "figure of the mother" who embodies "both paralyzing dread," since Christabel's mother has died, and "self-transforming power," which Coleridge's heroine fears to activate.[16]

The psychoanalysis of Romantic texts, in other words, has moved from revealing the deepest drives within the imagination and the conscious obfuscation of them to exposing the subject and its imaginings as layers of expression and repression that lead only to signs of signs of signs that never reach ultimate objects or depths. These layers intimate, while also keeping their distance from, what Lacan calls "the Real," the welter of sheer chaotic physicality (including the most primordial pre-language in the body) – the unavailable otherness that Kant termed the "Thing in itself" – which remains removed from and yet desired by any and all representation. Now that this shift in theory has occurred, we may have arrived at an understanding, as Joel Faflak argues in *Romantic Psychoanalysis* (2008),[17] of the many similarities between the layers in Romantic writing and the process of psychoanalysis that could help explain why Coleridge in 1805 was the first writer to use the term "psycho-analytical" (Faflak, *Romantic Psychoanalysis*, p. 7). Further developing the empiricism in John Locke's *Essay Concerning Human Understanding* (1690), Wordsworth, like several of his contemporaries, sees all remembered initial perceptions turning, like early memory-traces for Freud, into memorials of those very perceptions, including composites of them called "ideas," which can then associate with each other in combinations that can be projected back into later perceptions, especially in poetry's "state of excitement" when associations lend "colouring" to "life" as it has been observed. The Wordsworthian subject is therefore working through a layering of impressions, in which later ones become just as ghost-like as the memories from earlier years, because of which "the old consciousnesses that haunt the present self" lack just as much solid "ground" as the added associations.[18] Particularly when this layer-on-layer of impressions is again overlaid by readable verbalization, the desire in both psychoanalysis and many readers of the *Lyrical Ballads* for a basis of "closure to the work of the psyche" confronts the basis of this signifying-of-signifiers as phantasmal at every level and neither able nor inclined to face the "Real" head on; in much Romantic writing, therefore, "the psyche tenaciously resists closure" because it is more like a text of other texts than any sort of mental mirror simply reflecting external objects or internal sensations (Faflak, *Romantic Psychoanalysis*, p. 30).

At this point, though, psychoanalytic theory has moved beyond its transformation by Lacan. It has become influenced at least as much by the "way of reading" that Jacques Derrida came to call "deconstruction" by the late 1960s, a different extension of both Saussurean linguistics and existential phenomenology. For Derrida, especially in his sense of Freud,[19] the impression that becomes a memory-trace among other traces and is the basic mental reference to objects or "nature" in Locke, Wordsworth, Freud, and Lacan reveals that any such apparent "signified always already functions as a signifier" and that this signifier, even at a hypothetical "first moment," is always already in a relationship with other signifiers that it interprets and that interpret it (Derrida, cited in Rivkin and Ryan, *Literary Theory*, p. 304). This mobility of signifiers differing from and referring, indeed *deferring*, to other signifiers, Derrida reminds us, has long been associated in Western thinking, as it often was in the eighteenth and early nineteenth centuries, with what we normally call "writing," the visible and concrete arrangement of signifiers where figures differ from and defer to each other in order for us to read them. Writing, in turn, since it so differs from itself within itself, has long been thought to be an "exteriority" (p. 311) secondary to and outside of a "presence" at one with itself to which writing points, either inside minds (presence as an *idea*) or inside perceived objects (the *essence* of each object, as in the basic "tree-ness" of every tree). But "deconstruction" as a process of re-visionary reading shows that every attempt to assert a presence, even of mind – such as Coleridge's symbol-making "secondary imagination" that looks back to a more "primary imagination" that is God's act of creation pre-consciously repeating itself in each of us (see Coleridge, cited in Adams, *Critical Theory*, p. 478) – finds that no such presence can even be posited unless there is first a process of signifiers referring to signifiers, all of which refer to what is other than any of them. Coleridge, after all, grounds his "secondary" creativity by making it the signifier of a more "primary" one, which itself turns out to be a trace in the mind that defers to a level of creation beyond it (the level of God, which is *not* present). The movement back and forth among "traces" that is "writing" in the broadest sense, more primordial than the printed writing that is one consequence of it, is thus previous to and foundational for the grounds that are supposedly the basis of it.

Like most strict binary oppositions, the old notion of presence versus writing turns out to reveal that its "secondary" side underlies both the "primary" one and the whole dichotomy, which has repressively turned a basic and fluid movement across equal signifiers into a supposedly fixed (albeit fictional) scheme of hierarchical oppositions. Such a revelation about works such as Coleridge's have consequently led since 1970 to many rereadings of classic "Romantic" poems and prose texts as really driven by and ultimately revealing this self-deconstructing process. That is so much the case that, for the deconstructive view of the Romantic text, the internal dynamic of each one has become no longer a new-critical equipoise of oppositions, even though largely formal "close reading" remains the mode of analysis, but, in the words of Tilottama Rajan in 1980, "a disunified and contradictory structure tacitly [but visibly] involved in contesting its own meaning."[20] Like other theories we have noted, this *un*resolved dialectic finds precedents in Romantic writing, and not just at those skeptical moments when writers of this era explicitly doubt the immediate relation of signs to meanings. The Romantic period, as it happens, was an arena where a tug-of-war was waged between theorists of language who saw God, objects, and thoughts as prior to words, such as James Burnett, Lord Monboddo, and those, such as Horne Tooke, who posited words and their interrelations as necessary for the genesis and ordering of thoughts, making signifiers in some sense prior to the possibility of signifieds.[21] It was almost inevitable, given this debate, that Tooke's position would contend with Monboddo's, sometimes within the works of the same writer.[22]

It may be fitting, then, that the more recent deconstructive exposure of this tension in Romantic works has developed mainly in two directions that are essentially quite different. On the one hand, Paul de Man, from the late 1960s through to the 1980s, pioneered analyses of Romantic works that show their "constative" dimension, in which they strive to portray a world view with some "authority of sense and meaning," being countered by what makes that possible, the "performative" dimension, the level of "articulation ... prior to its signifying function" where each figure keeps displacing a predecessor and being displaced by a successor. Derrida's back-and-forth movement of every "trace" is now for de Man "the senseless power of positional language" in its "pure rhetoric" of signifiers, the "element in thought that [ultimately] destroys thought in [language's] attempt to forget" the "duplicity" in its making *and* un-making of meanings.[23] In this view and those that echo it, there is finally no escape from the dependence of emerging significance on a meaningless "rhetoricity," even in Coleridge's valuation of the "symbol" over "allegory," one of those binaries where the second term really underwrites and undermines the first. For de Man the Romantic symbol is an attempted concrete universal made possible and put in question by the process most fundamental to allegory (what Coleridge calls a "picture language"): the reference of the most visible figures to other signs or texts, as when some earthly icon, such as a rose, is made to refer to some counterpart in scripture or philosophy or code of chivalry.[24]

On the other hand, there are counter-practitioners of deconstruction who prefer showing how the ever-disruptive movement of signification can enable a return from repression of the re-creative powers of language to transform its older constructs. In this approach, Derrida's exposure of how any "trace's" reference in backward- and forward-looking directions can open sentences and works to their widest ranges of "intertextual" allusion means that the significance of symbols is never *strictly* hemmed in by their most immediate context and that they can be shifted from one order of meanings to others, just as they have been in a past they always echo. This view sees special value, for example, in the sense of great poetry in P. B. Shelley's *Defence* as reopening "afresh the associations" that have been suppressed by hegemonic constructs so that "vitally metaphorical" activations of language's intertextual and reformative possibilities can help us envision the "unapprehended relations of things," which can break up the dominant schemes that have restricted the movement across different signifiers on which those norms are really based.[25]

Not all employers of deconstruction, to be sure, fall into only one of these two tendencies, but all of them are still vulnerable to a charge, also made against some new critics and psychoanalysts, that the underlying theory and any application of it stay at a level of purely textual or mental reference that ignores the struggles of material existence during the Romantic era between modes of economic production, methods of socio-economic exchange, and the conflicting interests of different social classes, the focal points for Marxist cultural analysis since the works from the 1840s to the 1860s of Karl Marx himself. Marx may echo the structure of Hegel's Spirit-matter dialectic and some early nineteenth-century arguments for cultural transformation, such as de Staël's *Literature Considered in Relation to Social Institutions* (1800), where the "relation of literature and society" is established as "one of mutual influence" (from the introduction to de Staël, cited in Adams, *Critical Theory*, p. 447). But Marx also finds the true cultural dialectic to be finally different from both of these. To him the "production of ideas" and "consciousness," including all forms of art, are the "direct efflux of ... material behavior" during a given span of time and in a particular social arena full of class conflicts and other tensions caused by newer modes of production struggling against older methods of exchange. For Marx the "phantoms formed in the human brain" at any time must therefore be viewed as "*sublimates* of ... material life process" – in chemical terms, shifts of concrete matter from a solid to a gaseous state – whereby the collations of beliefs that form "ideology" (non-material ways of interpreting and re-presenting material existence) must be seen as "reflexes and echoes of" a real "life process," particularly when "ideology," being so dependent on "phantoms" (like "memory-traces"), refigures "men and their circumstances upside down as in a camera obscura" (Marx, cited in Adams, *Critical Theory*, p. 625). Marxist analysis must consequently confront the tendency in ideology and its products, literature among them, to be a phantasmic "false consciousness" (or "superstructure") that distorts its material grounds (or "base"). Yet the same critique must press that anamorphic reconstruction back down to its very contentious social basis, which appears partly in the very act of distortion that tries to conceal it, somewhat as Freud's conscious symptoms both obscure and reveal unconscious drives, here transformed into a socio-political unconscious.

It is for these reasons in Marxist theory, then, that the surge in Marxist-"materialist" criticism in the 1930s, occurring alongside the resurgence of psychoanalysis, approached Romantic writing with a bias towards evaluating the basis and extent of its "false consciousness," including the deceptive unity of its "world-view" as "old" historicism has tried to construe it. According to Christopher Caudwell in 1936, most Romantic poems and their general mentality are nearly all productions of a "bourgeois dream" in largely middle-class writing about a desired but illusory "individualism" that strongly resists, and thereby reveals, "the contradiction" basic to the "bourgeois economy" that is the immersion of this class in conflicts with "lower" and "higher" ones at a time of blurring class boundaries. Even such an illusion for this Marxist, though, must and does eventually face the "lie" of a deceptive capitalism when "individualism" turns into a tragic vision of its always unsatisfiable desires, as in Keats's "La Belle Dame Sans Merci" (1819–20), and so makes readers turn to "freedom as the life-won consciousness of social necessity," a drive towards transformations beyond bourgeois dominance such as Marx envisioned in the nineteenth century (Caudwell, cited in Gleckner, *Romanticism*, pp. 108–24). By the 1950s and

1960s, however, Marxist analyses have acquired greater scope and have thus expanded their understandings of the social dynamics being refigured in Romantic literature and the range of literature of this era to which analysis should be applied. In *Culture and Society* (1958), the British neo-Marxist Raymond Williams may accept Caudwell's sense of the "Romantic artist" as resisting immediate history insofar as poets of this type hold up "certain human values" that can "be set above the clamor of the writer's actual relations with society." To this end these authors fashion an ideology of "culture" as the "embodied spirit of a People" and a "court of appeal in which real values [can be] determined" beyond politics and economics (Williams, cited in Gleckner, *Romanticism*, pp. 273–5). But at the same time Williams, who views ideological constructs as "effluxes" of deeper "structures of feeling" that arise in people as *part* of their material struggles, sees the Romantic poeticizing of certain values as reflecting widespread "apprehensions" about "the essential significance of the [emerging] Industrial revolution." These efforts also reveal that "the production of art was coming to be regarded as one of a number of specialized kinds of production" that were all contesting the same cultural space, so much so that the "idea of the independent creative writer" now came into being, but without any genuine autonomy from "a large new middle-class reading public" and a growing "institution of commercial publishing" (pp. 271–4).

Though the idea of one conceptual period mentality is still being challenged here, Romantic writing is not simply "false consciousness" any longer but, first, a literary engagement with competing ideologies that range between pre-industrial beliefs and others nostalgic for older hierarchies and, second, a troubled quest for a supposed "free play of genius" within an array of conflicting market factors and modes of public expression (Gleckner, *Romanticism*, p. 285). This more nuanced sense of the Romantic work in its social contexts has therefore been the most common one in the Marxist analyses of Romanticism since 1960, and these more recent variations have therefore developed in several different directions, sometimes even within the career of one Marxist critic (my example being Daniel P. Watkins). One direction reads the corpus of a Romantic writer or a group of poems to show, in the very style and the imagery of the writing as well as its references to immediate social conditions or texts about them, that the "individualism and subjectivity" in the poetry "is a sign of the fragmentation of bourgeois life," including the reactionary and progressive ideologies pulling that life in opposite directions at once.[26] Another direction accepts, far more than Abrams, the deep involvement of most Romantic writers in the highly contentious quarrels over degrees of revolutionary change and even the gender- (along with class-) politics of the 1790s and after, yet it concentrates on how the resulting works articulate the power-relations that waning or rising ideologies tacitly endorse or question, as when the "romantic rejection of capitalism" embraces the latter's continuations of gender inequality enough that many writings in this vein display "masculinist tendencies" to construct the Romantic "subject" by way of deceptive subjugations of woman.[27] A third variation reminds us of the jostling among multiple genres, as well as class-based discourses, at this time in Britain so that the critic may question the focus primarily on lyric poetry in most of Romantic scholarship through 1970 and see the ideological struggles of this era manifested quite powerfully in many prose fictions (see chapter 9 of this volume) and in the highly social and commercial realm of Romantic-era drama.[28] Though psychoanalysis and deconstruction have begun to shatter the unity of the Romantic subject and text affirmed in old historicism and new criticism, Marxism, in turn, breaks the Romantic "I" into the many social relations that constitute it and the Romantic period into a wide variety of discourses in economic and political conflict with each other.

### III   The revolutions of gender criticism, "new" historicism, and cultural studies

The most thoroughgoing dispersions of the Romantic text, subject, and period, however, have really come from the arguments of feminism and gender-theory and the ways in which they and some of the schemes already discussed have become contributors to even more recent complexes of theory and criticism, the ones we now call "new" historicism and cultural studies. The women's movement for genuine equality in the 1960s and after, though it did draw attention back to precursor-texts that included Mary Wollstonecraft's *A Vindication of the Rights of Woman* (1792), took until about 1975 to take substantial hold in the academic study of literature in the English-speaking world. When it did, it quickly shattered the established boundaries of the "Romantic period" that only Marxism had really begun to unsettle. A new imperative to recover and analyze long-suppressed writing by women of the past soon exposed the astonishing amount of published and performed works by women in Britain from the 1780s to the 1830s (see chapter 8 of this volume). This true revolution thereby exploded the "spirit of the age" as somehow epitomized only by the "Big Six" male poets and the genres in which they wrote, the view so long enabled by the sidelining of the few recognized female authors of that time as throwbacks to the eighteenth century (Jane Austen) or as writers of *non*-literature (such as the *Vindication*) or as mere disciples of men (Mary Shelley) only slightly concerned with issues tied to their femininity (even though Mary was Wollstonecraft's daughter). One major result has been not just the welcome reprinting of many long-lost texts by women of this era but the thorough reassessment of all their works, even "classic" ones such as Austen's and Shelley's, as deeply imbued with the actual life-struggles of being a woman in a male-dominated culture (see Curran on Austen in chapter 8, below), with critiques of the oppressive problems for both sexes that stem from the constructs of male dominance (as in *Frankenstein*, where a man "gives birth" without benefit of woman while failing to see how much his mother's death actually drives him), and with the need for women to couch their writing in a "double-voiced discourse" that forces their "muted" word-patterns and themes to be articulated at least partly in the "dominant" language of men demanded by both literary tradition and most publishers of the time.[29]

Another important result, though, recalling and extending Wollstonecraft's theoretical claims, has been the theorizing of what these positionings of "woman" really mean within "the more general cultural ideology that conditions both the behavior patterns and the modes of discourse available to men and women."[30] The dominant Anglo-American approach to such theorizing – what Showalter has called "gynocriticism" (*New Feminist*, p. 248) from the Greek *gune* meaning "woman" – has emphasized how women writers, double-voiced as nearly all must be, have still written out of a "distinctive female literary tradition with its characteristic themes and forms," always adjusted under the pressures of class or race and often conveyed in "noncanonical" genres ranging from letters, diaries, and conduct books to tracts, children's literature, books of folklore, and subsets of the novel, popular drama, and poetry (Mellor, *Romanticism and Feminism*, p. 4), all of which now need to be read and reassessed *as literature* and as in fact more prevalent during this era than the lyric or narrative poetry of internalized male quests. Indeed, it can now be argued that these mainly feminine "themes and forms," some begun in much earlier women's writing, reveal an entirely different "Romantic period" than any codified by Dowden, Lovejoy, Wellek, Abrams, or Bloom:

> Instead, women Romantic writers tended to celebrate, not the achievements of the imagination ... but rather the workings of the rational mind, a mind relocated ... [firmly] in the female as well as the male body. They thus insisted [not only] on the fundamental equality of women and men ... [but] on what Carol Gilligan has recently taught us to call an ethic of care which insists on the primacy of the family or the community ... and on a cooperative rather than a possessive interaction with a Nature troped as a female friend or sister ... [all through] a gradual rather than violent social change ... that extends the values of domesticity into the public realm.[31]

Though Anne Mellor recognizes, here in 1993, that these are synoptic generalizations about what some women writers advanced in conservative and others in more liberal ways at the time, she offers extensive evidence that these were central concerns in the writings of Austen, Mary Shelley, the Gothic "romancer" Ann Radcliffe, and the noted playwright Joanna Baillie as much as in the texts of, among others, Charlotte Smith, Hannah More, Dorothy Wordsworth, Mary Robinson, Felicia Hemans, and Letitia Landon. If there is any dominant "period mentality" in their era, we have to "discriminate" among Romanticisms once again, Mellor and others argue, now by accepting at least two: a "masculine" (the traditional) and a "feminine" (the above) Romanticism that appear to have occupied often separate spheres generically and ideologically but are ultimately as equal in aesthetic and historical importance as they are coterminous over the late eighteenth and the early nineteenth centuries.

Meanwhile, another whole line of feminist thinking, the French-based theory associated by Alice Jardine with "gynesis,"[32] has taken the groundless and centerless differing-and-deferring of signifiers seen as primordial to all discourse by Derrida and shown how that "otherness" has long been associated in the West with an unstable femininity against which supposedly grounded and centered male discourses of "presence" have arisen to provide illusory stability and all-controlling authority. If women's writing is double-voiced in this view, a female author can offer an answer to male dominance by bringing forward the repressed "gynetic" mobility across differences – the primordial Feminine – on which all writing, gender-divides, and thus even men are based. The French psychoanalyst Julia Kristeva has called this mobility the "semiotic" level (like Lacan's pre-linguistic body-language), at which point there is not yet full separation of the child from the body of the mother, and has more recently linked that primal chaos with the "abject," the primordial condition of differences blurring into and out of each other (like the male child being inside and outside the mother at birth and genders thus being in some sense indistinct) which has to be "thrown off" (abjected) if a subject, particularly a man seeking power, is going to assert a coherent "identity" in constructions of a "self."[33] Critics in this vein have consequently found women writers, and even a few men, of the Romantic era asserting a counter-discourse in multiple genres in the ways they hint at a "presymbolic language," the "literal" as opposed to Lacan's public language of the "symbolic," as when Margaret Homans in 1986 reveals Dorothy Wordsworth in her diaries writing out quite semiotically the feminine "natural" descriptions that her brother then turns into the "literal" level of his very masculine nature poems.[34] As Anne Williams has shown in 1995,[35] too, this tense interplay between the feminine/semiotic and the male/symbolic drives in Western culture appears quite sharply in the uneasy relationship of "Romantic" writing to the so-called "Gothic" fictions and dramas from the 1760s through to the 1820s that "high" Romantic poets often drew into their works while claiming to be scornful of such "low"-level writing. The Gothic from Horace Walpole's *Castle of Otranto* (1764) to Radcliffe in the 1790s and beyond, Williams reminds us, is the literature of dead primal mothers, known mainly from obscured vestiges of writing, who return from repression in some spectral or monstrous form as the "unruly female principle" – the "abject," as in the figure of Geraldine who harbors all the deathly contradictions of "innocent" Christabel or the face of Frankenstein's creature that resembles his dream of embracing his decaying mother's body – to show the foundation of most internal quests to be this feminine multiplicity that is just too basic to be overcome despite all male *and* female efforts to keep "her" buried from view (see Williams, *Art of Darkness*, pp. 108, 176–9).

Eventually, though, this tug-of-war between a level of mobile, blurring differences and a symbolic process of turning these into codified public schemes, including fixed gender oppositions, has to beg some profound questions: if distinct "gender" (the cultural categorizing of sexes that are both really fluid) is a construct repressive of a more complex body-language in women and men – and is thus far more social and conventional than "natural" and inevitable – what does that mean about "gender" as a category and not just about the unnatural hierarchy of "male" over "female"? What, too, do such blatant constructs reveal about all such distinctions, such as those that have for centuries tried to stigmatize homosexuality, the interplay of body-languages between people both sexed male or both sexed female? These questions prompted by French feminism, but also by Anglo-American constructivist sociology and Foucault's *History of Sexuality* (1976–84), led by the later 1980s to the expansion of feminist theory into the wider study of gender as a social problem for all sexes, culminating in the 1990 publication of both Judith Butler's *Gender Trouble* and Eve Kosofsky Sedgwick's *Epistemology of the Closet*. In these theoretical statements, "gender" is never "predetermined by some manner of interior essence" but continuously constructed in a Lacanian, largely public, and theatrically "*stylized repetition of acts*" by which a person, sexed male or female, comes to "embody" a "set of historical possibilities" encoded in the realm of symbolic interactions, so much so that there is no challenging this process, even if it misrepresents the complexities of one's variable body-language, except by alternative actions of performance that act out a "modality of gender that cannot be readily assimilated into existing categories" (Butler, cited in Rivkin and Ryan, *Literary Theory*, pp. 900–1008). At the same time, though, Sedgwick insists, "human sexuality," even when forced into this process, ought to be recognized as a multiplicity beyond description that "extends along so many dimensions," and so differently within and between individuals from day to day, that such a plural "it" is never "well described in terms of the gender of object-choice" or any fixed public norm (Sedgwick, cited in Rivkin and Ryan, *Literary Theory*, pp. 912–21). Both arguments mean that histories of "female" versus "male" oppositions, however useful for a start – including the dichotomy of "feminine" versus "masculine Romanticism" – are but an incomplete way of dealing with the struggle of myriad sexual possibilities with the symbolic order of cultural constructs that enforce both gender-opposites and prohibitions of same-sex relationships.

Such theories have consequently encouraged a variety of post-feminist but highly gender-based studies of Romantic writers. Among these, admittedly, are continuations of the initially feminist approach to how Romantic male subjects construct their textual selves via the symbolic "othering" of the feminine, thereby revealing their own subjugation to an entirely fictional process (see Alan Richardson and Marlon Ross, for example, in Mellor, *Romanticism and Feminism*, pp. 13–51). Since the mid 1980s, though, these studies have been joined by ones on mostly male Romantics encountering the multiplicity of possible sexual roles, including homosexual ones, in the ways their chosen schemes of self-stylization place them in oscillations among sexual tendencies because of historically layered features *in those schemes of performance* and not just in the orientations of the authors themselves.[36] In addition, there have come to be accounts of the ways Romantic-era men, concerned about the gender-process confining them even if it is not as restrictive as what has limited women, have tried to rewrite the gender codes for both sexes in the face of powerful but aging social norms. Tim Fulford's *Romanticism and Masculinity* (1999),[37] for example, has shown how "a crisis of gender" in the 1790s, in the wake of revolutions that had destabilized the locus of "authority" with the help of the *Vindications* of Wollstonecraft and others, led to constructions of "a different kind of manliness" in place of "traditional models" that "had been discredited without being successfully replaced" (Fulford, *Romanticism*, pp. 5–11). Gender theory has set the stage, it turns out, for analyses of Romantic "masculinity" as much as "femininity" insofar as both are symbolic categories of containment that can be put in question by examining the histories of their unstable constructions, ultimately for the benefit of women, men, and all those who cross the traditional boundaries that culture keeps trying to impose on sexuality.

Fulford, however, could not make the thorough case he does without linking his debts to gender-theory with what he admits to be the "new historicism" that began to declare itself clearly around 1980 (Fulford, *Romanticism*, p. 22). Every text he treats is "contextualized and historicized" within all the different and conflicting discourses that impinged upon each at the time it was written (*ibid.*). Fulford, like many others by the year 2000, is denying the unified period mentality of "old" historicism, the quasi-organic coalescence of contraries in the "new critical" sense of a text aesthetically transcending its time, and the notion that the deepest layers of individual subjectivity are mainly internal to the subject itself, the view of most strictly Freudian psychoanalysts. New historicist subjectivity is more of a crossroads where choices are made among culturally situated discourses that also help form every subject's ways of construing its "nature." This approach harkens back to many discourses itself: those Marxist dialectics focused on the contesting voices of different classes at any one time, partly as recast by the Russian Mikhail Bakhtin in his "heteroglossia" of the differing discourses within a social space; the anthropologist Clifford Geertz's analysis of societies by a "thick description" of all the stories, gossip, special terms, and small rituals dovetailing into any cultural activity; Lacan's and Butler's throwing of the subject into the contentious crucible of the Symbolic order that is the path to self-presentation; the "intertextuality" of Derridean deconstruction *without* the acceptance of a performative level where signs carry no ideological baggage with them; Anglo-American feminism's opening of established and recovered texts, not only to their double-voicing through dominant male discourses but to echoes in them of muted writings by women in their racial and class contexts; and the later Foucault's sense of all organized discourses as seeking *power* over the "knowledge" and the groupings they help to form in very local, as well as large-scale, exercises of attempted control that also arouse discourses of resistance with similar aims. Most of these strands were conflated first by the American professor Stephen Greenblatt and several of his colleagues in "early modern" literary studies, starting most clearly in his *Renaissance Self-Fashioning* (1980), though they were soon joined by the more directly Marxist Alan Sinfield and Jonathan Dollimore among scholars of the early modern in Britain. The key common ground of their approaches, as in Fulford's, is "a refiguring of the socio-cultural field" that "resituates" any work or artistic display "in relationship to other genres and modes of discourse" alongside relevant "social institutions and non-discursive practices," all in cultural play over a particular span of time. The purpose of each refiguration is to show in the work or display and its interconnections "the patterns of consonance and contradiction" and the jockeyings for "ideological dominance" among the *dis*-united "values and interests" affecting the author, the group(s) most immediately affiliated with him or her, and the larger society of that time and place.[38]

The movement of this approach into British Romantic scholarship began accelerating in the early 1980s, and it has since become, with its genuine openness to related "schools," the dominant critical mode in Britain and America – with even a manifesto-volume in 1989 by some of its best practitioners[39] – for interpreting writers and cultural performances of the Romantic period, however much this perspective rejects the coherence of a "period" in the "old historical" sense. One direction "new historicism" has taken, to be sure, extends the Marxist view of imaginary transcendence as "false consciousness" into texts of Wordsworthian Romanticism where even their intertextual references to "non-literary" discourses and events help them to achieve an illusion of rising above the immediately historical, to such an extent that these "strong denials of history" can be shown to be "the deepest realizations of history."[40] This direction has been both defined and critiqued by Jerome McGann's *The Romantic Ideology* (1983),[41] which shows how attempts at dissipating social conflicts in sublimations of them by poetry can indeed be found in works by most of the canonized male "Romantics" – but also how considerable modern criticism, from "old" historicism even to deconstruction, has too easily accepted this ideological gambit by imitating it to the point of effacing the complex range of historical conditions relevant to any text.[42] McGann has then gone on to demonstrate himself a far wider range of new-historical approaches to Romantic and other poems, especially in analyses of all the points at which a text-in-the-making is "in circulation," engaged in exchanges between the author and his/her colleagues and their ideologies, the authors and the genres or the pertinent texts of the past *and* the present, the author and his/her publishers and editors, these publishers/editors and their targeted readers, readers (including the larger "public") and the authors (particularly when the author revises) – all of the foregoing *within* the economics of publishing and marketing – and even the work after the author's death and all the "framings" that inform the subsequent readings of it, from editions to source studies to influential interpretations.[43] At about the same time, too, Marilyn Butler in Britain, most of all in *Romantics, Rebels, and Reactionaries* (1981),[44] has reminded us that all writers of this era, given the burgeoning rise in the printing as well as the circulation of writing, usually wrote not as the solitaries of "Romantic ideology" but as members of groups with ideological orientations in conflict with other such groups, all of whom had relationships with previous group versions of their positions and with publics they sought as their audience in a world of rapid socio-economic change and feverish contests among opposed beliefs.

Between them, McGann and Butler have consequently helped to launch several mini-revolutions in Romantic scholarship that have lasted to this day. Among these are studies of Romantic-era works as quite often collaborative, rather than just personal, achievements;[45] thorough research into the growing reading public of the time and its effect on what was written, published, staged, and reviewed;[46] new ecological understandings of how Romantic "nature" poetry and prose engaged with the environmental debates of both its day and ours;[47] revelations about the parallels between the imagination in poetry and the mind and brain as conceived by the science and medicine of the time;[48] and greater attention to the Romantic-period awareness of the conventions in many specific genres – prose, theatrical, and critical, as well as poetic – as authors, given the ideologies and even the gender affiliations linked to different forms, wrestled with tensions between maintaining and changing the types of writing they chose to rework from the distant or immediate past.[49] In all of this, it can be (and has been) argued that scholarship is getting closer than ever before to the real conditions and multiplicity of the Romantic period, even if the effect is to question Romantic notions of *Zeitgeist*. The British Romantic era, we have long known – and not just in the historical novels and poems of Sir Walter Scott – was a time deeply immersed in thoroughly rearticulating the history of Britain, Europe, and "the East"; in advancing the idea of the self (say, in Wordsworth's *Prelude*) as an organically developing entity evolving through, but also retaining some, history; *and* in holding widely published debates among different ideologies of what history is and what it should include.[50] Hence we can now be in dialogue with more aspects of the Romantic era, and with a greater variety of texts and intertextual relationships, because some of these have helped to set in motion the perspectives *beyond* the "Romantic ideology" through which we can now view them.

I would even argue that this volume itself makes extensive use of what is now possible because of new historicism and the related approaches that have contributed to it. What we offer here are windows into large ranges of cross-textual and socio-political interrelations that are fundamental to the widened range of Romantic-era texts that we have now come to value. The following essays show us, in fact, several emergent arenas of focus in Romantic studies that have all been encouraged by new historicism: the intertextual references back and forth between early nineteenth- and eighteenth-century texts that show much closer ties than we used to accept between trends we now call "Romantic" and much of the "Enlightenment" that led to them (see chapter 2, below); a more expansive view of the complex political scene in Britain after the French Revolution that explains the tensions in many kinds of writing between defenses of tradition and calls for greater freedom (see chapter 3); the broad range of similarities and differences – not Wellek's uniformity – between German idealist philosophy after 1780 and British responses to it (see chapter 4); the controversies at the time about how language works, which stretched well beyond Monboddo and Tooke, as these appear in the references of this era's poets to linguistic theories only recently tied to them (see chapter 5); the interactions of nearly all published genres with the magazines and papers that reviewed them incessantly from the eighteenth into the nineteenth century, a very political and contentious set of exchanges that was the "spirit of the age" as much as any other (as Butler shows in this volume – see chapter 6); the many vagaries of the publishing business and the different publics for different literatures that writers of this era had to anticipate at several stages of their work (see chapter 7); the hitherto little-noticed relationship between the growing ranks of female *readers*, with their circulating libraries and favorite publishers, and the increasing publications by women across a broad spectrum of genres (see chapter 8); the remarkable and frequently politicized range of numerous prose fictions at this time, too long undervalued during the concentration on poetry in older Romantic scholarship (see chapter 9); the many and layered cultural conditions, from a range of available genres to the class-positions attached to different types of writing (hardly one mind-set), from which the poets of the Romantic period, male and female, did arise and develop (according to Curran – chapter 10); and the conversations between the visual, performing, and printed verbal arts at this time, once studied as separate, if parallel, spheres, that now can be seen as producing a series of interpenetrations, inside but also outside the illuminated books of Blake, that were enabled by several factors from changing market tastes to the support or disdain of public institutions (see chapter 11).

Concurrently, though, we should also note that many of the impulses that helped to drive new historicism have also led several recent scholars of Romantic writing to read it through the interlocking perspectives most often labeled "cultural studies," which include new or revived theories and analyses focused on marginalized groups, "subaltern" races, and colonized or post-colonial civilizations. The name "cultural studies" comes principally from the Centre for Contemporary Cultural Studies, founded in 1964 at the University of Birmingham in England, which began, according to one of its founders, Stuart Hall, as a "discursive formation" torn between long-standing aspects of Marxism, such as "the complex relations" of capital, class, and power as these imbue many "different domains of life," and the rejection by what was then the "New Left" of the Marxist "model of base and superstructure" as inadequate to the description of real social interactions.[51] This tension, Hall claims, was somewhat resolved by greater academic attention to oral, written, visual, and material "textualities" of all kinds, with street talk, carnivals, rock and roll, and anti-colonial protest journalism being just as relevant as literature, "legitimate" theatre, or film. Indeed, "culture" as Hall came to define it by 1986 refers to "the actual, grounded terrain of practices, representations, languages and customs of any specific historical society" (S. Hall, as quoted in Grossberg *et al.*, *Cultural Studies*, p. 5). All these textualities, according to Catherine Hall, allow people or groups to construct "identity," but always in a "society" that must be exposed as "cross-cut by complex social and political antagonisms" from those of "class" and "gender" to those of "race and ethnicity." The exposure of all this reveals, as in Foucault, how any "regime of knowledge constructed" out of such contested and contesting discourses manifests "relations of dominant and subordinate," whether the analysis is about small community tensions or the relations between colonizers and the colonized or even masters and slaves (C. Hall, also from 1990, cited in Grossberg *et al.*, *Cultural Studies*, pp. 240–3). While this approach joins new historicism in seeing any "text" as in circulation among composers, contributors, and different classes of readers or respondents, all of which are caught in rivalries among discourses affiliated with class, gendered, and racial positions, the emphasis of cultural studies is usually on how the subordinated "low" or marginal in any of these encounters struggles with the dominant "high" or central, and vice versa, in local, national, or international discourse-exchanges of many kinds.

Particularly as this emphasis has spread and been transformed in migrations across Europe and the Atlantic, it has therefore been concerned most often with the ways contested cultural positions can and do articulate themselves, simultaneously asserting and blurring boundaries, within the claims of "certainty and stability" from some "dominant" quarter as it succeeds or fails in "mask[ing] conflict, insecurity, and resistance" that is always there in "ever-shifting and historically specific" forms (C. Hall, cited in Grossberg *et al.*, *Cultural Studies*, p. 241). Catherine Hall herself, for example, in her concentration on British missionary forays into colonized and enslaved outposts before the middle of the nineteenth century, shows how numerous missionary discourses asserted a new "order" based on the abolition of slavery, yet still manifested "the cultural racism of the anti-slavery movement" enough to make protesting slaves describe the oppression they faced only through the words of a quite "particular male, middle-class, English imagination" (pp. 244–5). With such revelations, cultural-studies analysis can discover once-hidden frames of reference even in the earlier nineteenth-century writing of authors now described as exemplary "Romantics." Coleridge's poem "Fears in Solitude" (1798), for instance, condemns both the slave trade of his own time and the imposition of British prerogatives on virtually all their foreign victims when his speaker laments how "we have gone forth / And borne to distant tribes slavery and pangs, / And, deadlier far, our vices, / whose deep taint / With slow perdition murders the whole man" ("Fears," lines 49–52). Indeed, Coleridge was one among many "Romantic" models, men and women, who openly prefigured the posture that present-day cultural studies now asks of its practitioners: the role of the "engaged intellectual" who always combines theory with practice, matching refashioned styles of writing and criticism with genuine engagement in social issues and political action.

This standard, of course, has not gone unnoticed or unpracticed by present-day scholars of Romanticism. But since cultural studies is so deliberately unstable, boldly eclectic, and quite far-ranging, the recent Romanticists who have adopted forms of it, often with features of new historicism, have done so on a variety of fronts that are still being developed and will undoubtedly increase.[52] One vein continues the connection with gender criticism at Birmingham by analyzing the explicitly marginalized woman before and after 1800 and how she both challenges and is used by dominant groups for either cultural validation or pointed exclusion.[53] Most of the scholarship in this cultural-studies revolution, though, stems from two overriding concerns thus far. One of them is how writing of the Romantic era responded to many elements of the slave trade and the issues of race linked to it, given the much-publicized debates over slavery that led Britain's Parliament to outlaw the trade, though not to emancipate the slaves, in 1807. The other is how criticism has dealt with the widespread use in Romantic writers of "the East" as it was constructed by both proponents and critics of the British imperialism that had conquered India and would bring a quarter of the world under British control by 1820, now that scholars of literature have been alerted to the West's numerous misconstructions of this very "Orient" by Edward Said's landmark study so aptly called *Orientalism* (1978). Though the pervasiveness of enslavement and "othered" races in many texts of this period started to be surveyed some time ago, often in the writings of abolitionist women, an intense scrutiny of "the slave question" based in cultural-studies and post-colonial theory has been applied to many well-known and newly recovered Romantic works by Helen Thomas in 2000[54] and Debbie Lee in 2002,[55] as well as in other books focused more on single authors of this period. These studies follow the cultural-studies effort to show the "dominant" discourse having to face the "insecurities," as well as the tyrannies, of its own situation, by revealing, as Lee says, how the contradictions in the best-known Romantic stance – between the sympathetic humanism it inherited from "sensibility" and its visions of human progress often appropriated by pro-capitalist and imperialist arguments – force Romantic writers, in the face of slavery and its consequences, to see themselves, like their civilization, as internally divided and *not* finally organic. Ultimately the constructed "self" that would be "unified" in Britain turns out to be based on the "othered" and the "alienated" on whom that construction depends for its socio-economic foundations and its cultural supremacy.[56]

Perhaps not surprisingly, a similar understanding of such writers appears in the recent new attention to Romantic orientalism and its many ties to imperialism, especially in such studies as Saree Makdisi's in 1999,[57] Alan Bewell's of the same year,[58] and Nigel Leask's in 2002.[59] As Leask puts the matter, most of the "Romantic discourse of the Orient" exhibits "more anxieties and instabilities ... than positivities and totalities." Such authors as Byron, P. B. Shelley, and Thomas De Quincey, we find, "neither" tried completely "to subvert the imperialist project," despite their and other critiques of it, nor "simply to endorse it," given their British guilt over the fact and brutalities of slavery, the spread of European contagions to races of other lands, and Britain's pillaging of natural and aesthetic resources from conquered civilizations (Leask, *British Romantic Writers*, pp. 2–3). The writing that results, then, even when the "imperialist Self" seems brought "level with its Oriental other," finally "perpetuates the prejudice of the East/West binary opposition whilst attacking the ideology of empire which it empowers," thereby showing the fundamental "antagonisms" undergirding dominance that cultural studies always pursues (pp. 4–5).

Even if we can still accept, as the goals of some, the striving of the imaginative self for at least poetic wholeness and its hopes for an organic re-fusion of mind and nature once both regressive tyranny and the violence of revolution are past – an aspiration that still justifies the label "Romanticism" – those constructs, themselves competitors among others at the time (as Marxism, feminism, and new historicism have shown), are now revealed by cultural studies to be built on a base of deep social conflicts, national and international, that no ideology of transcendence can finally escape or entirely subsume – the reality that any future study of Romanticism must admit and face, complicating and enriching what that label means from now on. The scholarly effort just recounted that accelerated at the start of the twentieth century to secure post-Enlightenment Romanticism as a cultural confluence of ideas and poetic devices useful for asserting a coherent Western culture has been shown by the dawn of the twenty-first century to be a self-deceiving fabrication remarkably parallel to the attempt of some Romantics themselves to achieve "totalizing aspirations" in "poetry and politics" (Leask, *British Romantic Writers*, p. 6; see also Gonsalves, "Problematic Configurations"). The future of Romantic studies must consequently acknowledge and engage the pulls in both these directions even as it confronts the tug-of-war between conservative nostalgia and progressive revolution in most of the British texts we reread or uncover in struggling with what "Romanticism" does and should mean. Cultural studies and its tributaries are already starting to be challenged, as we have found to be the fate of all the earlier "schools" of theory and criticism.[60] Yet, whenever the resulting changes come to be focused on Romantic writing and the cultural contestation from which it emerges, they will still begin – because of this entire history – with a vibrant field of enquiry and a rich array of literatures that are just as ready to be revised as the Romantic era itself asked to be in its own revisions of the genres and the issues that prompted its striking transformations of Western culture.

## NOTES

1. Hans Eichner, ed., 'Romantic' and Its Cognates: The European History of a Word (University of Toronto Press, 1972), p. 5.
2. William Wordsworth, Selected Prose, ed. John O. Hayden (New York: Penguin, 1988), pp. 281–2.
3. See Harold Bloom, ed., Romanticism and Consciousness: Essays in Criticism (New York: Norton, 1970), pp. 3–24.
4. See Stephen Copley and John Whale, eds., Beyond Romanticism: New Approaches to Texts and Contexts, 1780–1832 (London: Routledge, 1992), pp. 1–3.
5. Aidan Day, Romanticism (London: Routledge, 1996), p. 5.
6. George Whalley, "England: Romantic – Romanticism," in Eichner, 'Romantic,' pp. 157–262.
7. Taine, cited in Hazard Adams, ed., Critical Theory Since Plato, rev. edn. (Philadelphia: Harcourt Brace Jovanovich, 1992), p. 612.
8. Robert Gleckner, ed., Romanticism: Points of View, 2nd edn. (Detroit: Wayne State University Press, 1975), p. 18.
9. Ferdinand de Saussure, Course in General Linguistics, eds. Charles Bally and Albert Sechehaye, trans. Wade Baskin (New York: McGraw-Hill, 1959), pp. 65–70.
10. Julie Rivkin and Michael Ryan, eds., Literary Theory: An Anthology, 2nd edn. (Oxford: Blackwell, 2004), p. 22.
11. M. H. Abrams, The Mirror and the Lamp: Romantic Theory and the Critical Tradition (New York: Norton, 1958).
12. M. H. Abrams, Natural Supernaturalism: Tradition and Revolution in Romantic Literature (New York: Norton, 1971).
13. Harold Bloom, The Anxiety of Influence: A Theory of Poetry, 2nd edn. (New York: Oxford University Press, 1997).
14. Michel Foucault, The Order of Things: An Archeology of the Human Sciences (New York: Random House, 1970), pp. 236–53.
15. For examples of both, see Barbara Schapiro, The Romantic Mother: Narcissistic Patterns in Romantic Poetry (Baltimore: The Johns Hopkins University Press, 1983).
16. Charles J. Rzepka, "Christabel's 'Wandering Mother' and the Discourse of the Self: A Lacanian Reading of Repressed Narration," Romanticism Past and Present 10 (1986): 23.

17. Joel Faflak, *Romantic Psychoanalysis: The Burden of the Mystery* (Albany: State University of New York Press, 2008).

18. Laura Quinney, "Wordsworth's Ghosts and the Model of the Mind," *European Romantic Review* 9 (1998): 300.

19. See Jacques Derrida, *Writing and Difference*, trans. Alan Bass (University of Chicago Press, 1986), pp. 196–231.

20. Tilottama Rajan, *Dark Interpreter: The Discourse of Romanticism* (Ithaca: Cornell University Press, 1980), p. 17.

21. See Hans Aarslef, *From Locke to Saussure: Essays on the Study of Language and Intellectual History* (Minneapolis: University of Minnesota Press, 1982), and William Keach, *Shelley's Style* (New York: Methuen, 1984), plus his essay below (see chapter 5).

22. As noted, for example, in Robert N. Essick, *William Blake and the Language of Adam* (Oxford: Clarendon Press, 1989), pp. 28–103.

23. De Man, cited in Harold Bloom *et al.*, *Deconstruction and Criticism* (New York: Seabury Press, 1979), pp. 50–66.

24. See Paul de Man, "The Rhetoric of Temporality," in Charles S. Singleton, ed., *Interpretation, Theory and Practice* (Baltimore: The Johns Hopkins University Press, 1969), pp. 173–209.

25. See Shelley, cited in Adams, *Critical Theory*, p. 517, and Jerrold E. Hogle, *Shelley's Process: Radical Transference and the Development of His Major Works* (New York: Oxford University Press, 1988), pp. 3–27.

26. Daniel P. Watkins, *Keats's Poetry and the Politics of the Imagination* (Rutherford, New Jersey: Fairleigh Dickinson University Press, 1989), p. 25.

27. Daniel P. Watkins, *Sexual Power in Romantic Poetry* (Gainesville: University Press of Florida, 1996), pp. xii–xiv.

28. See Daniel P. Watkins, *A Materialist Critique of English Romantic Drama* (Gainesville: University Press of Florida, 1993), especially pp. 1–20.

29. Elaine Showalter, ed., *The New Feminist Criticism: Essays on Women, Literature, and Theory* (New York: Pantheon, 1985), p. 263.

30. Anne K. Mellor, ed., *Romanticism and Feminism* (Bloomington: Indiana University Press, 1988), p. 4.

31. Anne K. Mellor, *Romanticism and Gender* (New York: Routledge, 1993), pp. 2–3.

32. See Alice Jardine, *Gynesis: Configurations of Woman and Modernity* (Ithaca: Cornell University Press, 1985).

33. See Margaret Homans, *Bearing the Word: Language and the Female Experience in Nineteenth-Century Women's Writing* (University of Chicago Press, 1986), p. 6, and Julia Kristeva, *Powers of Horror: An Essay on Abjection*, trans. Leon S. Roudiez (New York: Columbia University Press, 1982), pp. 1–10.

34. Homans, *Bearing the Word*, pp. 40–67; see also Mary Jacobus, *First Things: The Maternal Imaginary in Literature, Art, and Psychoanalysis* (New York: Routledge, 1995).

35. Anne Williams, *Art of Darkness: A Poetics of Gothic* (University of Chicago Press, 1995).

36. See Louis Crompton, *Byron and Greek Love: Homophobia in Nineteenth-Century England* (Berkeley: University of California Press, 1985); Christopher Z. Hobson, *Blake and Homosexuality* (New York: Palgrave, 2000); and Andrew

Elfenbein, *Romantic Genius: The Prehistory of a Homosexual Role* (New York: Columbia University Press, 1999).

37. Tim Fulford, *Romanticism and Masculinity: Gender, Politics and Poetics in the Writings of Burke, Coleridge, Cobbett, Wordsworth, De Quincey and Hazlitt* (New York: Palgrave/ St. Martin's, 1999).

38. Louis Montrose, cited in Aram H. Veeser, ed., *The New Historicism* (New York: Routledge, 1989), pp. 17–19.

39. See Marjorie Levinson *et al.*, *Rethinking Historicism: Critical Readings in Romantic History* (Oxford: Blackwell, 1989).

40. Alan Liu, *Wordsworth: The Sense of History* (Stanford University Press, 1989), p. 32.

41. Jerome McGann, *The Romantic Ideology: A Critical Investigation* (University of Chicago Press, 1983).

42. See also Clifford Siskin, *The Historicity of Romantic Discourse* (New York: Oxford University Press, 1988), pp. 15–56.

43. See Jerome McGann, *The Beauty of Inflections: Literary Investigations in Historical Method and Theory* (Oxford: Clarendon Press, 1985), pp. 17–65, 135–72.

44. Marilyn Butler, *Romantics, Rebels, and Reactionaries: English Literature and Its Background, 1760–1830* (Oxford University Press, 1981).

45. See Jack Stillinger, *Multiple Authorship and the Myth of Solitary Genius* (New York: Oxford University Press, 1991).

46. See Jon P. Klancher, *The Making of English Reading Audiences, 1790–1832* (Madison: University of Wisconsin Press, 1987).

47. See James C. McKusick, *Green Writing: Romanticism and Ecology* (New York: St. Martin's Press, 2000), and Timothy Morton, *Ecology Without Nature: Rethinking Environmental Aesthetics* (Cambridge, Massachusetts: Harvard University Press, 2007).

48. As in Alan Richardson, *British Romanticism and the Science of the Mind* (Cambridge University Press, 2001).

49. See Siskin, *Historicity*, pp. 67–147; Stuart Curran, *Poetic Form and British Romanticism* (New York: Oxford University Press, 1986); Julie Carlson, *In the Theatre of Romanticism: Coleridge, Nationalism, Women* (Cambridge University Press, 1994); and Alan Bewell, cited in David L. Clark and Donald C. Goellnicht, eds., *New Romanticism: Theory and Critical Practice* (University of Toronto Press, 1994), pp. 71–100.

50. See McGann, *The Beauty*, pp. 255–333; Steven Bann, *Romanticism and the Rise of History* (New York: Macmillan, 1995); and Jerome Christensen, *Romanticism at the End of History* (Baltimore: The Johns Hopkins University Press, 2000).

51. S. Hall from 1990, cited in Lawrence Grossberg *et al.*, eds., *Cultural Studies* (New York: Routledge, 1992), p. 279.

52. As in the wide range visible in Alan Richardson and Sonia Hofkosh, eds., *Romanticism, Race, and Imperial Culture, 1780–1834* (Bloomington: Indiana University Press, 1996).

53. As in Debbie Lee, *Romantic Liars: Obscure Women Who Became Imposters and Challenged an Empire* (New York: Palgrave Macmillan, 2006).

54. Helen Thomas, *Romanticism and Slave Narratives: Transatlantic Testimonies* (Cambridge University Press, 2000).

55. Debbie Lee, *Slavery and the English Romantic Imagination* (Philadelphia: University of Pennsylvania Press, 2002).

56. See Lee, *Slavery*, pp. 29–43, and Joshua D. Gonsalves, "Problematic Configurations of the Nation as I-land: A Phenomenological Report on Half-Knowledge from 'Any Island of Lethe Dull'," *Studies in Romanticism* 45 (2006): 425–66.

57. Saree Makdisi, *Romantic Imperialism: Universal Empire and the Culture of Modernity* (Cambridge University Press, 1999).

58. Alan Bewell, *Romanticism and Colonial Disease* (Baltimore: The Johns Hopkins University Press, 1999).

59. Nigel Leask, *British Romantic Writers and the East: Anxieties of Empire* (Cambridge University Press, 2002).

60. See William Warner and Clifford Siskin, "Stopping Cultural Studies," *Profession* (2008): 94–107.

# 2

MARSHALL BROWN

# Romanticism and Enlightenment

The new age proclaims itself to be fleet of foot, with wings on its soles; the dawn has put on seven-league boots – Long has lightning flashed on the horizon of poetry; the heavens have collected their stormy might into a powerful cloud; now the thunder has resounded mightily, now it has retreated and flashed only in the distance, now it has returned yet more fearsomely: but soon we shall speak not of a single storm, but the entire sky will break out into flame, and then all your petty lightning rods will avail no longer. Then the nineteenth century begins in earnest ... Then there will be readers who can read.

Friedrich Schlegel, "On Incomprehensibility"

## I Romanticisms and Enlightenments

The readers of this volume will find Arthur O. Lovejoy's famous essay "On the Discrimination of Romanticisms" amply confirmed: Romanticism cannot be defined. To include an essay called "Romanticism and Enlightenment" seems to be an impossibility compounded. On any reasonably comprehensive view the eighteenth century was not dramatically more uniform than the early nineteenth. Indeed, in one crucial respect it was less so, for no fact so inescapably galvanized the Enlightenment mind as that of revolution did the mind of Romanticism. There are many versions of Enlightenment – aristocratic and bourgeois, rationalist and empiricist, modernist and classicist, mercantilist and *laissez-faire*, urban and pastoral, religious and secular. Properly speaking, this chapter should be entitled "Romanticisms and Enlightenments," a multiplicity that leaves the student no hook except the little word "and" to hang a hat on.

That is what I propose to do. Though it may not be feasible to define either Enlightenment or Romanticism, there may be better prospects for defining their relationship. To be sure, an approach focusing on the process rather than the materials or the product will not furnish objective determinations. Avoiding the quest for some kind of essence of historical periods, I will treat the "and" of my title as a vector without a precise location. And I will compound the turn away from a goal of "objectivity" by asking how the Romantics sensed their relationship to the preceding generations rather than by attempting to ascertain the external facts.

For the truth is that the facts are contradictory. It is a truism, on the one hand, that the Romantics rebelled against their predecessors. The typical Romantic – so conventional wisdom runs – went to extremes. He was a godless revolutionary in his youth and, if he lived long enough, an orthodox traditionalist in his age, but in neither case an Enlightened progressive. Somewhere along the line, humanist tolerance lost its appeal, giving way on the one hand to the libertinism of a Shelley or a Byron, on the other to the bigoted Catholicism of several of the older German Romantics. A common intellectual enemy was Newtonian rationalism, whose desiccated narrowness was attacked by Blake, by Keats (in "Lamia"), and, with otherwise uncharacteristic savagery, by Goethe in his vast *Theory of Color.* Romanticism, on this view, attacked Enlightened, classicizing, conformist rationalism in recognition of unstated emotions and unconscious instincts.

The evidence for the Romantic attack on Enlightenment lies everywhere at hand. The antirationalism of a De Quincey comes late enough that one might hesitate to identify it as an original impulse of Romanticism. But already among the first generation of Romantics one finds the geologist and poet Novalis (Friedrich von Hardenberg, 1772–1801), who, before his early death, composed the *Hymns to the Night,* the dream-dominated medievalizing romance *Heinrich von Ofterdingen,* the mystical, orientalizing story *The Apprentices at Sais,* and the aphorisms entitled *Pollen* and *Belief and Love,* most famous among them being the utterance "The secret way goes inward." Novalis is the subject of influential early essays by Carlyle, he was widely admired in mid nineteenth-century France, and he has been taken (by Hugo Friedrich) to be, like Poe, a fountainhead of symbolist and expressionist poetry.[1] If there is one Romanticism confronting one Enlightenment in all of Europe, Novalis is it, and the two are simple contraries like night and day. Were that the case, the story would be quickly told.

That too simple story, finally, could be easily corroborated in the British context. On the one hand, Blake assaulted all the canons of eighteenth-century art along with all the preconceptions of Lockean empiricism, as Wordsworth vilified the diction of eighteenth-century poetry. On the other hand, supernatural sensationalism, such as Fielding reduces to ridicule in *Tom Jones* (8.11; 12.11; 16.5), became the norm in the Romantic novel in Britain, France, Germany, and America, and, so this story goes, Enlightened cosmopolitanism gave way to nationalism and the revival of indigenous mythologies. The eighteenth century wrote satire in heroic couplets, moral odes, local poetry, and extended didactic poems in Miltonic blank verse; the Romantics wrote sonnets, blank-verse meditative lyrics, ballads, mythological or metaphysical odes, and first-person epics. Eighteenth-century novels were picaresque or epistolary; Romantic-era novelists satirized the picaresque or else wrote social, historical, or Gothic fictions. Eighteenth-century philosophy was empiricist and materialist; Romantic philosophy, after passing through the inhuman rigors of neo-Spinozism, became (as Thomas McFarland documents in *Coleridge and the Pantheist Tradition*) transcendental and idealist.

Much in that conventional account is true. But inevitably a closer look complicates the picture. Writers like Morse Peckham and Virgil Nemoianu have shown how many Enlightenment values persisted despite the changed atmosphere of the nineteenth century. Voltaire's ideal of tolerance continues in the writings of the Schlegels, of Shelley, and of French revolutionary thinkers – contemporaries often more different from one another than they are from their common ancestor. Popean satire is not only reborn in Byron, but also strongly colors Blake's prophecies and leaves traces in some of Shelley's works and even a few of Keats's. Neoclassicism, which was a formative element in the Enlightenment, remained a powerful if variable current in Goethe (who translated two of Voltaire's tragedies), Schiller, the later Schlegels, the artists of the French Revolution, Shelley, Keats, and the later Wordsworth ("Laodamia"). The mythological works of Keats, Shelley, and Hölderlin in many respects remain faithful to the syncretic (comparatist) and euhemerist (historically rooted) traditions of the Enlightenment, partly because they draw on many now forgotten seventeenth- and eighteenth-century mythographic compendia.[2] The development of stage drama is too complicated to examine in detail here, but broadly it may be said that both in Britain and in France the main forms of Romantic drama (melodramatic tragedy, domestic comedy, and opera) grow continuously out of eighteenth-century traditions, and in Germany, where there is a marked shift in style beginning around 1760, it is more a turn from French to British models than an advance from Enlightenment to Romanticism. Nor did the Romantic novel simply reject earlier forms: Austen modeled her moralism and her meticulous prose on Johnson, while the epistolary novel survived, largely through the mediation of Goethe's *Werther*, in Hölderlin's *Hyperion*, Foscolo's *Jacopo Ortis*, Scott's *Redgauntlet*, and numerous others. Formal philosophy, which becomes transcendental in Germany, remains rationalist with a tinge of mysticism in the French ideologues, and rationalist with a tinge of metaphysics in both the British tradition that leads from Hartley to Godwin to Bentham and the later Scottish school of Reid, Stewart, and Hamilton. Wordsworth's aesthetics, through the influence of Archibald Alison (*Essays on the Nature and Principles of Taste*, 1790), remains strongly in the associationist tradition. These manifestations add up to a great deal of important writing in the Romantic period that prolongs Enlightenment paradigms, even while the mainstream of Romantic lyric, Romantic mythological closet drama (*Manfred, Prometheus Unbound, Faust*), and also the familiar essay of Lamb and Hazlitt differs profoundly from Enlightenment norms. The first objection to the simple view of Romanticism as a rejection of Enlightenment is that it delivers a woefully impoverished picture of what was actually written by major figures in the decades after 1800.

A second, related objection, which has long found a place in traditional literary histories, is that, conversely, many elements of Romanticism are present in writers of earlier generations. Romantic nature feeling – affectionate dwelling on particulars, along with dreaming or daydreaming in dark grottoes, amid vast wildernesses, or on high mountains – is widespread in the writing of the second half of the eighteenth century, and it can easily be traced further back, to Thomson and Young, to moments in Pope's "Windsor Forest" and "Eloïsa to Abelard," or, on the Continent, to such works as the precise descriptive poems of Thomson's German translator, Barthold Heinrich Brockes (1680–1747). The ballad revival, the Spenserian revival, the Gothic novel, the cult of sentiment, all date from the middle of the eighteenth century. Blank verse lyric really begins not with Wordsworth and Coleridge, but with Akenside and his circle. Wordsworth's attack on poetic diction is foreshadowed in Goldsmith's *Life of Parnell* and again in chapter 8 of *The Vicar of Wakefield*, with its criticism of the "false taste" of the period that admires "a string of epithets that improve the sound without carrying on the sense." Counter-currents of Enlightenment culture, on this view, become main currents of Romantic thought: Swedenborg and Young lead to Blake, who illustrated Young's *Night Thoughts* and appears to have modeled the nine parts of *The Four Zoas* (as Shelley would the structure of *Queen Mab*) on Young's nine nights; Berkeley funnels into Coleridge, Klopstock's biblical dramas into Byron's, and Rousseau and Diderot (virtually exact contemporaries of Johnson, Gray, and Hume) into everybody. These counter-currents, it often used to be said, constituted a pre-Romanticism that coexisted with the official Enlightenment.[3]

To be sure, few scholars still use the term pre-Romanticism in the old way. Dislodging individual themes and motifs from the contexts where they occur gives a distorted picture of their significance: however steadily Brockes and Thomson may look at their subjects, devotional descriptions of birds and flowers do not really greatly resemble Wordsworth's personal memory poems. And isolated and imperfect anticipations, such as Akenside's blank-verse "Inscriptions" or Walpole's *Castle of Otranto* (written in 1764 but, as Mehrotra showed in his study of its influence, not really influential until about the time of Ann Radcliffe),[4] or even the handful of nature sonnets written by William Lisle Bowles in the years around 1790, do not equate with the prolific and controlled achievements of the Romantics.

"Pre-Romanticism," though widely diffused, turns out to be an unwitting and accidental by-product of other impulses, and hence radically different from the consciously worked out aims of the various Romantic writers, richly elaborated in a coherent body of works.

Nevertheless, accounts of an eighteenth-century pre-Romanticism and of a Romantic post-Enlightenment conjointly remain valuable. What they lack in a spurious coherence they make up in a genuine complexity. They have shown that many forces, often clashing, were at play in both periods and that traditional period concepts need to be viewed, as Jerome J. McGann says, more "critically." From Arnold to Yeats and beyond, Wordsworth and Shelley alike (let alone Keats and Blake) had been treated as elite, essentially private poets. A scholarly counterwave in the 1950s and 1960s stressed the fashionable, popular or populist dimensions of their writing. Yet subsequent criticism – partially returning to and contextualizing some Arnoldian themes (such as that poetry is the criticism of life) – more adequately acknowledged how fashions respond to countervailing fashions. (This was evident in the German case, where the "Romanticism" of Novalis and the Schlegels encountered the simultaneous "classicism" of Goethe, Schiller and Humboldt in a sometimes loyal, sometimes embittered opposition.) Recognizing what I would like to call post-Enlightenment values has meant learning again to highlight the oppositional elements in Romantic poetry. Wordsworth praising peasants, Shelley free love, Blake intellectual warfare, Byron libertine heroism, or Austen the traditional virtues of agrarian society – these all mean something different in the abstract from what they mean in a world of growing industrialism and antirevolutionary turmoil and repression.

Whatever one's assessment of individual arguments, critical and ideological readings of Romantic works have greatly increased the perception of covert and implicit meanings embodied within them. But they have also greatly complicated the task of the literary historian. It was all too easy to take Romantic values as the new and Enlightenment values as the old – or, worse, as the wave of the future and the past respectively in a world perpetually lacking a present. But if writing is oppositional (designed, one might simply say, to persuade someone of something), then it constitutes a clash of contemporaneous values whose historical dimension remains to be investigated. The same considerations apply to the now outmoded accounts of pre-Romanticism. Pre-Romantic traits are undoubtedly present throughout the eighteenth century, and gratitude is owed to the scholars who pointed them out. But these traits are oppositional features of the Enlightenment itself, not glimmerings of a new dawn; they need to be referred to their contemporary context in order to be understood. The Enlightenment can no more be limited to the *Essay on Man* than Romanticism to the more private dimensions of *Lyrical Ballads*.

And that is just as well. The traditional historical picture suffered from the illusion that some features of a period could simply be assigned to some other period. But the procedure is obviously circular. We need to know which values are Romantic in order to disentangle Romantic writing from post-Enlightenment writing, or pre-Romantic from Enlightenment. But we need first to have disentangled them in order to know which values are Romantic. And the separation, could it be performed, is inimical to historical understanding. It tells, at most, the difference between Enlightenment and Romanticism, but it does not explain the relationship between the two. Enlightenment, to use M. H. Abrams's terms, is the mirror of wit, Romanticism the lamp of genius; Enlightenment is collective and social and Romanticism private and individual (or, in accounts like Max Horkheimer's and Theodor Adorno's *Dialectic of Enlightenment*, the reverse); Enlightenment is universalizing, Romanticism historicizing – any such characterizations obscure the processes by which Romanticism emerges out of Enlightenment. A taxonomic approach to periodization denies the rights of history.

For all these reasons, I propose here a more dialectical idiom. The thesis is that, in both the antithetical senses of the idiom, Romanticism grows out of Enlightenment. The new turns against the old, but it does so from a historical logic already inscribed in the old, and still preserved in the new. The historical thrust of Enlightenment and the historical memory of Romanticism must alike be recognized if their succession is to be comprehended. Romanticism and Enlightenment differ from one another in consequence of the ways in which each differs internally from itself – in which Enlightenment is driven towards its opposite and in which Romanticism incorporates its antithesis.

## II   The darkness of Enlightenment

From a certain perspective it appears natural to pit the optimism or elation of the post-Restoration decades against the satiric impulse that dominated in the early eighteenth century. While the party of faith reacted to the Restoration with the resignation of the blind Milton, typified by the gloomy classicism of *Samson Agonistes*, or else with the bitterness of Marvell's "Last Instructions to a Painter," the party of Enlightenment welcomed what it called the Glorious Revolution in a mood of exalted panegyric. Dryden served as its spokesman, for despite the ever-popular *MacFlecknoe* and *Absalom and Achitophel* he was only occasionally a satirist. It can easily be made to seem, then, as if the radiant fabric of Enlightenment gradually unraveled, with didacticism steadily giving way, for better or worse, before satire. With *The Rape of the Lock* leading to *The Dunciad*, Pope to Johnson, and the bright Augustan age to the gloom of Sensibility, the pattern seems to continue. From this scheme derives the over-simplified account, discussed in the first section of my essay, which treats Romanticism as the rejection of Enlightenment and as the embrace of darkness.

By recognizing that there is also a darkness at the heart of Enlightenment, we can rearrange and clarify the received historical picture. If Dryden is at all representative, the mood of elation at a new age preceded the facts that were to justify it, for he celebrated Cromwell as a bringer of peace in the *Heroic Stanzas* before celebrating Charles in the same role in *Astræa Redux*. Enlightenment rationalism existed as an anticipatory cast of mind, even before it had any genuine reason to celebrate. And the hopes proved to be excessive, as genuine hope must always be. In that excess already lay the seed of the self-division that characterizes Enlightenment and that eventually destroyed it.

Here, from Dryden's *Annus Mirabilis*, his greatest poem of the 1660s, are some euphoric stanzas that portray the Royal Society.

> This I fore-tel, from your auspicious care,
> Who great in search of God and Nature grow:
> Who best your wise Creator's praise declare,
> Since best to praise his works is best to know.
>
> O truly Royal! who behold the Law,
> And rule of beings in your Makers mind,
> And thence, like Limbecks, rich Idea's draw,
> To fit the levell'd use of humane kind. (657–64)

The bravado of this mood lies in its ready linkages of the divine and the human. The explosive formula of Spinozistic pantheism, *deus sive natura* ("God, i.e., nature," as it might be rendered), lurks close at hand. Milton's Adam, a year later, was to seek what the Archangel Raphael calls "knowledge within bounds" (*Paradise Lost*, 7.120). His aim closely resembles Dryden's; he desires revelation in order, as he says, "the more / To magnifie his works, the more we know" (7.96–7). Yet Adam's priorities are clear: knowledge exists to further praise. Dryden's "and"s, by contrast, obscure the priority of God and nature, praise and knowledge, the rationality of law and the authority of rule. Likewise, the "is" in line 660 – an uncommon and pointedly vague usage in Dryden's early style – obscures the relationship between present accomplishment and future potential: reason prevails at the expense of any clear ordering of values. And the last two lines run further risks in their implicit correlation of science with commerce, speculation with profit. "Reasoning I oft admire," Adam was soon to say, "How Nature wise and frugal could commit / Such disproportions, with superfluous hand / So many nobler Bodies to create, / Greater so manifold, to this one use" (8.25–9). Raphael immediately corrects Adam's rationalism with the injunction to "be lowlie wise" (8.173); there are many mysteries, he says, and the lights of heaven do not exist solely to enlighten man's mind. Reason reduces all things to man's measure.

Dryden in 1666 was no Leveller. The specious humility of his word "levell'd" betrays reason's dangerous reductions. Immediately, the perils of conflict arise to haunt the smooth progress of mind: "But first the toils of war we must endure" (665). Reason's alchemy promises to put all things on an even keel, but its anticipated glorious dawn is irremediably shadowed by the unpredictable terrain of experience. (The mixed metaphors are implied by Dryden's text and combine with the willed simplicity of the diction to constitute the complex strength of his style and of his insight.) Enlightenment begets self-scrutiny: the greater the aspirations of reason, the more difficult it is for humans to realize them. Thus does the elation of the 1660s prepare the way for the "unpolish'd, rugged Verse" (*Religio Laici*, 453) of Dryden's doctrinal poems and of his fables.

> Dim as the borrow'd beams of Moon and Stars
> To *lonely, weary, wandring* Travellers,
> Is *Reason* to the *Soul*: And as on high,
> Those rowling Fires *discover* but the Sky
> Not light us *here*; So *Reason's* glimmering Ray
> Was lent, not to *assure* our *doubtfull* way,
> But *guide* us upward to a *better Day.*
> And as those nightly Tapers disappear
> When Day's bright Lord ascends our Hemisphere;
> So pale grows *Reason* at *Religions* sight;
> So *dyes*, and so *dissolves in Supernatural Light.*
>
> (*Religio Laici*, 1–11)

Whether in religion or in politics, the Enlightenment yearned for the splendor of the sun. But it never forgot that light is born out of darkness. Charles II, Dryden says, began subject to a "black Star," and the "thaw" in 1660 – so Dryden wishfully writes – came as but a heightening of the palette of experience.

> Yet as wise Artists mix their colours so
> That by degrees they from each other go,
>   Black steals unheeded from the neighb'ring white
> Without offending the well cous'ned sight:
> So on us stole our blessed change; while we
> Th' effect did feel but scarce the manner see.
>
> (*Astræa Redux*, 113, 134, 125–30)

It was never a world basking in light, but a world groping its way out of the darkness or seeing feelingly. The great philosophical image of the age was that of Descartes, sitting in the wintry darkness of Germany and seeking out reason by the light of his stove, "like a man who walks alone and in the shadows" (*Discourse on Method*, part II). Like Dryden some decades later, Descartes too was writing out of an experience of religious warfare with one claimant to sovereignty pitted against another (as he expresses it in the opening sentences of *Discourse*, part II), but he acknowledges the violence and the homelessness that Dryden conceals. He will not, he tells us, preach a revolution that would overthrow the foundations of the state, but he will throw down the house of his own experience in order to build it afresh. Locke, to be sure, never talks this way, but he too is very unsure of his ground in the "vast Ocean of *Being*" (*Essay Concerning Human Understanding*, 1.1, 7), and his famed cautiousness, as Leo Strauss beautifully put it, "is a kind of noble fear."[5]

Part of the oversimplification that neglects the dark, "Romantic" side of Enlightenment results from concentrating on one or at most two genres at a time. While Dryden was writing poems in praise of reason, the nation, art, and science, comic playwrights – Dryden prominent among them – were excoriating the dissoluteness of the age. After 1700 the comic stage grew more sentimental and polite, and the Addisonian manner made the harsh polemics of a Jeremy Collier or a John Dennis unfashionable in essays. But in the verse satire of Swift, Pope, and, later, Charles Churchill, the Juvenalian mode increased in importance (even – as Howard Weinbrot has shown – in imitations of Horace),[6] becoming ever more personal and even vulgar in its attacks on vice and on vulgarity. And yet, on a comprehensive view the overlap between satire and sentimentality remains great: Pope and Thomson are the leading masters of eighteenth-century poetic diction; Pope and his older contemporary Young were closely associated in the popular mind; and it is not even difficult to find cases of the same poem appearing in both couplet and Pindaric dress (John Dyer's *Grongar Hill*) or in ironic and sentimental styles (Shenstone's Spenserian imitation, *The Schoolmistress*). As the end of the century approaches, the temptation to compartmentalize grows ever greater. Vulgar spoofing, claimed for the novel by Fielding, was exemplified in his wake by Sterne's *Tristram Shandy* and Smollett's *Humphry Clinker*. The heritage of Richardson went its own separate way to fuel the explosive emotionalism of writers like Frances Burney and Elizabeth Inchbald. Satire, in Johnson and Goldsmith, turned increasingly towards an exaltation of feeling in recognition of what *Rasselas* calls "the uncertain continuance of reason." Yet stage comedy enjoyed a revival noted for its decorousness of language and situation and its traditional values.

A less insular perspective can show that these disparate phenomena must all belong to a single complex of values. In Germany, for instance, Klopstock's emotional religion and nationalism combined with Lessing's liberalism to beget the violent antics of storm and stress (*Sturm und Drang*) drama; in France, Diderot was the century's most extravagant admirer of both Richardson and Sterne, the responsible editor of the *Encyclopédie*, which was the great summa of Enlightenment thought, and yet the founder of a theatrical tradition that led to the proto-revolutionary farces of Beaumarchais (the French Sheridan, who was at once formally even more conservative than his British counterpart and yet politically far more dangerous). The various literary traditions of the later eighteenth century in Britain will continue to look like the frayed ends of the Enlightenment until they are seen as various positions in a continuum of values that, without ever being fully articulated, regulated the thought processes of the entire period.

Historically the bright sides of Enlightenment dominated at first, and the dark sides – satire and then sentiment – prevailed later, especially after 1740. But the ideological and emotional precedence goes the other way. Before Charles II entered the limelight, he was under a "black Star." That star – as Dryden's text makes extraordinarily plain underneath its decorative obscurity – was as much his personal dissoluteness as his political destitution.

> Such is not *Charles* his too too active age,
> Which govern'd by the wild distemper'd rage
> Of some black Star infecting all the Skies,
>    Made him at his own cost like *Adam* wise.
>                         (*Astræa Redux*, 111–14)

The more fully elaborated sequence of *Alexander's Feast* (1697) leads music through rape, drunkenness, "joyless" military victory, the "pain" of erotic desire, nightmare and madness, before Cecilia brings harmony to earth. The melancholy overview in Dryden's last poem, *A Secular Masque* (1700), images the completed century as a succession of bestial revelry, pointless war, and faithless love. Dryden began his career by claiming or implying that a new age has dawned:

> Some lazy Ages lost in sleep and ease
> No action leave to busie Chronicles;
> Such whose supine felicity but makes
> In story *chasmes*, in *Epoche's* mistakes;
> O're whom *Time* gently shakes his wings of Down
> Till with his silent sickle they are mown:
>    Such is not *Charles* his too too active age ...
>                         (*Astræa Redux*, 105–11)

He ended, literally on his deathbed, by wishing for that new age in the gloomy recognition that "supine felicity" has been the best of man's experiences hitherto: "'Tis well an old age is out, / And time to begin a new" (*Secular Masque*, 90–1).

Given the consistent pattern and the regression of confidence, the "black Star" passage of 1660 can serve as a commentary on the stage comedies of the Restoration in relationship to the ideals of Enlightenment. Even though many of the leading playwrights were also elevated poets (Dryden, Congreve, Wycherley) or respected statesmen (Etherege, Vanbrugh), the comedies can most readily seem an outlet that vented energies antithetical to Enlightened rationalism. Such readings underrate the integrity of the age and the comprehensiveness of its vision. The plays generate happy endings out of immoral, foolish, and chaotic actions. There is little logic in this progression, but in that respect they can be taken to echo the equally illogical yet psychologically compelling progressions of Dryden's poems. "Apollo's ... drunk ev'ry Night," sings Sir Wilfull Witwoud in Congreve's *The Way of the World* (1700), "and that makes him so bright." "The Sun's a good Pimple, an honest Soaker, he has a Cellar at your *Antipodes*" (4.10). That is Dryden's black star all over again, and as willful and wishful as *The Secular Masque* of the same year. Mirabell, Congreve's more thoughtful spokesman, especially in soliloquy, has this to say of the force of reason and of its habitation:

> To think of a Whirlwind, tho' 'twere in a Whirlwind, were a Case of more steady Contemplation; a very Tranquility of Mind and Mansion. A Fellow that lives in a Windmill, has not a more whimsical Dwelling than the Heart of a Man that is lodg'd in a Woman. There is no Point of the Compass to which they cannot turn, and by which they are not turn'd; and by one as well as another; for Motion not Method is their Occupation. To know this, and yet continue to be in Love, is to be made wise from the Dictates of Reason, and yet persevere to play the Fool by the force of Instinct. (2.6)

The lesson of stage comedy, which is also the lesson of the greatest poetry of the age, is that reason and instinct, wisdom and passion, must coexist, and that their dwelling place is a frantic bosom or a turbulent windmill.

The poet Dryden and the comic playwrights should be taken conjointly to represent the spirit of the age. In his meager refuge from the Northern cold Descartes has to tear down before he rebuilds; that is, he is a satirist before he is a rationalist. The contents of Hume's philosophy are different, but the founding gesture is the same: he must tear down the house of epistemology before he can build those of sociability and morality. What Norman O. Brown called Swift's "excremental vision"[7] haunts even so complacent-seeming a work as Goldsmith's *She Stoops To Conquer*. The disorderly house with its unruly servants here may seem too tame to count as prefigurations of Beaumarchais's riotous *Marriage of Figaro*. But when Kate possesses herself of her hereditary jewels stolen from the locked casket of Aunt Hardcastle, in a sequence that leads to a wild night-time ride ending, for the Aunt, in the horse-pond at the bottom of the garden, the dark passions at the perimeter of human rationality are unmistakably acknowledged.

"Wherefore," Walter Shandy asks at the conclusion of Sterne's masterpiece, "when we go about to make and plant a man, do we put out the candle?" (9.33). *Tristram Shandy* is arguably the century's profoundest response to Locke. Historically, readers have argued whether it is an application, a commentary, or a critique of Locke. I do not think the question has as much importance as has sometimes been thought because Locke's *Essay Concerning Human Understanding*, like any great book, undertakes a self-critique of its own illuminations. It too has a generative darkness in the background. *Tristram Shandy* compounds the Lockean *tabula rasa*, or sheet of blank paper, with various pages that contain no text, but are eloquent in their silence. The first is the black page that covers the dead Yorick (1.12). Much later comes the white page belonging neither to perceptivity nor to reason, but to the imagination that is left free to represent its own desire as a picture of the Widow Wadman (6.38). Whiteness likewise represents vacancy in the omitted chapters 9.28–29. When these chapters are later incorporated in 9.25, they prove to contain Toby's abortive proposal to the Widow, with its confusion of discourse with "the REAL PRESENCE," in the belief "That talking of love, is making it." A whole century, we realize, talked of reason too, without necessarily making it. In between the black and white pages comes the mottled page of 3.36. "Without *much reading*, by which your reverence knows, I mean *much knowledge*, you will no more be able to penetrate the moral of the next marbled page (motly emblem of my work!) than the world with all its sagacity has been able to unravel the many opinions, transactions and truths which still lie mystically hid under the dark veil of the black one." It was Wordsworth who wrote that, "'mid all this mighty sum / Of things forever speaking, / The eye it cannot choose but see" and that one should not fear "That nothing of itself will come" ("Expostulation and Reply," lines 25–6, 17). The Enlightenment was less confidently open and took the marbled page as its motley emblem. In modern reprints that page is black and white and looks like an image produced and reproduced. But in the first edition it is an actual piece of beautifully marbled paper, seamlessly inlaid into the book. It is an emblem, but it is also the thing itself, a real presence that brings the self-image of the age bodily into our chamber. For once, in a way perhaps possible only in a book, the image is at one with the object, in ambiguous fulfillment of age-old yearnings for a self-begetting clear and distinct idea.

The images that I have been tracing regulate the fundamental impulses of epistemology, psychology, and politics alike in the Age of Reason. Yet they are rarely acknowledged in their full extent – perhaps only in Hume and Sterne, which may be what makes those the two most disturbing authors of the age. The story I have told is one of the concealment of darkness under a Utopian optimism and of the gradual and reluctant acknowledgment of the darkness – let me now call it the Romantic darkness – at the origin of life. It is the story of an age coming to know itself. The knowledge, at last, burst upon it in ways that were never entirely comfortable. That self-knowledge of Enlightenment is what we know as Romanticism.

## III  The great awakening

My first section demonstrated how both Enlightenment and Romanticism contain similar contradictions within them. The second section discusses the genealogy of reason in the Enlightenment. That genealogy is implicit in Enlightenment texts, but recognized only in incomplete or fragmentary ways. Far from being a repudiation of Enlightenment, Romanticism was its fulfilling summation. Of all Enlightenment authors Hume comes closest to an overview of the dialectic of Enlightenment, and Kant (in the introduction to the *Critique of Pure Reason, his Prologomena to Any Future Metaphysic*) credits Hume with awakening him from his dogmatic slumber. Romanticism, I will suggest, is the fulfillment and awakening of Enlightenment.

To see what this formula entails, I begin with the early Wordsworth poem I have just quoted. Matthew, the aged schoolmaster who is Wordsworth's interlocutor in the poem, represents the wisdom of an earlier generation. In the companion poem, "The Tables Turned," Wordsworth disparages his "meddling intellect," his "science," and his "art." Both poems are bantering in tone; these lines do not state settled doctrines or reflect a fundamental antipathy between the two friends, but they do associate Matthew – who appears throughout the poems devoted to him as a figure of light – with the Enlightenment. What, then, does Wordsworth mean by telling Matthew, "The eye – it cannot choose but see?" The eye, after all, is the one sense organ that can be closed off. And, indeed, Wordsworth's eyes in this poem must be either closed or at least vacant, for he is "dream[ing] my time away." His reverie is devoid of cause and effect or of what Keats was to call "consequitive reasoning" ("You look round on your mother earth, / As if she for no purpose bore you"), and it appears to be thoughtless ("When life was sweet I knew not why"). Yet he says it is full, not empty.

The debate between Wordsworth and Matthew – that is, I believe, between Romanticism and Enlightenment – is rooted not in alienation or incomprehension, but in a common ground. For it is Enlightenment doctrine that Wordsworth turns against his teacher. Ever since Descartes, the principle that the soul always thinks had been espoused by Enlightenment rationalists and empiricists alike. As applied to the sense of sight, that principle was interpreted to mean that the eye is always on the watch, whether the lid is open or shut. Even when nothing registers, as Leibniz had said in the preface to his *New Essays on Human Understanding*, we still have an unending stream of "little perceptions," though we may be unaware of them. "This mighty sum / Of things forever speaking" is the full, punctual world of empiricism, a world without empty space. "Methinks, it should have been impossible / Not to love all things in a world so fill'd," Coleridge wrote in 1817, in the lines added to "The Eolian Harp" as a reflective summing up. In "Expostulation and Reply" Wordsworth does not think (he only "deem[s]" and "dream[s]"), but he enjoins Matthew to "think" in order to accede to the totality of Enlightened experience. That is the message addressed by Romanticism to its forebears.

One mistake often made is to link Romanticism too closely with the world of dreams. *L'Ame romantique et le rêve* – Armand Béguin's title (1937) is virtually a cliché. Yet the French tradition in which he wrote traces Romanticism well back before the generation of '98. Reverie – empty dreaming or daydreaming – was at its most fashionable around the 1780s, with writers like Rousseau and William Cowper. The writers whom we know as Romantics are distinguished from this earlier generation by virtue of the fact that they tell their dreams, and, indeed, the more haunted they are (as with De Quincey's opium reveries), the more they try to share and illuminate their hauntings. It is not dreaming that is the distinctive emblem of Romanticism – for even Dryden had his "black Star" – but the moment of awakening in which the dream is preserved.

Such moments are ubiquitous in Romantic poetry. There are the literal awakenings like the Arab Dream in book v of *The Prelude*, "Kubla Khan," Lambro's awakening of Haidée and Don Juan in canto iv of Byron's poem, the apocalyptic moments that conclude Blake's major epics, or the image of Adam's dream in Keats's letter of November 22, 1817. Equally prevalent, especially in the younger poets, are failed or uncertain awakenings like those in "The Idiot Boy," "Christabel," the "Ode to Psyche," the "Ode to a Nightingale," "Hyperion," and "The Triumph of Life." Moneta, the warner in "The Fall of Hyperion," admonishes Keats that "The poet and the dreamer are distinct, / Diverse, sheer opposite, antipodes" (1, 199–200); most of Keats's narratives involve struggles to awaken, and the earliest, "Sleep and Poetry," contrasts the good, imaginative sleep that leads to the dawn with the self-deluding imaginative death of neoclassical "handicraftsmen" who work in "The name of one Boileau" (200, 206). Just in the weeks when he was avidly attending Hazlitt's lectures on the eighteenth-century poets, Keats penned a blank-verse sonnet ("O thou whose face") that ends with the line, "And he's awake who thinks himself asleep." The full scope of mind necessarily encompasses an alertness to dreams. The Enlightenment's limitation was to think itself awake.

The schema of awakening or of failure or struggle to awake is repeated even more often by analogy and metaphor. Before further considering the implications of this schema, I will present two familiar examples at somewhat greater length. The first is Wordsworth's "Tintern Abbey." The earliest experiences described in this poem are "The coarser pleasures of my boyish days / And their glad animal movements." The earliest stage of genuine humanity is Wordsworth's interpretation of empiricism: it is all elementary perceptions ("Their colours and their forms") and generically classified objects ("The sounding cataract," "the tall rock," etc.). Pope – of whose poetry Wordsworth knew thousands of lines by heart – uses the phrase "The language of the heart," and Wordsworth, nostalgically, speaks of "The language of my former heart" as he attributes to Dorothy the "shooting lights" and the natural eyes associated with Enlightenment.[8] Beyond mere empiricism comes – and here Wordsworth quotes and acknowledges Young – "the mighty world / Of eye and ear, both what they half-create, / And what perceive." Half-creation is not pure imaginary guesswork, "As is a landscape to a blind man's eye," but rather a dream-world that recomposes the perceived world, when "we are laid asleep / In body, and become a living soul: / While with an eye made quiet by the power / Of harmony, and the deep power of joy, / We see into the life of things." The dark world is at once memory, dream, and imagination. Through it Wordsworth passes beyond the mechanistic and empiricist psychology of "An appetite: a feeling and a love, / That had no need of ... any interest, / Unborrowed from the eye," towards the revived humanism of the active mind. In the fourth paragraph of the poem, as Wordsworth recomposes the genesis of his current maturity, "thought" is introduced as the key term, and reasoning processes begin to govern the poem's rhetoric (paragraph 4 has "And so," "For," "Therefore," whereas the "If" in paragraph 3 lacks its consequent "then"). Yet the earlier stages of feeling, the "gleams / Of past existence," are preserved and honored, not rejected. "Day-light" is "joyless," and so Wordsworth wishes the light of the moon on his sister, yet the development leads to a renewal of vision (as the verbs of sensation in the first paragraph proceed from "hear" to "behold," "view," and finally "see") and a return to the now tamed "light of setting suns." Romanticism comes into its own by recapitulating its prehistory. "Tintern Abbey" means a great many things, and in pointing out these elements of structure I have not begun to interpret the poem. Even from the purely epistemological perspective an interpretation would need to account for the various elements in Wordsworth's assessment of empiricism: why, for instance, does he link elementary perception with such eagerly appetitive feelings? The coming-to-consciousness of Romanticism is not itself the content of Romantic belief; rather, it is the ground on which Romantics arrived at their often conflicting assessments of the world they experienced. It is the grammar, not the text of their thinking.

Shelley's *Prometheus Unbound* depends on a more abstract version of the same grammar of consciousness. It alludes chiefly to political history (the French Revolution and the *Ancien Régime*) rather than to intellectual history, and its judgments of past eras differ from those of "Tintern Abbey." But it too portrays – indeed repeatedly – the dawning of a new age and the awakening of a new humanity. The necessitarian tyrant Jupiter is resisted darkly by Prometheus. Yet Prometheus is unable to free himself: mere denial is servitude, not liberation. It is, of course, a grave simplification of Shelley's multiple perspectives to identify Jupiter with light and Prometheus with night, and consequently an even graver one to present the play as the triumph of the Romantic imagination (or of revolutionary freedom) over Enlightenment reason (or aristocratic tyranny). For the victory of one power would merely perpetuate a cycle, whereas Shelley's concluding vision is of an everlasting day (4.14: "We bear Time to his tomb in eternity"), modeled on the dance of lights in Dante's *Paradiso*. It is not the evil past that is vanquished by present good, but rather the entire Miltonic conflict of evil and good that is transcended.

Critics often treat the play as a lyrical effusion whose dramatic conflict ends in the very opening speech, when Prometheus says, "Disdain? Ah no! I pity thee" (1.53). Could the authority of the past be so easily put down, the force of history would be very weak indeed. But the pity is in fact both mutual (Mercury, Jupiter's messenger, twice says, "I pity thee," 1.356 and 428) and ineffective: Jupiter moans in his only appearance that Demogorgon, who eventually has the last word in the play, has "No pity" (3.3, 64). Both Prometheus and Jupiter live in the post-Saturnian world where time appears as a shadow (2.4, 33–4) that opposes past to present, necessity to desire. Asia's long narration in 2.4 (the center of the play) describes how Promethean invention mastered time and how Jovian law then mastered invention. But neither did away with the temporal cycle of negation and domination that is Shelley's real concern.

The psycho-historical dynamic issues in a characteristically Shelleyan punning ambivalence. Immediately after expressing his pity, Prometheus says, "The curse / Once breathed on thee I would recall" (1.58–9). Prometheus's recall, like his pity, is inferior because it remains oppositional. Though masked as a retraction, it is really a negation. As in Freud's account of negation, it serves as a pretext to recollect what he has forgotten. Prometheus wishes to deny power to Jupiter, but not to eliminate the whole idea of power (e.g., 1.272–3). In the process he shows his likeness to Jupiter in many ways, such as in the exultation that he condemns yet often seems to express, as well as in his victory over the Furies ("Methinks I grow like what I contemplate, / And laugh and stare in loathsome sympathy / ... Yet am I king over myself, and rule / The torturing and conflicting throngs within, / As Jove rules you" [1.450–1, 492–4]). Reminded of the curse at last, he repents (1.303: "It doth repent me"); falteringly, he asks to change his state. In all these ways he is wrong, even as he pities Jupiter. In the closing speech Demogorgon preaches a forgiving retraction or else an enduring resistance before which oppressive evil merely vanishes:

> To forgive wrongs darker than death or night;
>   To defy Power, which seems omnipotent;
> To love, and bear; to hope till Hope creates
>   From its own wreck the thing it contemplates.          (4.571–4)

Far from terminating with Prometheus's expression of pity, the play's dramatic action only begins there; it proceeds via a complex process of development leading to Demogorgon's corrective concluding injunction, "Neither to change, nor falter, nor repent" (4.575).

If that process is Prometheus's way of dealing with his past, it is also symptomatic of Romanticism's way of dealing with its past. Repudiation and triumph are its most visible gestures, which have led to conventional accounts of the war of Romanticism against Enlightenment reason. Pitying condescension is another gesture that is not infrequent in writings about Enlightenment figures by second-generation Romantics. But all these gestures are surface signs of a yet more complex process that was the Romantic working-through of its roots. What was to be overcome had to be thoroughly remembered. And if the chain of necessity is overthrown, the Promethean rebellion too must give way to the eternal day of rectified reason.

In her narration Asia speaks as if all value derived from Prometheus: "He gave man speech, and speech created thought, / Which is the measure of the universe" (2.4, 72–3). But Earth speaks differently in the closing scene – more impersonally as well as with a reformed priority that puts thoughts before an ordering language rather than after a creative language. His is the play's considered judgment of the birth of consciousness. "Language is a perpetual orphic song, / Which rules with daedal harmony a throng / Of thoughts and forms, which else senseless and shapeless were" (4.415–17).

The "Godlike," "divine" (2.4, 79, 82), creative ambitions of a Promethean Romanticism give way in the play to the synthetic and syncretic dance of all forms, thoughts, and eras with one another in the coadunative imagination. Much in Asia's praise of music replays Dryden's various shadowed panegyrics on the celestial mission of the arts, whereas Earth calls to mind their grounding and paves the way for Demogorgon to "waken Oblivion" (4.543).

The deluded "all-prophetic song" (2.4, 76) that Asia recounts is really a denial of the past. The destiny of Romanticism was to proceed beyond this immature or premature stage towards a reconciliatory recollection. English provides the fortunate puns recollect and remember. The Enlightenment, as I have proposed, aimed at masking and forgetting the itinerary by which it arrived at reason. Its self-knowledge was therefore only partial. Romanticism, with the same goal, undertook a synthetic itinerary. Collecting the members of the path of reason, it aimed at knowing the light through knowing the dark and the present by means of the past. Locke and Kant, for instance, shared the desire to clarify the mechanisms of consciousness. But Locke begins with perception, that is, with the bright or visible part of the process, without studying the faculties that precede and empower perception. Kant's theory of knowledge, by contrast, focuses specifically on the preexisting, imperceptible structures that beget conscious perception. And philosophy beyond Kant concentrated increasingly on the paths leading from the predisposing structures towards fully developed cognition – on what Hegel called the history of consciousness – as well as on analogously idealized histories of society and of nature. The heroines of Austen, the heroes of Scott, and the great Romantic poets all know themselves by remembering what they have experienced. That distinguishes the novels even from picaresques like those of Defoe, whose narrators recount their errors in order to segregate the renegade past from the reformed present. And it distinguishes poems of return like "Tintern Abbey" or Mörike's "Besuch in Urach" even from Gray's "Ode on a Distant Prospect of Eton College," which masks childhood recollections in an allegorical vision of future woe, an "all-prophetic song."

> Mr Bentham's method of reasoning, though comprehensive and exact, labours under the defect of most systems – it is too topical. It includes every thing; but it includes everything alike. It is rather like an inventory, than a valuation of different arguments. Every possible suggestion finds a place, so that the mind is distracted as much as enlightened by this perplexing accuracy. The exceptions seem as important as the rule. By attending to the minute, we overlook the great; and in summing up an account, it will not do merely to insist on the number of items without considering their amount. (*Works*, 11.14)

Such is William Hazlitt's judgment on Jeremy Bentham, a transitional figure and the eldest of the notables portrayed in *The Spirit of the Age*. Bentham forgets nothing and hides nothing, but he also synthesizes nothing. Such indiscriminate visibility, says the great Romantic portraitist, is not true Enlightenment. "By attending to the minute we overlook the great": that is the charge leveled by Romanticism at even the most inclusive minds of the eighteenth century. Hogarth was another such. Though a notorious hater, Hazlitt treasured Hogarth. Yet even Hogarth failed to satisfy the hunger for imagination of even the most empirically minded of the great Romantics.

> He had an intense feeling and command over the impressions of sense, of habit, of character and passion, the serious and the comic, in a word, of nature, as it fell within his own observation, or came within the sphere of his actual experience; but he had little power beyond that sphere ... [to] make the dark abyss pregnant ... making all things like not what we know and feel in ourselves, in this "ignorant present" time, but like what they must be in themselves, or in our noblest idea of them, and stamping that idea with reality ... : this is the ideal in art, in poetry, and in painting. (*Works*, 6.146)

In the long passage from which these phrases are excerpted, Hazlitt challenges Hogarth to bring the dark abyss to light, to lift the world around us into "the empyrean," and to give ideas reality by raising them "above the ordinary world of reality." The best of the Enlightenment, as Hazlitt saw it, was striving towards a Romantic potential.

There is no way to reduce the diffuse prose and the incommensurate ambitions of Hazlitt's critique of Enlightenment to a formula or a common denominator. Its virtue, rather, lies in its comprehensiveness. Thus does Romanticism claim not to reject, but to refine, subsume, and transcend its predecessors.

## IV   Revolution

Sheridan was the great Georgian playwright who then became a leading Romantic politician. His politics looked forward, whereas his dramaturgy looked backward, to the comic playwrights of the Restoration. Yet when he became manager of Drury Lane Theatre in 1776, his most important reform was to increase the number of new plays produced. So representative a figure looks backward and ahead at once.

Lamb, in his permanent nostalgia, seems to me less representative of his age. Still, his comments on the comedies he saw in his youth are telling. Utterly unreal because utterly amoral, they were (as he says in "On the

Artificial Comedies of the Last Century") a dream-world to which audiences repaired "to escape from the pressure of reality." They were relaxing because they were aggregates without a synthesis.

> For what is Ben [in Congreve's *Love for Love*] ... but ... a dreamy combination of all the accidents of a sailor's character ... But when an actor comes, and instead of the delightful phantom ... displays before our eyes a downright concretion of a Wapping sailor ... when ... he gives to it a downright daylight understanding, and a full consciousness of its actions ... we feel the discord of the thing; the scene is disturbed; a real man has got in among the dramatis personae, and puts them out.[9]

Let us call that real man, Romanticism. It was an awakening from the comic dreams of Enlightenment. Yet that awakening entailed (to Lamb's regret) a "full consciousness" of what had been superseded. You cannot look ahead if you do not know which road lies behind you.

And let us call the process of awakening, revolution. Lamb's language for the artificial comedy of the last century bears a remarkable resemblance to Carlyle's language for the artificial society of old France: "Such visual spectra flit across this Earth, if the Thespian Stage be rudely interfered with: but much more, when, as was said, Pit jumps on Stage, then is it verily, as in Herr Tieck's Drama, a *Verkehrte Welt*, or World topsyturvied" (*The French Revolution*, 2.1.10). In the first paragraph of this essay I said that all the Romantics shared a consciousness of revolution. By that I did not mean only of the French Revolution. For one thing, the Revolution itself – as Carlyle's masterpiece shows – was many different things at different times, in different places, to different people. And, for another, the course of political revolutions was and is often guided by revolutions in ideas, feelings, behavior, the Industrial Revolution, Kant's Copernican Revolution in philosophy, revolutions in life style, even in poetic style. For much of Wordsworth's life the revolution in Cumberland mores preoccupied him far more than did events abroad. Even Carlyle, in the midst of proclaiming the French Revolution "the crowning Phenomenon of our Modern Time," recognized that revolution is permanent and ubiquitous.

> All things are in revolution; in change from moment to moment, which becomes sensible from epoch to epoch: in this Time-World of ours there is properly nothing else but revolution and mutation, and even nothing else conceivable. Revolution, you answer, means *speedier* change. Whereupon one still has to ask: How speedy? At what degree of speed; in what particular points of this variable course, which varies in velocity, but can never stop till time itself stops, does revolution begin and end; cease to be ordinary mutation, and again become such? It is a thing that will depend on definition more or less arbitrary.
>
> (1.6.1)

But if we say that, claiming that Romanticism was the revolutionary reawakening of Enlightenment implies recognizing that revolution meant something different in 1800 from now. The word meant a turning back before it meant a turning away. In the seventeenth century revolution was the opposite, not the consequence of rebellion, and it retained some of these connotations even into the nineteenth century. When Hazlitt wrote that Home Tooke "had none of the grand whirling movements of the French Revolution, nor of the tumultuous glow of rebellion in his head or in his heart" (*Works*, 9.53) he continued to reflect a sense that revolution is greater and more embracing than rebellion. Even Carlyle, for whom "Time is rich in wonders, in monstrosities most rich; and is observed never to repeat himself, or any of his Gospels" (2.5, 1), projects an affinity of the whirling of the Revolution with the great cycles of nature. His monumental book of memory, perhaps the first historical essay to treat modern times as a receding experience that must be reconstructed archeologically (as Koselleck understands the process), was prompted by a passion to return to what Wordsworth had called "the fountain light of all our day."

> Understand it well, the Thing thou beholdest, that Thing is an Action, the product and expression of exerted Force: the All of Things is an infinite conjugation of the verb *to do*. Shoreless Fountain-Ocean of Force, of power to *do*; wherein Force rolls and circles, billowing, many-streamed, harmonious; wide as Immensity, deep as Eternity; beautiful and terrible, not to be comprehended: this is what man names Existence and Universe; this thousand-tinted Flame-image, at once veil and revelation, reflex such as he, in his poor brain and heart, can paint, of One Unnameable, dwelling in inaccessible light! From beyond the Star-galaxies, from before the Beginning of Days, it billows and rolls, – round *thee*, nay thyself art of it, in this point of Space where thou now standest, in this moment which thy clock measures. (2.3, 1)

Such is the sense in which Romanticism was revolutionary. It had its moments of rebellion, yet it was not fundamentally a rebellion against its predecessors. Rather, it was revolutionary in that older and more encompassing sense in which a revolution gathers up and recollects, as it sweeps all with it towards the future.[10]

## NOTES

1. Hugo Friedrich, *The Structure of Modern Poetry: From the Mid-Nineteenth to the Mid-Twentieth Century*, trans. Joachim Neugroschel (Evanston: Northwestern University Press, 1974). Consult as well Maurice Besset, *Novalis et la pensée mystique* (Paris: Aubier, 1947).

2. See Stuart Curran, *Shelley's Annus Mirabilis: The Maturing of an Epic Vision* (San Marino, California: Huntington Library Press, 1975), ch. 2; E. B. Hungerford, *Shores of Darkness* (New York: Columbia University Press, 1941).

3. The best case is made by Henri Monglond, *Le Préromantisme francais*, 2 vols. (Grenoble: Arthaud, 1930).

4. K. K. Mehrotra, *Horace Walpole and the English Novel: A Study of the Influence of "The Castle of Otranto" 1764–1820* (Oxford: Basil Blackwell, 1934).

5. *Natural Right and History* (Chicago and London: University of Chicago Press, 1953), p. 206.

6. See Weinbrot, *The Formal Strain: Studies in Augustan Imitation and Satire* (Chicago and London: University of Chicago Press, 1969); see also Thomas Lockwood, *Post-Augustan Satire: Charles Churchill and Satirical Poetry, 1750–1800* (Seattle and London: University of Washington Press, 1979).

7. Brown, *Life against Death* (Middletown, Connecticut: Wesleyan University Press, 1959), pp. 179–201.

8. Robert J. Griffin, "Wordsworth's Pope: The Language of His Former Heart," *ELH* 54 (1987): 695–715.

9. "On Some of the Old Actors": 2:140, in *The Works of Charles and Mary Lamb*, ed. E. V. Lucas (1903; reprinted, New York: AMS Press, 1968).

10. For elaboration of this notion of revolution, see my essay, "Errours Endlesse Traine: On Turning Points and the Dialectical Imagination," *PMLA* 99 (1984): 9–25, and Reinhart Koselleck, "'Neuzeit': Remarks on the Semantics of the Modern Concepts of Movement," in *Futures Past*, trans. Keith Tribe (Cambridge and London: MIT Press, 1985), pp. 231–66.

# 3

P. M. S. DAWSON

# Poetry in an age of revolution

Poets are no more insulated from political events and controversies than are any other class of people. Indeed, they are less so, in that poets work in *language*, the same medium in which political concepts and demands are formulated, contested, and negotiated. If this is generally true it is of particular relevance in periods of significant historical change, when political issues impress themselves with increased urgency on all sections of society and give rise to vigorous debates concerning fundamental political principles. The period between 1780 and 1830, during which the great Romantic poets came to maturity and produced their most important works, was such a period, as they were all aware. Wordsworth told an American visitor that "although he was known to the world only as a poet, he had given twelve hours thought to the conditions and prospects of society, for one to poetry."[1] Coleridge and Southey were both active as political journalists, and Coleridge produced a number of significant works of political theory. Byron spoke on political issues in the House of Lords, as well as satirizing political opponents and the political situation in general in his poetry.[2] Shelley wrote to his friend Peacock, "I consider Poetry very subordinate to moral & political science, & if I were well, certainly I should aspire to the latter" (Shelley, *Letters*, II, 71). His interest in politics is evidenced by the political pamphlets he wrote. William Blake could express regret that his countrymen should "trouble themselves about politics" and state "Princes appear to me to be Fools Houses of Commons & Houses of Lords appear to me to be fools they seem to me to be something Else besides Human Life" (Blake, *Poetry and Prose*, p. 580). Yet, as David Erdman has shown, his poetry is saturated with political concerns. Even Keats, the most apolitical of the great Romantic poets, published a sonnet to celebrate the release from jail of the liberal political journalist Leigh Hunt and began a political satire on the Prince Regent, "The Jealousies: A Faery Tale" (also known as "The Cap and Bells"). An example of arrogance to an inferior moved him to exclaim, "O for a recourse somewhat human independant of the great Consolations of Religion and undepraved Sensations, of the Beautiful, the poetical in all things – O for a Remedy against such wrongs within the pale of the World!" (Keats, *Letters*, p. 33). Poetry was Keats's life – but like all the Romantics he suspected that there were times when poetry was not enough.

In this essay I wish to place the political concerns of the Romantic poets within the context of the events, social movements, and ideas of their age. Against this background their political attitudes and stances will make more sense than when considered in isolation. But I also wish to argue that they did not merely reflect their age. Their political concerns were also shaped by their particular role as poets, though in ways which are often ambivalent. In *A Defence of Poetry* Shelley claimed that "Poets are the unacknowledged legislators of the World" (*Poetry and Prose*, p. 508). This claim would have been endorsed by all the Romantics insofar as they believed that poets contributed to political understanding and action in ways that went beyond their role merely as concerned citizens. It is a claim that we should treat with both respect and caution. Their belief in it gave the Romantics a crucial self-confidence without which they would have been lesser poets. At the same time it forms part of an ideology – the Romantic ideology – that reflects certain inevitable deficiencies in the Romantics' understanding of themselves and their age.

Before we consider this topic, however, it is necessary to sketch briefly the historical events and tendencies of the period. The central event is beyond question the French Revolution, "the master theme of the epoch in which we live," as Shelley called it, hinting to Byron that he might take it as the subject for a poem; in the event Shelley himself treated it in fictional form in his *Laon and Cythna*, later revised as *The Revolt of Islam* (Shelley, *Letters*, I, 504). Its effects, both positive and negative, on British political attitudes were far-reaching and lasting. In assessing the reactions to it we must, however, take into account certain differences that determined how individuals reacted. In terms of their social origins the Romantics ranged from the aristocracy (Byron, a peer, and Shelley, the heir to a baronetcy and son of an MP), through the middle class (Wordsworth, the son of an attorney, and Coleridge, the son of a clergyman) and lower middle class (Keats, the son of a stable owner), to the artisan or upper working class (Blake, the son of a hosier, who earned his own living as an engraver), and even the rural proletariat (John Clare, an agricultural laborer). The extent to which the canonical Romantics shared a common outlook indicates that whatever their origins they shared as men of letters and intellectuals a new and uneasy social position: "Literary men," Bulwer-Lytton noted, "have not with us any fixed and settled position *as* men of letters."[3] None of these Romantics lived entirely from their literary earnings, but their status as literary producers affected their sense of their own identity more than any other economic affiliations.

One crucial point of distinction among the Romantics concerns what we may call their generational position. It is customary to distinguish two generations of Romantic poets: an older generation of writers born in the early 1770s, including Wordsworth (born 1770), Coleridge (1772), and Southey (1774), who were initially fervent supporters but later resolute opponents of the French Revolution and what it represented; and a second generation, born around 1790, including Byron (1788), Shelley (1792), and Keats (1795), who were consistently liberal in their politics and can be seen as supporters of the Revolution, if with qualifications. (As a member of an earlier generation Blake, born 1757, is, in this as in other respects, anomalous.) We must remember that public events are also personal events to the individuals living through them, so that such factors as age and previous experience weigh heavily in their reactions, and the testimony they offer often reflects the personal as much as the public significance of events. A telling example very much to the point here is the fact that Wordsworth's fullest and most moving account of the revolutionary ferment of the early 1790s is offered in *The Prelude*, whose central theme is the growth and development of his own mind. In *The Excursion* (1814) he again treated the events of that period in terms of their impact on a single individual, the figure known as the Solitary. Thomas De Quincey was later to take Wordsworth to task for assuming prematurely the failure of the French Revolution in his account of it. For De Quincey, writing in 1845, the Revolution "has succeeded; it is far beyond the reach of ruinous reactions; it is propagating its life; it is travelling on to new births – conquering, and yet to conquer" (De Quincey, *Works*, xv, 235). De Quincey was a great admirer of Wordsworth and politically conservative to the point of reaction – but he was born in 1785, and this allowed him to see the events of the 1790s in a different historical perspective than was available to the elder generation.

For those who, like Wordsworth, came to maturity at the time of the French Revolution, it was the culmination of a decade in which beneficial and progressive reforms had come to seem a real possibility. The loss of the American colonies at the end of the War of American Independence in 1783 was a national disaster, but the Americans' success served if anything to encourage those who wished to reform the British political system. Blake in *America, a Prophecy* (1793) saw the war as a struggle between liberty and despotism and as presaging the European revolutions of the 1790s. For the second generation of poets, after the defeat of the revolutionary struggle, the continued existence of the American republic was one of the few sources of encouragement – "a People mighty in its youth ... Where, tho' with rudest rites, Freedom and Truth / Are worshipped," in the words of Shelley's Laon (*The Revolt of Islam*, XI.xxii). The American slogan "No Taxation without Representation" had relevance for the mother country, whose unrepresentative political system was increasingly called into question. Its defenders argued that the system did effectively represent the leading "interests" of the nation, rather than individual voters or constituencies. But it was undeniable that it favored the aristocratic landed interest to the detriment of the rising commercial, financial, and industrial interests. Those excluded from the political process were increasingly inclined to dismiss the opposition of Tory and Whig as merely a factional struggle for power and profit. Influential and respectable groups were agitating for the reform of Parliament, and it was known that even the Prime Minister, William Pitt the Younger, favored it. The prospects of changing society for the better were promising, and there sprang up a variety of humanitarian movements for such causes as the abolition of slavery, the reform of the prison system, and the education of the poor. The liberal sensibility of the 1780s is well represented by the poetry of William Cowper, particularly his *Task* (1785). The optimism of progressives in Britain was initially encouraged by the events of 1789 in France. It was at first assumed that France, for so long a byword for despotism and political benightedness, was finally following the Enlightened example of Britain. The destruction of the notorious prison of the Bastille in July 1789 was greeted with rapture by, among others, the young Coleridge who penned "An Ode on the Destruction of the Bastille." The London Revolution Society, whose pro-French activities were to provoke Edmund Burke's monumental attack on the whole revolutionary movement, had in fact been founded to celebrate the Glorious Revolution of 1688–9 which had established the Protestant succession and a balanced system of government in Britain. After the civil wars and political upheavals of the seventeenth century the Revolution settlement had inaugurated a century of domestic peace and economic growth under William and Mary, Queen Anne, and the Hanoverian Georges. War abroad had increased Britain's colonial possessions, while increasing prosperity at home fostered increased agricultural productivity and the growth of industry. Ironically enough, this prosperity probably helped to undermine the political stability that had produced it. Those classes who had increased their economic strength now wanted a share of political power, and the old aristocratic system seemed increasingly outmoded and restrictive. The first serious challenge to this system was the agitation surrounding John Wilkes in the 1760s, when London mob violence began to take a disturbing political turn. By the 1780s discontent was being expressed even by sections of the ruling class. Once the political debate had been opened in this way, the radical ideas that had lain dormant since the seventeenth century were revived among literate artisans and working men, including William Blake. In the 1790s working-class radicalism began to organize itself in the form of societies, of which the most famous was the London Corresponding Society, which established contact with the Jacobin clubs in France. Those who wished for change at home naturally felt their cause was the stronger when they saw British ideas of liberty exported first to America and then to France. Now, surely, was the opportunity to see that the mother of freedom did not lag behind other countries.

To be aged around twenty with such ideas and such hopes and faced by events like those occurring in France was to be in a situation of unique opportunity – and unique vulnerability. Wordsworth recognized the significance of the conjuncture of historical and personal factors when he wrote:

> O pleasant exercise of hope and joy,
> For great were the auxiliars which then stood
> Upon our side, we who were strong in love.
> Bliss was it in that dawn to be alive.
> But to be young was very heaven! ...
> Not favoured spots alone, but the whole earth,
> The beauty wore of promise, that which sets
> (To take an image which was felt, no doubt,
> Among the bowers of Paradise itself)
> The budding rose above the rose full-blown.
>
> (*The Prelude* [1805], x.690–4, 702–6)

But this is a retrospective view. When he wrote these lines Wordsworth was aware that the extravagant promises had not been kept – the glorious dawn, like that in his "Ode: Intimations of Immortality," had faded "into the light of common day" (76). The elder Romantics did not (as is sometimes claimed) abandon all hope of human betterment. They did, however, come to see it as involving a much longer time span and trusted increasingly to morality and religion rather than political reform to bring it about.

The elder Romantics' disillusion is in many respects understandable. As events unfolded, the French Revolution turned out to be a Pandora's box, with despair rather than hope left at the bottom. Its internal development, its repercussions in Britain, and its activities abroad all shocked or appalled its initial supporters. Those who had applauded it as a bloodless reform along the lines of the Glorious Revolution had then to come to terms with the September Massacres of 1792, the execution of Louis XVI in 1793, the Terror, and the rise of Robespierre. The latter's fall was celebrated dramatically by Coleridge and Southey, and Wordsworth was to recall the relief it gave him in *The Prelude* (x.515ff.). But he had already entered the mythology of politics, and John Clare (who was only two when Robespierre was guillotined) was a generation later to defend his mistrust of "revolution and reform" by recalling that "there was a Robspiere, or somthing like that name, a most indefatigable butcher in the cause of the french levelers" (Clare, *Autobiographical Writings*, p. 26). The spectre of mob violence, particularly ominous to those who remembered the Gordon Riots of 1780 in London, was to haunt the minds of liberals for a generation and strengthen the determination of conservatives to refuse any kind of reform. The conservative backlash was intensified by the outbreak of war between France and Britain in 1793, which, as recorded by Coleridge in his "Fears in Solitude" (1798) and by Wordsworth in *The Prelude* (X.229–305), created an intolerable strain on the sympathies of liberals. The imminent prospect of a French invasion in the early 1800s completed their transformation into British patriots. The war was to last, with insignificant intermissions, for over twenty years, becoming in the words of a *Times* correspondent "a war of no common description – a war of system against system, in which no choice is left us, but victory or extirpation."[4] It was the first "modern" war in a number of respects, not least the ideological commitment of the two sides. While prosecuting the war abroad Pitt's Tory government and its successors were also determined to deal with dissent at home. The demand for reform was fueled by economic distress both during and immediately after the war. Liberals who had looked forward to a reform "from the top," carried out by respectable and educated men like themselves, were easily alarmed by the sight of the people attempting to take part in the political process on their own behalf, though it seems likely that the reformers, by enlisting working men in political activities, acted to avoid a revolution rather than to provoke it. Another source of alarm was the danger that discontent in Ireland might provide an opportunity for a French invasion.

The government response to such dangers was repression, by force when necessary, and by the widespread use of spies, informers, and *agents provocateurs*. Liberals soon found how isolated they were in a society whose mistrust of innovation was exacerbated by the fear of invasion from without and revolution from within. The net of suspicion and paranoia enveloped even respectable opponents of the government, as some among the poets were to find. In 1792 Robert Burns's gift of artillery to the French National Convention led to an investigation by his superiors in the Excise. In 1796 a Home Office agent was shadowing Wordsworth and Coleridge in their wanderings (they were suspected of spying for the French) and trying to take down their conversation for his masters (Coleridge, *Biographia*, I, 193–7). In 1803 Blake quarreled with a soldier, Private Schofield, who accused him of making seditious and even treasonable statements – an accusation that could well have cost Blake his liberty if not his life, had he not had respectable friends to speak for him at his trial. Blake suspected that the incident was a deliberate attempt to entrap him.⁵ In 1812 Shelley's correspondence from Ireland was being opened and his case came to the attention of the Postmaster General, the Home Secretary, and the Irish Secretary. It was no doubt the respect due to the son of an MP and grandson of a baronet that saved him from prosecution; his servant was actually arrested and imprisoned for distributing his pamphlets.⁶ Following the death of his first wife Shelley lost the custody of his children, a virtually unprecedented judgment, for which his published views on religion and marriage were largely responsible. The general ideological intolerance of British society in matters moral and political – "cant" as it was known – made Shelley and Byron glad to live abroad.

It was not, however, upper- or middle-class liberals who bore the main brunt of government repression but working-class radicals. In 1793–4 a number of leading reformers were tried in Scotland and given sentences of up to fourteen years' transportation to Botany Bay in Australia – events that probably lie behind Burns's anthem to "the cause of TRUTH and Liberty," "Scots, wha hae wi' Wallace bled" (Burns, *Letters*, II, 235–6). In 1794 the government prosecuted leaders of the London societies for treason, but after the acquittal of Thomas Hardy, John Horne Tooke, and John Thelwall (a friend of Coleridge's) – an acquittal at least partly due to a masterly pamphlet by William Godwin – they were forced to back down. The suspension of *habeas corpus* between 1794 and 1801 and again in 1817–18 allowed the arrest of scores of radicals without the uncertainty and embarrassment of a trial. In 1812 the government deployed more troops against the Luddite framebreakers (on whose behalf Byron spoke in the Lords) than had been sent to the Iberian Peninsula four years earlier to fight the French. The riots that followed the Spa Fields meetings organized by the Spenceans in December 1816 led to their leaders being prosecuted for high treason, while the sailor Cashman was hanged for his part in the riots opposite the shop kept by William Godwin. In 1817 three Derbyshire radicals were executed for their part in a rebellion instigated by a government spy, prompting Shelley to write one of his most powerful political pamphlets, *An Address to the People on the Death of the Princess Charlotte*. In 1819 a large demonstration of reformers at St. Peter's Field in Manchester was attacked by the local Yeomanry, who were congratulated by the government for their action; Shelley's response this time was another pamphlet, "A Philosophical View of Reform," and the poem *The Mask of Anarchy* (both remained unpublished in his lifetime). It can be seen that the apparatus of government oppression had outlasted the war, which was finally brought to an end with the Battle of Waterloo in 1815. In an ironic gesture the slaughter at Manchester was dubbed "Peterloo," rather as every political scandal now is given the suffix "-gate."

The war also obliged the government to do something about the long-standing problem of Ireland. During the American war Henry Grattan's middle-class Volunteer Movement had forced significant concessions from the English government. During the war with France the society of United Irishmen with their radical aims and French sympathies was an obvious target for repression. Following the Irish rebellion of 1798 and a French landing, the government reasserted direct rule over the sister-island with the Act of Union (1801), dubbed by Byron "the union of the shark with his prey" (*Works*, II, 441). Largely owing to George III's opposition this was not accompanied, as Pitt had intended, with a measure of Catholic emancipation. The continued denial of full civil liberties to Catholics (while Britain supported her Catholic allies in Portugal and Spain) was a scandal for liberals up until the repeal of the Test and Corporation Acts (1829) and prompted Shelley's trip to Ireland in 1811–12. As the Irish poet Thomas Moore wryly commented in 1809, "Rebels in Cork are patriots at Madrid" ("The Sceptic: A Satire," 58, in Moore, *Poetical Works*, p. 143). It should however be noted that George III was more in step with the country at large (including the older Romantics) than were the liberals on this issue.

At a period when Christianity was considered to be part of the law of the land, political and religious issues were virtually inseparable. Dissent from the established Church of England (whether by Catholics or Protestant Dissenters) was seen as going hand in hand with dissidence, and the French were blamed for infidelity as much as revolution. The speech to the Revolution Society that provoked Burke's *Reflections on the Revolution in France* was delivered by the Dissenting intellectual Richard Price. Another Dissenting supporter of the Revolution, Joseph Priestley, saw his house and laboratory destroyed by a Birmingham mob under the slogan "Church and King." The followers of "old" Dissent – the Baptists and Unitarians – were regarded with suspicion because of the actions of their forebears in the seventeenth century, and while few of them were potential regicides their continued exclusion from public office and other civil rights made their academies a natural breeding ground for political opposition. Godwin and Hazlitt were both sons of Dissenting ministers, and Coleridge contemplated a career as a Unitarian minister. Modern historians have tended to identify the "new" Dissent of Methodism as politically conservative, though it was hardly welcomed as such at the time. Outright atheism, as in the case of Shelley, went hand in hand with a more radical rejection of the established order; Shelley attacked God as a "prototype of human misrule." Not surprisingly those Romantics who, like Wordsworth, Coleridge, and Southey, finally returned to a defense of the established political order also devoted themselves to defending the Established Church.

The government's policies towards France and towards radicals at home would not have been possible without ideological justification. The government was assiduous in its efforts to manipulate the existing media, whether by prosecuting journalists like William Cobbett, William Hone, Richard Carlile, and Leigh Hunt and his brother John, or by bribing and priming journalists on the government side. A member of Pitt's government and future Prime Minister, George Canning, was the moving force behind *The Anti-Jacobin* (1797–8), a weekly journal that attacked the French and their British sympathizers, and whose merciless satires of Wordsworth, Coleridge, and Southey in their democrat phase are still remembered. In the *Quarterly Review*, founded in 1809 as a deliberate counterweight to the liberal Whig *Edinburgh Review* (founded 1802), William Gifford, editor of the *Anti-Jacobin*, again took up the Tory cudgels against the poets of the younger generation, who were also assailed by the wits of *Blackwood's Edinburgh Magazine*. Throughout this period political considerations weighed heavily in the reviewing of poetry. The partisan treatment meted out to Keats prompted Clare to ask "is polotics to rule genius – if it is – honesty & worth may turn swindlers & liberty be thrown to the dogs & worried out of existance." But Clare well knew that "to escape the hell of party-political critisism is impossible" (Clare, *Letters*, pp. 189–90).

The government's most valuable support was secured by conviction rather than interest. The leading conservative ideologue was Edmund Burke, author of *Reflections on the French Revolution* (1790) and other works and pamphlets of the 1790s.[7] As an opponent of the American war and of royal absolutism Burke's liberal credentials were impeccable. Yet he broke with many of his fellow Whigs by his total opposition to the French Revolution and its British supporters. Rejecting the philosophy of abstract rights of the French revolutionaries, he offered a vision of human society as essentially hereditary, "a partnership not only between those who are living, but between those who are living, those who are dead, and those who are to be born."[8] When the first generation of poets awoke from their dream turned nightmare it was to Burke's principles that they turned. Burke's greatness, appreciated even by liberal critics like William Hazlitt, consists in having elevated the political debate to the level of a debate of principle. His appeals to tradition, sentiment, and chivalry were open to question, but at the same time they served to call into question the values of reason, progress, and efficiency to which Burke's opponents appealed. As we shall see, not even the most radical of the Romantics would find it easy to resolve this clash of principles.

The other side of the ideological debate is represented by one of the replies to Burke's *Reflections*, Thomas Paine's *Rights of Man* (I, 1791; II, 1792). A veteran of the American Revolution, Paine not only defended the principles of the French Revolution but called for their implementation in Britain. Against Burke's appeal to the hereditary principle, Paine insisted that "Every age and generation must be as free to act for itself, *in all cases*, as the ages and generations which preceded it."[9] His writings had their greatest impact among working-class radicals, and his influence among this audience alarmed the government so much that they prosecuted him for seditious libel, obliging him to flee to France. The story that he was advised to escape by Blake is, alas, almost certainly apocryphal.[10] In France Paine was imprisoned under the Terror, when he occupied himself by writing *The Age of Reason* (I, 1794; II, 1795). This anti-Christian work was actually intended to counter the French tendency to atheism by offering instead a pure Deism. But Paine's "infidel" religious beliefs were almost more scandalous in Britain than his revolutionary politics, and publishers were prosecuted in the 1810s and later for republishing his religious works.[11] Paine's influence has much to do with the free-thinking tendency of nineteenth-century British radicalism. Religious and political issues were intimately connected in this period because of the conservative posture of the established church and the ideological use to which it put Christian doctrine. Shelley charged that the accusers of the Deist publisher Richard Carlile cared for religion "only as it is the mask and the garment by which they are invested with the symbols of worldly power" (Shelley, *Letters*, II, 143). Blake accused Bishop Richard Watson, who wrote against Paine, of being "a State trickster," and attributed "the English Crusade against France" to "State Religion." Blake himself was no infidel and wished to defend what he considered true Christianity against its self-seeking spokesmen – he thought that "Tom Paine is a better Christian than the Bishop."[12]

If Paine spoke to and for the radicals while Burke put the conservative case, the liberal intelligentsia had their textbook too in the shape of William Godwin's *Political Justice* (1793). Although he had been a Whig journalist in the 1780s, Godwin aspired to produce a true political philosophy rather than mere party polemic. He certainly opposed the political principles of Burke, and his rejection of all authority or tradition led him to an anarchist position. At the same time he rejected the activism of Paine and considered that the resort to revolutionary action posed as great a threat to intellectual independence as did acquiescence in the established order. The combination of theoretical extremism and practical restraint made Godwin the perfect theorist for intellectuals, and his work had a great influence among young liberals in the 1790s, including the first generation of Romantics, as William Hazlitt (not without malice) was to recall a generation later.

> No work in our time gave such a blow to the philosophical mind of the country as the celebrated Enquiry concerning Political Justice. Tom Paine was considered for the time as a Tom Fool to him; Paley an old woman; Edmund Burke a flashy sophist. Truth, moral truth, it was supposed, had here taken up its abode; and these were the oracles of thought. "Throw aside your books of chemistry," said Wordsworth to a young man, a student in the Temple, "and read Godwin on Necessity."
>
> (*Works*, XI, 16–17)

It was believed that it was in consideration of the high price of the work and its intended address to the educated that the government decided not to prosecute it – an equivocal compliment. Godwin's initial fame was followed by later obscurity, and many of his early admirers, including Wordsworth, did not care to be remembered as such twenty years later. But he did have one significant disciple among the younger poets – his son-in-law, Shelley.

By the time Shelley was eagerly studying *Political Justice* the elder poets had transferred their allegiance to Burke. Shelley understood the disillusion from which they suffered, though he did not share it. In the preface to *The Revolt of Islam* he wrote:

> on the first reverses of hope in the progress of French liberty, the sanguine eagerness for good overleapt the solution of these questions, and for a time extinguished itself in the unexpectedness of their result. Thus many of the most ardent and tender-hearted of the worshippers of public good have been morally ruined by what a partial glimpse of the events they deplored, appeared to shew as the melancholy desolation of all their cherished hopes. Hence gloom and misanthropy have become the characteristics of the age in which we live, the solace of a disappointment that unconsciously finds relief only in the wilful exaggeration of its own despair. This influence has tainted the literature of the age with the hopelessness of the minds from which it flows.
>
> (*Poetical Works*, pp. 33–4)

Shelley wrote *The Revolt of Islam* in order to understand and come to terms with what he accepted as the temporary failure of the revolutionary movement. He could see this failure as a lesson of history, to be learnt in order to guide future action. For the younger generation the historical debacle did not involve the frustration of personal hopes, nor did it oblige them to curb their aspirations for the future.

The polemical exchanges between the two generations in the 1810s can obscure the fact that the political differences between them are often matters of degree rather than of kind. The elder generation's experience of political violence led them to view with horror the revival of the popular radical movement after 1815. Southey, writing in 1817 to the then Prime Minister, was scandalized to note that the "spirit of Jacobinism" that had seduced him and fellow middle-class liberals in the 1790s had now "sunk into the rabble."[13] But the younger poets' attitude was at best ambivalent. Byron shared Southey's fantasies of a new Jacobin tribunal presided over by radical leaders like William Cobbett and Henry Hunt. Even Shelley, the most sympathetic to the radical cause, was torn between two imperatives: to rouse the people to resistance, and simultaneously to moderate and guide them towards peaceful means of change. The refrain of *The Mask of Anarchy* – "Ye are many, they are few" – reflects his ambiguous attitude: do the odds guarantee victory in an armed struggle, or make such a struggle unnecessary? Whatever their sympathies with the poor and oppressed, the poets were for the most part upper- and middle-class intellectuals who could only fear what the oppressed might do to right their wrongs.

Another factor common to the two generations is the Romantic commitment to national independence, a commitment whose importance and conservative tendency is well known in the case of Continental Romanticism. (See the essay by Peter Thorslev in the present volume.) In Britain nationalism took a more liberal direction that stressed the rights of a national community to political self-determination. It provided a bridge over which the elder Romantics could cross from defense of revolution to support of reaction. In 1796 Southey published *Joan of Arc*, written in collaboration with Coleridge. The point of the choice of subject is clear – England had no more right to interfere in the affairs of the French republic in the late eighteenth century than it had had to meddle with the kingdom of France in the fifteenth. In 1814 Southey, freshly crowned as poet laureate, published *Roderick, the Last of the Goths*, with an equally pointed political moral – Britain's defense of Spain and Portugal against French imperialism was as holy a cause as Roderick's defense of Spain against Moorish invasion. Southey could argue that he opposed the French in 1814 for the same reasons for which he had sympathized with them twenty years before. Southey and Byron had little enough in common, but canto 1 of the latter's *Childe Harold's Pilgrimage* (1812) shows Byron too as a sympathizer with the Portuguese and Spanish. Britain's involvement in the Iberian Peninsula from 1808 also gave Coleridge and Wordsworth the opportunity to speak out in favor of the war against France, Coleridge in the columns of *The Courier*, and Wordsworth in a long pamphlet on *The Convention of Cintra* (1809). Their unhappiness with French foreign policy was not a new thing; the crucial event was probably the French invasion of Switzerland in 1798, which inspired Coleridge's "France: An Ode." In this poem Coleridge had to disavow his earlier enthusiasm for France as a champion of liberty, now that it had invaded the land of William Tell and republican independence.

French imperialism was symbolized by the figure of Napoleon, who entered popular mythology as a bogeyman (see figure 3.1). In the eyes of the elder Romantics he was a descendant of Milton's Satan (see figure 3.2). As "the child and the champion of Jacobinism" (Coleridge, *Essays on His Times*, 1, 185) Napoleon exposed the hollowness of the French republican rhetoric of freedom for all nations. The younger generation had no more liking for Napoleon, whom they saw as yet another tyrant, perhaps a great one in comparison with his opponents, but still a tyrant rather than a liberator. For Byron Napoleon was an exemplary tragic figure, a historical embodiment of the contradictions Byron perceived within himself (*Childe Harold's Pilgrimage*, III. sts. xxxvi–xlv). His notorious self-identification with Napoleon (he even acquired a replica of the Emperor's old coach) implies no endorsement of his actions. In his "Ode to Napoleon Buonaparte" (1814) Byron reserves his warmest praise for "The Cincinnatus of the West," George Washington. In Blake's mythological system Napoleon can be identified as the revolutionary Orc who ended by turning into the tyrannical Urizen whom he had initially opposed. For Shelley he was the man who threw away the unparalleled opportunity to be the liberator of mankind when he yielded to the temptation of "greatness" in the bad old sense ("The Triumph of Life," 215–24).

In Shelley's words, Napoleon's "grasp had left the giant world so weak / That every pigmy kicked it as it lay" (226–7). His fall ushered in the age of the "Holy Alliance," the league of Russia, Austria, and Prussia, who, in the eyes of the liberals, had defeated Napoleon only in order to reimpose their own tyranny on Europe. Britain was not a member of the Holy Alliance but had formed a Quadruple Alliance with its members. Not surprisingly, if not entirely fairly, the Foreign Secretary, Lord Castlereagh, was detested by the liberals for his support of European despotism as well as for his earlier activities in Ireland. He was the first of the three government leaders savaged by Shelley in *The Mask of Anarchy* (the others were the Home Secretary, Lord Sidmouth, and the Lord Chancellor, Lord Eldon), and Byron wrote some particularly vicious epigrams on the occasion of his suicide in 1822. The younger poets detested the Holy Alliance for its oppression of nationalist liberation movements. Even Keats spoke on behalf of nationalism by publishing a sonnet "To Kosciusko," the Polish patriot who led a rebellion against Russia (a leading member of the Holy Alliance) in the 1790s, and who had also been celebrated in verse by Coleridge and Leigh Hunt. Byron and Shelley saw the suppression of nationalist movements at first hand during their years in Italy, once more under the control of Austria and its Italian

3.1 "The Beast as described in the Revelations Resembling Napolean Buonaparte," engraving, 1808, by Sauley and Rowlandson.

3.2 "Boney's meditations on the Island of St. Helena, or The Devil addressing the Sun," engraving, 1815, by George Cruikshank.

puppet-states. Byron's sympathy with the revolutionary Carbonari extended to allowing them to store arms in his cellar, and his activities brought him to the attention of the Italian authorities.[14] Shelley was more circumspect, but he shared with Byron the liberal English view of Italy as the home of the great medieval republics and was prepared to remind British reformers that, via the influence of Italian literature on English poets, "we owe among other causes the exact condition belonging to [our own] intellectual existence to the generous disdain of submission which burned in the bosoms of men who filled a distant generation and inhabited another land" (Shelley, *Prose*, p. 231). In such poems as "Lines Written among the Euganean Hills" (published 1819), "Ode to Liberty" (1820), and "Ode to Naples" (1820) he celebrated Italy's republican tradition, lamented its extinction, and hailed its resurgence. One of the most explicit statements of his own anarchist position, the sonnet often known as "Political Greatness" was actually addressed to the short-lived republic of Benevento, which tried to establish its independence from papal rule in 1821. Byron's "Ode on Venice" (published 1819) and *The Prophecy of Dante* (1819) also lament the political decline of Italy; though his two verse dramas *Marino Faliero, Doge of Venice* and *The Two Foscari* (both published with the *Prophecy* in 1821) show Byron's preference for the aristocratic republicanism of Venice and his preoccupation with the political dilemma of the dissident patrician.

If Italy had a strong hold on the English political imagination, Greece had a stronger. In the preface to *Prometheus Unbound* Shelley speculated that "If England were divided into forty republics, each equal in population and extent to Athens, there is no reason to suppose but that, under institutions not more perfect than those of Athens, each would produce philosophers and poets equal to those who (if we except Shakespeare) have never been surpassed" (*Poetry and Prose*, p. 134). The Hellenism of the younger Romantics also served as a code for the preference of a pagan amorality over the asceticism of Christianity. In this respect Keats is less detached from political controversy than he is usually taken to be. Wordsworth was responding to the subtext of the "Hymn to Pan" in Keats's *Endymion* when he sneered that it was "a Very pretty piece of Paganism."[15] Those trained to admire the cultural and political achievements of classical Greece could not but lament its modern degradation under Turkish rule, as Byron did in canto II of *Childe Harold's Pilgrimage* (1812). It is therefore not surprising that the liberal poets welcomed the beginning of the Greek War of Independence in 1821. Shelley translated Prince Ypsilanti's "Cry of War to the Greeks" for publication in English newspapers and wrote *Hellas* (published 1822) to promote sympathy for the Greek cause. Byron again carried sympathy into action, committing himself and his financial resources to the struggle, and dying of a fever at Missolonghi.

If nationalism provides a point of contact between the two generations, there are nonetheless important distinctions. The elder Romantics had more in common with the mystical nationalism of Continental Romanticism and its conservative bias. The younger poets were liberal nationalists, whose nationalism was a form of cosmopolitanism. Shelley supported the struggles for independence of the Irish, the Italians, the Spaniards, and the Greeks because he hoped that eventually they would liberate themselves not only from their external oppressors but from their own narrowly national prejudices, particularly those connected with religion. His political ideals, derived from the Enlightenment and Godwin, are universalist and abstract. Wordsworth, as he describes it in book x of *The Prelude*, reacted against the abstraction of the Godwinian philosophy and replaced it with other ideals: the organic unity and the sacredness of the particular community, as can be seen even in his relatively early poems on the local community of the Lake District, "Michael" and "The Brothers" (both in the second volume of *Lyrical Ballads* of 1800). In 1801 Wordsworth drew the attention of a prominent politician to these poems, expressing his sense of the unique value of the particular community and its way of life, which he saw as under threat from such modern developments as "the spreading of manufactures through every part of the country ... Workhouses, Houses of Industry, and the invention of Soup-shops &c &c." The defense of tradition against modern innovation is Burkean; yet Wordsworth was actually writing to the liberal Whig leader, Charles James Fox, whose support of the French Revolution had led to a break between him and his former ally Burke (Wordsworth, *Early Years*, pp. 313–15).

Wordsworth no doubt wished to see a continuity between his youthful liberalism and his growing conservatism. But the contradiction represented by his letter is symptomatic of what is problematic in the attitude of all the Romantics to progress. The debate between Burke and Paine had established the central political issue of the age as the tension between tradition and freedom. Burke defended the traditional political institutions of society as the result of an organic process of development expressing a collective wisdom not to be improved on or called into question by any individual who was the product of that society. Paine vindicated the right of any society – and by extension of any individual – to decide all such questions for itself and thus to liberate itself from the claims of prescription and the dead hand of the past. Between these two options the Romantic poets could choose in different ways; but none of them could escape the tension they generated. The early revolutionary enthusiasm of the elder Romantics showed that they had appreciated the claims of freedom, if finally they saw the defense of tradition as the most urgent concern. It is perhaps less obvious but equally true that the younger poets felt the force of the appeal to tradition. Poets are after all badly placed to reject such an appeal, as they work to find their roots and their place in the traditions of British and European literature. And the struggle for liberty has its own tradition, as Shelley and Byron's interest in the heritage of Greek and Italian republicanism testifies. The tradition could itself be a site of contestation. Burke agreed with Price in his reverence for the Glorious Revolution, but differed totally in his interpretation of it. When Shelley in *A Defence of Poetry* recalled "the last national struggle for civil and religious liberty" (*Poetry and Prose*, p. 508) he was implicitly invoking the authority of such republican writers as Milton and Algernon Sidney – an authority conservatives like Wordsworth could also invoke to bolster their nationalistic support for England in her struggle with France.

As upper- and middle-class intellectuals, all the principal male Romantic poets found themselves carried along on movements of social change with whose consequences they were in various ways forced to quarrel. These movements were in the last analysis economic, comprising what have become known as the Agricultural Revolution and the Industrial Revolution, with their accompanying changes in attitude. The war promoted the growth of industry by increasing demand for many manufactured goods and giving British manufacturers (thanks to British naval superiority) a monopoly of overseas markets. The wartime increase in food prices also favored agricultural improvement and provoked a fresh wave of enclosures of common land by act of Parliament. These economic developments lie behind the codification of the new "science" of political economy in the writings of Thomas Malthus (*An Essay on the Principle of Population*, 1798, enlarged 1803) and David Ricardo (*On the Principles of Political Economy, and Taxation*, 1817). Malthus was actually spurred to produce his thesis that the increase of population must inevitably set limits to human progress by the Utopian speculations of writers like Godwin. His conclusion that the poor should be left at the mercy of economic forces made him anathema to all the major Romantics. The economic and social life of the nation was changing radically, in ways that alarmed conservatives like Wordsworth and troubled progressives like Shelley. The pressure for political and social reform came primarily from those who had profited from these economic changes and who wished to use their economic prominence to press their claims to a greater share of political power and to promote their own middle-class, liberal, and progressive values. They were able to enlist political allies both from those of the old aristocratic ruling class who had profited by astute investment in new forms of economic enterprise, and from the new, mainly urban working class, brought into being by the spread of industrialism and becoming aware that its economic interests could only be protected by gaining a share of political representation. By using such universal human values as freedom and equality as the slogans under which to forward their own class interests, the bourgeoisie were able to gain support from classes with whose interests theirs were finally at odds. They could not of course control the consequences of this strategy. While middle-class reformers were largely satisfied with what they gained with the first Reform Act (1832), their working-class allies had formed expectations that led them to continue pressing for further reform throughout the nineteenth century.

Insofar as they espoused the values of liberty and equality the Romantics could be seen as ideologues for the bourgeois revolution, helping to obscure the class nature of middle-class political demands, which as Marx was to show were implicitly calls for economic *laissez-faire* and the unrestricted operation of the market. But we must recognize that what were slogans to the politicians were matters of genuine concern to the poets; they took the universal claims of middle-class liberalism seriously, and this had important consequences. It meant that the radical working-class reformers could draw on the liberal poets to define their own political demands and aspirations, left unfulfilled by the success of the bourgeois revolution. Byron and Shelley enjoyed a high reputation with the radical Owenites and Chartists. It also meant that the poets could offer a penetrating critique of the practice of the bourgeoisie by comparing it with its own professed values.

The Romantic attitude to industrialism can be caricatured as an aesthetic distaste for smoking chimneys and noisy factories and a preference for the idyllic charms of the countryside. In actual fact the Romantic imagination responded powerfully if ambivalently to the sublimity of the new industrial landscape.[16] The real focus of the Romantics' critique of their age is on the moral and social values in whose name both the increase of industry and the rationalization of agriculture took place. These social tendencies implied a redefinition and a revaluation of human nature and of the human person to which the poets were all finally opposed. In revolutionizing the British economy and British society the middle-class reformers seemed resolved to throw out the human baby along with the outdated social and political bathwater. The poets' problem was how to rescue the former without seeming to defend the latter. Responses to the new order could often be little better than nostalgia, which fueled the growing interest in medieval themes, to be found in Burke's lament that "the age of chivalry is gone. – That of sophisters, oeconomists, and calculators, has succeeded" and in the radical Cobbett's accusation that the Reformation had destroyed the old order of feudal loyalty and monastic charity.[17] The reactionary position that provided a refuge for such unlikely bedfellows could also be laid to the charge of the poets. There is some point in Peacock's malicious accusation that "While the historian and the philosopher are advancing in, and accelerating, the progress of knowledge, the poet is wallowing in the rubbish of departed ignorance, and raking up the ashes of dead savages to find gew-gaws and rattles for the grown babies of the age."[18]

We must recognize that a number of the Romantics' distinctive concerns are polemical themes in their long-running struggle with what they saw as the dominant philosophy of the age, a philosophy to which we can refer under the shorthand term of "utilitarianism."[19] A philosophy that reduced human action to the calculation of consequences and the pursuit of self-interest and valued hard facts over fine fancies was bound to touch poets on a sensitive spot. Keats sneered that the capitalistic brothers in his *Isabella; or, the Pot of Basil* thought "redlined accounts / Were richer than the songs of Grecian years" (st. xvi). But the sales figures of Keats's own Grecian romance, *Endymion* (1818), seemed to indicate that the reading public shared their tastes. If the Romantics were fond of recalling that other societies had considered the poet a seer or prophet, it was a defensive reaction to a society that saw them as mere entertainers at best and self-indulgent triflers at worst. This negative view of poetry in the modern age was expounded with some glee (and an indeterminate amount of irony) by Shelley's friend Peacock, whose account shows how easily a low estimate of poetry could be reconciled to political liberalism.

> [W]hen we consider that the great and permanent interests of human society become more and more the main spring of intellectual pursuit; ... and that therefore the progress of useful art and science, and of moral and political knowledge, will continue more and more to withdraw attention from frivolous and unconducive, to solid and conducive studies ... we may easily conceive that the day is not distant, when the degraded state of every species of poetry is ... generally recognized.    ("The Four Ages of Poetry," p. 131)

Peacock's attack stung Shelley (who had himself, as noted earlier, once put "moral and political knowledge" above poetry) to respond with his *Defence of Poetry*. That the poets had a real case to answer is clear from the views on poetry expressed by the great liberal spokesman Thomas Babington Macaulay, writing with no irony at all.

> We think that, as civilisation advances, poetry almost necessarily declines ...
>
> Perhaps no person can be a poet, or can even enjoy poetry, without a certain unsoundness of mind ...
>
> In a rude state of society men are children with a greater variety of ideas. It is therefore in such a state of society that we may expect to find the poetical temperament in its highest perfection ...
>
> He who, in an enlightened and literary society, aspires to be a great poet must first become a little child, he must take to pieces the whole web of his mind.[20]

This is the nightmare of Blake come true, a narrow rationalism that excludes and stigmatizes everything it cannot incorporate within itself. In the light of Macaulay's remarks we can see why Romantic poetry is so often concerned with childhood, madness, the socially inferior, myth, and superstition – with everything that was marginalized by the dominant philosophy of progress and utility.

In 1818 Keats crossed from economically backward Ireland to prosperous Scotland and encountered the central tension between tradition and progress within his own experience. In a startling prefiguration of Max Weber's thesis concerning Protestantism and the rise of capitalism, Keats attributed the economic progress of Scotland to the influence of the Calvinist "kirk-men" who "have made Men, Women, Old Men Young Men old Women, young women, boys, girls and infants all careful … regular Phalanges of savers and gainers." But by the same token they had "banished puns and laughing and kissing" – for Keats the fate of Burns was a powerful indictment of Scottish asceticism. He concluded, inconclusively:

> I have not sufficient reasoning faculty to settle the doctrine of thrift – as it is consistent with the dignity of human Society – with the happiness of Cottagers – All I can do is by plump contrasts – Were the fingers made to squeeze a guinea or a white hand? Were the Lips made to hold a pen or a kiss? And yet in Cities Man is shut out from his fellows if he is poor, the Cottager must be dirty and very wretched if she be not thrifty – The present state of society demands this and this convinces me that the world is very young and in a verry ignorant state – We live in a barbarous age. (Keats, *Letters*, p. 118)

But in pointing to the "young" and "barbarous" state of the world Keats is implicitly invoking the very doctrine of progress that was undermining the poetic values of love and pleasure to which he was committed.

Simply by being poets, then, the Romantics were fated to be reactionaries, in at least one sense of the term. William Hazlitt, who had his own reservations concerning the "new" reformers of the utilitarian school of Bentham, concluded that poetry itself was by its nature opposed to liberal political values.

> The language of poetry naturally falls in with the language of power. The imagination is an exaggerating and exclusive faculty: it takes from one thing to add to another: it accumulates circumstances together to give the greatest possible effect to a favourite object … The principle of poetry is a very anti-levelling principle … Poetry is right-royal. It puts the individual for the species, the one above the infinite many, might before right. (*Works*, IV, 214–15)

Hazlitt opposes the imagination, "a monopolising faculty, which seeks the greatest quantity of present excitement by inequality and disproportion," to the understanding, "a distributive faculty, which seeks the greatest quantity of ultimate good, by justice and proportion." The opposition of imagination and understanding or reason is a commonplace in Romantic literary theory. But, as Hazlitt shows, there are political considerations that make the issue less clear-cut than it might appear. In his reply to Burke Paine had seen an intimate connection between the latter's imaginative power and literary graces and his reactionary politics. Those who thought of themselves as political reformers, like Paine, could make the choice between reason and imagination in favor of the former. For the poets this was an impossible choice, and the recognition of its necessity was agonizing. This recognition of a disjunction of values lies behind the Furies' taunt to Prometheus that

> The good want power, but to weep barren tears.
> The powerful goodness want: worse need for them.
> The wise want love, and those who love want wisdom;
> And all best things are thus confused to ill.
>
> (*Prometheus Unbound*, 1.625–8)

In Shelley's last major poem, "The Triumph of Life," the narrator grieves

> to think how power and will
> In opposition rule our mortal day –
> And why God made irreconcilable
> Good and the means of good;          (228–31)

The narrator of Keats's "The Fall of Hyperion: A Dream" faces a similar dilemma, between Moneta's description of him as one "of the dreamer tribe" (1.198) and his admiration for those

> Who love their fellows even to the death;
> Who feel the giant agony of the world;
> And more, like slaves to poor humanity,
> Labour for mortal good.          (1.156–9)

The narrator hopes that a poet can be "a sage; / A humanist, physician to all men" (1.189–90), and Moneta agrees – but Keats can have no confidence that he is this kind of poet. The healing of the division between "Good and the means of good" is a central concern of Shelley in his *Defence of Poetry*, where he replies to Peacock's elevation of understanding over imagination by arguing that the imaginative visions of poets (in the widest sense) must serve to guide the labors of the reformers (*Poetry and Prose*, pp. 500–1).

Was it realistic to believe that poetry could have this kind of influence in the modern world? The Romantics recognized that as writers their task was the spreading of ideas and the changing of minds. Faced by the incomprehension of the reading public, Wordsworth proudly reminded his correspondent "that every great and original writer, in proportion as he is great

or original, must himself create the taste by which he is to be relished"
(Wordsworth, *Middle Years*, I, 150). By influencing his readers the poet could
free them from what Blake memorably called their "mind-forg'd manacles"
("London," 8). The Romantics' faith in the power of imaginative vision to
transform the world is the source of some of their greatest achievements.
To it we owe *The Prelude*, "The Ancient Mariner," the prophetic poems of
Blake, *Prometheus Unbound*, and the odes and "The Fall of Hyperion" of
Keats. But it is not a faith we can easily share. To rely on vision to transform the world is to be limited to transforming it in vision while leaving it
untouched in reality. The Romantic assumption that the mind creates its
world neglects the extent to which the converse is true. If the social world
determines our mental being, then the extent to which poets, or any writers,
can change the conditions of existence is severely limited, though they are
naturally reluctant to recognize this. Not all the Romantics would have
endorsed Coleridge's view of society, but they would probably have agreed
with his thesis that society's ills stemmed from an erroneous philosophy,
and that it was the business of responsible intellectuals to oppose that philosophy.[21] Yet it seems more likely that economic and social developments
had brought about the philosophy than vice versa. Coleridge's dream of an
independent class of intellectuals, the "clerisy," not involved in struggling
for particular interests and thus able to educate and legislate for society as a
whole, is the typical fantasy of a writer.[22] Such a body could only come into
existence as the product of the kind of material interests it was supposed
to oversee and would only be able to deal with symptoms it would be condemned to mistake for causes.

The Romantics in general remained under the sway of what Marx and
Engels were to call "the German ideology." Their strictures on their Young
Hegelian colleagues apply to these poets too.

> Since the Young Hegelians consider conceptions, thoughts, ideas, in fact all the
> products of consciousness, to which they attribute an independent existence,
> as the real chains of men … it is evident that the Young Hegelians have to fight
> only against these illusions of consciousness. Since, according to their fantasy,
> the relations of men, all their doings, their fetters and their limitations are
> products of their consciousness, the Young Hegelians logically put to men the
> moral postulate of exchanging their present consciousness for human, critical
> or egoistic consciousness, and thus of removing their limitations. This demand
> to change consciousness amounts to a demand to interpret the existing world
> in a different way, i.e. to recognize it by means of a different interpretation.[23]

As Marx put it in the eleventh of his "Theses on Feuerbach": "The philosophers have only interpreted the world in various ways; the point, however, is

to change it" (p. 620). The Romantic poets called on their readers to imagine the world anew in order to transform it – but the social world would have to be transformed first if the possibilities of imaginative vision were to be available to any but a privileged few. The error is more pardonable in poets than in political philosophers; and on Marx's own principle that "It is not the consciousness of men that determines their existence, but their social existence that determines their consciousness,"[24] it is futile to castigate individuals for the errors of their time and class. These errors preserved them from despair and allowed them to at least record their protest against conditions they rightly considered to be inhuman. Their position is most sympathetically seen as one of responsibility without power. The "escapism" of which they have sometimes been accused is rather a strategy of compensation, an attempt to lodge themselves (and their readers) in more congenial worlds of their own creation to console them for their inability to transform this world, "the very world which is the world / Of all of us, the place in which, in the end, / We find our happiness, or not at all" (*The Prelude*, x. 725–7). There is a danger that the resort to vision may cut the visionary off from the human community, and this is a frequent theme in Romantic poetry – in the Urizen of Blake, in Wordsworth's *Excursion*, in Coleridge's "Kubla Khan" and "Ancient Mariner," in Shelley's "Alastor" (1816) and "Triumph of Life," in Byron's *Childe Harold*, *Manfred*, and *Cain*, in Keats's "La Belle Dame Sans Merci" and "Fall of Hyperion." The danger was ever-present because it seemed that the alternative to visionary escape could only be acquiescence in the conditions of the world as it was and a lapse into custom and habit. In a society whose practices and beliefs constituted a denial of human imagination and creativity it was the poets' role to keep open a sense of alternative possibility. This perhaps is the crucial political function of the imagination, and in this respect all true poets are, as Shelley argued at the end of *A Defence of Poetry*, politically progressive, whatever their ostensible political beliefs.

### NOTES

1. Quoted in F. M. Todd, *Politics and the Poet: A Study of Wordsworth* (London: Methuen, 1957), p. 11.
2. For Byron's speeches in the Lords, see Byron, *Works*, II, 424–5. He spoke on the Framework Bill (1812), on Catholic Emancipation (1812), and on Parliamentary Reform (1813). His most important political satires are *Don Juan* (1819–24), *The Vision of Judgement* (1822), and *The Age of Bronze* (1823).
3. *England and the English* (1833), ed. Standish Meacham (Chicago and London: University of Chicago Press, 1970), p. 98.
4. Quoted in Clive Emsley, *British Society and the French Wars 1793–1815* (London and Basingstoke: Macmillan, 1979), pp. 159–60.

5. See David V. Erdman, *Blake: Prophet against Empire*, rev. edn. (New York: Doubleday, 1969), pp. 403–11.

6. See Kenneth Neill Cameron, *The Young Shelley: Genesis of a Radical* (London: Victor Gollancz, 1951), pp. 167–9, 172–7.

7. Burke was also the author of *A Philosophical Enquiry into the Origins of Our Ideas of the Sublime and Beautiful* (1757), an important source for the development of the Romantic aesthetic of sublimity. The political implications of the sublime are explored in Ronald Paulson, *Representations of Revolution 1789–1920* (New Haven and London: Yale University Press, 1983).

8. *Reflections on the Revolution in France*, ed. Conor Cruise O'Brien (Harmondsworth: Penguin, 1968), pp. 194–5.

9. *Rights of Man*, ed. Henry Collins (Harmondsworth: Penguin, 1969), p. 63.

10. See Erdman, *Blake: Prophet*, pp. 154–5.

11. Shelley's *Letter to Lord Ellenborough* (1812) and a letter intended for publication in the *Examiner* written in 1819 (Shelley, *Letters*, II, 136–48) were both prompted by the prosecutions of radical booksellers for publishing *The Age of Reason*.

12. *Poetry and Prose*, pp. 612–13, 620. Watson was actually a liberal bishop, but he fell afoul not only of Blake but also of Wordsworth, whose most outspoken (though not published) political pamphlet was *A Letter to the Bishop of Landaff* (1793).

13. C. D. Yonge, *The Life and Administration of Robert Banks, Second Earl of Liverpool*, 3 vols. (London: Macmillan, 1868), II, 298–9.

14. For the police reports on Byron, see Byron, *Works*, IV, 454–64; for his address to the Neapolitan insurgents, v, 595–6.

15. B. R. Haydon's account, quoted in Walter Jackson Bate, *John Keats* (London: Oxford University Press, 1963), p. 265.

16. See Francis D. Klingender, *Art and the Industrial Revolution* (1947; reprinted, London: Granada, 1972).

17. Burke, *Reflections*, p. 170; William Cobbett, *A History of the Protestant "Reformation," in England and Ireland; Showing How That Event Has Impoverished and Degraded the Main Body of the People in Those Countries* (1824–6).

18. "The Four Ages of Poetry" (1820), in *Memoirs of Shelley and Other Essays and Reviews*, ed. Howard Mills (London: Rupert Hart-Davis, 1970), p. 128.

19. The founder of utilitarianism is usually considered to be Jeremy Bentham, the radical legal and political reformer; but Bentham systematized ideas and attitudes that were common currency among progressive thinkers at the time. See Elie Halévy, *The Growth of Philosophical Radicalism* (1928), trans. Mary Morris (London: Faber and Faber, 1972).

20. "Milton" (1825), in *Critical and Historical Essays*, 2 vols. (London: Dent, 1907), I, 153–6.

21. See his letter to the Prime Minister, Lord Liverpool, July 28, 1817; Coleridge, *Letters*, IV, 757–63.

22. See *On the Constitution of the Church and State*. The subsequent history of the idea is traced in Ben Knights, *The Idea of the Clerisy in the Nineteenth Century* (Cambridge University Press, 1978).

23. Karl Marx and Friedrich Engels, *The German Ideology* (1845–6; reprinted, Moscow: Progress Publishers, 1976), pp. 35–6.
24. Preface to *A Contribution to the Critique of Political Economy* (1859); Karl Marx, *Early Writings*, trans. Rodney Livingstone and Gregor Benton (Harmondsworth: Penguin, 1977), p. 425.

# 4

PETER THORSLEV

# German Romantic Idealism

Im Anfang war die Tat! (In the beginning was the act.)
*Faust*, part I

Die Weltgeschichte ist das Weltgericht. (World history is the Last Judgment.)
*Schiller*

## I

When the elegant exercises of Hume's skeptical empiricism woke Kant from the dogmatic slumbers of his Continental rationalism, surely no one could have predicted the prodigious symphonies of German Transcendental Idealism to follow. Not, of course, that these were composed by Kant himself, but his "Copernican Revolution" in epistemology prepared the way for them, as surely as the German compositions of the later Mozart prepared the way for Beethoven and Brahms – and, eventually, for the monstrous syntheses of Wagner. David Hume's secure place in the history of philosophy rests not on the construction of any philosophical system: quite simply, his essays constitute the most thorough job of deconstruction in modern intellectual history. (It is a pity, attributable, perhaps, to the French origins of the critical school – in French tradition, Locke has always been respected, Hume ignored – that modern deconstructionists have so neglected Hume. There are so many lessons available there, not only in the elegant simplicity of his arguments, but in the admirable lucidity of his Enlightenment prose.) In the third canto of *Childe Harold's Pilgrimage* Byron speaks of Gibbon, the most eminent of Enlightenment historians, as having "Sapp[ed] a solemn creed with solemn sneer" (III, st. 107). I have always liked to think that Byron's metaphor implied not that Gibbon with his (in-)famous fifteenth chapter of the *Decline and Fall* had drained the vital fluids from Christian doctrine, but that Gibbon was indeed a "sapper," that he had undermined the foundations of established dogma and planted an intellectual charge that he intended would blow the religious establishment to kingdom come. If this is Byron's metaphor, however, one must say that Gibbon laid a long fuse. It was not until the later decades of the nineteenth century that the twin charges of the

Higher Criticism and evolutionary theory left Matthew Arnold with only a "melancholy long withdrawing roar" ("Dover Beach," 25).

Hume, however, with his sensible Scottish inheritance and his Enlightened common sense, was never solemn, and one cannot imagine him with anything so forthright as a sneer. Nevertheless, with his quietly constructed essays he undermined not only the last certitudes of rationalist dogma – in this he had his predecessors in the English empirical tradition of Hobbes, Locke, and the early Berkeley – but the certitudes of the empirical tradition as well. His most notorious and long-lasting attack struck at the very foundations of empirical science: indeed, twentieth-century scientific philosophy, many scholars concede, has yet fully to recover. The venerable law of cause and effect, Hume concludes, rests on foundations no more secure than the perception of "constant conjunction" (the Necessitarian Godwin, between the first and the third editions of *Political Justice*, read or reread his Hume, and carefully changed all references to "cause and effect" to "constant conjunction"). Indeed, Hume suggests, cause-and-effect relationships are perhaps evidence of no more than a "laziness" of the human mind. The most devastating of his charges, however, Hume reserved for a posthumous publication: he was, after all, a respectable public citizen, and for all his philosophical radicalism, concerned for his "character," as he called it, or his public reputation. In his *Dialogues on Natural Religion* he ironically deconstructs all of the "proofs" for the existence of God: the rationalist proofs, including the venerable ontological argument, and the major "empirical" proofs as well, including the argument from design (the existence of the watch presupposes the watchmaker).

The possible devastating social effects, however delayed, of his deconstructive efforts Hume seems not to have taken very seriously. Pierre Bayle, the Huguenot whose famous *Dictionnaire historique et critique* (1697–1702) served for well over a century as a source-book for skeptics and atheists, nevertheless confessed himself a fideist (one who believes that no intellectual proofs are necessary for Christian belief). Following the example of his notorious precursor, Hume attempted to cover his exposed and blasphemous posterior with a confession of Christian fideism, at the conclusion of his *Dialogues*, but perspicacious readers were not long deceived: Samuel Johnson, for one, and even Scots nationalist and apologist Boswell considered him no better than an atheist. When he turned from his desk, however, Hume could retire to play backgammon with his friends – and in his politics he remained something of an unreconstructed Scots Tory. Perhaps, shored up by the "sympathy ethics" he adopted from the third earl of Shaftesbury and from Francis Hutcheson, he felt secure in the Enlightened faith that if only the mind is set free from dogma and cant, ethics will take care of itself. In any case, and so far as the immediate future of the English-speaking world was concerned, he had no great need to worry. Successive editions of William Paley's *Evidences of Christianity* took for granted the argument from design, as if Hume had never written his *Dialogues*; the young Shelley, who did take Hume's arguments seriously in his *Necessity of Atheism*, was summarily sent down from Oxford.

Immanuel Kant, however, in his provincial capital of Königsberg, to his everlasting credit also took Hume's arguments seriously, and, moreover, he seems to have sensed the horrendous ethical, social, and political consequences of Hume's skepticism. After Hume's demolition derby, Kant took it upon himself to pick up the pieces. He did not attempt, however, a frontal attack on Hume's ultimate skeptical empiricism. Instead, he began the painstaking construction of a new system of philosophical reasoning, an engine that to this day remains a marvel of German intellectual engineering. That his disciples amongst the Romantics should take it as a new chariot of fire in which they could ascend to the unattainable heights of Absolute Idealism was not of his doing, nor done with his consent.

In his first great critique, the *Critique of Pure Reason*, Kant conceded Hume's major antimetaphysical thesis. We cannot attribute the extension of time and space, or the relations of cause and effect (to take only the most ready-to-mind of Kant's "categories") to the objects of perception, to the things-in-themselves, as Hume had demonstrated, for if we do, we become inevitably involved in confusion and contradiction (Kant's famed "antinomies"). On the other hand, it seemed perhaps to Kant's Prussian mind too dismissive, too flippant, to attribute these categories to mere "lazy" habits of perception. The categories, Kant maintained, are inevitable, built into the mind; they are also the *a priori* conditions of all intelligibility. In this (much simplified) assertion consists the Copernican Revolution in epistemology that inaugurated the Romantic age. Concepts without percepts are empty, Kant conceded, but percepts without concepts are blind. Thenceforth, the phenomenal universe became a something that, in Wordsworth's memorable phrase, we "half-create, and [half-] perceive."

Yet there are no absolutes in Kant's first critique; one might almost say that what Kant did was to systematize and rationalize Humean skepticism. We cannot attribute any ontological status to the categories of the mind, and on the other hand we can make no definitive predications of the things-in-themselves as they really are without *using* the categories of the mind. We can assert their existence – they provide the (involuntary) "contents" of our "percepts" – but we can say almost nothing more. The first critique did provide a framework and a *Lebensraum* for the natural sciences of the day: in the realm of the phenomena, of the world of experience as organized by the understanding operating with the *a priori* categories, eighteenth-century science (read Newtonian physics) reigned supreme. Metaphysically speaking, however, Kant's first critique provided no more than a holding action against the onslaughts of Humean skepticism: he liberated science by carefully prescribing its limits. Hume's deconstruction of the law of cause and effect, for instance, is based quite simply on a misapplication of the categories. Hume was attempting to find some basis for causal relationships in the realm of the "noumena," of things as they are in themselves, and this attempt, in Kant's terms, is an illegitimate enterprise. The law of cause and effect is an *a priori* category of the understanding and applies only in the realm of the phenomena. So Kant dropped an iron curtain between physics and metaphysics, between the phenomena and the noumena, and established a philosophic dualism that was to frustrate and challenge Continental philosophy for more than a century.

Still, Kant was not only an Enlightenment follower of Newtonian physics, he was also a Lutheran pietist in his ethics, and he was quite aware that man does not live by bread alone. We must act not only in the realm of scientific discovery, but also in the realm of ethical imperatives. In his second great critique, that of *Practical Reason*, he concedes that it may not be intellectually (or cognitively) absurd to deny the existence of God, or of a free (and moral) will, or even of an afterlife of rewards and punishments, but it is morally absurd to do so, and moral absurdity should be as repugnant to the mind of man as intellectual absurdity. The self is not, as Hume had seemed to maintain, a mere succession of "phenomenal" and passive subjective impressions; we have an immediate intuition of an active self that is indeed "noumenal," that is free and responsible, and that cannot be subjected to the categories of the analytic understanding. And just as in the second critique he liberated the realm of ethics from the rigid categories of "scientific" and phenomenal laws, so in his third critique, the *Critique of Judgment*, he liberated the realm of aesthetics. If morality has its own operating procedures and makes its own demands, so does beauty. Organic or teleological form, for instance, which presents a conundrum to the analytic understanding, finds its home in the creation and the appreciation of works of art.

The next generation of post-Kantian Transcendental Idealists – Fichte, Schelling, and Hegel are the main prophets – were not much inspired by the first critique. In it, Kant had provided a living space for Newtonian science, but the Idealists were not much interested in Newton – or, indeed, in the careful analyses of mathematico-descriptive science in general. (Indeed, some modern philosophers of science still consider German Idealism to have introduced a new dark age and to have set back genuine scientific investigation on the Continent for a half century or more.) When new discoveries in science did obtrude on their philosophizing – in magnetism, Galvanism, the mechanics of perception, even Mesmerism – they served mainly as launching-pads for vast theories on dialectic principles from which, as Coleridge writes, in his *Theory of Life*, they could "construct a universe." (Mathematical reasoning, Coleridge maintains in the same treatise, is inimical to such "true" science, which must deal with qualities, not quantification.) The trajectories of these intellectual rockets – besides Coleridge's essay, see for instance Schelling's *Von der Weltseele*, and even Goethe's *Metamorphosenlehre* – only briefly lit up the night sky, and their detritus now litters the intellectual landscape of the age – or glows dimly in the studies of present-day followers of Rudolf Steiner and anthroposophy.

Kant's second and third critiques, however, provided the Romantic Idealists with the license they needed for new metaphysical explorations, in the realms of ethics, aesthetics, and grand theories of history. It is this decisive shift in emphasis that is emblematized in the first epigraph above from *Faust*. "Im Anfang war das Wort," writes St. John (in Luther's translation): the mind, the Word, Logos, Being. Not so, responds Faust in a "strong" misreading: "Im Anfang war die Tat": the will, the deed, the act, Becoming. In some respects German "Idealism" can be a misleading term, if one thinks of Plato's (static) realm of transcendent, eternal, immutable Forms or Ideas. Coleridge's term, in the *Biographia*, the "Dynamic Philosophy," seems more appropriate. For these Romantic philosophers the great ideals exist not in any abstract realm of transcendent being, but are immanent in the progress of the individual mind, and in the history of mankind: they were indeed, in Wordsworth's phrase, a something "evermore about to be."

Fichte was the closest to Kant, and felt himself a disciple: indeed, when Kant came to think that Fichte had gone too far, and moved to repudiate his follower, Fichte somewhat tartly responded that perhaps he was the better Kantian of the two. In any case, Fichte took advantage of the opening in metaphysics of the second critique: for him, the essence of life was the striving of the moral will – individually, socially, and politically – and this he made also the essence of his philosophy. The phenomenal world (in Kant's terms) is but the unconscious creation of the (noumenal) Ego, posited to provide the will with obstacles to overcome. It is the moral duty of the Ego to overcome these obstacles to understanding, and the conclusion of the struggle – although in most of Fichte's writings this ideal seems on an ever-receding horizon – should come in the Ego's realization that all obstacles are Ego-created and therefore subject to the enlightened will. (The parallel with Blake's "mind-forg'd manacles," which it is also our duty to overcome, is both striking and apposite: not a matter of influence, of course, but of a common climate, and common sources – especially, perhaps, in the mystical philosophy of Jakob Böhme.) In our own day we have come to associate the concept of *praxis* so exclusively with Marxism that it is good to be reminded that for Fichte also the practical reason took precedence: the reason is an instrument of the will, no end in itself. Fichte was one of the founders of German nationalism, and he thought it his duty to rouse the German peoples to resist not only Napoleon's armies, but also the incursions of "French" Enlightenment.

Schelling is not so close to Kant as was Fichte, but in his aesthetic idealism he nevertheless took advantage of the opening to metaphysics of Kant's third critique and posited as his first principle the creative rather than the moral will. If for Fichte man's saviour was the prophet, the patriot, the moral preacher who rouses us to salvation as moral strife, for Schelling it is above all the artist, who with the products of the creative imagination brings us to the realization that all of nature as well as all human artifacts are productions of the same Creative Will, of the World Soul.

From Hegel, finally, we have the Grand Synthesis, the Ring Cycle of Romantic philosophy. The moral and the creative will become one: the Absolute, the World Spirit, for which he appropriates the name of Reason – having nothing whatever to do with the "reason" of Enlightenment philosophy, the "mere analytical understanding," as Coleridge also so dismissively names it. If Fichte's vision is moral, if Schelling's is aesthetic, Hegel's is historical: if for Fichte the moral prophet is the saviour of humanity, and for Schelling the artist, for Hegel it is the philosopher of history. Hegel, however, adds a very important reservation: the philosopher-historian does not *affect* history, he interprets it, after the fact. The World Spirit realizes itself in and determines all of history; it uses (Hegelian) heroes, world-historical individuals (*Weltgeschichtliche Menschen*), but these heroes, like Carlyle's, know not what they do. The World Spirit becomes conscious of itself in philosophy, but only in retrospect: "The Owl of Minerva," as Hegel puts it in the preface to *The Philosophy of Right*, "flies only at twilight."[1] World-historical heroes determine history, all unconsciously, in accordance with the will of the World Spirit; philosophers understand history, but they cannot affect it. That said, however, the daring, the range, and the sheer intellectual effrontery of Hegel's vision can hardly be overestimated. He could truly say, with Terence, "Nothing human is alien to me." Every episode in the intellectual, political, artistic, and religious history of mankind is grist for Hegel's philosophic mill. His is a selective reading of history, to be sure: events that further the realization of the grand design of history are "essential"; those that do not are "accidental" (*zufällig*). The true effrontery of Hegel's vision, however, becomes apparent in the fact that in his view he has no opponents in all of the history of Western philosophy, even among his immediate predecessors, Kant, Fichte, and Schelling: he has only precursors. In Harold Bloom's appropriate term, what Hegel presents us with is nothing less than *the* Romantic "strong misreading" of Western intellectual-artistic-political history. In so doing, of course, he also presents us with a kind of secular theodicy, or, in M. H. Abrams's instructive coinage (in *Natural Supernaturalism*), a "biodicy." "All things work together for good," as St. Paul says, or, as Wordsworth puts it, in *The Prelude* (XIV.389), "all['s] gratulant if rightly understood." This is no naively optimistic interpretation of history, however: as Hegel put it in another of his aphorisms, "Reason" (the realization of the Idea in history) "is the rose in the cross of the present" (he was thinking of Luther's logo for the Reformation: a black cross set in a white rose). We mere mortals, engaged in a strife-torn history, can bear our crosses with resignation, if not with equanimity, in the vision of the white rose of the ultimate realization of the Absolute Idea.

## II

The technical details of these grand Romantic syntheses, and their arcane terminologies – the Ego and the non-Ego of Fichte's system, and the *Anstösse* through which this dichotomy is overcome; the varied manifestations of the Absolute in Schelling's pantheism ("the night in which all cows are black," as Hegel derisively described it); the intricacies of Hegel's new and "dynamic" logic, in which contradictories become *aufgehoben* in ever-new and productive syntheses, carrying within them "the seeds of their own destruction" – these we can perhaps safely leave to the professional historians of philosophy. But what can the general student of Romanticism learn from a study of the basic presuppositions of German Romantic Idealism?

Schiller and Goethe were deeply and decisively influenced by Kant's second and third critiques. Schiller, for instance, attempts in his concept of the "Beautiful Soul" a kind of reconciliation of the moralism of the second critique and the aestheticism of the third. Goethe, who fancied that his name would survive longer as a *Naturphilosoph* than as a poet, was much taken with the concept of organic form in the third critique and attempted a kind of transcendental application of it to the organic world in his *Metamorphosenlehre*; and in his *Farbenlehre* he launches a direct attack on Newton, the prince of Enlightenment science, for his color theories in the *Optics*. (In his study entitled *The Damnation of Newton*, Frederick Burwick suggests that so far as perception theory goes, at least, Goethe may now be seen to have had the better of the argument.[2]) The German *Romantiker* proper – Novalis, Hölderlin, Friedrich Schlegel – were even more closely involved, in action and reaction, with the post-Kantian Idealists. Novalis takes off from Fichte, but develops a philosophy of Nature not so very different from that in the early Schelling. Hölderlin suggests an organic and aesthetic philosophy of Nature that not only anticipates Schelling, but was deeply influential on the philosophy of his friend and fellow student at Tübingen, Hegel. Friedrich Schlegel's philosophy, on the other hand, was witty, allusive, epigrammatic, and utterly unsystematic, and his "Romantic irony" feeds on Kant's antinomies – and remains a thorn in the side of Hegel's theory of art: pure aestheticism, Hegel complained, that denies all the moral imperatives of history. Among the English Romantics only Coleridge, De Quincey – and Carlyle, if one considers him a Romantic (and he shares his birth-year with Keats) – were directly and deeply influenced by Kant and the post-Kantians. Coleridge acknowledges his debt to Kant freely and openly; about his debt to Schelling he is perhaps less candid, but it is now even more apparent.

Of far greater significance, however, than any study of direct influence might suggest – however fascinating such studies are – is the fact that the German Romantic Idealists present us with a discursive and philosophical account of the dominant Romantic *Weltanschauung*, of the set of presuppositions, of working axioms, the literature of the period represents in imagery, myth, and symbol. It is enlightening to see that Blake, in his idiosyncratic mythology, provides us with a kind of analogue of Fichte's moral philosophy: as Fichte's Ego all unconscious creates the phenomenological world, in order to provide an "other" in which the Ego may see itself in opposition and come to see its own salvation in the realization that the phenomenal world is its own creation, so Urizen, split off from Los, creates a Newtonian universe that is restrictive and binding and that Los must overcome in the vision that sees it as a creation of his fallen and divided self. The parallels, indeed, can be made even more specific: both Fichte and Blake were at first enthusiastic supporters of the French Revolution, in spite of the fact that both were (or became) the most virulent critics of that Enlightenment philosophy (Locke, Newton, Voltaire, Rousseau) of which the Revolution was in some sense an expression. Fichte – and with some good reason, since Napoleon's armies were at the gates – came to see it as the duty of the German people to educate the world in the new Romantic gospel. Blake was no such chauvinist, and yet there is perhaps some element of xenophobia in the fact that the New Jerusalem will rise in England's green and pleasant bowers (*Jerusalem*, plate 77), and that, at the close of the prophecy, a chastened Locke and Newton are allowed inside, but Voltaire and Rousseau are not. (In a series of studies, David Punter has drawn illuminating parallels between Blakean and German Romantic dialectics, although he sees a closer affinity between Blake and Hegel than between Blake and Fichte.[3])

So long ago as 1960, E. D. Hirsch provided us with what in his sub-title he called a "Typological Study of Romanticism" (*Wordsworth and Schelling* – Punter acknowledges the line of succession). Here there could also be no question of influence, and yet, as Hirsch persuasively argues, there is an "astonishing spiritual closeness" between the Schelling of the *Ideen zu einer Philosophie der Natur* (1797) and the Wordsworth of the great decade of 1796–1806, which produced the first complete (1805) *Prelude*. What Schelling and Wordsworth share is a philosophy of "mutual inclu-siveness": the I and the not-I of Fichtean opposition become parallel, even mirror-image expressions of the same *natura naturans*, the World Soul.

The true monument in this kind of philosophical-literary scholarship, however, remains Abrams's *Natural Supernaturalism*, and the centerpiece of his study is a brilliant and detailed parallel reading of Wordsworth's *Prelude* and Hegel's *Phenomenology*. Both works, he argues, are *Bildungsgeschichte* of the human spirit; both present us with a new theodicy, or a "biodicy," of the individual life, and, by extension, of the human spirit. Both present an organic and evolutionary, a teleological view of the journey of the human spirit, and at its destination, both pilgrims come to the Wordsworthian con-clusion that "all['s] gratulant if rightly understood." Not, as Pope with his rationalistic optimism had asserted, "Whatever is, is right," but rather "what-ever is about to be, is right." Abrams might have carried his parallelism one step further: for both Wordsworth and Hegel this vision of pattern, mean-ing, and significance is always and only retrospective. The deliberative and philosophic mind has no part in the furtherance of the process; Nature (for Wordsworth) and the World Spirit (for Hegel) operate in man and through man, but without the acquiescence, and often in spite, of man's conscious will. This unconscious working of the World Spirit is what Hegel refers to as the "cunning of Reason," and what Wordsworth demonstrates as that secret and caring ministry of Nature that leads him, in spite of his wayward will, to the realization that the end vision of the pilgrimage more than justifies the many episodes of suffering and disillusion that preceded it.

Abrams's study represents the acme of this kind of historical scholarship on German Idealism and Romanticism. Moreover, this scholarship (and Abrams is representative) did not merely present a neutral description of the Romantic synthesis: it is unabashedly apologetic. The Romantic celebration of life, joy, and transcendence still had meaning, even validity, in the later twentieth century: it is, in Yeats's ringing phrase, a "monument of unageing intellect" ("Sailing to Byzantium," 8).

Not so, the New Historicists inform us: the Romantic *Weltanschauung* must not be so "represented" or recapitulated; it must be restored to its "pastness"; and then seen for what it is, or was: the Romantic Ideology.

In this view, Abrams's work must be viewed not only as a monument *in* the scholarship of the Romantic *Weltanschauung*, but as a monument *to* it. Admittedly, however personal and moving the close of Abrams's work is, with its confession of faith in the eternal relevance of Romanticism, it does have about it an elegiac tone, as if this world view might be more apposite in the rural landscape and long winters of upstate New York than in Manhattan, or London, or Los Angeles. In any case, the way had been prepared for such a reassessment: some years earlier (1964), in a very influential work on Wordsworth (*Wordsworth's Poetry 1787–1814*), Geoffrey Hartman had "deconstructed" Wordsworth's organic vitalism: all the poet's protestations to the contrary, Wordsworth is not so much a poet of Nature as a poet who was led to reject nature in favor of an "unmediated vision" of the transcendent. Paul de Man in his famous essay on "The Rhetoric of Temporality" suggested that both Wordsworth and Coleridge were guilty of ontological "bad faith" in their espousal of a transcendent idealism they must or should have known does not square with the facts of experience. Indeed, so long ago as the mid thirties, I. A. Richards, in *Coleridge on Imagination*, had made a valiant attempt to see what could be salvaged in Coleridge's aesthetic theory if one ditched its transcendentalist superstructure (a good deal, as it turned out).

Still, one might say, *Weltanschauung* or Ideology: a rose by any other name … Contemporary transcendental idealists are a rare breed, and surely few would deny (and Abrams not among them) that the ideology – or the ideologies – of Romanticism were historically determined, even if there might be a great deal of disagreement as to what the determining factors were. The difficulty with the New Historical assessment comes not with its terminology, but with its sources and its presuppositions. Jerome J. McGann, in his widely influential manifesto for what has in Romantic scholarship at least come to be called the New Historicism (*The Romantic Ideology* – the definite article is significant), took his title and his cue from Marx and Engels's *The German Ideology*, but if Abrams's work is in part at least an unabashed apology for Romantic Idealism, Marx and Engels's work is just as certainly a rather heavy-handed polemic, and the view they present is perhaps even more likely to be distorted.

McGann takes as one key text, for instance, a paragraph from *The German Ideology* in which the authors describe the axioms and procedures by which Hegel arrives at his "idealist" conception of history:

Once the ruling ideas have been separated from the ruling individuals and, above all, from the relationships which result from a given stage of the mode of production, and in this way the conclusion has been reached that history

is always under the sway of ideas, it is very easy to abstract from these various ideas "*the* idea," the notion etc. as the dominant force in history, and
thus to understand all these separate ideas and concepts as "forms of self-
determination" on the part of *the* concept developing in history. It follows
then naturally, too, that all the relationships of men can be derived from the
concept of man, man as conceived, the essence of man, *Man*. This has been
done by the speculative philosophers. Hegel himself confesses at the end of the
*Geschichtsphilosophie* that he "has considered the *concept* only" and has represented in history the "true *theodicy*" ... Now one can go back again to the
producers of the "concept," to the theorists, ideologists and philosophers, and
one comes then to the conclusion that the philosophers, the thinkers as such,
have at all times been dominant in history: a conclusion, as we see, already
expressed by Hegel.[4]

A few paragraphs later the authors make the last argument more specific:

Whilst in ordinary life every shopkeeper is very well able to distinguish between
what somebody professes to be and what he really is, our historians have not
yet won even this trivial insight. They take every epoch at its word and believe
that everything it says and imagines about itself is true.

This is not merely a bad caricature of Hegel's philosophy of history, it is
a travesty of it. Moreover, it seems a travesty that is patently ideologically
determined: were the authors to present an accurate picture of Hegel's procedures and presuppositions, they would be forced to acknowledge what
they have in common with him: (Romantic) historicism.

Hegel did not postulate some common and "essential" nature of man and
from that deduce a philosophy. It is a distinctive feature not only of Hegel's
philosophy but of German Idealism in general that there is no such thing as
a stable and "essential" Man: in every aspect of our selves we are timebound
and historically determined. As Hegel puts it in the preface to the *Philosophy
of Right*: "Whatever happens, every individual is a child of his time; so philosophy too is its own time apprehended in thoughts. It is just as absurd to
fancy that a philosophy can transcend its contemporary world as it is to
fancy that an individual can overleap his own age, jump over Rhodes."[5]
Moreover, although Hegel was an "idealist," and spoke of the process of
history as a gradual revelation of the "absolute Idea," this "idea" (pattern,
process, "meaning") is never available to the consciousness of those acting
in history: it is only and always immanent in history, and available to consciousness only in retrospect. Far from saying that "philosophers ... have at
all times been dominant in history," Hegel insists that philosophers cannot
affect history. In his memorable phrase from the same preface, "philosophy
comes always too late," and when it "paints its gray on gray," the green tree
of life has "already grown old." Finally, Hegel was very well able to make

the "shopkeeper's" distinction between what a man thinks he is or professes to be doing, and what he "really" is and "really" does: it is the very essence of Hegel's doctrine of the "cunning of Reason" to assert that not merely shopkeepers and their customers but even "world-historical individuals" like Caesar or Frederick the Great may think they are acting on professions of faith, or for the glory of the state, when in "reality" they are acting to further the realization of the progress immanent in history. What the Romantic Idealists (especially Hegel) and Marx share is an organic or vitalist conception of history: that there is a driving process apparent in history that is indifferent to, and for the most part beyond the reach of, our conscious perceptions of it and that works its way with or without our wills.

To put it another way: what Hegel and Marx reject (and what Marx seems to be accusing Hegel of in this passage) are the twin doctrines of an Enlightenment ideology. First, that there is indeed a common and essential nature of man, that this essence is rational, and that it is both self-interested and "sympathetic." Second, that there is indeed such a thing as the disinterested mind.

Recently the Enlightenment "myth" of the disinterested mind has once more, in literary-historical circles, at least, fallen into disrepute. McGann can go so far as to say that anyone today who seriously defends it is either naive or hypocritical. Years ago the eminent philosopher-naturalist Michael Polanyi wrote that among biologists, the concept of teleology is like a loose woman whom biologists deny in public but consort with in private. The same can now be said, perhaps, in post-modernist literary circles, of the myth of the disinterested mind: we may be so intimidated by Marxist or other critics of historiography that we deny the concept in public, but when we retire to our studies, it becomes once more our familiar. Actually, I suppose one should not say that Hegel denies the *possibility* of the disinterested mind: presumably the philosophic mind that brings to self-conscious realization the "Idea" in history is truly disinterested, but then it is so only in retrospection, in second thoughts. But if he does not deny the possibility of the disinterested mind, he does deny its efficacy. (Marx, presumably, denies not only the efficacy, but the possibility.)

In any case, Hegel makes it perfectly plain, in the *Philosophy of Right*, but also in the much earlier *Phenomenology*, who these proponents of the myth of the disinterested mind are or were, those philosophers who presume to "transcend [their] contemporary world." They were the *philosophes* of the "French" Enlightenment, and the inevitable result of their presumption was the Revolution and the Reign of Terror. With their intellectual guillotines (the metaphor is his) these *philosophes* attempted to "abstract" man out of the concretion of his history, and with what results recent history

demonstrated. "Such men," Coleridge writes of the same French philosophers in his *Biographia*, "need discipline, not argument; they must become
better men, before they can become wiser" (*Biographia*, I, 123). For at least
a hundred years the Revolution became the bugbear with which to frighten
off anyone who might be tempted by such visions of "social engineering" –
the term is not Hegel's, but the concept assuredly is! (Indeed, one might
argue that Marxism, as the new revolutionary dogma, became palatable
only because Marx could "coopt" Hegel and suggest that Marxism does not
"abstract" us from history but replaces us in a new vision of it, one founded
not on Absolute Idealism but on dialectical materialism.)

In *The Prelude* Wordsworth demonstrates none of that vindictiveness or
vituperation one finds in Hegel, perhaps because Wordsworth had himself
once shared that vision: "Bliss was it in that dawn to be alive, / But to be
young was very heaven" (1805, X.693–4). The mature works of Hegel, at
least, show no trace of such youthful enthusiasm. Wordsworth's ultimate
message in *The Prelude*, however, is the same: the painful withdrawal from
and disillusionment with the faith that "human Reason's naked self" might
"in self-knowledge and self-rule,"

> shaking off
> The accidents of nature, time, and place ...
> Build social freedom on its only basis,
> The freedom of the individual mind,
> Which, to the blind restraints of general laws
> Superior, magisterially adopts
> One guide, the light of circumstances, flash'd
> Upon an independent intellect.          (1805, X.821–30)

This vision of the disinterested mind, however intoxicating it may seem at
first, is fatally flawed: it leads to an abstraction of man from history and
from nature, as, "knife in hand," we "probe / The living body of society /
Even to the heart" (873–7). (Indeed, as in "The Tables Turned," "Our meddling intellect / Misshapes the beauteous form of things; / – We murder to
dissect.") Our only salvation must be to return man to "The laws of things
which lie / Beyond the reach of human will or power; / The life of nature"
(XI.97–100).

In the passage from *The German Ideology* quoted above, Marx is obviously accusing Hegel of "abstraction," but it is a charge Hegel would have –
with some justice – vigorously denied. The casual reader of the Romantics,
faced with the capitalized powers and personifications of Blake's *Jerusalem*,
Coleridge's *Biographia*, and Hegel's *Phenomenology*, might be excused
for thinking that some vast process of abstraction is taking place, but the
Romantic Idealists insisted that all their powers and principalities were

the objects of immediate experience. Their contention is borne out, to some degree, by a disinterested observer in the other camp: John Stuart Mill, in his essays on Bentham and Coleridge as "seminal minds" of the nineteenth century (essays that should still be required reading for any student of Romanticism: Mill, like Alfred North Whitehead in a later generation, was able to appreciate many of the "corrective" virtues of Romantic concreteness), places Bentham in the tradition of (Enlightenment) "abstraction," and Coleridge in the tradition of Romantic "concreteness." In some respects the Enlightenment tradition did try to "abstract" a concept of man that should be valid for all time, as Bentham, for instance, tried to construct legal systems for nations he had never visited; the first generation of Romantics, on the other hand, insisted on seeing man in the concrete actuality of history. The organic "metaphor" is not arrived at by any process of abstraction, but by an immediate intuition of analogy, even of identity. Moreover, it predates German Idealism, both in its alliance with nationalism and in its conservatism.

The Romantic age did not invent history, as scholars of Romanticism seem sometimes to suggest: it did invent historicism. Ernst Cassirer, in his definitive *Philosophy of the Enlightenment*, calls Pierre Bayle "the spiritual leader of the Enlightenment," and, at the same time, the "founder of modern historiography."[6] Voltaire, the Encyclopedists, Montesquieu – all were historians as well as natural and political philosophers. Hume wrote a six-volume history of Britain from Caesar to the Glorious Revolution, and it can surely be argued that Gibbon's *Decline and Fall*, as the crowning achievement of Enlightenment historiography, surpasses any product of the Romantic age. But these Enlightenment historians believed in a common nature of man that does not change with history, and, above all, they believed in the power of the disinterested mind to discover historical "fact."

The Romantic-organic view of history, on the other hand, begins with two almost exact contemporaries, neither of whom survived into the age of German Idealism: Johann Gottfried Herder and Edmund Burke. Both hated Enlightenment "abstraction," and both had a reverence for national cultures and institutions as unconscious and organic expressions of a people's "soul." As men they were very different indeed: Herder, a gentle religious enthusiast (he was court chaplain at Weimar) was a follower of Kant who nevertheless could not stand the analytic abstractions of the first critique and who opted rather for a romanticized and mythicized Spinoza, whose "God" became not the rationalist body of almost geometric rules of Spinoza's *Ethics* but rather the vital Will and Soul that finds its expression in the world of nature, but above all in the gradual evolution of human history. Burke, on the other hand, was foremost a man of action and a pragmatic politician, but his abiding faith in the organic unity of national cultures and his deep distrust of any philosopher, revolutionary, or administrator who would think to tamper with these organic cultures led to his seemingly contradictory stands on public issues: his speeches in favor of the impeachment of Warren Hastings, whose administration in India imposed alien "reforms" on an ancient and indigenous culture; his defense of the American colonists, who were, as Burke saw it, acting in accordance with their rights under the British "constitution" George III and his corrupt ministers were subverting; and, above all, his brilliant orations in defense of the French monarchy, which surely did a great deal to establish in the English mind the Revolution as that nightmare warning against all attempts at radical political reform. Wordsworth adds to *The Prelude* in 1832 – ironically, the year of the First Reform Bill – his ringing tribute to the "Genius of Burke," which "forewarns, denounces, launches forth, / Against all systems built on abstract rights," and

> the majesty proclaims
> Of Institutes and Laws, hallowed by time;
> Declares the vital power of social ties
> Endeared by Custom; and with high disdain,
> Exploding upstart Theory, insists
> Upon the allegiance to which men are born –    (1850, VII.512, 523–30)

The Enlightenment ideology, for all the occasional dullness of its emphasis on uniformity and abstraction, was always determinedly internationalist. The Romantic ideology, for all its enthusiasm for infinite variety and transcendence, was at its core concrete, experiential, and nationalist. If one were pressed to find a socio-political determinant for organicist historicism, surely it is to the rising tide of nationalism that one should look. Enlightenment internationalism culminated in the Revolution. The Napoleonic era represents the watershed, whether one sees Napoleon himself as the grand evangelist for revolutionary doctrine or as the symbol of a renascent French nationalism. (Hazlitt and Byron, to their credit, I think, saw him as both.) In any case, the spectre of the Revolution, reinforced by the depradations of the Napoleonic wars, inspired a renascence of nationalist sentiment – and perhaps the spirit of imperialism, its bastard son – all over Europe, but especially in a divided and subject Germany, so long denied any concrete manifestation of national identity. In such an environment it seems only natural that a philosophy that promised a new sense of transcendent destiny, grounded not on transient expressions of popular opinion ("mechanical ballot-boxes," Carlyle called them), but immanent in the very process of history itself, should find a welcome audience and should, in one form or another, dominate much of Europe, at least until the First World War.

## III

Still, the Enlightenment ideology did not die in the French Revolution and its aftermath, nor did it wither away in the blasts of German Idealism.[7] Jeremy Bentham died in the year of the first Reform Bill, and William Godwin outlived all but Wordsworth among the major English Romantics. William Hazlitt, an older contemporary of the second generation, in his critical essays, at least, championed the virtues of the "disinterested mind" against all Romantic "egoisms" whatever (even if in some of his historical essays – in his account of Napoleon's career, for instance – he allowed his revolutionary interests to sway his native good judgment). More to the point for literature, one can argue that the Enlightenment faith enjoyed a renascence in the second generation, particularly in the poetry of Byron and Shelley – an Enlightenment faith tempered and chastened, of course, by what had intervened, with none of the intellectual arrogance so characteristic of the French before the Revolution or of the emotional aridity and insensitivity so common in the writings of Godwin and Bentham. Unlike John Stuart Mill, Byron and Shelley did not need to be "converted" to the importance of feeling by discovering Wordsworth: they grew up reading him – and Rousseau. They grew up also in an age of reaction, political and intellectual. The depth of that reaction can be gauged by the sympathetic account Hazlitt gives of the trajectory of Godwin's reputation, in his essay on him in *The Spirit of the Age*. Of the first publication of *Political Justice* (1793) Hazlitt writes: "No work in our time gave such a blow to the philosophical mind of the century ... Tom Paine was considered for the time as a Tom Fool to him; Paley an old woman; Edmund Burke a flashy sophist." Twenty-five years later, however, "Mr. Godwin's person is not known ... his opinions are not asked ... he has no train of admirers ... he is to all ordinary intents and purposes dead and buried" (*Works*, XI, 16–17). Indeed, in his first communication with him, Godwin's future son-in-law all but said that he thought Godwin had been dead for years.

One scarcely needs to make a case for Shelley. *Queen Mab* is a veritable encyclopedia of the central ideas of the French and English Enlightenment, and, as recent scholarship suggests, Shelley never deserted these skeptical ideals for any Romantic monism or historicism. He did indeed displace his hopes onto an ideal future, as the New Historicists suggest, but then so did his early mentor Godwin, and it is important to note that neither of them suggested that these hopes are given any guarantee or sanction in the processes of Nature or in an inexorable progress of world history. The creative force Mont Blanc symbolizes is indeed ineffable and mysterious, but the lesson the disinterested mind can learn from the contemplation of that mystery is "to repeal / Large codes of fraud and woe" (Shelley was perhaps thinking of the similar enlightened purpose of Lucretius's *De Rerum Natura*). Tyrannies like Jupiter's may return – we have no guarantees against them – but if and when they do, we have still the weapons of an unfettered mind to deal with them – that, and a faith in the basic good will of our common nature.

The case for Byron raises different issues. The "gloomy egoism" (the phrase is Hazlitt's) of the heroic poetry undoubtedly appealed to an age of reaction and disillusionment, of escape from disappointed hopes. Yet, even here, Sardanapalus (in the drama of that title) is the very portrait of the skeptical and benevolent mind, tragically brought down by established forces of nationalism and tradition; in the third canto of *Childe Harold's Pilgrimage* Byron presents incisive and sympathetic portraits of three of the most maligned heroes of the Enlightenment – Voltaire, Rousseau, and Gibbon; in the fourth canto he includes a ringing affirmation of faith in the disinterested mind that might have come from Voltaire, Godwin – or Shelley:

> Yet let us ponder boldly – 'tis a base
> Abandonment of reason to resign
> Our right of thought – our last and only place
> Of refuge; this, at least shall still be mine:
> Though from our birth the Faculty divine
> Is chained and tortured – cabined, cribbed, confined,
> And bred in darkness, lest the Truth should shine
> Too brightly on the unprepared mind,
> The beam pours in – for Time and Skill will couch the blind.
>
> (IV, st. 127)

*Cain* is the closest of all of Byron's works to the spirit of Voltairean iconoclasm, and it evoked a more vociferously hostile reception from the establishment than any other work of the age – a reaction that, despite his protestations to the contrary, Byron probably enjoyed. *Cain* has also a serious moral, however, and that moral, more than any superficial echoes of plot and argument, allies it with the "Spiritual leader of the Enlightenment," Pierre Bayle. Beleaguered between the unthinking dogma and cant of his parents, and the hypocritical casuistry of Lucifer, the lesson Cain learns, too late, is that he has a loving obligation to his brother that supersedes all supernatural sanctions or intellectual misgivings. Bayle was notorious in his own day and long afterwards for his repeated contention that a community of atheists might be as moral as a community of Catholics, or even of Huguenots (his own persuasion). If God is dead, all things are possible, says Ivan Karamazov. Not so, responds Bayle: we have still our common humanity.

Bayle and Byron bring one inevitably to the issue of irony in Romantic scholarship. Romantic irony, especially as propounded by Friedrich Schlegel, was a by-blow of German Idealism, bred by enthusiastic minds on the body of Kant's first critique, but a bastard son most heatedly repudiated by Hegel, the inheritor of the Romantic Ideology. Repudiated also, however, by a master ironist who was Hegel's most energetic opponent: Søren Kierkegaard.[8] Surely Hegel and Kierkegaard were right: irony pursued as an end in itself, or as a means for a vacuous freedom from all intellectual and ethical imperatives, leads only to the irony of ironies, in an infinite regress – and to aestheticism and ennui. For Bayle and Byron, however, irony is not an end but a means: in Kierkegaard's terms, not the Truth but a way. It is the sign of the disinterested mind.

It has always seemed a mystery that so many modernist and post-modern critics alike have persisted in seeing Byron's *Don Juan*, surely one of the most resilient and life-affirming poems in the language, as an epic of negativism, as a "myth of despair." Perhaps the reason is that if it is to be perceived for what it is, it must be acknowledged as a simple affirmation of faith in the disinterested mind: if we rid our minds of cant and hypocrisy, ethics will take care of itself. A parallel between *Don Juan* and Bayle's great historical *Dictionary* may seem at first far-fetched, but let us pursue it. Both works proceed crabwise by digression: Bayle's text, as such, is but a ribbon of twenty-four-point type at the top of his folio pages, an index to his forever digressive footnotes, in which all his wisdom lies. Bayle's *Dictionary* began not as a compendium of received facts and opinion, but as a compilation of errors, ancient and modern, to be refuted by his dialectic method; *Don Juan* too is an ironic exposure, sometimes caustic, sometimes half-indulgent, of the follies of his age. Both works depend for their unity not on their matter, but on style, tone, and personae. Their irony is pervasive, but also reflexive, and it creates a stance of disillusioned or unillusioned common sense: in conceding their faults and idiosyncrasies, they rise above them, and disarm their critics. Both resist system and closure, and instead perform virtuoso mental exercises on the topics of their day. Finally, both authors were fascinated with and devoted to history – "But then the fact's a fact – and 'tis the part / Of a true poet to escape from fiction / Whene'er he can" (*Don Juan*, VIII, st. 86) – history not as grand theory or as evidence of sanctioning patterns and meaning, but history as a disinterested and ironic account of human follies and human virtues. They were perhaps too much concerned with idiosyncratic and even esoteric detail – both confess this weakness – but then only in the very particularities of history does one come near the evidences of our common humanity.

## IV

It is surely fair to say, then, that the second generation of the British Romantics rejected the "Romantic Ideology," or the organic-historicist-idealist tradition of thought discursively presented in the major philosophical works of German Idealism (in what Coleridge in the *Biographia* called the "Dynamic Philosophy") and poetically presented in much of "High Romantic" literature. Shelley respected Wordsworth as a poet and shows his influence, and scholars persist in seeing in the third canto of *Childe Harold's Pilgrimage* evidences of Byron's brief flirtation, at least, with Wordsworthian "naturalism." Neither poet, however, shows in his mature poetry evidence of any settled faith in a transcendent "idea" realizing itself in nature and in history, driven by an inexorable will. The second generation did not, however, reject this philosophical tradition because it was "idealist" rather than grounded in the material conditions of history. Shelley's *Queen Mab* may have enjoyed a *sub rosa* renaissance as a sacred text for the Chartists, and Byron's late *Age of Bronze* is as trenchant a satire on British political and financial institutions as any poem of the age, but it would be absurd to see either Shelley or Byron as precursors of dialectical materialism.

It seems clear that their rejection of this organicist tradition came about in their realization – for them made evident in the later careers of Wordsworth, Coleridge, and Southey – that it was in its essence, through the very force of its organic metaphor, culturally, socially, and politically antireformist, antiintellectual (i.e., opposed to the conscious analytic reason), and profoundly conservative. They returned to the Enlightenment principles of the American and French Revolutions. It is emblematic of that return that when Byron, Shelley, and Leigh Hunt (Keats's political mentor) set up a poetic-political journal-in-exile, in Pisa, they named it *The Liberal*, a term then used, in its political sense, only to refer to those underground enclaves of radicals in France, Italy, and Spain (the *liberales*) who remained firmly committed to antimonarchist and revolutionary principles.

The great English proponents of this idealist tradition, then, are Blake, Wordsworth, Coleridge – and Carlyle, who carried it through the Victorian age. Blake is a special case: more of an individualist and iconoclast, he never made his peace, as did his colleagues, with the Established Church or state. He was also, however, a more determined *idealist* than the others: a theory of history based on changes in the material means of production would have made no sense to him; even in a land of dark Satanic mills, he maintains, our manacles are "mind-forg'd," and only through mind, in renewed imaginative vision, can they be broken. Wordsworth and Coleridge – and Carlyle – on the other hand, not only made peace with the Establishment but became important apologists for it, by denigrating "abstract," analytic, reformist reason; by emphasizing organic, unconscious, and evolving tradition; and by giving this tradition sanction in a vision of transcendence.

This "idealist" tradition has perhaps always had more critics than apologists. One can certainly argue, for instance, that in the "Ruined Cottage" – a poem Coleridge praised as one of the greatest in the language – Wordsworth and his spokesman, the Pedlar, overlook or evade the (in some respects) remediable material and political causes of Margaret's suffering: indeed, even the reactionary De Quincey complained that the Pedlar ought simply to have written a letter to the War Office on Margaret's behalf. Wordsworth's purposes, however, were not those of social or political protest; the Pedlar presents Margaret's suffering as a part of a larger pattern, as inexorable as the passing of the seasons and the gradual encroachment on cottage and garden of the "calm oblivious tendencies / Of nature." And surely the power of the poem lies in the persuasion of consolation in the Pedlar's final "image of tranquility," of "the high spear-grass on the wall, / By mist and silent raindrops silvered o'er," so that

> all we feel of sorrow and despair
> From ruin and from change, and all the grief
> The passing shews of being leave behind,
> Appeared an idle dream that could not live
> Where meditation was ...                    (514–24)[9]

We have surely become more, not less, aware, in this our own time, that there is indeed that in Nature which transcends merely human purposes, an infinite order and creativity we perceive only dimly and ignore at our peril. The greatest works of High Romantic Idealism restore some sense of wonder, even of reverential awe, to such visions of transcendence and attempt also to find a place for man within them. A noble purpose, at least, and one that can never be made quite irrelevant, whatever the pressures of practical science or of political praxis.

## NOTES

1. *Hegel's Philosophy of Right*, trans. T. M. Knox (Oxford University Press, 1952), p. 13.
2. Frederick Burwick, *The Damnation of Newton: Goethe's Color Theory and Romantic Perception* (Berlin and New York: Walter de Gruyter, 1986).
3. See especially *Blake, Hegel, and Dialectic* (Amsterdam: Rodopi, 1982).
4. McGann quotes this paragraph in *The Romantic Ideology: A Critical Investigation* (University of Chicago Press, 1983), p. 9; I quote here and in the following paragraph from Karl Marx and Frederick Engels, *The German Ideology*, ed. C. J. Arthur (New York: International Publications, 1985), pp. 66–7.

5. Hegel, *Philosophy of Right*, p. 11.
6. Ernst Cassirer, *The Philosophy of the Enlightenment*, trans. Fritz C. A. Koelln and James Pettegrove (Princeton University Press, 1951), especially pp. 207–9.
7. The parallel between Byron and Bayle I have drawn at greater length in "Byron and Bayle: Biblical Skepticism and Romantic Irony," in *Byron, the Bible, and Religion*, ed. Wolf Z. Hirst (Newark: University of Delaware Press, 1991), pp. 39–57. For greater detail on the relationship of Shelley and Byron to the Revolution and to the Enlightenment, see my "Post-Waterloo Liberalism," *Studies in Romanticism* 28 (1989): 437–62. For a study relating all of the English Romantics in novel ways to the Enlightenment, see Andrew M. Cooper, *Doubt and Identity in Romantic Poetry* (New Haven: Yale University Press, 1988).
8. For Hegel's discussion of Romantic irony, see especially *The Philosophy of Fine Art*, trans. F. P. B. Osmaston (London, 1920), I, 89ff., 398ff.; for Kierkegaard, see *The Concept of Irony with Constant Reference to Socrates*, trans. Lee M. Capel (Bloomington and London: Indiana University Press, 1965), especially pp. 289ff.
9. I quote from the reconstructed "Ruined Cottage" as printed in *William Wordsworth*, The Oxford Authors (Oxford and New York: Oxford University Press, 1984), pp. 31f.

# 5

WILLIAM KEACH

# Romanticism and language

Questions about linguistic theory have assumed striking prominence in critical work on Romanticism. This is in part because literary criticism over the past several decades, like philosophy for a much longer time, has taken a distinctly linguistic turn. But in addition to this pervasive preoccupation with theoretical understandings of the linguistic sign and of verbal representation, more particular circumstances, at least in the United States, have focused attention on Romanticism and language. Romantic texts, most notably Wordsworthian texts, were among the first to be read through the linguistic turnings of poststructuralist criticism in its American guise. Jacques Derrida's extended critique of Rousseau's *Essay on the Origin of Languages* in *Of Grammatology*, along with his readings elsewhere of Shelley and other eighteenth- and nineteenth-century writers, cast an even greater glamor on Romanticism's role in theoretical formulations. And since many Romantic texts, verse as well as prose, turn out to contain powerful, agitated broodings on their own status as language, poststructuralist readers have often found their theoretical concerns anticipated, not merely reflected back to them, in Wordsworth or Coleridge or Shelley.

Important as the poststructuralist focus on Romanticism and language has been, it has at the same time encouraged attitudes or dispositions that now need to be put under more consistent, more exacting historical pressure. On the one hand, in our eagerness to accommodate Romanticism to our own linguistic turn, we sometimes obscure or minimize crucial differences between ourselves and writers who suddenly seem modern or relevant in new ways – differences of philosophical assumption or terminology, differences of broader cultural placement or determination. On the other hand, our discovery of similarities between our own thinking about language and that of Romantic writers may still be distorted and restricted by persistent misconceptions about British Romanticism itself – misconceptions about a Romantic repudiation of Enlightenment ideas and achievements, about the alleged preeminence of German Idealist philosophy in shaping British

Romantic values. Another way of putting this latter point is to suggest that our current theoretical investment in language is as tellingly anticipated in Enlightenment as in Romantic writing, and that British and French rather than German linguistic theory generates the most important lines of continuity running from the seventeenth and eighteenth centuries through Romantic into modern (including poststructuralist) thinking.

The primary aim of this essay is to establish a historical sense of how Romantic writers themselves conceptualized key issues of verbal representation – how they thought about the relation of words to thoughts and to things, about the social and historical processes through which language is formed and changed, about the connection of ordinary speech to formal prose and verse. Such a historical sense can make us critically aware of our distance from Romantic theorizing about language, while at the same time giving us a fuller, more accurate understanding of the ways in which important, unresolved questions in current theory and criticism were already at stake in the Romantics' rethinking of the philosophies of language they inherited from the Enlightenment. With its emphasis on the empiricist[1] tradition in Britain and France, my approach here is deeply indebted to Hans Aarsleff, whose *The Study of Language in England: 1780–1860* (1967) and *From Locke to Saussure: Essays on the Study of Language and Intellectual History* (1982) have established the historical basis from which all subsequent work on Romanticism and language must proceed. Aarsleff's work is polemical as well as informative, and in claiming this kind of centrality for it I am not urging endorsement of all its particular judgments and emphases. Crucially important alternative approaches need to be recognized: Olivia Smith's revealing analysis of the struggle between "vulgar" and "refined" discourse in *The Politics of Language 1791–1819*, Murray Cohen's and Stephen K. Land's contributions to the history of linguistic theory in the eighteenth and nineteenth centuries, Michel Foucault's provocative epistemic "archaeologies" in *The Order of Things*. But anyone who cares about Romanticism and language needs to begin with, or go back to, Aarsleff's indispensable scholarship.

I

*From Locke to Saussure*: Aarsleff's collection of essays begins with Locke because *An Essay Concerning Human Understanding*, and especially the third book entitled "Of Words," created the central tradition in the philosophy of language for subsequent centuries, including our own. But for students of Romanticism, beginning with Locke as anything other than a foil for Romantic ideas about the creative imagination may seem very strange.

After all, Blake rages prophetically against the cold mechanistic universe of Locke and Newton, and Coleridge condemns Locke for making the mind an essentially passive receiver and arranger of sense data. The Blakean and Coleridgean characterizations, or caricatures, of Locke are so powerfully embedded in received notions about Romanticism that it comes as a shock to learn that Wordsworth and Shelley shared little if any of this antipathy to the most influential philosopher of the preceding era. Whatever its strengths and weaknesses, Locke's account of language in the *Essay* was still the most influential force in British Romantic thinking about the topic. With this acknowledged, we should go back to the *Essay*, as many Romantic writers themselves did, for a fresh look.

It will come as no surprise to anyone to see that Locke's approach to language is grounded in his empiricism, in his assumption, as he says at the beginning of book II of the *Essay*, that "From *Experience* ... all our Knowledge is founded, and from that it ultimately derives it self" (II.i.2). What students of Romanticism may find surprising, however, is that Locke's concept of experience is not limited to the senses, as so many commentators on his work have claimed. Experience, he goes on to say, is double; it generates ideas from two "Fountains of Knowledge" – from "external, sensible Objects," and from "the internal Operations of our Minds, perceived and reflected on by our selves." Locke designates the mental activities that produce ideas from these two sources: "Sensation" and "Reflection." While ideas of sensation have a kind of genetic or temporal priority in that simple ideas of this sort are what our minds are first capable of producing, ideas of reflection soon come to have equal status and increase in significance for Locke as he directs his analysis to more complex mental operations.

Locke's empiricism, it has often been remarked, is a "way of ideas":[2] nothing is immediately present to the mind but its own ideas of sensation and reflection. Locke assumes the existence of an external physical world of things, but that world can be perceived and known only through its transformation into the mental world of ideas. And while the mind has immediate access to its own ideas, it can have only mediate access to ideas produced by other minds. This mediate access happens through language. The first founding principle of Locke's treatment of language in book III of the *Essay* is that it originates in the human capacity for social as well as for individual experience: "God having designed Man for a sociable Creature, made him not only with an inclination, and under a necessity to have fellowship with those of his own kind; but furnished him also with Language, which was to be the great Instrument, and common Tye of Society" (III.i.1). What does it mean for Locke to say that humanity is endowed with the capacity for language? It means not just that we are "by Nature ... fashioned, as to be *fit to frame articulate Sounds*," but also that we "should be able to use these Sounds, as Signs of internal Conceptions; and to make them stand as marks for the Ideas within [our] own Mind, whereby they might be made known to others" (III.i.2). These remarks pave the way for the second major founding principle in Locke's philosophy of language: "*Words* ... come to be made use of by Men, as *the Signs of* their *Ideas*; not by any natural connexion, that there is between particular articulate Sounds and certain *Ideas*, for then there would be but one Language amongst all Men; but by a voluntary Imposition, whereby such a Word is made arbitrarily the Mark of such an *Idea*" (III.ii.1).

Locke's insistence on the "arbitrary" relation between the two aspects of the linguistic sign – the phonetic mark and the idea it signifies – may sound strikingly modern, but it was not original even with him. Hobbes had used the same term, and so had other seventeenth-century philosophers. It is Locke, however, who most conspicuously establishes this principle and passes it on to subsequent theorists of language. And it is in Locke's *Essay* that the potential instability of this notion of the "arbitrary" becomes apparent. Is the distinction between "natural" and "arbitrary" adequate to cover all the ways in which language may be connected to the material world? And how does the "arbitrary" institution of particular words square with Locke's assumption of a social impulse to communicate? It is often taken for granted that Locke's phrase "by a voluntary Imposition" refers to linguistic convention or compact. But he never directly says so – and in English usage "arbitrary" is a very different kind of word from "convention," "compact" or "common use" (see John Barrell's discussion in chapter 2 of *English Literature in History 1730–80*). The arbitrary sign is such an important – and for many later thinkers troublesome – concept not just because it denies that linguistic meaning is a matter of any "natural connexion" between words and the world, but because it also harbors powerful tensions about the social and political formation of language.

In Locke's system words stand primarily for ideas and only secondarily for things, and he was aware that this view gave language a precarious purchase on the material world. He recurrently attacks simplistically optimistic assumptions of a "double conformity" between our ideas and the words we use to represent them on the one hand, and between our ideas and the things or actions from which they derive on the other. Though originating in a social impulse, language for Locke has an irreducibly subjective aspect: "Words in their primary or immediate signification, stand for nothing, but the Ideas in the Mind of him that uses them" (III.ii.2). Given a claim such as this we can understand why Stephen Land designates the theory of language expounded in Locke's great empiricist *Essay* as "idealism."[3] We can also see links between Locke's theories of language and epistemology and the liberal individualist ideology that underlies his theories of economy, politics, and government. In Locke's view, language is always threatening to become merely subjective or private. It can fulfill the social impulse from which it springs in the first place only through a continuous process of clarification or rectification, in which one individual's grasp of the correspondences between word and idea and between idea and thing is compared to and tested against that of other individuals. Locke places little confidence in the ongoing practice of ordinary common speech as a context in which significant clarification or rectification can take place, a point we shall return to later in the discussion of Wordsworth. Instead, Locke appeals to the systematic rational analysis of correspondences among terms, ideas, things – and in this crucial respect his empiricism is entirely consistent with the values and practices of Cartesian rationalism, to which it is so frequently contrasted. For Locke, it would seem, the common human capacity for communicating through language can only be realized in philosophical discourse, and even then it is susceptible to the inevitable limitations of having to depend on words established by arbitrary imposition.

Language in Locke's *Essay* is at once an indispensable and an inherently imperfect means for communicating thought. At times it is also more – it is indispensable or intrinsic to thinking itself. For while Locke often writes as if ideas in the mind preexist the words we use to represent them, he sometimes gives words a constitutive role in our having ideas in the first place. The positive account of this constitutive function of language emerges most clearly in the discussion of those complex ideas Locke calls "Mixed Modes and Relations." Such ideas, he says, illustrate most fully "the Workmanship of the Mind" and are entirely "of Men's making" (III.v.4): "this union, which has no particular foundation in Nature, would cease again, were there not something that did, as it were, hold it together, and keep the parts from scattering. Though therefore it be the Mind that makes the Collection, 'tis the word which is, as it were the Knot, that ties them fast together" (III.v.10). Locke is a nominalist in his conviction that the reality of complex general ideas consists entirely in the mind's drawing together and giving a name to otherwise unconnected qualities or phenomena. Some of his eighteenth- and nineteenth-century followers will go further in showing how far language is intrinsic to thinking, but it is important to recognize that in doing so they are extending an impulse already there in the *Essay*. Locke's favorite figure of words as knots that tie together otherwise scattered external or internal perceptions, homespun though it is, carries fascinating implications for later theories of how versions of reality get woven together in language, and of how they get undone.

In fact, it is worry about thought being undone by language – what we might call the negative perspective on language's constitutive relation to thinking – that dominates Locke's linguistic theory. At the end of book II, he explains why he will devote all of the following book to questions of language: "I find, that there is so close a connexion between *Ideas* and Words; and our abstract *Ideas*, and general Words, have so constant a relation one to another, that it is impossible to speak clearly and distinctly of our Knowledge, which all consists in Propositions, without considering, first, the Nature, Use, and Signification of Language ... " (II.xxxiii.19). Throughout the *Essay* Locke is concerned with what he calls "the Abuse of Words" because he understands it also as the abuse of thinking, particularly of the kind of formal, systematic philosophical thinking implied in the aim "to speak clearly and distinctly of our Knowledge, which all consists in Propositions."

Locke's terms here indicate strongly the broader intellectual and cultural context of his treatment of language. They should remind us both of Descartes's rationalism and of the spirit of late seventeenth-century scientific discourse. Locke was himself a qualified physician and deeply interested in physical science. He became a fellow of the recently created Royal Society in 1668 and was close to men such as Thomas Sydenham, a pioneer in modern clinical research and epidemiology, and Robert Boyle, the founder of modern chemistry. Locke's concern with language does not, it must be said, attribute priority to observation and experiment. His primary concern, as we have seen, is the relation between words and ideas, and only secondarily between words and things. Nevertheless, his preoccupation with the ways in which so much of what we say and write interferes with the formation of clear and distinct ideas articulated as propositions does reflect his participation in the ideology of the Royal Society. That ideology is obvious in Locke's notorious denunciation of figurative language in the last two chapters of book III: "if we would speak of Things as they are, we must allow, that all the Art of Rhetorick, besides Order and Clearness, all the artificial and figurative application of Words Eloquence hath invented, are for nothing else but to insinuate wrong *Ideas*, move the Passions, and thereby mislead the Judgment; and so indeed are perfect cheat" (III.x.34). The fellows of the Royal Society may have been pleased to read this, and we need to imagine that Locke had them very much in mind when he wrote it. But the passage does not fully reflect Locke's attitude towards language, or his own reliance on "artificial and figurative application of Words." "Let us then suppose the Mind to be, as we say, white Paper, void of all Characters" (II.i.2); "'tis the word which is, as it were the Knot" (III.v.10) – some of the pivotal moments in *An Essay Concerning Human Understanding* turn upon figures of speech self-consciously deployed ("as we say," "as it were"). Locke's concern with the "abuse of words" does not blind him to the fact that what may look like abuse to those intent on speaking "of Things as they are" may be necessary to the philosopher whose central aim is to show "whence the Understanding may get all the *Ideas* it has" (II.i.1).

Locke left much to be worked out in what he calls, at the very end of the *Essay*, "σημειωτική [semeiotike], or the *Doctrine of Signs*, the most usual whereof being Words, it is aptly enough termed also λογική, Logick" (IV.xxi.4). The suggestive indeterminacy of Locke's "Doctrine of Signs" is part of its pervasive influence. In his introduction to the standard edition of the *Essay* Peter Nidditch calls attention to some of its more familiar rifts and discrepancies and observes that "the divisions and oppositions in his thought ... may well have been creative: without them, he might not have been driven to pursue his problems as persistently and devotedly as he did" (p. x). The comment is worth bearing in mind as we move on to imagine how he was read by later eighteenth-century and Romantic writers.

## II

The century that separated Locke's fourth revised edition of *An Essay Concerning Human Understanding* (1700) and the preface to *Lyrical Ballads* (1800) produced an astonishing amount of theorizing about language – about its epistemological status, its origins, its relations to other modes of thinking and practical behavior. Locke had set the main direction and principal terms for the most important developments, but not to the exclusion of alternative, even antagonistic, approaches. A traditional Christian view of language continued to be variously asserted and would eventually find new life in the speculations of some Romantic writers. According to Christian tradition language was not a system of signs arbitrarily established through the workmanship of the human mind, but rather a nomenclature or inventory of creation divinely established by God and first given to man – only secondarily to woman – in the original state of Edenic innocence. The "Adamic" view held that before the Fall there was a single language that perfectly represented the created universe. This original Adamic language was lost in the confusion of tongues after Babel, but it might someday be recovered through proper spiritual insight.

Such ideas were often held literally by the naive and the mystical. But they were also explored with philosophical sophistication by Leibniz and his followers. Leibniz read Locke's *Essay* with remarkable intensity and formulated his agreements and disagreements with it in *Nouveaux Essais sur l'entendement humain* ("New Essays on the Human Understanding," written 1703–5 but not published until 1765). In opposition to Locke's principle that words are arbitrary and not natural signs of ideas, Leibniz argues that many words have their origin in imitations of natural sounds (onomatopoeia), and more generally "that there is something natural in the origin of words that indicates a relation between things and the sounds and movements of the vocal organs … words have come into being as occasion arose from the analogy of sound with the disposition of the mind that accompanied the perception of the thing. I am inclined to believe that Adam did not impose names in any other fashion."[4] Leibniz's resuscitation and transformation of Adamic theory in opposition to Locke's "Doctrine of Signs" looks forward to an important strain in Romantic thinking, and to Coleridge in particular.

Other philosophers and theorists of language departed from Locke in ways that were not overtly Adamic. Berkeley begins his *Treatise Concerning the Principles of Human Knowledge* (1710) by attacking Locke's account of the role played by language in forming abstract general ideas. And in a passage that anticipates Edmund Burke's emphasis on the affective or emotive capacity of language in *A Philosophical Enquiry Concerning the Origin of Our Ideas of the Sublime and Beautiful* (1757), Berkeley denies Locke's premise that words are necessarily signs of ideas: " … passions … arise, immediately in [the] mind upon the perception of certain words, without any ideas coming between" (introduction, paragraph 20). Of still broader potential significance is the place of language in Berkeley's account of reality as composed entirely of mind and its ideas and notions. For Berkeley as for Locke, language is composed of signs for ideas and other mental events. But those ideas and mental events have no relation to a nonmental material world. They derive instead from a world that exists as the continuous creative perception of God's infinite mind – a world whose order Berkeley repeatedly characterizes as the divine language of nature. Reality is determined less importantly by individual signs within this divine language of nature than by the regular ways in which its signs are related, by what we might call a divine grammar. In Berkeley's view, human language is but an imperfect reflection of the signs and grammar of a world whose mode of existence is already linguistic.

An emphasis on grammar rather than individual signs links Berkeley's radical Christian idealism to the rationalist idealism of "universal grammar," a tradition in Enlightenment language theory that became freshly famous with the publication in 1966 of Noam Chomsky's *Cartesian Linguistics*. Chomsky was looking to find historical antecedents for his own belief in rules or norms common to all languages and deriving from innate organizing principles in the human mind. He found them, plausibly, in seventeenth-century theories of "universal grammar," and particularly in the *Grammaire générale et raisonnée* of Antoine Arnauld and Claude Lancelot (1660), commonly known as the "Port Royal grammar." Chomsky's celebration of Descartes as providing the philosophical foundations of "universal grammar," and especially his denunciation of Locke as having consolidated a tradition in which language was the product of a mind passively dependent on sense data, have been decisively challenged by Aarsleff, who shows that in the seventeenth and eighteenth centuries Cartesian rationalism and the Lockean "way of ideas" were accurately understood to have much in common.[5]

An inventive return to classical metaphysics – to Aristotle and Anaxagoras as well as to Plato – distinguishes the *Origin and Progress of Language* (1774–92) of James Burnett, Lord Monboddo, another eighteenth-century theorist whose acceptance of many of Locke's principles is sometimes belied by a distinctively un-Lockean vision of mental life. Neither of Monboddo's premises – that language is "the expression of the conceptions of the mind by articulate sounds" (1, 3) and that language is not "natural" but "acquired" (1, 12) – conflicts fundamentally with Lockean convictions. But Monboddo attacks Locke's distinction between "ideas of sensation" and "ideas of reflection," arguing that all ideas, as ideas, arise reflexively from the operations of the mind. And he works from the above premises to the conclusion that language itself is the most elaborate of all the human "arts," that it is a purposive creation of rational thought, and that as such it could not have come into being in the first place without a vast amount of prior social and intellectual development. Monboddo denies language the degree of constitutive relation to thinking already attributed to it in Locke's *Essay*: not only sensation and recollection, but comparison, abstraction, and generalization must all have existed in human culture before language could have been invented. This position is in some respects reactionary. But by treating thought and language as sequential and separate rather than as reciprocal and interdependent, Monboddo took an important step towards isolating the formal system of language as an object of study *per se*. In this respect his work points beyond Romanticism to the nineteenth-century science of philology.

The most powerful and influential thinking about language in the eighteenth century came not from writers whose metaphysical commitments were at odds with or skew to Locke, but from those who deliberately set out to explore the full implications of what he had done. The key mid-century figure is the greatest of Locke's many followers in France, Etienne Bonnot de Condillac. Condillac's *Essai sur l'origine des connaissances humaines* (1746) takes as its main task an attempt to show that in the evolution of human consciousness, Locke's two sources of ideas – sensation and reflection – have a common origin in sensation. But in arguing for what Aarsleff calls "a gradual rise from sensation to reflection,"[6] Condillac does not deny that reflection remains for him, as it was for Locke, a source of knowledge in its own right. Reflection is the condition of the mind in its full potential, and its emergence from sensation and perception is unimaginable, according to Condillac, without the simultaneous development of linguistic signs. The mental progress from simple perception through selective attention, imagination (the retrieval of absent sensations), and memory to reflection parallels the linguistic progress from a primitive, involuntary "language of action" through "natural cries" used involuntarily and then voluntarily as "natural signs" to the voluntary institution of arbitrary signs. Reflection becomes possible only when the mind learns to invent signs for its own use. And in turn, the subsequent development of a system of "instituted signs" depends upon the very powers of reflection such signs make possible. In contrast to Monboddo's hierarchical insistence on the priority of highly developed thought to the invention of language, Condillac shows that thinking cannot evolve beyond the elaborations of memory without the creation of language as we know it. His argument, the complex suggestiveness of which has attracted Derrida (*The Archaeology of the Frivolous*), is a brilliant genetic exfoliation of the suggestions in Locke's *Essay* about language's constitutive relation to thinking.

Near the end of the century Locke's theory of language underwent a second and in several respects more radical revision in John Horne Tooke's "*ΕΠΕΑ ΠΤΕΡΟΕΝΤΑ, or, the Diversions of Purley* (vol. I appeared in 1786, vol. II in 1805). Horne Tooke's point of departure is a distinction latent in Locke's assertion that the purpose of language is not only to communicate thoughts, but "To do it *with* as much ease and *quickness*, as is possible" (III.x.23). Not all words, Horne Tooke says, are "*immediately ...* the signs of ideas" – "many words are merely *abbreviations* employed for dispatch, and are the signs of other words" (III.i.14). Locke's *Essay Concerning Human Understanding* is really an essay on one of the primary functions of language, Horne Tooke goes on to say: "if he had sooner been aware of the inseparable connexion between words and knowledge" (i.e., before coming to this awareness near the end of book II), Locke "would not have talked of the *composition of ideas*; but would have seen that it was merely a contrivance of Language: and that the only composition was in the *terms*" (I. ii.18, 19). Horne Tooke attempts nothing less than to prove that all mental activity is really linguistic activity.

This radical reduction of Locke was to pose a major challenge to Romantic writers such as Coleridge and Shelley, who read and responded directly to *The Diversions of Purley*. The challenge, as Olivia Smith shows in chapter 4 of *The Politics of Language 1791–1818*, was political as well as philosophical: Horne Tooke was a well-known radical activist, several times tried and once imprisoned for views hostile to the government. Although his pursuit of linguistic and political principles led at times to eccentric extremes (much of *The Diversions* is given over to elaborate etymologies, some of them outrageously contrived), Horne Tooke released a potential in the Lockean philosophy of language that unsettled Romantic writers, and should unsettle us.

One further development in late eighteenth-century thinking about language, roughly contemporary with Horne Tooke's, needs to be acknowledged before we turn directly to British Romantic writers themselves. Following the violent upheavals of the Revolution and the Reign of Terror in France, during the government of the Directory (1795–9), intellectual life was dominated by a group known as the *idéologues*. The most prominent and influential member of the group was the politically progressive aristocratic philosopher Destutt de Tracy, who in a presentation before the reorganized Institut National des Sciences et Arts in 1795 proposed that the new term "ideology" be used to designate the analysis of sensations and ideas that was to be central to the work of the Institut's division of moral and political sciences. For Tracy, Locke was the Copernicus and Condillac the Kepler of the tradition of philosophical analysis that he and his colleagues sought to extend and institutionalize. Foremost in Tracy's understanding of that tradition was Condillac's conviction that, as Tracy puts it, "language is as necessary for thought itself as for giving expression to it."[7] Tracy and the *idéologues* made the debate over the constitutive function of language absolutely fundamental to the Institut National's program of intellectual and educational reform. Although they varied in their degree of materialist or sensationalist emphasis, the *idéologues* agreed on two closely connected and potentially antagonistic principles: the ineluctable subjectivity of language on the one hand, and the impulse towards social communication that rectifies or redeems the inherent limitations of language on the other. The ascendancy of Tracy and the *idéologues* was short-lived. Napoleon distrusted their critical, antireligious rationalism and soon after his *coup d'état* in 1799 set about discrediting and marginalizing them. But their impact on Continental and British thinking about language was already considerable and would extend into the early decades of the nineteenth century.

## III

William Wordsworth first visited France in the summer of 1790 when, as he says in *The Prelude*, the country was "standing on the top of golden hours, / And human nature seeming born again" (1850, VI.340–1). He returned in

November 1791 and stayed for more than a year, during which time it is quite likely that he was exposed to the philosophy of Condillac, then at the height of its importance in French revolutionary intellectual culture (Aarsleff, *From Locke to Saussure*, pp. 372–81). He may also have become familiar with the elaboration and extension of Condillac's ideas about language in the early thinking of the group who would come to be known as the *idéologues*. The preface to *Lyrical Ballads* (1800), for all its claims to signaling a new departure in poetic practice rooted in a new conception of poetry's authentic linguistic base, bears the stamp of Lockean and Condillacian principles. When Wordsworth begins the preface by saying that "a systematic defence of the theory, upon which the poems were written" would depend on his showing "in what manner language and the human mind act and react on each other" and on his "retracing the revolutions, not of literature alone, but likewise of society itself" (*Prose*, 1, 120), he is echoing a conviction that had dominated theorizing about language since the appearance of Locke's *Essay*. Throughout the preface Wordsworth adheres, if only implicitly at times, to the view that words, like thoughts themselves, are at once inherently private or subjective and dependent on a process of communal validation or "rectification" (the latter is Destutt de Tracy's term). Language necessarily reflects its social determinations as well as the individual acts of mind of a particular speaker or writer; speech and writing are to an important degree relative productions of a particular language culture, whether local or national. Although these ideas were prominently articulated in Germany by Johann Gottfried Herder and developed later by Wilhelm von Humboldt, they were first broached by Locke, Condillac, and their followers, and it is on them that Wordsworth is drawing in the preface.

Yet to insist that what has long been regarded as the founding critical document of English Romanticism is importantly indebted to empiricist thinking is not to deny that Wordsworth is at the same time resistant to, mistrustful of, certain tenets and practical consequences of that thinking. Aarsleff puts the complications this way: "Wordsworth rejected the poetic practice and the dominant poetic theory of the last century, but he built his own critical theory on the philosophy of the same century that had given language a central role in our understanding of the ways of knowing, communication, and the potentialities of expression" (*From Locke to Saussure*, p. 373). But the situation would seem to be even more pointedly conflicted than this. Consider the fundamental Lockean principle that words are arbitrary signs of ideas. Wordsworth continually appeals to an ideal that words may be naturally rather than arbitrarily related to thoughts, and through thoughts to things. For him, the arbitrariness of language is viciously evident in "what is usually called poetic diction"

(*Prose*, I,130) and in self-consciously new poetic artifice. He sets himself defiantly against those who "indulge in arbitrary and capricious habits of expression" (*Prose*, I, 124), against "false refinement or arbitrary innovation." His poems in *Lyrical Ballads* may be "an experiment," but their innovations are grounded in two principles meant to counter the arbitrariness of language. One of these is emotive and expressive: "all good poetry" takes its origin in "the spontaneous overflow of powerful feelings" (*Prose*, I, 148). The other is, or would appear to be, social: Wordsworth's poems are written "as far as was possible in a selection of language really used by men" (*Prose*, I, 123) – particularly by "men" from "Low and rustic life" who "speak a plainer and more emphatic language," whose "passions ... are incorporated with the beautiful and permanent forms of Nature," who "hourly communicate with the best objects from which the best part of language is originally derived" (*Prose*, I, 124). In an attempt to escape from "arbitrary and capricious habits of expression," Wordsworth has revised the two cardinal assumptions of empiricist theory. He makes a special virtue of the ineluctable subjectivity of language by assuming that genuine feeling can either transcend or transvalue the arbitrariness of language. At the same time, he offers an account of the social "rectification" or valorization of language by appealing to an idealized rustic community whose thoughts and words are both "incorporated with the beautiful and permanent forms of nature" – that is, with a Nature that exists beyond or outside language and can therefore legitimize authentic references to it.

But Wordsworth is not naively optimistic about the power of language to incorporate thoughts and feelings, or to be incorporated with or by nature. Near the end of the preface he acknowledges that his own language, even in being "a selection of language really used by men" from "Humble and rustic life," may nevertheless "frequently have suffered from those arbitrary connections of feelings and ideas with particular words and phrases, from which no man can altogether protect himself" (*Prose*, I, 152). This is the characteristic Wordsworthian attitude towards language: a desire on the one hand for a new kind of natural link among words and thoughts and things, and on the other a recognition of what in *The Prelude* he calls, at a moment when the imagination is forced to recognize its separation from nature, the "sad incompetence of human speech" (1850, VI.593). It is an attitude most arrestingly articulated in the remarkable *Essays upon Epitaphs* (1810–12), where Wordsworth locates in verses inscribed on tombstones in provincial country graveyards instances of what he calls "the general language of humanity" (*Prose*, II, 57), by which he means language expressive of unembellished powerful emotion and at the same time sanctioned by particular communities living close to nature.

The complications implied in Wordsworth's looking to commemorations of the dead as embodiments of his linguistic ideal are finely drawn out in Frances Ferguson's *Wordsworth: Language as Counter-Spirit* (1977). Ferguson's title derives from a crucial passage in the third of Wordsworth's *Essays*:

> Words are too awful an instrument for good and evil to be trifled with: they hold above all other external powers a dominion over thoughts. If words be not (recurring to a metaphor before used) an incarnation of the thought but only a clothing for it, then surely will they prove an ill gift; such a one as those poisoned vestments, read of in the stories of superstitious times, which had power to consume and alienate from his right mind the victim who put them on. Language, if it do not uphold, and feed, and leave in quiet, like the power of gravitation or the air we breathe, is a counter-spirit, unremittingly and noiselessly at work to derange, to subvert, to lay waste, to vitiate, and to dissolve. (II, 84–5)

Having haunted graveyards, with their instances of language that seem to him "like the power of gravitation or the air we breathe," Wordsworth is himself haunted by recognitions of an antithetical vision of linguistic power. This antithetical vision is not that of Locke and Condillac, with their sense that arbitrary, humanly instituted linguistic signs are intrinsic to thought, but of Dryden and Pope, for whom (as Wordsworth has previously pointed out) words are "a clothing" for thought ("True wit is nature to advantage dress'd"). Wordsworth's longing for words to be "an incarnation of the thought" is so strong and yet so vulnerable that he opposes it not to alternative ways of conceiving the reciprocal interdependence of language and thought, but to commonplace views that words are powers as "external" to thought as clothes are to the body. The underlying irony of Wordsworth's asserting that words must incorporate or embody thoughts in essays where the bodies in question are all corpses suggests just how unresolved his attitude towards language can be.

Wordsworth was of course not alone in being caught between a desire to embody his thoughts in language as essential to human existence as gravity or air and a recognition of "the sad incompetence of human speech." Some versions of this tension may characterize all Romantic poets – maybe even all poets. What is distinctive about Wordsworth's linguistic practice are the powerful swings in its implied attitudes towards its own resources. Wordsworth can, of course, give us a profound sense of the pressure and action of the material world and of the physical significance of writing itself – what Christopher Ricks has called (borrowing Wordsworth's own line) "A pure organic pleasure from the lines." But for all his appeal to language as the incarnation or incorporation of thought, Wordsworth's words frequently gesture towards a realm of pure spirit where gravity and air move with the power of mind. This is especially the case when he is writing about writing. In book v of *The Prelude,* the book on "Books," he wonders, "why hath not the Mind / Some element to stamp her image on / In nature somewhat nearer to her own?" (1850, v.45–7). The answer to this speculative question comes to be located in an ideal of books as "things that teach as Nature teaches" (v.231), in "the great Nature that exists in words / Of mighty Poets" (v.594–5). But as this latter passage continues, the Nature to be found in poetic language dissolves into a force strangely like the "counter-spirit" of the *Essays upon Epitaphs*:

> Visionary power
> Attends the motions of the viewless winds,
> Embodied in the mystery of words:
> There, darkness makes abode, and all the host
> Of shadowy things work endless changes, – there,
> As in a mansion like their proper home,
> Even forms and substances are circumfused
> By that transparent veil with light divine,
> And, through all the turnings intricate of verse,
> Present themselves as objects recognised,
> In flashes, and with glory not their own.          (v.595–605)

The "transparent veil" of words here, working "endless changes" in a mysteriously paradoxical realm of "darkness" and "shadowy things," is disturbingly akin to the image of words as "poisoned vestments ... unremittingly and noiselessly at work to derange, to subvert, to lay waste, to vitiate, and to dissolve." We have come a long way from the ideal of a poetic language selected from "the real language of men" – unless that "real language," no less than the language of "mighty Poets," has the power to dissolve into darkness as well as bring to light the thoughts it would embody. A book, even a book like *Lyrical Ballads*, may be but a "Poor earthly casket of immortal verse" (v.164).

## IV

Coleridge shared Wordsworth's desire that words be more than arbitrary signs of thoughts. On September 22, 1800, he wrote to William Godwin:

> I wish you to *philosophize* Horn Tookes System, and to solve the great Questions ... Is *thinking* impossible without arbitrary signs? & – how far is the word "arbitrary" a misnomer? Are not words &c parts & germinations of the Plant? And what is the Law of their Growth? – In something of this order I would endeavour to destroy the old antithesis of *Words* & *Things*, elevating, as it were, words into Things, & living Things too.          (*Letters*, I, 625–6)

This letter echoes a sentence from Wordsworth's note to "The Thorn" in the second edition of *Lyrical Ballads*, where "repetition and apparent tautology" are seen to be capable of becoming "beauties of the highest kind" because of "the interest which the mind attaches to words, not only as symbols of the passion, but as *things*, active and efficient, which are of themselves part of the passion" (*Prose*, II, 513). Coleridge's insistence that words can embody and not just stand for thoughts and things is, however, consistently more exuberant and untroubled than Wordsworth's. Where Wordsworth can find an ultimate linguistic integrity in silent inscriptions commemorating the dead, Coleridge puts his linguistic faith in words as "living Things" – as plants, as live bodies: "The focal word has acquired a *feeling* of *reality* – it heats and burns, makes itself be felt. If we do not grasp it, it seems to grasp us, as with a hand of flesh and blood, and completely counterfeits an immediate presence, an intuitive knowledge."[8]

In the letter to Godwin we can see Coleridge resisting "Horn Tooke's System," even as by implication he takes that system to represent the most advanced formulation of recent linguistic thinking. In his study of *Coleridge's Philosophy of Language* (1986), James C. McKusick traces Coleridge's "close intellectual relationship" to Horne Tooke, a relationship that began in the mid 1790s when Coleridge came to know Tooke personally and developed an admiration for his progressive politics as well as for his work on language. By 1801 Coleridge was changing his mind about Tooke's politics, but according to McKusick, "his admiration for Tooke's scholarship remained unaffected by these feelings." Unaffected? Here is an entry from Coleridge's *Table Talk* for May 7, 1830:

> Tooke affects to explain the origin and whole philosophy of language by what is, in fact, only a mere accident of its history. His abuse of Harris [James Harris's *Hermes, or a Philosophical Inquiry concerning Universal Grammar* appeared in 1751] is most shallow and unfair. Harris, in the Hermes, was dealing – not very profoundly, it is true, – with the philosophy of language, the moral and metaphysical causes and conditions of it, &c. Horn Tooke, in writing about the formation of words only, thought he was explaining the philosophy of language, which is a very different thing.[9]

The fact of the matter is that Coleridge rejected Horne Tooke's radical effort to understand all mental processes as processes of language. Coleridge certainly exploited *The Diversions of Purley* for metaphysically suggestive etymologies – of "mind" from "the motion of the Scythe in mowing," or of the noun "thing" from the verb "to think." But this latter etymology clearly shows Coleridge's opposition to Tooke, who had derived the verb "to think" from the noun "thing."

Coleridge repudiates the cardinal principle of the Lockean tradition, that language is the arbitrarily and historically contingent "workmanship" of the human mind. Instead, he elaborates a conviction that words can become at once natural things and the thoughts we have about things, and that their being so is an expression of the coalescing of things and thoughts, of nature and mind, in a transcendent power called "the Logos." In the famous condensation of his thinking on these matters in chapter 13 of the *Biographia Literaria*, Coleridge defines both the Primary and Secondary Imagination as essentially linguistic, or more specifically vocal, powers – as a repetition and an echo, respectively, of that originary reflexive utterance, "I AM," through which the infinite divine mind expresses itself as the existing universe and thereby creates it. The summarizing formulations of chapter 13 are offered, Coleridge tells us via a patently fake letter of advice "from a friend," in place of – by way of deferring – a full articulation of his ideas, which will be reserved for his "announced treatises on the Logos or communicative intellect in Man and Deity." These "treatises" were never published, but Coleridge did leave behind a manuscript which has come to be known as the *Logic*, and which was finally published in 1981 as a volume in the ongoing Princeton University Press-Routledge edition of his works. In his illuminating chapter on the *Logic*, McKusick regards it as a systematic philosophy of language. Despite the fact that long sections are translations or paraphrases of Kant's *Critique of Pure Reason*, it is the most sustained and philosophically erudite treatment of language by any British writer of the Romantic period. That Coleridge at one point considered calling his treatise "EΠEA ζώοντα" ("living words"),[10] an obvious variation on the Homeric epithet ("winged words") used by Horne Tooke in the title of his great work, "*EΠEA ΠΤΕΡΟΕΝΤΑ, or, the Diversions of Purley*," shows that he still conceived of his project in part as a reply to Tooke.

In the *Logic* Coleridge is preeminently concerned not with the semiotic dimension of language, with the ways in which words signify thoughts or refer to things, but with "grammatical discourse," with grammar as a formal relational system that "reflects the forms of the human mind" (p. 18). He thus positions himself squarely within the line of thinking that runs from the doctrines of universal grammar expounded in the Port Royal Grammar and in Harris's *Hermes* to Chomsky's recent work. Coleridge's postulation of universal linguistic categories bypasses the pseudo-historical reliance on an original Adamic language in favor of a more technically elaborate appeal to the "infinite I AM" – to a divine, transcendental act of language in which subject and object, mind and world, are eternally united. "This primary mental act," he writes, "which we have called the synthetic unity or the unity of apperception, is presupposed in … all consciousness" (*Logic*, p. 76). The original word of God is constitutive at once of all existence and of all thinking. Berkeley is an important influence on this idealist conception. But where Berkeley asserts that human language is "arbitrary," unlike the divine language of nature to which it imperfectly refers, Coleridge entertains the belief that human language too, in its highest forms, echoes or reflects transcendentally constituted links between ideas or perceptions and things. It is most emphatically in the "symbol," with its "translucence of the special in the individual or of the general in the especial or of the universal in the general," and "Above all by the translucence of the eternal through and in the temporal," that human language triumphs over those "empty echoes which the fancy arbitrarily associates with apparitions of matter" (*Lay Sermons*, p. 30).

The theoretical speculations worked out during the 1820s in the prose of the *Logic* begin to take shape early in Coleridge's career – not just in lectures, letters, and notebook entries, as we have seen, but in his poetry as well. The ideal of a divine natural language emerges at a key moment in "Frost at Midnight," as the speaker imagines that his infant son will have an upbringing far different from his own childhood "In the great city, pent 'mid cloisters dim":

> But thou, my babe! shalt wander like a breeze
> By lakes and sandy shores, beneath the crags
> Of ancient mountain, and beneath the clouds,
> Which image in their bulk both lakes and shores
> And mountain crags: so shalt thou see and hear
> The lovely shapes and sounds intelligible
> Of that eternal language, which thy God
> Utters, who from eternity doth teach
> Himself in all, and all things in himself.          (54–62)

Coleridge might seem to come close here to Wordsworth's conviction in the preface to *Lyrical Ballads* that people from "Low and rustic life … communicate with the best objects from which the best part of language is originally derived." But already we can discern the grounds for Coleridge's differences with Wordsworth, differences elaborated in the famous attack on the linguistic tenets of the preface in the *Biographia Literaria*, chapter 17: "The best part of human language, properly so called, is derived from reflection on the acts of the mind itself. It is formed by a voluntary appropriation of fixed symbols to internal acts, to processes and results of imagination" (*Biographia*, II, 54). The argumentative formulations of 1815–17 are latent in the poetic longings of 1797–8. While the child in "Frost at Midnight" is situated along with the rustics among what Wordsworth calls "the beautiful and permanent forms of nature," he learns to speak not by listening to the language of rustic society, but by communicating directly with a natural world that is already linguistic – with the "eternal language" that is nature understood as God's self-utterance. And that "eternal language" of nature in "Frost at Midnight" is figuratively seen to contain those "reflection[s] on the acts of the mind itself" which, for Coleridge, constitute the "best part of human language": the child will perceive not just "lakes and sandy shores," "crags," and "clouds," but the "processes and results of imagination" by which these natural forms echo or reflect each other: "the clouds, / Which image in their bulk both lakes and shores / And mountain crags." Yet, the conventions of ordinary, arbitrary human language resist this drive towards an all-encompassing "eternal language." The "voluntary appropriation of fixed symbols to internal acts" in which the child in "Frost at Midnight" will participate may not be as untroubled as his father wishes: "Great universal Teacher! he shall mould / Thy spirit, and by giving make it ask" (63–4). But "ask" in what kind of language? In an immediate echo of the Great universal Teacher's "eternal language" of natural forms? The father's fond hope obscures difficulties that his child will be given to asking, difficulties registered in the grammatical tension of the father's own idealizing verse.

## V

It is a distinctive sign of Percy Shelley's differences from and with Wordsworth and Coleridge, and of his very different intellectual relationship to empiricist philosophy, that he exuberantly accepts the arbitrariness of language. Early in *The Defence of Poetry*, comparing the expressive potential of language to that of "colour, form, and religious and civil habits of action," he says that "language is arbitrarily produced by the Imagination and has relation to thoughts alone" (*Poetry and Prose*, p. 483). Nowhere is Romanticism's positive appropriation and transformation of empiricist discourse more striking than in this passage of the *Defence*. Shelley takes the Lockean insistence on the ineluctable subjectivity of language ("Words in their primary or immediate Signification, stand for nothing, but the Ideas in the Mind of him that uses them") a radical step further with his insistance that it is "the Imagination," not just the understanding, that produces language. There is considerable evidence to suggest that it was Locke to whom Shelley was responding. He had read Locke avidly, along with Hume, very early in his career, when he thought of him as a sensationalist, as the predecessor of the French materialists whom he admired (Holbach, Volney, Cabanis). Then, in the autumn of 1815, he appears to have begun a serious rereading of Locke's *Essay*, at a time when the new skeptical and idealist philosophical reading he had done since 1812 – the year in which he met William Godwin and ordered the writings of Monboddo, Horne Tooke, and Sir William Jones from his bookseller – was beginning to open up new questions about language and the mind's experience of the world and of itself. Shelley returned to Locke after the famous Switzerland summer of 1816 and, according to Mary Shelley's journal, read the *Essay* regularly from mid November 1816 to January 1817. He read Locke again in March 1820, less than a year before beginning the *Defence*.

While Shelley's boldly optimistic appropriation of Locke's principle that words arbitrarily signify "thoughts alone" is characteristic of his intellectual bearings and allegiances, it is at odds with his prevailing attitude towards language. When focused on the actual temporal and historical condition of language rather than on its ideal potentiality relative to other media of expression, he tends, like Locke, to emphasize its limits and imperfections. "You say that words will neither debauch our understandings, nor distort our moral feelings," he says in a letter to Godwin:

> But *words* are the very things that so eminently contribute to the growth & establishment of prejudice: the learning of *words* before the mind is capable of attaching correspondent ideas to them, is like possessing machinery with the use of which we are so unacquainted as to be in danger of misusing it. But [although] words are merely signs of ideas, how many evils, & how great spring from the annexing inadequate & improper ideas to words.
>
> (*Letters*, 1, 317)

Although this letter, written July 29, 1812, shows Shelley's thinking about language at a very early stage, it demonstrates a profoundly mistrustful recognition of the constitutive power of language that will prevail and complicate itself in his later writing. On the one hand, Shelley wants to maintain a clear distinction between words and ideas, and to insist on the latter's independent priority; on the other, the passage is energized by his acknowledging, in what he believes to be opposition to Godwin, that words commonly hold a devastating power over "correspondent ideas" – that the machine of language, to turn a Coleridgean phrase in the Shelleyan direction suggested here, is diabolical rather than blessed.[11]

This troubled apprehension of language's power over thought haunts some of the most famous passages of Shelley's *Defence*, such as the celebration of the creative authority of "poets, in the most universal sense of the word":

> Their language is vitally metaphorical; that is, it marks the before unapprehended relations of things, and perpetuates their apprehension, until the words which represent them, become through time signs for portions or classes of thoughts instead of pictures of integral thoughts; and then if no new poets should arise to create afresh the associations which have been thus

disorganized, language will be dead to all the nobler purposes of human intercourse.                                                          (*Poetry and Prose*, p. 482)

Shelley's account of the generative cultural force of metaphor deviates from
its apparent celebratory trajectory at the temporal conjunction "until," with
its anticipation of the historicizing phrase "through time." The history of
discourse, for Shelley, follows the institutional consolidation and normal-
ization of vital metaphor into the signs of ordinary language. The arbitrary
production of language by the imagination, which two paragraphs later
Shelley will claim as an originary power for the individual poet, comes to
be seen here, in the course of a single sentence, as an arbitrary power of a
very different kind. Once the "before unapprehended relations" marked by
poetic metaphor get absorbed into the language they perpetually enrich,
they lose their generative vitality. The passage from imaginative life to death
is inherent in the historical condition of language; the possibility of poetic
revitalization is, in this crucial moment of the *Defence*, precariously and
challengingly tendered as a conditional "if."

Shelley encourages us to believe that "new poets" will always arise. But
they will necessarily have to work as much "to create afresh the associations
which have been thus disorganized" by the inevitable process of linguistic
institutionalization as to originate "vitally metaphorical" language. Another
way of putting this would be to say that the poet in history must take advantage of the potential in the arbitrary relation between words and thoughts
to turn language against its own tyrannical and capricious "dominion"
(Wordsworth's word) over thinking. This aspect of the poet's work is both
artistic and political, and it becomes increasingly difficult when, as is often
the case, Shelley's understanding of "the before unapprehended relations of
things" contradicts common cultural assumptions about what "things" are.

"[N]othing exists but as it is perceived," he says in the fragmentary essay
"On Life," following the seemingly nonsensical but nonetheless irrefutable
claims of empiricist philosophy in its radically idealist (Berkeley) and skeptical (Sir William Drummond) modes against the "shocking absurdities of
the popular [dualistic] philosophy of mind and matter" (*Poetry and Prose*,
p. 476). What Shelley attempts to confront in this essay, and recurrently in
his poems, is the fact that language as it exists does not and perhaps cannot be made to conform to "the most refined deductions of the intellectual
philosophy." The dualism of mind and matter inheres in the very structure
of our language, and Shelley's or any other writer's desire to dissolve it must
risk violating not only such formal coherence but such practical social and
cultural efficacy as existing language may be deemed to offer: "By the word
*thing* is to be understood any object of thought, that is, any thought upon

which any other thought is employed, with an apprehension of distinction" (*Poetry and Prose*, p. 478). What becomes of those "before unapprehended relations of things" that are "mark[ed]" by "vitally metaphorical" language when the distinctions or differences essential to such relations are entirely a matter of perception or "apprehension," without any other ontological ground? Shelley's provoking such a question is an indication of why his writing has been the focus of so much deconstructive criticism – some of it, particularly Jerrold Hogle's *Shelley's Process* (1988), brilliantly revealing. But his own attitude towards what is at stake in trying to dissolve false differences and the identities they depend on is very different from the characteristic deconstructive appeal to the play of language:

> The words *I*, and *you* and *they* are grammatical devices invented simply for arrangement and totally devoid of the intense and exclusive sense usually attached to them. It is difficult to find terms adequately to express so subtle a conception as that to which the intellectual philosophy has conducted us. We are on that verge where words abandon us, and what wonder if we grow dizzy to look down the dark abyss of – how little we know. (*Poetry and Prose*, p. 478)

Shelley may sometimes push his writing towards "that verge where words abandon us" because he delights in playing on the brink. But even there we find him working – not just desperately, but with determined resourcefulness – to overcome the sheer dizziness that his skeptical intellectual convictions produce in himself and in his readers.

The categories of distinction and unity built into language that Shelley wants to undo and replace with "before unapprehended" distinctions and unities are political as well as grammatical and philosophical. Language can only be revitalized from within, by making a virtue rather than a vice of the arbitrary signifying processes on which language depends. One of Shelley's most striking political representations of this activity of liberating the potential of language from within its very constraints occurs in canto VII of *The Revolt of Islam* (1818), a poem that addresses itself, in the words of the preface, to the "panic which, like an epidemic transport, seized upon all classes of men during the excesses consequent upon the French Revolution." And all classes of women too: Cythna, the poem's heroic female protagonist, recalls her long isolated imprisonment in a cave beside the sea:

> My mind became the book through which I grew
>   Wise in all human wisdom, and its cave,
> Which like a mine I rifled through and through,
>   To me the keeping of its secrets gave ...

> And on the sand would I make signs to range
> > These woofs, as they were woven, of my thought;
> Clear, elemental shapes, whose smallest change
> > A subtler language within language wrought:
> > The key of truths which once were dimly taught
> In old Crotona. (VII.3100–13)

Cythna's creative linguistic activity here is inseparable from her condition of isolated imprisonment, and in this respect she is a figure of the poet – of Shelley himself as he recurrently imagines his own position within language. That Cythna's activity is historical is made evident by her unlocking "truths which once were dimly taught / In old Crotona"; that it is textual (a matter of "mark"-ing, as Shelley says in the *Defence*, not just saying) is suggested by the precarious image of making signs on the sand to articulate her weavings of thought. Weaving, an image traditionally associated with the work of confined women, is here woven into a new text of self-sustaining power and subtlety (the word "subtle" once meant "woven fine," Latin *subtilis* from *sub-tela*, and has its root in the verb *texere*, "to weave"). Shelley sees Cythna's liberating herself from within language as it comes to her historically not as an act of violent repudiation but as an expression of "Clear, elemental" difference, as an elaboration of "smallest change" into her own self-empowering idiom.

This moment in *The Revolt of Islam* engages in complicated ways the central questions about women's place in romantic writing that have been posed by Margaret Homans, Mary Jacobus, and other feminist critics. Cythna is undeniably a male writer's image of women's access to linguistic power; her weaving "A subtler language within language" is itself woven by Shelley into the Spenserian stanzas of an epic tradition and of a visionary political allegory that set the terms for what she can and cannot accomplish. Yet Cythna offers a very different figure of women's relation to language and writing from anything we find in Wordsworth or Coleridge. In saying that the terms of her working within language, including her working in isolation, are Shelley's own, we are recognizing that those terms extend even as they question and reimagine the empiricist view of language as an inherently constrained yet incompletely determined and therefore transformable product of human culture.

## NOTES

1. I have used "empiricist" and "empiricism" throughout because they are the common modern terms for the philosophical tradition stemming from Bacon, Hobbes, and Locke. But it is worth noting that in the seventeenth and eighteenth centuries these words (along with "empiric" and "empirical") had pejorative meanings and

were used to designate outmoded, unscientific medical practice, or any practice guided by mere experience, without scientific knowledge (see Samuel Johnson, *Rambler* no. 183). Only in the nineteenth century did "empiricist" and "empiricism" develop their modern philosophical senses; the first such use of "empiricism" cited in the *Oxford English Dictionary* is from an 1803 number of the *Edinburgh Review*.

2. See John Yolton, *John Locke and the Way of Ideas* (London: Oxford University Press, 1956).

3. See *The Philosophy of Language in Britain* (New York: AMS Press, 1986), pp. 31–78.

4. "Brevis designatio meditationum de Originibus Gentium ductis potissimum ex indicio linguarum," *Miscellanea Berolinensia* (1710), p. 2; quoted in the English translation by Hans Aarsleff, *From Locke to Saussure: Essays on the Study of Language and Intellectual History* (Minneapolis: University of Minnesota Press, 1982), p. 91.

5. "The History of Linguistics and Professor Chomsky," first published in *Language* 46 (1970): 570–85, and reprinted in *From Locke to Saussure*, pp. 101–19.

6. *The Study of Language in England: 1780–1860* (Princeton University Press, 1967), p. 19; see Aarsleff's essays on "The Tradition of Condillac" and "Condillac's Speechless Statue," in *From Locke to Saussure*, pp. 146–224. Condillac's *Essai* was translated into English as *An Essay on the Origin of Human Knowledge* in 1756 by Thomas Nugent; it was subtitled *A Supplement to Mr. Locke's "Essay On the Human Understanding."*

7. "Mémoire sur la faculté de penser" (1796), *Mémoires de l'Institut National. Sciences morales et politiques* (1798) 1, 318, quoted in the English translation by H. B. Acton, "The Philosophy of Language in Revolutionary France," *Proceedings of the British Academy* (London: Oxford University Press, 1959), p. 200. Acton's account of Tracy should be supplemented, and in some instances corrected, by Aarsleff, *From Locke to Saussure*, pp. 344–5, 375–6.

8. From a notebook entry in MS. Egerton 2801, fo. 145, quoted in *Inquiring Spirit: A Coleridge Reader*, ed. Kathleen Coburn (London: Routledge and Kegan Paul, 1951), p. 101.

9. Quoted from *Specimens of the Table Talk of the Late Samuel Taylor Coleridge*, ed. H.N. Coleridge (London, 1835); see McKusick, *Coleridge's Philosophy of Language* (New Haven: Yale University Press, 1986), p. 43.

10. From Notebook 29 (the "Clasped Vellum Notebook"), Henry W. and Albert A. Berg Collection, New York Public Library, fo. 39v.; quoted in McKusick, *Coleridge's Philosophy*, pp. 123–4.

11. In *The Friend* (1818), Coleridge claims that one of the purposes of his metaphysics is "to expose the folly and the legerdemain of those who have thus abused the blessed machine of language." This last phrase provides the title of Jerome Christensen's provocative book, *Coleridge and the Blessed Machine of Language* (Ithaca: Cornell University Press, 1981).

# 6

MARILYN BUTLER

# Culture's medium: the role of the Review

During the last quarter of the twentieth century social historians and historical critics cautiously developed a language for studying the arts that breaks out of a narrowly aesthetic vocabulary. We became interested not so much in literature or art or music, not even in "the arts" altogether, but in a given society's cultural production. The full consequences for our sense of how individual arts or artists operated at any particular point in time will take a very long time to absorb.

Part of the problem here is that old-style "literary history" and "art history" constructed a continuous narrative with claims, which now seem remarkably fragile, to explain where art came from. Powerful figures within the art world were held to wield the influence of despots. In order to understand younger artists it was enough to show who they copied and who they reacted against. Cultural history is of course far more impersonal than this. It also registers types of event, and of historical change, held by literary history to be of secondary significance, such as the passing or the repeal of laws affecting state censorship or copyright, and the two or three major advances in the technology of book-production. During the eighteenth century a combination of legal, financial, and industrial factors produced a huge expansion in the bulk and influence of print culture, working one of those transformations that truly deserve the term revolutionary: yet the century in which it took place is notorious for being one of the quietest on literary-historical record.

Old-style literary history saw no problems in getting from the seventeenth to the eighteenth centuries, long conventionally run together as "the Augustan age." The polite culture surrounding the Stuart court and still visibly represented by the eighteenth-century stately home was held to speak poetically through the country house and landscape poem, the elegy and the ode, the "poems of state" and what Louis Bredvold called "the gloom of the Tory satirists." Yet somewhere along this well-engineered highway relations between writers and readers certainly changed, if only because printers identified, created, and reached a market for printed books and periodicals. The chief means of marketing and a key to the perception of books in the later eighteenth century is the journal or, increasingly, the specialized literary Review. This essay aims to pursue the question of how journals, journalists, readers, and "creative" writers interacted in a period in which book-production boomed and the prestige of writers arrived at new heights – the period known in the old aesthetic terminology as Romantic.

The cultural historian John Brewer has produced an admirable, succinct summary of the transformation of all forms of British cultural production in the century or so following the restoration of the monarchy in 1660. At that point both literary and artistic activity still centered on the court, with the result that it was greatly hampered by lack of funds and by the desire of a centralized government to control the expression of opinion. The publishing industry suffered from both prior censorship and legal monopoly, which notionally restricted the number of printing presses to twenty. In these circumstances poetry, especially, was likely to be produced for private circulation in manuscript. There were no newspapers, periodical journals, reviews, almost no professional authors, and no "public," in the sense of a market for books and culture generally. During the next century a leisured class emerged, serviced but also developed and defined by its leisure industries, of which the booming print culture was probably the most significant and influential part.

When the Licensing Act lapsed in 1695, printers were able to set up for the first time in provincial towns, and the effect on publishing in London was dramatic. As Brewer puts it,

> In Charles II's reign fewer than 200 men were employed in the London printing trades. By the end of the eighteenth century over 3,000 employers, apprentices and journeymen operated more than 600 presses. The newspapers, periodicals, pamphlets and books they printed were distributed and sold by 300 bookseller/publishers whose capital and organisation secured a national market for every sort of imprint. Over the course of the eighteenth century the publishing industry averaged over 3,000 titles each year; if we make the very conservative assumption that imprints averaged 500, then between 1700 and 1800 over 150 million books were published, at a time when the population of England and Wales was less than nine million.[1]

The periodical, long the least prestigious and most nearly invisible element in this cultural effort, is in fact its matrix. It is through journalism that writing for the market becomes a viable way of making a living, and that new prose forms emerge, novels as well as diverse kinds of "journalism," from the essay to rapportage. For the first time the public became aware of written discourse in its printed form as both a commodity to be purchased and possessed and a leisure pursuit.

To some extent the newspaper and the miscellaneous journal gave "discourse" a disarmingly natural form. Within the covers of a single unbound periodical readers encountered a lively, eclectic mix of fables, dreams, letters, poems, travels, natural science, history, and biography; of book-reviews in any of these fields; of obituaries and tables listing the prices of commodities. To us it looks as though the eighteenth-century journals accomplished remarkable feats of homogenization, creating a market for the booksellers and a single English-speaking culture, straddling the Atlantic, of which readers themselves could have had no apprehension before. But the impact of the journals was paradoxical, since they were so organized as to underline the compartmentalization of knowledge and its increasing specialization. Though not quite so fragmented as the dictionary and the encyclopedia, they did not distinguish one field above another or otherwise attempt to group, still less to hierarchize, knowledge. The impression of disorder left by journals as well as reference-books was evidently disquieting, for it is caught in satires on modern knowledge throughout the period, from Shadwell's *The Virtuoso* (1676), via Swift's *Laputa*, Pope's *Dunciad* and Sterne's *Tristram Shandy* to Peacock's *Headlong Hall* (1815). The journal's influence on the way knowledge was conceptualized will be one of the leading themes of this essay.

Seventeenth-century journals tended to be the productions of learned societies dedicated to the new secular fields, such as the sciences or the historiography of developing nation states. The pioneer was the *Journal des sçavans* (Paris 1665), followed in the same year by the *Philosophical Transactions* of the Royal Society in London. But the first of these printed abstracts of scholarly enquiries in many fields, the second research-papers and scholars' letters, and the level was too specialized for the public, in Britain at least. One key innovation, associated with the public space of the coffee-house in which it could be read, was the urbane and conversational *Tatler* and *Spectator* of Richard Steele and Joseph Addison. Another breakthrough came a generation later in the second quarter of the eighteenth century, with the founding of the peculiarly British and crucial institution of the "serious" general magazine or Review.

Early Reviews were commercial ventures, initiated by bookseller-publisher-distributors who traded in books nationwide. The targeted reader was not someone already knowledgeable about books, but anyone who might be induced to read or buy them. A staple element in the magazine and the sole element in the Review was the report on a book just published – which was plainly aimed not at selling the individual book (for on the whole there was little direct "puffing"), but at creating and developing an audience for "literary intelligence." Just as all modern advertising stimulates the public's appetite both to acquire things and to win the prestige that comes from acquiring the right things, so the journal works most effectively at a level on which the interests of booksellers are not visibly involved. Through hidden arts of persuasion readers are merely taught to value the current knowledge, speculations, and ideas carried in print culture.

In France, the largest European cultural entity, and in Germany, the third after Britain, institutions of learning mattered more than in Britain, journals and journaled book culture mattered less. The French had their academies, including provincial ones, while legally produced printed materials suffered from strict state censorship. Books on forbidden topics like politics, religious infidelity, pornography, and scandal had to be smuggled in across the frontier, from distributors and ultimately printing presses in Amsterdam, the Rhineland and Switzerland; in 1789 Malesherbes, Louis XVI's censor, remarked that a Frenchman who had read only legal books would be a hundred years out of date.[2] In a Germany divided into small states, princes supported a university for reasons of prestige, while no journal succeeded in achieving really general circulation; there was still a much larger public for books in French than in German. By the end of the eighteenth century pan-German nationalism had emerged, well in advance of national unity. Then and afterwards, it was largely in the universities, through learned discourses like the new nationalist literary one, Romanticism, that the German spirit found self-expression. Both in France and Germany, eighteenth-century culture and knowledge were still associated with the patronage of princes or of the aristocracy. In Britain, after the appearance of the *Gentleman's Magazine* in 1731 and of the *Monthly Review* in 1749, court and aristocratic patronage was of negligible importance for literature.

The *Gentleman's Magazine and Historical Chronicle* was launched by the printer Edward Cave, son of a Rugby cobbler, as an encyclopedia of current affairs and contemporary opinion. Its forty-eight (soon to be fifty-six) pages were sold unbound at 6d, for binding as an annual work of reference: "an outstanding bargain," as R. D. Mayo observes.[3] Though the title page archly names an author, "Sylvanus Urban, Gent.," much of the contents were statistics and even articles pirated (legally) from other serial publications. Later in the century the bulk of a monthly number was made up of a series of short articles in the form of letters from readers addressed to Mr. Urban. This main section, occupying perhaps sixty of eighty pages, was followed by regular items assembled by the editor and his assistants: a summary of parliamentary bills, lists of new publications, prices of commodities, death notices expanded into obituaries where the deceased was a local worthy. It is only after 1765 that the list of New Books appears "with remarks," that is, short reviews or summaries of a few select items.

The *Gent's Mag*, as it became known, had interests implied by the name of "Sylvanus Urban, Gent.": these straddled town and country, and were unmistakably bound up in serious money-making, not the feminine sphere of leisure. So readers' letters typically swopped information on new processes, such as the use in agriculture of what were known as "arts." Arts meant what it signified in the title of the (London) Society of Arts, an institution that gathered and disseminated information about engineering, mechanics, new implements, and new methods for use in farming or manufacturing – and not, therefore, what it signifies in the title Arts Council, the modern body in Britain that subsidizes theatres, orchestras, museums, and some creative writers. But the *Gent's Mag*'s more erudite readers were also interested in natural history, including botany and geology, and in cultural history, which they generally called "popular antiquities," including ballads, folk customs, superstitions, and dialect words. At first sight the magazine's range looks generously eclectic, until one notices that its popular miscellany has actually displaced more traditional kinds of knowledge. Do not call here, its ugly, cluttered format announces, for information on biblical or classical learning, or the collecting of expensive *objets d'art*, the interests of the wealthy patron or of the traditionally bookish cleric.

Without having a radical editorial stance, the *Gent's Mag* managed by its very representativeness to reflect middle-class attitudes that could become egalitarian and oppositional (in relation to an aristocratic government) in the last three decades of the century. The selection of poems it published had pastoral or provincial settings and benign humanitarian attitudes that hinted at the changing social composition of the growing leisured class, and at its links with commerce and Nonconformity. By their frequent recourse to phrases like "the spread of enlightenment," correspondents helped to sustain the impression that the public sphere was widening and an irreversible "progress" under way. Other incidental expressions betray the presence of new values. One reader writes in 1795 to ask for biographical information about William Cowper, "that king among our eighteenth-century poets" (p. 733), a phrase that elevates writers and scales down acquired notions of kingship. But then the *Gent's Mag* had been partly edited since 1778 and wholly edited since 1792 by its printer-owner John Nichols, who was not only the author of an eight-volume *History and Antiquities of Leicestershire* (1795–1815), to which George Crabbe contributed the natural history, but the compiler of a *Biographical Dictionary* (1784) and of innumerable obituaries of writers and scholars in the magazine, some of which make the staple of his massive *Literary Anecdotes of the Eighteenth Century* (9 vols., 1812–15). Unevaluative, implicitly friendly and respectful towards writers because of its belief in the value of their calling, Nichols's *Anecdotes*, like the magazine he edited until his death in 1826, did much to populate "the republic of letters," and to turn poets into favorite middle-class worthies for the nineteenth century.

In launching the *Monthly Review* in 1749 the publisher-bookseller-distributor Ralph Griffiths filled the most important gap in the *Gents Mag*'s diagnosis of readers' interests – books. Seven years later one of Griffiths's contributors, Tobias Smollett, emerged as editor of a rival with the same format, the *Critical Review*. For the rest of the century these two Reviews, the first Whig, the second generally Tory, competed for the loyalties of the new public for literature, though they were soon joined by others. Their tone matched that of the *Gent's Mag*, but they limited their coverage to anonymous notices of poetry, novels, drama, belles-lettres, as well as of travels, biography, science, and some popular theology. To more abstruse theology, and to scholarly work in learned languages, the Reviews gave much less attention. The impression made by their contents and organization was egalitarian. "Who an author was" did not matter (though in practice reviewers, mostly men, tended to patronize women and men risen from the "lower orders"). The fitness of readers was similarly assumed. More than this, reading Reviews was itself a sign of cultivation, a ticket of entry to polite society.

The Reviews sold to the public through a national network of booksellers and distributors, and they were taken by local societies and by lending libraries, whose business they helped to encourage. The *Monthly Review* began in 1749 with a print run of 1,000, which by 1776 had reached 3,500. In 1797 it sold 5,000, a figure which kept it in front of its three rivals, the *Critical* (3,500), the *British Critic* (3,500), and the *Analytical Review* (1,500). Derek Roper gives these figures in his excellent study of the journals of the 1790s, *Reviewing before the "Edinburgh," 1788–1802*, commenting that they are impressively high:

> Much larger figures were to be achieved by the *Edinburgh* and *Quarterly*, but not for many years: in 1803 sales figures for the *Edinburgh*, then reckoned a dazzling success, were around 2,000, and in January 1805 its initial printing was still only 4,000 copies. Even the *Analytical*, which by 1797 was doing relatively badly, had a sale nearly equal to that of the *London Magazine* of Lamb, Hazlitt, and De Quincey in the greatly expanded market of 1821–25.[4]

Roper argues persuasively that journals had already reached a high point of their development and even perhaps the highest point of their influence before the end of the eighteenth century. The general reason for this is that nothing done by journalists *within* nineteenth-century culture could quite match the significance of their creation of that culture a century earlier.

But Roper also shows that the group of reviewers employed towards the end of the century by (say) Ralph Griffiths of the *Monthly Review* were often authorities in their fields; their judgments were generally fair and certainly not typically interested. A newcomer of 1796, the *Monthly Magazine*, owned by Richard Phillips and Joseph Johnson, employed writers of the same type and combined many of the best features of the periodicals of the century. It was a miscellany, but more intellectual and much more bookish than the *Gent's Mag*; hospitable to its readers, it nevertheless high-mindedly projected an ideal of liberal, middle-class intellectuality that anticipates both the innovative writing and the projected readership of nineteenth-century journals aimed at the thinking bourgeoisie, such as *Blackwood's* and *Fraser's*.[5]

Modern ideas of good reviewing practice are based on conventions established over two centuries and on the assumption that most readers of such articles have received some education relevant to literary and academic books. Modern reviewers focus on the performance of the author and compare it with that of other writers in the same field. Modern critics of early critics generally look out for evaluative judgments of that kind, and condemn reviews as unsophisticated if, instead, they summarize a book's contents or, worse, quote at length: the last practice is known as "padding." But the questions an eighteenth-century reviewer posed on behalf of amateur readers had to be more essential than the issue of the individual writer's expertise. The first requirement was a lucid and careful account of a book's contents, aimed at a reader with little or no prior knowledge of the field; indeed, the nature and the value of the field might itself become the matter the reviewer set out to investigate. For more obviously literary books, such as poetry and novels, comparative evaluation became the norm more quickly, but this does not mean that serious-minded contemporaries necessarily approved of it. Thomas Christie, the editor of the *Analytical* before it was taken over by its owner, the leading literary publisher Joseph Johnson, wanted his reviewers to concentrate on "objective" summary rather than on developing their own opinions.[6] The example of the *Edinburgh* was soon to show that there were in fact from the outset serious faults in the system of licensing the opinionated reviewer.

Isolating the general characteristics and impact of so large a body of writing is a difficult task, tackled acutely by Jon Klancher in his important study of journals in the Romantic period. Klancher shows that, on the one hand, by appearing regularly and opening their columns to readers, journals implied a community of discourse that united its scattered members and over time distinguished their idiolects from those of the national community. On the other hand, this comforting social identity was by definition also divisive; as journals proliferated, what they registered was the play within the community of different idiolects. Journals provided a notional "public sphere" deeply compromised from the start, since the egalitarian relationship of writer and reader and the classless status claimed for the reader were always sharply contradicted by the real world of widely unequal incomes, rank, and power.[7] In the very period in which "discourse" took on definition and offered itself as a subject for analysis, it was foregrounding, as Klancher shows, its own instability. Beguiling the reader with the pleasures and rewards of knowledge, the journals' mode of presenting knowledge – fragmentary, arbitrary, selective, contested – could never satisfy the more intoxicating promises of enlightenment.

Before the French Revolution a triumphalist tone regarding the spread of knowledge is very common. Klancher teases James Anderson, editor of a small new Edinburgh journal *The Bee*, for grandly seizing the opportunity afforded him by the spread of British trade: "By means of the universal intercourse which that trade occasions, and the general utility of this language, he hopes to be able to establish a mutual exchange of knowledge, and to effect a friendly literary intercourse among all nations ... till it shall comprehend every individual of the human race."[8] Another journal may be a source for this boastfulness, the memorable first number of *Asiatic Researches*, journal of the Asiatic Society of Bengal, in which the Society's founder-President Sir William Jones surveyed the fields the journal would cover with the grandeur of one of the great moghuls of the Enlightenment. One topic for self-congratulation was the fact that a small group (about thirty) of Jones's own countrymen, most of them employees of the East India Company in Bengal, were to take on this pioneering enterprise in their spare time. Another was the "ample space" they proposed to investigate, bound "only by the geographical limits of Asia" (if that), and encompassing "MAN and NATURE; whatever is performed by the one, or produced by the other." Reminding his original and future audience that the three branches of learning are History, Science, and Art, Jones goes on to lay down the program of the Society and its journal:

> You will investigate whatever is rare in the stupendous fabric of nature; will correct the geography of Asia by new observations ... will trace the annals ... of these nations ... and bring to light their various forms of government, with their institutions civil and religious. You will examine their improvements and method in arithmetic ... mechanics, optics, astronomy and general physics; their systems of morality, grammar, rhetoric and dialectic; their skill in ... medicine ... anatomy and chemistry. To this you will add researches into their agriculture, manufactures, trade; and, whilst you inquire with pleasure into their music, architecture, painting, and poetry, will not neglect those inferior

arts by which the comforts and even elegancies of social life are supplied or improved.[9]

This impressive account of what awaits discovery sketches the culture of Asia – a continent Jones has just defined as vaster in extent and older in terms of its written history than Europe. What Jones promises his middle-class, nonprivileged fellow members is a vaster sphere to move in and conquer than their own class-ridden and narrowly Continental world would traditionally have given them. The current of class contentiousness and heterodoxy, as well as the vision, of Jones's influential Discourse – an imitation and a parody of the Discourses of the President of the Royal Academy, Joshua Reynolds – is quite characteristic even of modest local journals in the age of the revolutionary dawn.

Two years later, Erasmus Darwin produced an extraordinary poem that may pick up this passage and certainly embraces the encyclopedic spirit of the culture of knowledge, as the journals now reflected it. "The Economy of Vegetation," the longer and more intellectually ambitious poem in Darwin's two-part *Botanic Garden* (1791), reads like a pastiche of creation-mythology in a variety of cultures, of which the most familiar are Hebraic (Genesis, *Paradise Lost*) and classical (Hesiod, Orpheus, Longinus); Eastern religions such as Hinduism are also occasionally introduced. Darwin maintains his seeming respect for the "traditional" body of his poem, insisting for instance that early poets are seekers after knowledge and interpreters of natural phenomena, just as scientists are. So he glosses the lines "When Love Divine, with brooding wings unfurl'd, / Call'd from the rude abyss the living world," by writing a note on the fossil record, along with some hints from Buffon on the evolution of species. "Through all his realms the kindling Ether runs / And the mass starts into a million suns" evokes a footnote that is actually a short essay on William Herschel's 1780s mapping of the solar system, cross-referenced to an article in the *Philosophical Transactions* of the Royal Society.[10] Like Jones, Darwin is a comparativist, and one who steadily uses the paraphernalia of modern learning (in Darwin's case, natural science) to unsettle and even unseat what the reader may take for received wisdom. Anyone trained by journal-reading to respect the latest learned intelligence (and the customary sign of its presence, the footnotes' parade of authorities) would begin to read the upstaged poem for its footnotes, rather than the other way round – a reader-response Darwin presumably hoped for. His poem has to share the page with a discourse that supersedes it; graphically the page-layout contrasts ancient and modern learning, and the modern is represented by a format and style familiarized in the more serious journals.

After this many of the most successful and intellectually ambitious poems of the period had footnotes, along with other features of *The Botanic Garden*: such as a narrative poem with an archaic, perhaps mythological setting and style, and footnotes, of necessity fragmented and nonholistic, that limited themselves to positivistic contemporary fact. Annotated poetic or more rarely prose "romances" with such an antinarration in the form of footnotes include Southey's *Thalaba the Destroyer* (1801) and *The Curse of Kehama* (1810), Scott's *Minstrelsy of the Scottish Border* (1802) and Waverley Novels (1814–), Byron's *Childe Harold's Pilgrimage* (1812) and *The Giaour* (1813), Shelley's *Queen Mab* (1813), and Moore's *Lalla Rookh* (1817). Another poem of the period with additional editorial matter was Coleridge's "Rime of the Ancient Mariner," where glosses (in a style of the seventeenth century) were added in 1817. My aim here is to point out how consistently the "romance" element in Romanticism was checked and undercut by a self-conscious modernity or a distancing intellectuality. Alternatively, it is the work of the poet's fantasy and creativity, the fictional world, that is contained within the parameters of the period's massive investment in knowledge.

The claims of Reviews in the few years before 1795 were more confident, all-encompassing and similar than they would be again. In the late 1780s English Dissenters, whose power-base lay in commercial London and in the rich provincial manufacturing centers of Bristol, Norwich, Birmingham, Derby, Sheffield, and Liverpool, were gathering their forces to win full political rights under a constitution secured throughout the past century for Anglicans. All four owner-editors of the journals dealing seriously with literary matters in 1790 – the *Monthly Review*, the *Critical Review*, the *English Review* and the *Analytical Review* – were Dissenters, and all these journals (including the hitherto Tory *Critical*) supported reform. In practice the war with revolutionary France that began in 1793 dashed Dissenters' hopes for the present generation. The journals' continued support for liberal causes, including peace with France, became all the more counter-cultural and elicited a powerful philistine backlash against literary culture from about 1796. Even the kind of liberalism that is expressed in one leader-column, with its mild hopes for "the return of peace, the extinction of animosities ... and the circulation of benevolence to an extent which may embrace every quarter of the globe" (*Gent's Mag*, preface, 1795), marked out the journals' culture to their opponents as tendentious and unpatriotic. All writers of any note associated with the reformist or pro-French publications of the first half of the decade – Godwin, Paine, Priestley, Price, Wollstonecraft, Hays, Coleridge, Lamb, and Southey – were ridiculed in the second, in caricatures, satirical novels, or the new satirical journal *The Anti-Jacobin*. The impact on creative writers can be felt, if not measured, during the next generation, by the compulsive self-portrayals, apologetic or defiant, of almost every significant literary figure of the period, from Godwin and Wordsworth to Byron and De Quincey.

One marker of the end of the bourgeois republic of letters was the jailing in 1798 of the doyen of publisher-booksellers, Joseph Johnson, for publishing a tract judged seditious. His *Analytical Review* collapsed, though the *Monthly Magazine* soldiered on by dint of some trimming under Phillips's editorship. But the Dissenter monopoly that gave late-century "literary London" such a misleading social and political coherence was already broken by the launching in 1792 of the Anglican *British Critic*. A much more significant journalistic event challenged the cultural status of London itself, the appearance in October 1802 of the *Edinburgh Review*.

The *Edinburgh* was founded at a time of national crisis by a group of young men anxious to make a national mark. It did not set out to serve the general public by extracting the contents of many books, but selected drastically in order to influence a more elite stratum of opinion. Its first challenger, the *Quarterly* (founded 1809), modeled itself on the *Edinburgh*. After one more middlebrow newcomer, Henry Colburn's *New Monthly Magazine* (1814), the next prestigious arrivals, *Blackwood's* (1817), the *London Magazine* (1820), and the *Westminster Review* (1824), differed in important respects, but nevertheless all visibly reacted to the *Edinburgh* which, despite its faults and the offence they often gave, remained the most famous periodical of the age.

If a single characteristic accounts for the supremacy of this journal, it is arrogance. The preface to the first number brashly states that it forms no part of the editors' object "to take notice of every production that issues from the press." Instead they mean "to confine their notice ... to works that either have achieved, or deserve, a certain portion of celebrity." Thus the first number of the *Edinburgh*, a quarterly, contains twenty-nine articles, mostly devoted to a single book, compared with the following numbers of books noticed in the same month in its three main rivals, all monthlies: *Monthly*, forty-four; *Critical*, sixty; *British Critic*, seventy-seven. But even this drastic retrenchment quickly came to seem insufficient, and by April 1804 the number of articles the *Edinburgh* carried was down to eighteen, only once again to rise higher; by 1810 twelve had become more usual. Francis Jeffrey, the Edinburgh lawyer who soon emerged as the sole editor, naturally represented this change not as an economy, but as a great advance towards intelligent and discriminating reviewing. Clearly we need not take his word for this.

The *Edinburgh Review* plainly set out to break the mould of existing journal culture. Its predecessors' show of inclusiveness in fact tacitly favored writings in new fields that appealed to the enlarged reading public. The *Edinburgh* challenged this indiscriminateness and banished the general magazine's crowded, miscellaneous appearance by an editorial policy that can be described as disciplined Whiggism. Its first fields for special "promotion" were academic, the specialisms for which Scottish universities were famous, especially the natural sciences, moral philosophy, and political economy. Next came matters of national political importance, such as foreign relations, the conduct of the war, geographically informed travels in the distant empire and territories contingent. Assuming that these fields were more likely to interest men with access to power than women or the middle orders, some of these editorial policies took a commercial risk.

Moreover, the *Edinburgh* largely excluded not only the classical and clerical "old learning" but also the technology previously aimed primarily at the new middle classes. It included, but treated satirically and destructively, certain types of writing encouraged by the eighteenth-century middle-class Reviews, such as most antiquities and most popular culture, both of which it found tendentious. The seductively readable style of "slashing" criticism for which the *Edinburgh* became famous was a weapon almost entirely reserved for popular writing, the last of these categories, and the field that distinctively marked off the new middle-class culture from older fields of learning.

This summary of the *Edinburgh's* contents will become clearer on inspection of the contents pages of the first four numbers, from October 1802 to July 1803 (see figure 6.1). Among the topics unusually well represented here are the sciences, for which the *Edinburgh* could call locally on experts. Astronomy, geology, physics, maths, and chemistry all appear, but special pride is taken in James Hutton's exciting *Theory of the Earth* (I.xxvi; IV.v), which substitutes for the description of the creation in Genesis and the chronology derived from it a slow, gradualist account of the forming of the earth's crust. Though the new geology is controversial and hotly contested, very explicitly so in Hutton's own writing, the reviewer's tone in these as in most scientific articles is judicious to the point of being bland. New facts about foreign lands are often welcomed in the same dispassionate style, as contributions to pure knowledge, without too much dwelling upon the fact that the regions most often covered (the Ottoman empire, Egypt, Persia, the West Indies, later India) are strategically crucial in the war with France and, moreover, the targets of Britain's own rapidly clarifying imperialist ambitions.

Meanwhile, works enthusiastic about the romance of the East, the beauty of its religions, or the importance of its languages will consistently

Contents of No. I.

Contents of No. II.

6.1 Summary of the *Edinburgh Review* contents pages.

be met with sarcasm, as are two books reviewed here on the remote past of the British Isles (Vallancey's *Prospectus of an Irish Dictionary*, III.xii, and *Vindication of the Celts*, IV.vii). Where the war with France is directly touched on, the tone tends to be studiedly "civilized," that is, bipartisan. The counterrevolutionary polemicist and translator of Burke, Friedrich von Gentz, is allowed his categorization of the errors of Napoleon in *L'Etat de l'Europe* (III.i), but also reminded that the Allied or anti-French powers were equally guilty when they partitioned Poland. The discussion of the "Crisis of the Sugar Colonies" (I.xxvii) treats slavery in the West Indies as an unacceptable institution, and to this extent favors the rebellious slaves in the old French colonies, but it also cautiously remarks that French and British colonists in the West Indies have more interests in common than interests driving them apart.

New writing by radical stalwarts left over from the 1790s is freely exploited by early reviewers in the *Edinburgh*. Godwin is ridiculed in I.iii, John Thelwall and Joseph Ritson in III.xiii, xxi. Poking suave, snobbish fun at the latter's vegetarianism, without overtly disclosing its connection with pacificism, helps to marginalize Ritson's very serious and influential role as a collector of ballads and popular traditions. The whole genre of "Public Characters," that biographical, typically self-identifying middle-class kind, is given half a page in the first number, to be disposed of (as far as the *Edinburgh* is concerned) for ever: "We suppose the booksellers have authors at two different prices, those who do write grammatically, and those who do not; and they have not thought fit to put any of their best hands upon this work" (I.122).

It is even more of a put-down to journals of the *Monthly Review* type to give such a very small showing to imaginative literature. Some numbers (e.g., v.ix, October 1804) review no new literary writing at all. The belles-lettres that appear often fall into one of two categories. The Scottish and/or utilitarian authors (Scott, Baillie, Edgeworth) earn praise for their wholesomeness. English "provincial" authors (Wordsworth, Coleridge, Lamb, and Southey) are generally identified as populists and are being reviewed in order to be attacked. The treatment of Southey's *Thalaba* in the first number makes it look certain that Jeffrey chose it in order to single out a whole group of writers. He had already reviewed *Thalaba* for the *Monthly* and, as Roper points out, did not find it necessary in that location to drag in the ideological issues with which he opens the topic in the *Edinburgh*.[11] Although *Thalaba* is a poem in a learned genre, a romance epic accompanied by scholarly footnotes, Jeffrey has plainly already made up his mind to assail a new "*sect of poets … dissenters* from the established systems in poetry and criticism," among whom he includes by name Wordsworth, Lamb, and Coleridge.[12]

He proceeds by gathering together the various criticisms made of Southey by, for example, George Canning in *The Anti-Jacobin* and John Ferrier in the *Monthly* – though these referred to the imitation ballads on strongly humanitarian subjects Southey published in 1797 and 1799. The probable reason for concocting this digressive review was to stir up a controversy that would win publicity for the new journal.

The founding editorial group that launched the *Edinburgh* included two Scots lawyers, Francis Jeffrey and Henry Brougham, plus the well-connected Anglican clergyman Sydney Smith. Their pool of occasional contributors is filled by academics in the secular-minded Scottish university system. The *Edinburgh*'s flavor became at once high-professional in the nineteenth-century scope of that term, in which the tone of social superiority once the prerogative of the gentry was adopted. In practice men from the law, medicine, and social science, backed by statistics, played a greater part than members of the old-gentry professions of church and armed forces.

Scottish universities in the eighteenth century had carved out a *modus vivendi* for themselves that consorted oddly with the fierce, Calvinistic, often philistine traditions of the Kirk. Academics like Hume managed to be notionally highly heterodox, skeptical, even atheistical, without challenging the present order in the state. It was the Kirk that was historically fundamentalist, radical, even revolutionary (back in the seventeenth century). Academics, like most Scotsmen of the professional and commercial classes, recognized that the 1707 Union with England opened the door to richer pickings for Scotland's large educated class, at home, in London, or abroad, than Scotland commanded alone. The *Edinburgh Review* continued that tradition, to which James Thomson and Tobias Smollett had belonged, of delivering advice to the English in tones of moral and intellectual superiority. More confidently than Thomson's generation, it spoke for the efficient, meritocratic, and socially progressivist Scottish professional class that increasingly either worked for the government and aristocratic opposition in London or built the empire in Canada and India. The sons of the English ruling class, notionally four hundred families and their networks, were prevented by the French war from going on the Continental Grand Tour; many went instead to Edinburgh and Glasgow, to lodge with the professoriate and learn the pragmatic science of government that became an orthodoxy for the next generations.

Potentially the *Edinburgh* seemed critical, because of its religious skepticism and its pro-French sympathies. In its first decade the young Thomas Love Peacock found in its apparently open forum for ideas a model for his intellectual prose satire – an extended series of dialogues in which currently fashionable notions are proposed (as in a series of articles on new books) and nothing gets resolved. But by 1818, when a crop of radical weeklies aimed at a dissatisfied lower-middle-class readership had emerged, Peacock objected to the political stance of both quarterlies. The Whig *Edinburgh Review* and the Tory *Quarterly Review* were really on the same side, he now found, that of the Establishment. "The best recommendation a work of fancy can have" for a reviewer in either "is that it should inculcate no opinions at all, but implicitly acquiesce in all the assumptions of worldly wisdom."[13]

The year after writing this Peacock became a senior administrator in the East India Company, the immediate subordinate in its London headquarters to James Mill, the philosophical radical and erstwhile aide to Jeremy Bentham. In an article in the first number of the utilitarian *Westminster Review* (1824), Mill seems to be developing Peacock's sardonic likening of the *Edinburgh* to the *Quarterly*. He opens by remarking acutely that aristocracy, the present system of government, cannot rule alone, but needs willing aides among the professional classes. It finds them above all in the law and the Church, the two professions that respectively dominate the two Reviews (213–14). Mill notices the extraordinary interest each journal shows from the start in the sphere of government. "Under the guise of reviewing books, these publications have introduced the practice of publishing dissertations, not only upon the topics of the day, but upon all the most important questions of morals and legislation" (206). As they perform one service, that of disseminating knowledge, they omit another, that of criticizing the *status quo*. The need of a journal to seem fashionable draws it to flatter leaders of opinion. "The favourite opinions of people in power are those that favour their own power … To these opinions periodical literature is under a sort of necessity … of serving as a pandar" (208). The *Edinburgh*, the journal of the Whig Opposition, appears superficially to be less aristocratic than the pro-government *Quarterly*, but it is merely a standard opposition feint to appeal to the many as to the few. "It is sufficiently evident, at last, on which side the winnings remain" (218).

Mill made his point in an impressive academic style by analyzing the contents of a number of articles from the early and middle runs of the *Edinburgh*, with the result that he spoke to readers as educated and rational as himself. Meanwhile, his point was partly subverted by the design and tone of the new journal – twelve long analytical articles, written in a voice of effortless superiority, in perfect mimicry of the prestigious quarterlies. A more broadly aimed critique of the two "aristocratic" journals came from the rivals that emerged following the *New Monthly* and after the war to reassert the tastes of the middle-class majority of readers, *Blackwood's Edinburgh Magazine* (1817) and the *London Magazine* (1820).

The *Edinburgh's* reign was finite, then; but for the first two decades of the century the metaphor of domination is appropriate. Much of its literary influence must have been negative. Where the earlier generation of journals supported writers on the middle-class/popular side, by giving the impression of a like-minded reading public, the *Edinburgh* warned off mere working writers who voiced heterodox opinions and sought to herd them into a literary ghetto that plainly lay outside the national public sphere. Probably Jeffrey helped to browbeat the isolated rural Wordsworth and the insecure urban Coleridge and Lamb out of the populism they were associated with in the 1790s. With Southey, his original target, he was less successful, for Southey became a genuine Tory populist, a writer and reviewer sympathetic to causes like Baptist missions, factory-children, Methodism, "our uneducated poets," which makes his tone distinctive in the Anglican environment of the *Quarterly*. More generally, working "literary London," the emerging, not unprosperous sub-profession of the hack writer that was Hazlitt's and became Dickens's, continued to grow in numbers and earning power, but went virtually unnoticed and not much employed by the two prestigious quarterlies. Neither of the quarterlies, as Roper remarks, ever played much part in spotting new talent. In fact the *Edinburgh's* opening statement of policy showed that it never intended to do so.[14] The roles of democratization and recruitment belonged to the eighteenth-century monthlies, several of which continued to exist, to some impressive Dissenting journals (most notably, the *Eclectic Review*), and from 1808 to the Hunt brothers' radical weekly *Examiner*. Leigh Hunt, equally political, specialized in finding radical talent; his partisan praise for Keats, Shelley, Reynolds, and others was more interesting critically than Jeffrey's reasons in 1802, 1807, and 1814 for grumbling at Wordsworth.

The *Edinburgh's* snobbish distancing of itself from mere writers and ordinary readers could also be positive. Just as the *Monthly*, the *Critical*, and the *Analytical* mediated between the writers of the 1790s and a supposedly sympathetic public, so the *Edinburgh* constructed an upmarket yet culturally receptive version of "the world," and helped train writers to address it. Would Byron and Shelley, Edgeworth and Austen, all born into the gentry, have written, or rather continued to write, for commercial publication, if they had not perceived that professional writing now rated as a refined activity? Successful creative writers visibly received the reward of social acceptance in the so-called Regency period. If Tom Moore, George Crabbe, and the Edgeworths were welcome at high-aristocratic Bowood or Holland House, it was surely because the *Edinburgh* reviewers had shown the way, by their pens and in person. James Mill gave only part of the case when he said that lawyers and churchmen made themselves useful to aristocracy: so did academics, journalists, and even poets, who all swelled the ranks of the new fourth estate. Byron and Shelley were schoolboys and students in the *Edinburgh*'s first unchallenged decade, and it taught them that the issues of the day were the war, disputed spheres of influence like the Middle East and India, and the new secular sciences that promised, at home, to help unsettle the influence of the Church. To a remarkable degree, the literal *contents* of the "younger Romantics" in the second decade of the nineteenth century, which are directly political to a degree unusual for poetry, repeat the contents of the *Edinburgh* in the first decade. Though this journal's scoffing did away with the naturalness, freshness, and feeling of the "popular" 1790s, it compensated by ushering in the intellectual, cosmopolitan, and political 1810s.

The story of the *Quarterly* overlaps that of the *Edinburgh*, since it was founded in 1809 by a group who included contributors to the *Edinburgh* (such as Scott). *Quarterly* writers disagreed with the *Edinburgh* on party politics, particularly on Jeffrey's "soft" policy on the war; but they were also "aristocrats," not by birth but in Mill's sense of wishing to maintain rule by an elite. In their notions of culture the principle of conservation rated as high as it did for Jeffrey. As the public's commitment to the war grew once in 1808 a large British land army became engaged in the Iberian Peninsula, the *Quarterly* launched itself at the opportune moment to win readers: its hearty will-to-win against France was plainly easier to put across than the *Edinburgh*'s languid stance of playing at most for a draw.

The *Quarterly* looks very like its parent – up to twenty substantial articles at the beginning, but the same tendency to drop down to about a dozen; a steady diet of informative, reasoned essays, with no "diary" or letters or other informal or volunteered contributions. But in fact, the *Quarterly*'s emphases are a little more familiar, traditional, reassuring, a little less intellectually strenuous. At least a third of the articles are usually literary, a considerably higher percentage than in the *Edinburgh*, though some discuss reprints of classics in Latin or Greek. Theology appears and plays a minor part, about the same as the scaled-down science (which, as in the *Edinburgh*, is academic rather than technological). In their early days the *Quarterly* reviewers do not look nearly so doctrinaire as their resolutely Scottish seniors. They keep their militancy for fighting the French and at first tend to treat their favorite topic of belles-lettres as though it is not a subdepartment of politics. Greater geniality as well as greater patriotism probably helped them in their circulation-war with the *Edinburgh*. Between 1812 and 1814, the sales of both journals topped 12,000, with the *Quarterly* claiming to be slightly ahead.

This late-war period gave the quarterlies a short, remarkable ascendancy, during which they exercised a lasting influence on the mainstream novel. Most late eighteenth-century novels were viewed as entertainments and as fodder for the female reader. The Edgeworth family took both quarterlies, Scott wrote for both of them: between 1809 and 1814 Maria Edgeworth and Scott "turned" the novel towards documentation and social realism and into that discourse of contemporary history and social analysis to which the serious nineteenth-century novel belongs. Edgeworth's *Ennui* (1809) and *The Absentee* (1812), the best-received of her Irish tales, appeared at just the right time to win accolades from both quarterlies. Naturally so, for these tales mirror the qualities and contents of the higher journalism. Firmly grounded in the Scottish science of society, they are composed in vivid, accurately observed scenes that seem to invite selection as quotations – that is, virtually to anticipate a second career in the columns of either or each quarterly. Following Edgeworth, Scott did more to resist appropriation, more to indulge his readers with the pleasures of story. Yet the nonfictional elements that make first Edgeworth so newsworthy, so much at home in these periodicals dedicated to the public scene, repeat themselves in Scott. Both novelists echo the quarterlies' commitment to social order and good government.

After the return of peace in 1815 the *Quarterly* developed a more active literary policy. Postwar political unrest soon found expression in cheap radical journals, such as T. J. Wooler's *Black Dwarf* (1817), and it became the turn of middlebrow Tories to worry about the infection that might be carried by culture. Robert Southey, himself the victim of the *Edinburgh*'s earlier crusade against populism, took a lead in the *Quarterly*'s. He had become interested during the war in the topic of the loyalty of the masses and how it could be secured. Where the masses in question had been Britain's new Indian subjects, he had concluded that there could be no sense of common interest unless there was a common religion, strongly believed in. He had therefore contributed to the first number of the *Quarterly* an article the *Edinburgh* would have been unlikely to print, on the desirability of sending missions among the Hindus to convert them to a popular revivalist Protestantism (vol. 1, February 1809, 193–225). Some similar reflections about securing the loyalty of the British masses to the state by means of Christianity occur in an article by Southey in the number nominally for October 1816 (XVI, 225ff.), which appeared the following February. At the end of a year of unemployment, low wages, high prices, and popular unrest, he was reviewing two examples of subversive literature, one in a form cheap enough for the lower orders to buy.

The first title Southey addressed was a substantial pamphlet, price 1s/6d: *Christian Policy*, by Thomas Evans, leading disciple of Thomas Spence, the agrarian communist and journalist of the French Revolution period. If he had known how to convey his vision of a communist Christian Utopia, Evans might, Southey warned, have subverted the loyalty of the common people much as Hinduism undercut it in India. He then turned to a work he did find formidable, William Cobbett's radical newssheet, the *Political Register*, which had once appeared as part of a newspaper and, being liable to a heavy tax, sold for a shilling. Cobbett's theme in 1816 was systemic corruption: not the misdeeds of this or that minister in an administration, but the inequity and rottenness of government by the few. In November 1816 he began the separate publication of the "leader" only on a single sheet, which evaded the tax, and could be sold for two pence. Southey, himself an outstanding journalist, shows a lively respect for Cobbett's unprecedented powers as a writer for the masses. The outcome of this article in one journal about another is an urgent call for censorship of the press.

We are most aware of the *Quarterly* for a handful of discussions of major volumes of poetry it carried in the "younger Romantic" years, 1814–22. The point is rather that in these years the journal conducted a comprehensive campaign on behalf of conservative, Christian, and family values, pursuing this with great rigor and pertinacity into most areas of current print culture. Where Jeffrey had mocked at a populist style in Wordsworth, the individual highbrow poet, the *Quarterly* hunted down "infidel," irreligious, or sexually explicit subject-matter in texts of all kinds. James Mill's gibe about its ties with the Church was a commonplace. From 1817 to 1822 its most typical and militant reviewers, after Southey, were ardent young Anglicans, several of them clergymen, such as Reginald Heber, H. H. Milman, Richard Whately, and Coleridge's nephew, the lawyer J. T. Coleridge.

Among celebrities Byron was far and away the most important target. But, just as Jeffrey had invented the myth of a Lake school, so the *Quarterly* team identified, in order to "demonize," an entire Satanic school of Byron camp-followers, to which Shelley, C. R. Maturin, and the anonymous author of *Frankenstein* were all recruited. At about the same time the *Quarterly* and *Blackwood's* established the profile of a middle-class Cockney school, headed by Leigh Hunt and including Keats, which was held to subvert morals through promoting sexual licentiousness.[15] The success of the *Quarterly* especially in shaking "liberal" poetry can be gauged by the fact that when a firmly liberal literary magazine emerged in 1820, the *London*, it dared not defend Byron: *Don Juan* and *Beppo*, said its leader-column, the Lion's Head, "trespass on the fences of society, and are therefore hazardous to its security" (II [1820]: 4–5). The campaign's secure base in public opinion is proved by the acquiescence of the *Quarterly*'s owner, John Murray, even though he was at the same time the unhappy publisher of *Don Juan*.

There is a neat symmetry in the fact that first the *Edinburgh*, now the *Quarterly*, threw their influence against the best young poets of the day as each generation arrived at maturity. Even though the quarterlies themselves drew culture into the political, they had no scruple in condemning political poetry. No wonder, one might think, that Peacock and Mill thought the journalists cynics. But then these two had been independent authors with radical, minority opinions; were their views of the world more true or more representative than those of journalists who were not paid by the state but had to find a considerable number of fellow citizens to sell to? Writers had been encouraged by the rhetoric of eighteenth-century Reviews to think themselves representative citizens of the world. In the more disillusioned (and more sociological) early nineteenth century, they were beginning to be identified as a marginal subgroup of the middling sort within a divided society.

"Posterity" (represented by more writers in later periods) has sympathized with the poets in this alienating quarrel, but too late. In the early 1820s the *Quarterly*'s campaign on behalf of middle-class "good taste" against "upper-class" license was as effective as the *Edinburgh*'s middle-class campaign against radical "vulgarity" had been. Byron and Shelley did not change their style; they were insulated at first by living in Italy, more permanently by dying in 1824 and 1822 before their unpopularity caught up with them. Their executors and editors had to resort to reinterpreting, censoring, and burning the documentary record in order to bring them into line with the more decorous and much less political literary norms of later generations. Well before his even earlier death in 1821, Keats was working to eliminate from his later poetry those elements in *Endymion* that a priestly critical movement was liable to take exception to, such as frank sensuality, vulgarity, and liberal politics. The success of the *Quarterly*'s clean-up campaign in the interests of the family reader is best measured by the taste and the critical norms of the second quarter of the nineteenth century. Byron, now perceived as Satanic, was toppled from his bad eminence, never (in the English-speaking world) quite to regain his critical respectability.

An ordered *separation* between literature, especially poetry, and independent or reformist or scientific thinking was in train by 1820. The more tendentious areas of scientific work, notably geology, experienced conflicts with public opinion, that is, with the vociferous clerical lobby within it. Like most of the literary free-thinkers, scientists in Charles Lyell's and Charles Darwin's generations learned to censor themselves. Thus, where the two great Reviews had differed, the spirit of the more concessive, cautious, and middlebrow *Quarterly* prevailed over that of the *Edinburgh*. Early Victorian literature and reviewing inclined to the *Quarterly*'s priorities: antiscientific, antiutilitarian, a sphere separated from money-making, social conflict, and heterodox politics.

Meanwhile, in tones very unlike those of the *Quarterly*, the resolutely middle-class *New Monthly*, *Blackwood's* and the *London Magazine* were already in the early 1820s shaping post-Romantic culture. More accurately, they became the main initiators of a culture to which we might agree to give the word "Romantic," which thus emerged as the world was robbed by death or physical decline of the main writers we call the "English Romantics." Colburn's *New Monthly Magazine* paid well and was thus able to get occasional pieces from some of the best journalists of the day, including Hazlitt, Leigh Hunt, and Lamb. The first two would not have written for Colburn if they had thought him illiberal, but he (or his effective editor, Cyrus Redding) might certainly have earned the censure of Peacock and Mill for frivolity. The *New Monthly* was one of that style of journal, very familiar since, which seemed to exist to catch "fashion as it flies." It was indeed so preoccupied with the epiphenomena of urban social life and amusements that it seemed to live by and for them, achieving the highest monthly sale for the highest price, as Redding boasted, indispensable to its readers on account of what Klancher describes as its "semiological one-upmanship."[16]

*Blackwood's Edinburgh Magazine*, another monthly, emerged in April 1817 as a popular, locally rooted middle-class alternative to the *Edinburgh Review*. Yet in 1820 its editor, John Wilson, succeeded to Edinburgh's prestigious chair of moral philosophy, and his journal was hospitable to other academic philosophers such as Alexander Blair. Out of its approximately one hundred and twenty pages, the first forty went to "Original Communications" from readers, in the style of the *Monthly Magazine*. These letters or "letters" turn out heavily weighted with antiquarianism, almost all of it Scottish. Other regular features include "Select Extracts" from current books, an "Antiquarian Repertory" (also dominated by Scottish material), a handful of short poems and reviews of four or five new books, of which one or two will be poetry. A section of "Literary and Scientific Intelligence" brings back into the foreground that group-portrait of working writers the quarterlies pointedly left out.

In the third year of its life *Blackwood's* coverage of the Scots literary scene was brought brilliantly to life by the introduction of "Noctes Ambrosianae," a kind of dialogic gossip column in which the editor Wilson, using the pen name "Christopher North," discussed current topics with contributors such as John Gibson Lockhart and James Hogg, the Ettrick shepherd. These are pages for browsing in, the place you go to find uneasy compliments to women poets and raw, demotic abuse of Hogg for his impenetrable accent and his bad manners: this teasing reads like eavesdropping, because it seems too lifelike to be anything else. In nineteenth-century literary history *Blackwood's* was remembered for occasional slashing reviews in Jeffrey's style, like Lockhart's snobbish advice to Keats to go back to his gallipots ("The Cockney Poets," vol. III [1818]). It got less and less credit for intellectuality, or for the humor, flair, and verve it brought to the task of shaping a self-consciously middle-class literary vehicle, or for its imaginative and up-to-date appeal to the solitary reader's experience. Its unpatronizing attentiveness to contemporary Scottish culture and writing must have made a real difference. Scott, the aristocratical lawyer, ceased to look representative after *Blackwood's* appeared center-stage. Within the next few years Galt and Hogg came into their own as novelists, and other highly successful Scottish journals, such as *Tait's*, appeared.

Where *Blackwood's* derived a distinctive character from its Scottish grass-roots, the *London Magazine* had more difficulty in differentiating itself from its two predecessors. It had the eclectic character of the other two, a strong literary focus, fashionableness (like the *New Monthly*), and an interest in both English classics and new work in European languages. The opening section of its "Miscellaneous Articles" includes poems and articles on topics such as James Shirley's plays. French, German, and Spanish books are regularly reviewed. After the first number it opens with "The Lion's Head," its literary gossip-column, an innovation trumped by the *Blackwood's* "Noctes Ambrosianae." Here and elsewhere the editor, John Scott, struggles to escape from the politically partisan style that the *Quarterly* was elevating into a near witchhunt.[17] Above all, the *London* picked up from the *New Monthly* an eye for the star journalist as literary celebrity. It poached Hazlitt, proudly featuring in its first number a series of his highly personal essays, "Table Talk," in barefaced imitation of the same writer's "Round Table" a few years before in the *New Monthly*. In the next few years it ran the more brilliant and more fully characterized "Essays of Elia," by Lamb, and De Quincey's *Confessions of an English Opium Eater*. Thus, the *London* testified to a new belief in being literary for its own sake. It did not cover, but merely listed, books on antiquities, science, law, political economy, and theology. The notion of a discrete, autonomous literary sphere was being visibly sustained within its covers. Mary Russell Mitford noted the immediate fashionable impact of the style:

> we are free and easy in these days, and talk to the public as a friend. Read *Elia*, or [Washington Irving's] *Sketch Book*, or Hazlitt's *Table Talk*, or any popular book of the new school, and you will find that we have turned over the Johnsonian periods and the Blair-ian formality to keep company with the wigs and hoops, the stiff curtseys and low bows of our ancestors.[18]

Mitford shows what a high place *literary* style (as carried in Reviews) occupied in the current conception of style generally.

Indeed, they had never before made such an impact, because they had never been so self-conscious, nor so conscious of a mass readership waiting to be recruited. After the Regency's highly politicized culture, the journals of the 1820s aimed at ordinariness, not in plainly class terms but more as a camaraderie that came to city-dwellers through shared experience. The greatest of their innovations was a sense of place. The late eighteenth-century journal evoked community, but as an abstraction. In the 1810s many in-group satires appeared, by Byron, Hunt, Moore, Horace Smith, and Peacock: these made no attempt to portray "literary London" as realizable people moving about real streets. Before 1820 there seems to have been no writing quite like Hazlitt's opening to his essay "The Fight" (*New Monthly*, February 1821), where he describes his walk down Chancery Lane one damp evening, looking for someone sharing his passion for "the Fancy" to tell him the time and place of the fight. After 1820 thick descriptions of London, the early prose-poetry of modern urban life written by Lamb, Hazlitt, and De Quincey, Piers Egan, Theodore Hook, and Thomas Hood, brilliantly use "the commonplace" to stand for that which is held in common – the all-important gatheredness which early journals supplied only in idea.

Largely because they are now seen as figures in a newly particularized, familiar setting, middle-class writers come into focus for the first time. Throughout the first century of the history of journals, and in spite of the ambivalence of the socially ambitious quarterlies, the professional advance of the writer had been at least a covert item on the agenda. The journals' own egalitarian ethos worked to advertise writing itself as that rare thing, a middle-class calling potentially open to talent regardless of gender, wealth, or access to patronage. By the end of the period, Reviews were getting *professionally* self-reflexive, in that articles and books on the lives and personalities of men and women of letters were filling the place once reserved for articles and books on statesmen or men of action. Writers by 1820 had to endure the scrutiny and the personal attacks of their own colleagues, attentions that the media of the twentieth century save for sportsmen, showbiz people, politicians, and royalty. Even the *Edinburgh* and the *Quarterly* grudgingly contributed to advancing the social prestige of (at least) the top writers, by creating the sense of a public sphere writers could take part in and then taking deeply seriously the threat their poems posed to public security.

The ordinary writer, who thus stepped into the place of the extraordinary Byron, was being brought close to the ordinary reader, for whom he provided a possible surrogate. Necessarily the observers, fashioners, forecasters of public attitudes and interests, journals now found an arrestingly new, internalized means, by mutual identification, to read their readers, and thus to enable readers to read themselves: as observant, alienated walkers in the city; as drunks, hacks, failures in love and worldly ambition; as a new kind of "character," quite unlike the idealizations of most formal literature. It was left to the new nineteenth-century personal essay, "talk," or "sketch" to advance, decisively, the commercial project launched by eighteenth-century journals: to capture who or what the public was. Klancher shows vividly how, through language, a mass audience was evoked in journals of the 1820s and 1830s and how its realization depended on a mix of introspection and rapportage. This mass was also, variously, men, women, young women, servants, the family circle, all notionally united by their access to the booksellers' network. Even Coleridge, who mistrusted the phenomenon, was writing of "the reading public" by 1817 in the singular.

Beyond writers and readers the journals had much to say about literariness, knowledge, culture. What that was has become less easy to see after a century of separating literary from nonliterary writing. The often nonliterary, eclectic materials surrounding each original article served to put not merely the discussion of literature, but literature itself, into a certain social and intellectual context, which seems to have wielded an influence at a deeper level than the individual value-judgments with which reviewing is associated in a later period. The short discussions within this essay of how poems and novels respond, formally and stylistically, to the holistic journal, barely introduce a large topic – which has to be that of Reviews rather than reviewing. To assemble together the reviews of one poet (as in, say, the *Critical Heritage* volume on Coleridge or Keats) is to disjoin each review from an expressive and very pertinent original location. For a general journal and a literary Review each proffered a version of the world, shaped by a schematic construction of knowledge and increasingly, as Klancher has shown, realized in a self-conscious and appropriate language. The journal in its entirety, as itself, needs a new and more functional style of criticism, for what it can tell us of the relations between literature and culture.

## NOTES

1. John Brewer, lecture delivered to *The French Revolution in Art*, symposium at the Clore Gallery, London, December 1989. I am grateful to Dr. Brewer for a copy of his lecture.
2. Quoted from Malesherbes's *Mémoires* by Robert Darnton, lecture, Bodleian Library, Oxford, June 1987.
3. R. D. Mayo, *The English Novel in the Magazines, 1740–1815* (Evanston: Northwestern University Press, 1962), p. 160.

4. Derek Roper, *Reviewing before the "Edinburgh," 1788–1802* (London: Methuen, 1978), p. 24. At its peak about 1815, the *Edinburgh* probably reached sales around 13,000. This compares with *Blackwood's*, also rated highly successful, which soon after its arrival in 1817 reached 6,000.
5. Roper, *Reviewing*, pp. 31–48.
6. *Ibid.*, p. 44.
7. Jon P. Klancher, *The Making of English Reading Audiences, 1790–1832* (Madison: University of Wisconsin Press, 1987), pp. 18–46.
8. *Ibid.*, p. 25.
9. William Jones, Discourse 1, delivered in 1784 to the Asiatic Society of Bengal, first published *Asiatic Researches* 1 (1789).
10. Erasmus Darwin, *The Botanic Garden* (1791) part 1, "The Economy of Vegetation," 1.101–2 and 105–6, and footnote to the latter.
11. Roper, *Reviewing*, p. 40.
12. [Francis Jeffrey], *Edinburgh Review* 1 (1802), reprinted in *Southey: The Critical Heritage*, ed. Lionel Madden (London: Routledge, 1972), p. 68. See Roper, *Reviewing*, pp. 101–11, for a fuller discussion of Southey and Jeffrey.
13. T. L. Peacock, "Essay on Fashionable Literature," *Halliford Edition of the Works of Peacock*, eds. H. F. B. Brett-Smith and C. E. Jones (London, 1924–34), VIII, 274. For Peacock's early debts as a satirist to the *Edinburgh*, see my *Peacock Displayed* (London: Routledge, 1979).
14. See above, p. 131, and Roper, *Reviewing*, p. 41.
15. The *Quarterly* reviewed Keats's *Endymion* in vol. XIX (April 1818) and *Frankenstein, or the Modern Prometheus* in vol. XIII (May [for January] 1818). The latter's dedication to William Godwin was enough to identify an "infidel" author. J. T. Coleridge, who had been at school with Shelley, wrote a very personal review in vol. XXI (April 1819) of Shelley's *Revolt of Islam*, in which he revealed the existence of the even more daring withdrawn version of the poem, *Laon and Cythna*. Some of the more effective slights heaped on Byron occurred when reviewers were supposedly dealing with other books. Cf., e.g., [R. Heber], "The Fall of Jerusalem. By the Rev. H. H. Milman," XXIII (May 1820): 225, in which Byron is incidentally accused of the "worser side of Manicheism."
16. Klancher, *English Reading Audiences*, p. 63.
17. Cf. the *London*'s attempts to defend a figure made notorious by Tory reviewing, Leigh Hunt. In a discussion of Hunt's "Hero and Leander" and "Bacchus and Ariadne," the reviewer states that the poet has been undervalued because "politics is the lord of the ascendant" (II [July 1820]: 45). The middle-class liberal journals of the eighteenth and nineteenth centuries tend to oppose politicized reviewing, most strongly when (as here) the issue is also one of class. The *London*'s remarks contrast sharply with the objections of Peacock and Mill that the aristocratic quarterlies are not political enough.
18. Mary Russell Mitford to Sir William Elford, June 22, 1824; *The Letters of Mary Russell Mitford*, ed. Richard Brimley Johnson (London: John Lane, 1925), p. 176.

# 7

STEPHEN C. BEHRENDT

# Publishing and the provinces in Romantic-era Britain

## I  Introduction: books and Romantic literature

Literary study focuses primarily upon literary texts, their authors, and the historical and cultural circumstances surrounding the origin, production, and assessment of those texts. The books themselves we customarily take for granted as the raw material for critical and theoretical analysis. But for their publishers, books are commodities possessing both real and virtual "value" in the public economic sphere. However authors and scholars may choose to see things, publishing has always been a "business," and publishers necessarily have wholly mercenary interests in the fortunes of the authors they publish. Already in the eighteenth century it was apparent that "even a sound work may depend on the publisher's exertions ... for securing a hold on the public mind."[1] An author's success – or failure – was tied as much to their publishers' marketing skills as to their own literary talent. Popular success required access to an interested readership, and publishers and booksellers were the gateway through which authors had to pass.

Although publishers had an obvious financial stake in the books they published, the authors were no less heavily invested. The Romantic era's greatest and most popular novelist, Sir Walter Scott, provides a good example. Although Scott had been Britain's most popular living poet, when *Waverley* appeared on July 7, 1814, his poetic star been eclipsed by that of the Regency's new literary sensation, Lord Byron, whose *Childe Harold's Pilgrimage*, cantos I and II, had appeared in March 1812, catapulting their author into immediate stardom. Scott's ambitious plans for his estate, Abbotsford, required substantial infusions of cash; he entered into a complex arrangement with several prominent publishers who then competed with one another first for the rights to his novels and then again for advantage in selling them in their own bookstores before the other partners could do so. Scott, who envisioned a more elite readership than the undiscriminating consumers of Regency popular fiction, was initially published in

Scotland by the powerful Edinburgh publisher Archibald Constable, whose son-in-law Robert Cadell in 1829 to 1833 published the reasonably priced *Magnum Opus* edition of Scott's Waverley Novels in initial printings of as many as 20,000 copies per volume. The London publishers wanted the profitable Scott, too: Longman and Company had already co-published *The Lay of the Last Minstrel* with Constable in 1805, and John Murray enlisted his Edinburgh agent William Blackwood to help secure Scott. The ensuing bidding and distribution contest among these publishers left the increasingly ill author hard pressed to produce enough fresh fiction for their hungry markets.

Sensational successes were the exception, though, not the rule: Scott and Byron during the middle years and Hemans later are good examples among the better-known poets. But the Romantic era saw many prolific authors nevertheless, like the novelists Jane and Anna Maria Porter, sensationalists like the pseudonymous "Rosalia St. Clair" and "Anthony Frederick Holstein," and poets like Robert Southey and Mary Robinson. The fortunes of such authors (or, more often, their lack of fortunes) were inextricably linked to their publishers, to those publishers' readerships (including the circulating libraries associated with many of them), and to the economic realities of the Romantic-era publishing industry that often dictated surprisingly small press runs. Percy Bysshe Shelley's books were usually printed in what now strike us as remarkably low numbers: *Alastor, and Other Poems* (1816), for instance, was published – at Shelley's own expense – in London by Baldwin, Cradock, and Joy in a press run of 250 copies, and copies remained unsold as late as 1820, while probably only 500 copies of his monumental *Prometheus Unbound, and Other Poems* (1820) were printed, and of these, too, many remained in 1824; while *The Cenci* (1819) did reach a second edition, it numbered only 250 copies.[2] Indeed, for most poets other than celebrated ones like Byron, Scott, Thomas Moore, and, later, Felicia Hemans, a press run of no more than 500 was fairly standard, and often the majority of those remained unsold years afterward, which indicates how little money was to be made by publishing, except for the fortunate few. Even Robert Bloomfield (1766–1823), whose best-selling 1800 poem, *The Farmer's Boy*, sold more than 25,000 copies in under three years, nevertheless died in abject poverty.

Scott's self-described brand of "superior" fiction held its own throughout its author's lifetime. The third Waverley Novel, *The Antiquary* (1816), printed in 6,000 copies, sold out within weeks, while the first edition of *Rob Roy* (1818) numbered an extraordinary 10,000 copies. This part of the publishing picture is relatively well known because Scott (like Byron) has long enjoyed canonical status. Less immediately familiar figures are the authors of the many "popular" and often sensational novels that were mass-produced especially by William Lane and his successors at the Minerva Press and disseminated through the many circulating libraries that Lane established throughout the country in addition to his vast central library in London. While publishers like Lane made huge profits from their successful publishing empires, the authors whose works drove their trade earned little. Minerva Press novelists were generally paid £25 or less per title, for example, even for multi-volume novels; everything else went to the publisher. This is not to say that real profit was not within the reach of an author who knew how to play the market. The prolific Hannah More, for instance, parlayed the public appetite for conventional moral tales and tracts to great advantage. Her lifetime profit from the sale of her copyrights has been estimated at as much as £30,000, a remarkable sum given that the pound was at that time worth more than twenty times its present value.

While major publishers flourished in population centers like London, Edinburgh, and Dublin, minor publishers abounded in provincial areas, often publishing the works of local authors for largely local audiences. While most novels were published in London, only slightly more than half of the poetry published during the Romantic era originated there, and some of this was co-published (or at least distributed) in conjunction with provincial publishers who held the copyright. The works of provincial authors therefore constitute a differently inflected "Romanticism" than that of the familiar canonical authors, especially in terms of the (often early) works published in the provinces. James Hogg ("the Ettrick Shepherd") published his *Scottish Pastorals* (1801) in Edinburgh and Sydney Owenson (later Lady Morgan) published her early *Poems* (1801) and her first novel, *St. Clair* (1803), in Dublin. With success came subsequent publication in London, and access to much differently constituted readerships. On the other hand, Thomas Moore, who contributed so much to the romanticizing of Irish identity, nevertheless published from the start among the Whig literati in London, as did the shoemaker poet Robert Bloomfield, while Robert Burns shrewdly crafted the persona of "ploughman poet," his literary sophistication and self-promoting strategies notwithstanding. Even so, the excitement generated by Burns's *Poems, Chiefly in the Scottish Dialect* (1786; published in Scotland and widely reprinted in England and pirated in Ireland) failed to preserve him from emotional and financial ruin. Even the Lake Poets, whose collective name implies their provincialism, in fact quickly progressed beyond their early publication in provincial centers (Coleridge in Cambridge and then Bristol, Southey in Bristol) to publication or co-publication by London publishers like Cadell and Davies or G. G. and J. Robinson, while Wordsworth *began* in London, with Joseph

Johnson. Perhaps the most distinctively "provincial" literature (much of it poetry) actually was produced by laboring-class writers like the Irishwoman Catharine Quigley (published in Dublin, 1813, and Monaghan, 1819), the Scotswoman Christian Milne (wife of a ship's carpenter, Aberdeen, 1805), or the Englishwoman Ann Candler (Ipswich, 1803), who resided in the Tattingstone workhouse. Works of this sort, perhaps because their readerships were small, local, and often both familiar and sympathetic, lend their humble, quotidian subject-matter and discourse an emotional and experiential authenticity that is largely missing from the grand generalizations of much of canonical Romantic writing.

## II  Printers, publishers, booksellers

Some aspects of the Romantic-era publishing industry may be unfamiliar to modern readers. First, there were both "publishers" and "booksellers," in addition to printers. Publishers dealt directly with (1) authors, purchasing the rights to their works; (2) printers and binders who produced the physical books; and (3) booksellers who distributed them to the consumers. Many publishers were also booksellers, selling their wares and those of other publishers in bookstores that were often large and sumptuous, especially in urban centers like London. Each publisher naturally gave priority to its own books; owning the rights to especially popular authors ensured a publisher/bookseller of first access to eager customers when new works appeared. Publishers first supplied their own stores and those of affiliated booksellers, and only later provided copies to other dealers. In addition, many publishers maintained circulating libraries, where for variable fees customers could borrow from a large and diverse stock of books. "Booksellers" were retailers who, whether they ran presses of their own or not, sold books principally by contract arrangements with various publishers. With the expansion of the Romantic-era periodical press, provincial newspapers became important cogs in the publishing wheel, printing advertisements for new books that urban publishers supplied (on commission or by individual orders) to provincial booksellers. Reviews in periodicals, many of which were directly affiliated with individual publishers, further whetted the appetites of curious readers.

"Books" were usually sold, especially after the 1790s, in stitched paper or cheap cardboard wrappers, rendering them very susceptible to damage and deterioration if their purchasers did not pay to have them rebound. Many books – like the ubiquitous chapbooks of sensational fiction – have disappeared as a result of wear, having been quite literally read to death. Even simple books were relatively expensive until late in the period, when more efficient production methods made cheaper editions possible. During the Regency, for example, the prices of new books were prohibitive even for readers in or above the "middle" class, while for the lower and laboring classes, book ownership was virtually out of the question. Hence the popularity of circulating libraries (for those who could afford subscriptions) and of pubs and coffee-houses where people might find copies or hear them read aloud. As consumer goods, books were mostly for the "well to do," not the ordinary working British citizen, although even illiterate citizens tried to have at least a few books visible when company called. As a result, books retained some of the elite status they had held in the eighteenth century. Even when booksellers like James Lackington (1746–1815) revolutionized the book trade by trading in secondhand and remaindered books (Lackington's London "Temple of the Muses" regularly housed as many as half a million volumes), books remained largely out of reach for the majority.

Printers were for the most part entirely separate parts of the industry, though their influence upon the publication process could be considerable. After 1799 English law required that the printer's name and address appear on the first and last pages of all books. Because this requirement, which William Pitt had urged upon Parliament amid government fears about an insufficiently regulated press in revolutionary times, made the printer liable for what was printed under his (and occasionally her) name, printers had a stake in any literary material that could provoke repressive government action like the prosecutions for treason and seditious libel that were pursued earlier in the 1790s. This impulse towards self-protection surfaces in the publication history of Percy Bysshe Shelley's *The Revolt of Islam* (1817, dated 1818). Originally titled *Laon and Cythna*, Shelley's poem was being printed for Shelley's publisher, Charles Ollier, when the printer noticed that it involved an incestuous relationship between the revolutionary siblings named in the title. He objected to Ollier, who in turn balked, forcing Shelley to withdraw and revise the poem to make it palatable to printer and publisher.

During the years 1800 to 1829 there appear to have been approximately 1,000 printers working at one time or another in London and the surrounding areas of Middlesex and Surrey. Because printers served whomever hired them, and for whatever needed printing, they could be engaged by individual authors willing to finance their books personally; in these cases the title page typically stated that the work was "printed by [printer's name] for the author." Often such arrangements, known as publication "on commission," involved books published by subscription, especially in provincial towns: authors (or their agents) would gather enough subscriptions (agreements in advance to purchase) from interested parties to cover the expense of printing and binding, with the publisher usually also taking a share of any profits, an arrangement that often left the naive author duped and over-charged. Sometimes these were purely vanity productions financed by their authors for the pleasure of seeing and distributing their works to friends and acquaintances. At other times, these printed-on-commission publica-tions were charitable projects undertaken (sometimes through public sub-scription, sometimes not) by philanthropic third parties for the benefit of authors who were physically disabled, indigent, or otherwise fallen upon hard times; Hannah More's sponsorship of "the Bristol milkwoman," Ann Yearsley (1752–1806), is a particularly well-known example, but such cases ran literally into the hundreds and were especially common in the provinces. *The Blind Poem*, by Mary Byrne, blind from birth, was published in Dublin in 1789 for the author's welfare, through the agency of an acquaintance. In England there was James Chambers, a celebrated but illiterate vagrant from the vicinity of Ipswich whose extemporized poems and acrostics, composed for drinks money, were twice published (in 1796 and 1820) by interested parties for his benefit. At the same time, established publishers frequently turned to subscription publication for authors who were relatively unknown or whose works had not yet proved to be reliably profitable. Even Charlotte Smith's publishers, Cadell and Davies, enlisted subscribers when her *Elegiac Sonnets* expanded to a second volume in 1797.

Usually, an author sold the copyright to her or his work to a publisher or to a consortium of them, agreeing to renounce all future financial claims to the work; sometimes an author might negotiate a profit-sharing arrangement rather than an outright sale of copyright. When a consortium of publishers was involved, the copyrights were divided into shares according to the size of each publisher's investment. Large publishing houses like Cadell and Davies or Longman and Rees owed much of their success to their careful manage-ment of investments in these joint ventures in publishing, which helped them offset losses from individual failures by providing a diversified portfolio of investments. Although the prices paid for manuscripts varied widely, they were usually very low. In 1797 Ann Radcliffe was paid the extraordinary sum of £800 for the copyright to *The Italian*, and John Murray paid Byron nearly £20,000 over the nine years of their association. But sums of that sort were the exceptions to the rule that saw struggling authors sometimes paid as little as £5 – and regularly in the £20–£25 range – for their efforts. Indeed, until the phenomenon of the literary "celebrity" emerged during the Regency and afterward, when better-known authors could command copy-right contracts into the thousands of pounds, the supply-and-demand condi-tions of the publishing industry typically kept authors in a position of nearly complete dependence: as already noted, even Scott was not immune.

## III   The early Romantic era

What we now think of as a publishing "industry" is a relatively recent phenomenon. During much of the eighteenth century, when books were produced in small numbers through a labor-intensive printing process, the publishing trade was dominated by relatively prosperous urban publishers like Jacob Tonson and Robert Dodsley, and the most prominent booksellers in London were to be found around St. Paul's Cathedral (especially in Paternoster Row), near the Temple Bar, and in the Strand. Provincial booksellers were for most of the eighteenth century few and far between. The principal sites were Birmingham, Bristol, Cambridge, Oxford, Bath, and Norwich, all of which had circulating libraries as early as mid-century, as well as York, where the printing industry had taken root early on. By 1800, however, it is estimated that there were nearly a thousand "booksellers" sprinkled throughout some 300-plus British towns and villages. These numbers, however, include establishments ranging from those devoted entirely to books to those dealing in "general merchandise" that might include as few as several dozen books.

Until 1800 Dublin was notorious for producing "pirated" (unauthorized) reprint editions. Ireland lay outside the jurisdiction of the Copyright Act of 1710, which held that copyright began when an author put pen to paper and that this copyright constituted a commodity that the author could cede to a publisher, with or without payment, for up to twenty-eight years. The law was enforced only haphazardly (probably by design), however, and the London-based book industry soon became a largely unregulated commercial monopoly at the expense of the authors upon whose work its prosperity rested. A landmark legal judgment in 1774 (*Donaldson* v. *Beckett*) declared perpetual copyright to be unlawful in England and Scotland, and the balance of the century witnessed dizzying chicanery as publishers attempted to circumvent legal obstacles to their reprinting all manner of both old and recent books. Book prices fell; by the 1790s there were fewer "fine books" (large, lavishly illustrated, and expensively produced volumes) and many more small, cheap editions in plain wrappers. The closely printed pirated Irish reprints, often cleverly abridged from the originals and printed on cheap paper, frequently sold for half the price of the London originals, and these cheap reprints even made inroads into the lucrative Scottish trade in reprinted editions. In reality, the Irish reprint business was aimed primarily at an Irish (or Anglo-Irish) rather than an English clientele, comprised both of private individuals bent on assembling libraries at the least cost and of circulating library proprietors similarly interested in inexpensive stock. The Act of Union of 1800, which forcibly brought Ireland into the United Kingdom, placed the book trade in

Ireland under the same conditions (including the copyright law) as those in England and largely eliminated the issue of Irish reprints after 1801.

By the mid 1780s publishing and bookselling had begun to change in response to the dawn of the modern age of mass production and mass consumption. The growth of literacy during the final two decades of the eighteenth century, coupled with technological advances (like mechanized paper manufacture and the steam-driven rotary presses introduced after 1810)[3] and the proliferation of periodicals aimed at both specialist and general readers, meant that the market for print materials of all sorts was growing exponentially by the century's end. The prominent publisher James Dodsley (1724–97), who had succeeded his elder brother Robert as a major publisher, published the first editions of Charlotte Smith's *Elegiac Sonnets* (at her expense) beginning in 1784. Thomas Cadell (1742–1802), the leading London bookseller until he retired in 1793, was succeeded by Cadell and Davies, consisting of his son Thomas Jr. (1773–1836) and William Davies (d. 1820). Cadell and Davies also published Smith, and the extant extensive correspondence among them illustrates both the financial pragmatism that characterized publishers' relations with their authors, on one hand, and the often desperate financial straits of even popular writers like Smith who had to depend upon their pens to support their families. Following the death of his father Charles Rivington (1688–1742), who had in 1711 founded the prestigious and theologically oriented House of Rivington, John Rivington (1720–92) maintained the firm's religious focus. As other publishers were beginning to do, however, Rivington saw the potential for building his profits by capturing part of the expanding readership for periodicals; in 1793 he established the reactionary monthly periodical *The British Critic*, with Archdeacon Robert Nares (1753–1829) as editor. Throughout the Romantic era, periodicals proliferated, and they were seldom free of political, religious, or other ideological ties; indeed, many were subsidized by particular partisan groups or other special interests. One result was that their literary reviews, which typically claimed a disinterested objectivity, were in fact fiercely partisan, praising or attacking works and authors for their politics under the guise of aesthetic judgment.

Meanwhile, various publishers had begun to capitalize on what we now call the "canon": the body of works by earlier writers for which the copyright terms were ambiguous or simply convenient to evade. By the mid 1770s many publishers turned to publishing (or reprinting) texts of earlier authors, for whom no copyright fees fell due. The Edinburgh publisher James Kincaid, for instance, in 1773 introduced a forty-three-volume set of *British Poets* that set the standard for the sort of uniform editions that still persist in modern book club and limited edition series offerings. Buoyed by

Kincaid's success in marketing his series (primarily in Scotland), fellow Scot John Bell published and sold a cheaper series, *The Poets of Great Britain*, at his London shop, beginning in 1777 and comprising a remarkable 109 volumes by the time of its completion in 1792. Pilloried as pirates by other publishers, Kincaid and Bell nevertheless prospered. Bell offered new series like *Bell's British Theatre* and *Bell's Shakespeare*, for example, and subsequently added newspapers and periodicals to his enterprise. Unable to defeat the successful Scots, London publishers opted to respond in kind during the 1780s, cooperating to produce *The English Poets*, with appended biographies by Samuel Johnson, although the series was neither representative nor broadly inclusive. Between 1792 and 1795 appeared the thirteen royal octavo volumes of *The Works of the British Poets*, published in Edinburgh by Mundell and Son and in London by John and Arthur Arch. Another compendious edition was *The British Essayists* (1803), assembled in forty-five volumes by the Scottish journalist and editor Alexander Chalmers (1759–1834) and published in London by Joseph Johnson. This was followed in 1811 by Chalmers's nine-volume edition of Shakespeare's plays, published in London by J. Nichols and Son. Prose fiction witnessed comparable projects like the uniform compendium editions published by the London firm of Harrison and Company during the 1780s that combined double columns of small print with engraved illustrations after prominent artists like Thomas Stothard. Later came the landmark fifty-volume set of *British Novelists* published in 1810 by John Rivington's sons Francis (1745–1822) and Charles (1754–1831), with biographical prefaces by Anna Letitia Barbauld. Reprinting the works of dead writers, rather than contracting with living ones, provided publishers with easy revenue and their growing readerships with material, but it did nothing for most contemporary authors, who would have to wait for their moment.

Particularly important in the late eighteenth century was the London publisher Joseph Johnson (1738–1809). Although his firm, founded in the 1760s, initially emphasized religious subjects, Johnson expanded his list to include medicine and children's works along with literature. Sympathetic to the republican principles of the French Revolution, by 1790 he was publishing political works and had founded the monthly *Analytical Review* (1788–98), an important voice for reform that included Mary Wollstonecraft among its regular contributors. By 1797 it had a circulation of about 5,000 – a sizeable number when we remember that individual copies were often read by (or were read aloud to) dozens of people in coffee-houses, pubs, and other public meeting places. One indication of how sensitive authors were to the politics of potential publishers – and to the access that those publishers could give them to large numbers of sympathetic readers – is the fact that it was to Joseph Johnson that the young William Wordsworth took his early long poem, *An Evening Walk* (1793). That relatively conventional narrative of a walking tour at dusk has embedded at its center a powerful anti-war message that must have struck a responsive chord both with Johnson and with his readers.

It is hardly possible to underestimate the impact of the Minerva Press upon the publishing – and therefore the reading – scene in early Romantic-era Britain. Horace Walpole's *The Castle of Otranto* (1765) had launched the craze for "Gothic" tales that swept all the arts in Britain and on the Continent and that lasted until well into the Regency and the publication of *Frankenstein* in 1818. In London, the charismatic William Lane (c. 1745–1814) founded the Minerva Press in 1790, issuing remarkable numbers of sensational novels until he was succeeded upon his death by his partner A. K. Newman, who continued the business (although he gradually dropped the "Minerva Press" name) through the 1820s. During the 1790s, Minerva published fully a third of all the novels produced in London. Lane and Newman published the work of numerous women novelists, many of whom, like Regina Maria Roche (1764–1845) and Eliza Parsons (1739–1811), were both prolific and popular in their day and then forgotten afterward until recent efforts to recover the lives and works of historically neglected Romantic-era writers. Indeed, the contemporary notoriety of the Minerva Press is evident from the fact that six of the seven titles that Jane Austen has Isabella Thorpe recommend to Catherine Morland in *Northanger Abbey* (1818) as examples of "horrid" novels were issued by that press in the 1790s. Like his contemporary James Lackington, who pioneered the practice of "remaindering" unsold books he purchased at a large discount and then sold for a still profitable fraction of their original prices, Lane turned an enormous profit from the seemingly insatiable public appetite for novels. Lane's profits were fed not just by the sales of books themselves but also by the considerable fees accumulated through circulating libraries.

By 1810 there were close to a thousand circulating libraries in Great Britain, many attached to bookshops so as to give customers the option to buy or to borrow. By 1820 the number had grown to some 1,500, with stocks ranging from several hundred books to tens of thousands in a library like the Minerva Press's great establishment in Leadenhall Street. Most circulating libraries were maintained by individual publishers and booksellers and consequently featured their books, often to the exclusion of others' books, so some readers subscribed to multiple libraries to stay current on all the latest offerings. The circulating libraries operated on a system of graduated fees, charging more for the latest works and less for older ones. But the fees also reflected the number of books one might borrow, the length of the loan period, and the subscriber's physical proximity to the library itself. Rural readers paid more, generally, than urban ones, and typically borrowed for longer periods. In 1820, the upscale bookseller William Sams bound at the backs of novels he published a prospectus for his circulating library in St. James's Street. The prospectus stipulates, "Subscribers paying 5£. 5s. od. the Year; 3£. 3s. od. the Half Year; or, 1£. 16s. od. per Quarter, are allowed 12 Volumes in Town and 24 in the Country; and are entitled to the newest and most expensive Works in the Library." At the other end of the spectrum, "Subscribers paying 3£. 3s. od. the Year; 2£. 2s. od. the Half Year; or 1£. 5s. od. per Quarter, are allowed 6 Volumes in Town, and 12 in the Country, but are not entitled to the immediate perusal of New Works." Nor was it just the books that drew crowds to the circulating libraries. From the start they had established themselves as important (and sometimes notorious) centers of social activity: places to see and to be seen, as evidenced by an 1811 print showing a small circulating library in Scarborough (see www.pemberley. com/janeinfo/circlibr.jpg – last accessed February 8, 2010).

Besides circulating libraries, there were also subscription libraries. These were fee-based, too, but they shunned popular fiction, providing instead a sterner diet of serious nonfiction, much of it directly related to local business, industry, history, and both civic and religious institutions. These establishments courted the business and merchant classes, presenting themselves as reputable, even distinguished, alternatives to the circulating libraries and their ephemeral bourgeois clientele.

By 1800 there were some 300 booksellers in London, a number that would swell to nearly 500 by 1820. While Dublin commanded the market for cheap reprints, Edinburgh remained the center of learning (and of books) that it had been for centuries, and publishing was thriving elsewhere. Bristol, for example, where Coleridge lived and worked in the mid 1790s, was the home of the poet and publisher Joseph Cottle (1770–1853), who published Coleridge and Southey, as well as Wordsworth and Coleridge's anonymous *Lyrical Ballads* in 1798. Before he gave up the book business, Cottle had also printed in Bristol (under the name of "Biggs and Cottle," as printed on the final page) Mary Robinson's 1800 *Lyrical Tales*: the title page links him, as printer, with T. O. Longman, the volume's London publisher. Stuart Curran has explained in his 1994 study of Robinson's collection how entrepreneurial relationships between "provincial" publishers like Cottle and their London counterparts worked to the benefit of both in the emerging mass market for poetry that featured new, young poets like Robinson, Wordsworth, Southey, Coleridge, and Cottle himself. Other major publishers were based in growing industrial and commercial centers like Birmingham, Manchester, and Sheffield, while still others were associated with centers of political dissent like Norwich and Belfast, and many of these likewise entered into partnerships with major urban publishers.

## IV  1800 and after

The increasingly competitive nature of the publishing industry after 1800 produced a new literary and commercial scene. Books were being produced by the thousands – if not the tens of thousands. One estimate places the total number of books published between 1801 and 1829 at no less than 27,000 titles.[4] Traditionally associated with the more refined tastes of the gentry (many of whom were book collectors), poetry accounted for well over 5,000 volumes in Britain between 1800 and 1830. Novels, the more populist (and popular) genre avidly consumed by the emerging bourgeois class, appeared at comparable rates: more than 2,500 new novels appeared between 1800 and 1830, including over 500 from the Minerva Press alone. Meanwhile children's literature, science, history, philosophy, economics, and all manner of religious, domestic, and agricultural texts poured from the presses (sermons were especially numerous), while the periodical press promoted, excerpted, and otherwise advertised them all to an increasingly diversified reading public. Even small but notorious publishers like the republican Richard Phillips (1767–1840) flourished. Phillips moved from Leicester to London, where he built a minor publishing empire by selling cheap educational books. In 1796 he established the *Monthly Magazine*, which shrewdly packaged its reformist agenda for the serious but intellectually curious middle-class reader who would form the core of the nineteenth-century British bourgeoisie. The wide range of subjects and authors treated in the *Monthly*'s pages constitute a barometer of the reading tastes of this emerging readership.

More important, though, were the "great" publishing houses whose fortunes controlled much of the literary production of the high Romantic era. John Murray had already established his publishing firm by 1780, specializing particularly in medical publications, but after his death in 1793 his young son (the second John Murray) took over the business, aided by his father's protégé Samuel Highley, who left the partnership when the younger Murray turned twenty-one in 1801. Murray's Tory sentiments attracted a conservative readership for the *Quarterly Review*, which he founded in 1809 to counteract the considerable influence of Archibald Constable's Whig quarterly, the *Edinburgh Review*, which had commenced in 1802. Murray is perhaps best remembered today for his long association with Byron, beginning with his publication in 1812 of the first two cantos of *Childe Harold's Pilgrimage* that turned their author into an overnight sensation and assured Murray's reputation. Interestingly, Byron's manuscript was initially rejected by both Constable and Longman, the two leading publishers, and it was Byron's friend Robert Charles Dallas who finally placed it with Murray. Murray's uncertainty about the poem is evident from the fact that the first edition numbered only a modest 500 copies. In 1816 he began publishing Felicia Hemans, whose first books had been published by Cadell and Davies and who would later be published in Edinburgh by William Blackwood and Sons. By 1817 Murray was rejecting 700 poetry manuscripts a year. In 1819 Murray published his first novel by Jane Austen, *Emma*, following with *Persuasion* and *Northanger Abbey* soon after.

Longman, which had been established in 1724 by Thomas Longman I and had built a considerable list in religious and educational books, became under Thomas Longman III perhaps the most extensive and prestigious London publisher during the Romantic period. Longman published both Scott's *Minstrelsy of the Scottish Border* (1802–3) and (in association with Constable) his *Lay of the Last Minstrel* (1805), and although he opened the door for Murray when he turned down Byron's *English Bards and Scotch Reviewers* (1809, published in multiple editions by the London publisher James Cawthorne), Longman seized upon the increasingly popular Thomas Moore, who published all but one of his books with that publisher. How important was the good relationship between authors and their publishers is indicated by the fact that Longman subsequently offered Moore the remarkable sum of £3,000 for *Lalla Rookh* (1817) before Moore had even begun composition. Longman published in all fields, its relatively conservative tastes reflecting the publisher's estimate of its customer base, and, like Murray, it was also a major player in the wholesale book trade. The Longman "group" included a number of partners during the period: its title pages included among the publishers' names at various points not just Longman's but also those of Hurst, Rees, Orme, Brown, and others. Although by the end of the Romantic era Longman largely abandoned literary publishing, its influence on the literary scene until then was profound.

Around 1807 Henry Colburn began publishing fiction in London and soon had a fashionable West End circulating library featuring attractive books for a decidedly upmarket clientele. He founded the *New Monthly Magazine* in 1814 and the weekly *Literary Gazette* in 1817; these periodicals kept Colburn's books in the public eye, and by the end of the 1820s he was the leading London publisher of fiction, publishing authors like John Banim, Anna Eliza Bray, and William Pitt Scargill.

Among the lesser London publishers were Baldwin, Cradock, and Joy, who published Charles Lamb's "Elia" essays in their journal, the *London Magazine*, and Thomas Tegg (1776–1846), who made a fortune with cheap reprints and chapbook redactions of popular novels. Tegg and others paid both authors and redactors to produce these chapbooks, whose radically abbreviated texts consisted primarily of the most luridly melodramatic passages from the originals. Produced and sold cheaply to a relatively unsophisticated readership, these works provided remarkably good profits for their publishers, although those who prepared the texts – like the prolific Sarah Scudgill Wilkinson (1779–1831), who wrote both long, multi-volume novels and abbreviated chapbook versions of them – typically were paid scandalously poorly for their efforts.

Late in the period, Edward Moxon began operating in London after learning the trade while working for Longman. Charles Lamb befriended the young Moxon and subsequently introduced him to Wordsworth in 1826. It was Moxon who in 1839 published the first authorized edition of Shelley's poetry, edited by the poet's widow, followed in 1840 by her selected edition of Shelley's prose. He also published poets like Southey, "Barry Cornwall" (Bryan Waller Procter), and Wordsworth himself in an edition of 1836–7. Mary Shelley's father, the Utopian anarchist philosopher and author William Godwin, began in 1805 with his second wife to publish works intended for children, most notably Charles and Mary Lamb's *Tales from Shakespeare* (1807). Interestingly, the controversial Godwin's name was not featured in the firm's business dealings or its publications, so as not to adversely affect the business.

In Scotland the key players were Archibald Constable (1774–1827) and William Blackwood (1776–1834), both in Edinburgh. Blackwood's signal achievement came in 1816 when he entered into an agreement with Murray to publish Walter Scott's *Tales of My Landlord* series, which proved a great moneymaker. But Scott proved unreliable in the long run, and the cagy Tory Blackwood wisely diversified his interests, including founding in 1817 a periodical to contest the influence of the Whiggish *Edinburgh Review*. The aggressively flamboyant *Edinburgh Monthly Magazine*, quickly retitled *Blackwood's Edinburgh Magazine*, was characterized by a slashing style practiced by major contributors like "Christopher North" (John Wilson, 1785–1854) and John Gibson Lockhart (1794–1854). Although Blackwood and Murray subsequently parted company over the direction of the journal, Blackwood continued to publish even authors whom his journal usually reviewed unfavorably, such as Byron and Shelley.

Scottish literary publishing increased sharply in the 1820s, with publishers releasing, either independently or in conjunction with other publishers, both more titles and increasingly large editions. Edinburgh's geographical proximity to both Ireland and the growing industrial north of England gave the Edinburgh publishers in particular a considerable market-and-supply advantage in these areas, and the number of Scottish printers also surged to keep up with this growing demand. These were not wholly boom times, however; both Constable and the printer James Ballantyne suffered bankruptcy in 1826. Walter Scott, who was closely involved in both these failures, was stunned; he devoted his final years to writing in an effort to satisfy the huge debts that he and his collaborators had incurred and that had led to their crash. The reversals involving Constable, Ballantyne, and Scott reflect the volatility of the industry in the 1820s. Although the market hit a high point in 1823–5, the following year witnessed widespread economic difficulties that seriously affected publishers. London firms like Hurst, Robinson, and Co., and others, fearful of a domino effect, turned cautious, electing to publish less in literature and more in history, science, moral and vocational instruction, and the domestic arts, for all of which there was now a ready market of bourgeois consumers.

In Ireland, the first decade following the Act of Union (1800) saw a dramatic reduction in publishers as the lucrative reprint market disappeared. But by the middle of the Regency several publishers were active in Cork, Belfast, Limerick, Newry, and especially Dublin. These latter included John Cumming, who partnered with Henry Colburn of London and George Goldie of Edinburgh to publish the popular novels of Eaton Stannard Barrett, Selina Davenport, and "Anthony Frederick Holstein," and the Irish nationalist poetry of J. S. Anna Liddiard. The road to success, in Ireland as in provincial cities throughout Britain, increasingly lay in collaborative publication, with publishers pooling their resources and their expenses to mutual advantage. Most often the "senior partner" in such consortia was an established London publisher like Colburn or Longman whose large capital and diversified list provided both security and visibility. Even so thoroughly "Irish" an author as Sydney Owenson (later Lady Morgan), who published her first poetic collection, *Poems* (1801), in both Dublin and London, turned for her second collection, *The Lay of an Irish Harp* (1807), exclusively to the London publisher Richard Phillips, who had already published both *The Novice of St. Dominick* (1806) and *The Wild Irish Girl* (1806). Nationalist sentiments notwithstanding, like many of her contemporaries Owenson learned early on the lessons of the marketplace and placed her work accordingly.

All of this is not to suggest that publishing was the exclusive domain of publishers in London, Edinburgh, and Dublin, and of the "lesser" centers of Oxford, Cambridge, Bristol, York, and Glasgow, for publishers abounded throughout Britain. In terms of poetry (which has been especially widely surveyed), probably 15 to 20 percent of all publications came from the provinces and represented more than 250 places of publication.[5] And while the majority of novels were published in London and Edinburgh, the publishers and co-publishers identified on their title pages represented no fewer that seventy towns and villages. The same was true for extra-literary works like sermons, histories, scientific writing, and domestic publications. Nevertheless, provincially produced works tended generally to be limited in number and scope of circulation. Friends and neighbors subscribed to one another's works, whether out of friendship, charity, or even genuine interest, but most of the books that issued from the minor provincial publishers never achieved sufficient visibility to distinguish their authors unless they were subsequently reissued by the major publishers, in which case the original author usually received no compensation and the provincial publisher very little. So while both novels and volumes of poetry continued to be published outside London between 1800 and 1830, many of these have vanished, while in other cases the few copies that remain are tucked away in remote collections, largely unseen, unrecorded, unread, and virtually "lost," their authors as obscure today as the books themselves.

## NOTES

1. Frank Arthur Mumby, "Part One: From the Earliest Times to 1870," in Frank Arthur Mumby and Ian Norrie, *Publishing and Bookselling*, 5th edn., rev. (London: Jonathan Cape, 1974), p. 154.
2. William St. Clair, *The Reading Nation in the Romantic Period* (Cambridge University Press, 2004), pp. 649–50. St. Clair's book provides a particularly detailed account of both the physical aspects of book production in Romantic-era Britain and the shifting intellectual, aesthetic, *and economic* dynamics of authorship and publishing.
3. Peter Garside suggests that although such innovations revolutionized the publication of newspapers (the London *Times* introduced steam-driven presses in 1814), their greatest impact upon the book trade came after the mid 1820s: Peter Garside, "The English Novel in the Romantic Era: Consolidation and Dispersal," in Peter Garside et al., eds., *The English Novel 1770–1829: A Bibliographical Survey of Prose Fiction Published in the British Isles*, 2 vols. (Oxford University Press, 2000), p. 39.
4. The number, based upon the *English Catalogue of Books*, is cited by Garside in "The English Novel," p. 21.
5. C. R. Johnson, "Preface," in *Provincial Poetry 1789–1839: British Verse Printed in the Provinces: The Romantic Background* (London: Jed Press, 1992), p. [ix]. This extensive bibliography documents the diversity of verse produced by provincial publishers.

# 8

STUART CURRAN

# Women readers, women writers

"Well, Miss Elliot ... we shall never agree I suppose upon this point. No man and woman would, probably. But let me observe that all histories are against you, all stories, prose and verse ... I do not think I ever opened a book in my life which had not something to say upon woman's inconstancy. Songs and proverbs, all talk of woman's fickleness. But perhaps you will say, these were all written by men."

"Perhaps I shall. – Yes, yes, if you please, no reference to examples in books. Men have had every advantage of us in telling their own story. Education has been theirs in so much higher a degree; the pen has been in their hands. I will not allow books to prove any thing."

(*Persuasion*, chapter 23)

Coming very near the end of Austen's last novel (1818), this sharp observation on the gender biases inherent in literary discourse has often been taken as a characteristically oblique expression of her feminism as well as a defense of her singular craft. Notwithstanding the truth that the passage reveals considerable self-reflection, the ironies (the pen is after all in Austen's hand) attending that traditional reading are manifold: it demands that we accept at face value what is, both in the novel and life, knowingly, wittily, undercut. Within the structure of the novel, this crucial exchange between Captain Harville and Anne Elliot is in some sense the turning point, as Anne, ostensibly asserting woman's constancy in the abstract, speaks over Harville's shoulder specifically to address Wentworth, who is across the room writing a letter. In essence her contrived indirect discourse allows him the objectivity needed to lay down that pen of self-centered inscription and at last "read" the truth of her love for him. The ironic reversal implicit in the passage likewise extends beyond the novel into the literary marketplace, where in the last months of her life, which is to say at this very point when she was asserting woman's veritable silence, Austen was at last well aware of her major artistic and popular success. The generations of critics who have here read Austen literally (or more exactly, have read Anne Elliot literally) have in the process authorized themselves, as the inscribers of literary history, to isolate her as a solitary feminine presence within their continuum of "masters" of the pen, as the first woman writer in English deserving serious attention. This removal has in turn authorized a second, in which Austen has been dislocated from her historical period back a full generation or more to speak for eighteenth-century stabilities against the storm and stress of Romantic Europe.

This is not to say that Anne Elliot is not right, that, as Janet Todd notes in linking with Austen's a similar comment made by the Duchess of Newcastle a century and a half earlier, "the image of woman conveyed to the modern reader is overwhelmingly made by men."[1] What is accentuated by the linkage of authors here, however, is the crucial place occupied by the person who "conveys" the image to another time. If the complaint of women authors about male control of their conception is already a century and a half old, another implicit corollary of Anne's indirect discourse is that we may have been trusting to the wrong conveyance all along. By the final third of the eighteenth century, at least, a man must have been, like Captain Harville (and, for that measure, Captains Benwick and Wentworth), rather a long time at sea not to be aware that the culture of writing was becoming rapidly feminized. Literary historians have in recent decades begun to attend seriously to the meaning of this remarkable shift in status as the woman writer created a profession for herself; and the consequences for a just history are yet by no means wholly apparent. As new technologies clear away the obstacles from bibliographical research and textual recovery, it has required continual, and in the end a major, adjustment of the record. At this point in the process we can assert two indisputable truths: one is that there were not mere dozens, nor even hundreds, but actually thousands, of women whose writing was published in Great Britain in the half-century between 1780 and 1830 that subsumes the Romantic period;[2] and the other is that until this generation we have known very little about it. What that says about the sociology of literary criticism is obvious to any reader and therefore need not occupy us further than to subjoin, if perhaps by stretching Austen's intent, her earlier proviso about Anne Elliot's amiable but patronizing mentor in literature: "Captain Harville was no reader; but he had contrived excellent accommodations, and fashioned very pretty shelves, for a tolerable collection of well-bound volumes ... "

## I

Women writers in England of the Restoration and early eighteenth century, for the most part, divided along lines of class and morality. A writer for the theatre, like Aphra Behn or her successor Susanna Centlivre, was understood to be compromised by the notorious moral laxity of the stage. The early novel inherited the tone, as it did the audience, of the Restoration, so that figures like Delarivier Manley and Eliza Haywood who specialized in *romans à clef* were personally tinged by the scandals they rehearsed in fiction. The social position of a professional woman writer, in other words, was little better than that of a mistress, and her precarious financial status indeed seems often to have reduced her to that level. On the other side were members of the aristocracy like the Duchess of Newcastle, the Countess of Winchelsea, Lady Mary Chudleigh, or Lady Mary Wortley Montague, all of whom made a marked imprint on the literary scene of the late seventeenth and early eighteenth centuries. Yet, the aristocratic woman, if at least relatively free to pursue her own interests, was in general an adjunct to the larger masculine circle in which her spouse figured. Although the type would survive into the Romantic age – Georgiana Cavendish, the Duchess of Devonshire, was a noted patron and author of the much circulated verses "The Passage of the Mountain of the St. Gothard" – the number of such titled women of letters was perforce too limited to sustain, let alone truly to define, a distinct feminine literary culture. That was left in England to a stratum of the upper bourgeoisie whose writing initially tended to a decorous piety, figures like Elizabeth Singer Rowe and Judith Madan. By the mid eighteenth century the small coterie for which such women wrote had greatly expanded, and in effect it split in two. An entire generation of evangelical women writers was energized and given patronage by Selina, Countess of Huntington: it is due to her exertions, for instance, that the black slave Phillis Wheatley's poetry was published in England not America. But the larger group, not openly less religious but certainly more attuned to the world, furnished the main channel for what in less than a generation became a flood of women seeking an identity, and sometimes an independence, through writing.

The Bluestockings formed in London in the 1750s and 1760s under the nominal leadership of Elizabeth Montagu and from the first prudently gathered into their activities such male luminaries of London's intellectual and literary worlds as David Garrick and Samuel Johnson. For the most part these were women of wealth and social position, evidence of the dramatically widening prosperity of the times. The Bluestockings were simply the extension into the distaff of the intellectual values and social etiquette of Enlightenment London. This logical development of the highly concentrated civilization of a capital city found its parallel in the eighteenth-century salons organized by women in other European centers, particularly Paris, Berlin, and Rome, though it might be said, by way of distinction, that the English Bluestockings, in accordance with the expectations of their culture, publicly distinguished themselves for their private virtues. Likewise, simple logic would dictate that this serious and privileged London elite would come to be emulated in England's regional capitals and even market towns, as the general economic well-being of the later eighteenth century exfoliated throughout the land. The by now notorious disengagement of bourgeois women from the necessities of work, which was surely welcomed then by many who envied the upper-class its luxuries, contributed directly to the spread of literacy and the appeal of the literary among these women. Reading and writing engaged the attention, stimulated the mind, and gave fashionable women something more to do than exchange visits. The Bluestockings set themselves no intellectual limitations: they debated moral questions, translated the classics, engaged in influential literary criticism. Although some later writers, notably Byron, disparaged their achievements, throughout the later eighteenth century they exerted a strong force on literary culture. From a purely economic perspective, their own wealth and refined connections allowed them to foster an audience large enough to contribute to the support of a number of women intellectuals. Among them was the paragon of learning, Elizabeth Carter, who secured £1,000 in subscriptions for her translation of the stoic philosopher Epictetus which appeared in 1758. The multiple further printings of this work, plus numerous editions of her poems and further writings, were sufficient to earn her a comfortable independence for almost a half century thereafter.

Although Epictetus fitted squarely within the then customary trade of London publishers, this translation did nothing to jar the assumptions underpinning male culture. Indeed, it underscored the primacy of classical learning and philosophical meditation, from which women had traditionally been excluded by their education. When the young Anna Aikin, later Mrs. Barbauld, came onto the scene with her highly lauded *Poems* in 1773, she indicated a similar alliance of interests, writing with a classical elegance and heading virtually every poem with a Latin epigram. The volume was in its fourth edition within another year, and she on her way to a literary career that would likewise span a half century. Generally speaking, the network sponsored by the Bluestockings succeeded by forging this kind of common cause with men of refinement, embracing the ends of a traditional university education (from which, of course, the women were wholly excluded) and of customary liberal and humanitarian ideals. So deeply committed were they to these values of the age that Hannah More, in two sprightly poems of the 1780s – "Sensibility" and "The Bas Bleu; or Conversation" – could suggest that the true upholders of England's Enlightenment civilization were Bluestocking women.

Given how comparatively few women had the education and means to devote themselves so unreservedly to high culture – and even Hannah More's commitment would not survive the stresses of the 1790s – there had to be other avenues for women writers. These too depended upon a newly enfranchised female readership, but one that was comparatively large and free of the elitist discriminations of the Bluestockings. These women readers virtually demanded a room of their own, to adapt Virginia Woolf's phrase, and what they got in response was the novel. That is to say, that by the last three decades of the eighteenth century the great first wave in the development of the English novel – dominated by Richardson, Fielding, Goldsmith, Smollett, and Sterne – had run its course, a course that, buttressed by the addition of Defoe at its beginning, has for years comprised the standard college curriculum in English eighteenth-century fiction. This modern feat of closure, however, it should be clear, has been managed by omitting the entire succeeding generation of fiction (with the occasional exception of Burney's *Evelina*), when the genre was virtually taken over by women. So wholly did the novel come to be identified as a woman's form that by the end of the century women seem to have accounted for well over half the novels written during it.

Similarly, they read what they wrote – and prodigiously. Men read novels too, of course, but the disease of reading life according to the conventions of fiction, from which Sheridan's Lydia Languish (*The Rivals*) and Austen's Catherine Morland (*Northanger Abbey*) are perhaps the best-known sufferers, was indicted as a particularly feminine affliction.[3] On a serious cultural level, however, the sudden emergence of the novel as a woman's genre had a dual significance. On the one hand, it testified that women had a grasp of quotidian reality every bit as detailed as men's; indeed, given their lack of professional liberation from day-to-day demands, they could be said to be wholly immersed in it (at least when they were not reading – or writing – novels). On the other hand, the rise of the novel threw starkly into relief the extent to which poetry had been sealed off as a male, upper-class fiefdom, requiring for its license not simply birth and breeding, but a common education and exclusive standards of shared taste.[4] That, of course, did not keep women from aspiring to it, whether like the Bluestockings by honoring the agreed terms or, like later women poets, by shifting the accepted grounds underneath generic expectations. By the 1820s, at the point that the term poetess attains common cultural currency, poetry too could be claimed to have become a woman's genre. When Tennyson's friend Trench criticized his early style – "Tennyson, we cannot live in art" – he was, in essence, demanding that his friend forsake the female space of enclosure, fantasy, and long past ages for a contemporary and necessarily masculine outdoors.

The emergence of the novel in the early Romantic period as a separatist genre is understandable; and its capacity to encode a separatist agenda, even if the denouement would be the inevitable marriage, can be glimpsed in the prime examples of the kind – like Burney's *Evelina*, Smith's *Emmeline*,

Inchbald's *A Simple Story*, and Austen's *Emma* – all of which reveal bright, frustrated, and manipulated young women who have no recourse but themselves to manipulate the males who exert power over them. But that the novel is not unique in this respect, that all the major genres tend to shift their grounds when women begin writing in them so as to reflect the problematic condition of women within family and social structures, accentuates the importance of textual recovery and historical reconception for the age. To cite another example from the early Romantic period, the theatre of the last two decades of the eighteenth century has until recent years been virtually ignored by students, and with that disregard has gone its central office as a social index to the culture. It is perhaps coincidental that the dominant voices writing for the stage during these decades are, in the 1780s, Hannah Cowley and, in the 1790s, Elizabeth Inchbald, who profited from the general improvement in the moral image of the theatre and were not called upon, like Behn and Centlivre, to sacrifice their good name for the curtain to rise. They too reveal a distinctly female perspective, which (since the texts have been until recently unavailable) has in general been gleaned only from explanatory notes to *Mansfield Park*, where it is discovered that the particular impropriety of the Bertram children's theatrical venture stems from the subject-matter of Inchbald's *Lover's Vows*, in which an unwed and abandoned mother returns to the scene of her seduction by an aristocrat and with her bastard son claims justice for herself and legitimacy for him. Hannah Cowley's *métier* was not this forerunner of the late Victorian problem-play but rather the comedy of manners. She was essentially Sheridan's successor in the genre, with the notable difference that her major creations are all vehicles for actresses, starting with an unknown Sarah Siddons who debuted in her first play, *The Runaway*, in 1776 (it was coincidentally David Garrick's last production). As with the novel, if one looks behind the obligatory bows to social custom, Cowley's plays continually reveal unexpected breaches of propriety. One of the main plotlines exemplifying her title, *A Bold Stroke for a Husband* (1783), has Victoria, left in the country while her husband philanders about Madrid, seize the initiative and go to the city, where she dons male clothes and seduces her husband's mistress away from him. Doubtless, this can all be justified, as Victoria reassures the audience, for the sake of her children, but that does not alter the fundamental questions her transvestism poses about the assumptions of cultural authority. This play and *The Belle's Stratagem* (1780), another of her comedies centering on shrewd female manipulation, were standard repertory pieces well into the nineteenth century; which is to say, they were understood as exemplary productions of their age. So, it goes without saying, was their author.

## II

What the foregoing survey of the late eighteenth century cursorily indicates is that the burst of activity by women writers that marks the 1790s was not so much a novel cultural phenomenon as a logical development of forces already in place. In the 1770s and 1780s women had moved to the forefront of the publishing world. What is surprising – even to the extreme – is how little real threat men seem to have felt at this determined incursion into their realm. Boswell's propensity for recording every snippy remark uttered by Johnson leaves us with the memory that he compared women preachers to dogs walking on their hind feet, but what should be emphasized is his constant presence among the Bluestockings and his general encouragement of Elizabeth Carter, Hester Thrale, and the young Helen Maria Williams. For Johnson the determining basis for judgment was likely to be politics not gender. It is certainly true that these years witnessed much satire upon scribbling ladies and a commonplace fear of the effects from their romantic novels on well-bred but innocent daughters. Yet, so stereotyped are these strictures that they appear mere ready-to-hand conventions: if a tone of condescension enters them, it seldom goes beyond the usual huff and puff of the patriarchy vaunting its institutionalized prerogatives. An objective chronicle of the 1780s would have to allow that there appeared ample room for women alike as readers and as writers in the rapidly expanding fortunes of the book trade and that no one strongly felt the need to stand in the way. By the end of the 1790s, however, as is indicated by Richard Polwhele's *Unsexed Females* (1798), which excoriated a series of prominent women writers as carrying out Mary Wollstonecraft's pernicious agenda and altogether constituting a serious menace to the existing state of things, the lines were drawn very differently. Perhaps the confrontation was inevitable and by nature could not be glossed over by the geniality of late Enlightenment manners. Still, the equation of writing women with demands for female equality and both together with all the excesses of the Terror in France, which was the product of, and the propaganda elicited by, the reactionary politics of the early years of warfare, determined much subsequent history, including the essential ideological control of the "Angel in the House" syndrome years after the Napoleonic Wars had receded into history.

But even such pressures could only divert or attempt to channel the essential flood of writing by women. The 1790s were heady times – "Bliss was it in that dawn to be alive," Wordsworth recalled – for women as well as men. There were a few casualties. The effortless and elegant *vers de société* that Lady Sophia Burrell produced for her circle at Tunbridge Wells or that Lady Anne Miller commissioned for various charities and printed over the years in four volumes of *Poetical Recreations at a Villa near Bath* no more than Boucher or Fragonard could survive the transition into the new realities of a revolutionary age. But for every loss there were a dozen gains. The 1790s in Britain form the arena for the first concerted expression of feminist thought in modern European culture: the terms of argument are heavily weighted by the conventional (which is to say, now long since exploded) wisdom of the age, which supported masculinist dominance by the twin pillars of female intellectual inferiority and the woman's essential role in the family. But Mary Wollstonecraft was by no means the only prescient vindicator of woman's rights, and the scope of agitation and its underlying cultural dynamics during this decade have yet to be fully explored. It is clear, however, that a wholly new sense of empowerment impels women writers, whatever the individual's political professions. Entire new genres dominated by women writers entered publishers' lists: one certain aspect of the feminist polemics of the 1790s was the intense debate that erupted over the education of children, particularly daughters. Conduct books tumbled forth, often assuming a newly polemical or adversarial tone. In *Practical Education* (1798) Maria Edgeworth with her father Richard initiated the rudiments of a modern, scientific approach to child development. Children's literature flourished, attaining with the new century and the verse productions of Ann and Jane Taylor and Adelaide O'Keeffe a new level of psychological and social realism and with the animal conclaves of Catherine Anne Dorset (Charlotte Smith's sister) an assured hold on the fantastic. Less innocent of ulterior purpose were Hannah More's *Cheap Repository Tracts*, which started forth in 1795 as the first concerted attempt to speak to the working poor in their own language and terms: the intent was undoubtedly reactionary, but paradoxically, the effect was revolutionary, embodying a new stylistic and social realism, stimulating a readership and a sense of cohesive identity among the working class.[5]

Something of the same dynamic of unanticipated inversion attends the birth of another genre without precedent, journalism from behind enemy lines. The 1790s, which saw all of Europe swept up for the first time in ideological warfare, elicited much skirmishing by paper as well. But if the grand debate on ideology is recalled from the clash between Burke and Paine (though Wollstonecraft was Burke's prior antagonist) and if the economic and purely political commentary were monopolized by men, the on-the-scene reportage fell by chance into the hands of women. Helen Maria Williams, confident as a poet and novelist of sensibility, adopted the tone of transcendent observer to chronicle her experiences in eight volumes of *Letters from France* between 1792 and 1798. Arriving in Paris just in time for the celebration of the Federation on July 14, 1790, she reacts with transport to the spectacle of a half million celebrants in the Champ du Mars: "it required but the common feelings of humanity, to become in that moment a citizen of the world" (*Letters*, 1, 14). Wollstonecraft's own account, *An Historical and Moral View of the Origin and Progress of the French Revolution and the Effect It Has Produced in Europe*, published in 1794 during the Terror, emphasizes her role as independent observer viewing events through the prism, thus from a distance, of history and morality. Like Williams, she casts herself as a citizen of the world, affirming against the debacle produced in France the certain necessity of representative government in modern Europe and refusing to throw any sop to Burke's argument for "virtual representation." Both women execrate Robespierre and exhibit something like pity for the reactionary fearfulness of Burke. Although they both were in danger, and Williams claimed her writings so infuriated Robespierre that she had to flee France for safety, the tone of absolute transcendence they adopt comes naturally, enforced by their having no personal stake beyond a moral one in the events unfolding before their eyes. Citizens of the world, like women in England, do not vote. Women doubtless will suffer the consequences (Williams is the foremost mythologizer of the heroic martyrdom of Madame Roland), but they do not make the political decisions that bring on revolutions and plunge countries into wars of empire. The implicit claim of Williams and Wollstonecraft, then, is that in such a fraught time only a woman can afford to be honest. Their dual assumptions – that the sole power women can claim comes from the pen, and that only the disinterested can wield moral authority – were by no means, however, limited to the urgent historical conditions that prompted their accounts, but have informed the polemical stance of women well into the modern age. Given the hovering presence of war and its effects throughout the Romantic period, this assertion of privileged authority might well be expected to survive the reaction against the feminism of the 1790s. It did so in a variety of modes, alike informing the dark jeremiad of Anna Barbauld, *Eighteen Hundred and Eleven* (1812), and flickering over the dazzling surface of Lady Morgan's atlas of the Bourbon Restoration, *France* (1816).

But the sense of impotence in the face of cataclysmic events can have far less self-assured consequences. Charlotte Smith, separated from her improvident husband and raising a large family by dint of her pen alone, during this decade produced novel after novel in which the dislocations of the European war result in exile and wandering, or are domesticated into the threat of financial ruin. Both themes coalesce in her lengthy blank-verse meditation of 1793, *The Emigrants*, in which she reads a collapsing European civilization through her own condition of helplessness before a legal system that is deaf to her just rights. The crippled Mary Robinson, whom Daniel Stewart, proprietor of the liberal *Morning Post*, dubbed "the English Sappho," similarly wrote across genres and against fate. She was a principal creator of the records of the marginalized that are most commonly exemplified in these years by the publication of Wordsworth and Coleridge's *Lyrical Ballads* in 1798. Her *Lyrical Tales*, printed in 1800 weeks before the second edition of their collection and her own premature death, by its title indicates its rivalry and in its contents reveals an extremity of condition often little short of existential. Smith and Robinson were perhaps the leading women writers of poetry and fiction during this decade, but their accent on the dispossessed and marginalized was widely replicated by the voices of other women, from Hannah More's working poor to the portraits of victimized women in Mary Wollstonecraft's unfinished *Wrongs of Woman; or Maria* (1798), Mary Hays's *Memoirs of Emma Courtney* (1796), Elizabeth Hamilton's *Memoirs of Modern Philosophers* (1800), or, in the next decade, Amelia Opie's *Adeline Mowbray* (1804). Like the moral stance of Williams and Wollstonecraft, this concern was centrally tied to the authentic condition of women, and, once voiced, was not to be repressed by domestic enclosure. By the 1820s, in the works of Felicia Hemans and Letitia Landon, women are abused and expire in such ingenious ways and with such inexhaustible plentitude that to a dispassionate reader of a later time their concentration on female suffering may seem simply macabre. In its historical context, however, it takes on other dimensions.

Within the ferment of women's writings in the 1790s the assimilation of the Gothic by women writers is a further development likewise deeply informed by notions of female impotence and repression. Perhaps it is because a later critical time takes such matters as significant cultural integers that the Gothic mode no longer merits condescension and, at least in the case of Ann Radcliffe, has even earned serious appraisal for its capacity to render psychic interiorities and the unexamined myths of power and submission undergirding modern society. If Radcliffe demystifies all her dark recesses by rational explanation and in the end defuses and domesticates every threat of chaotic excess in moves her male contemporaries "Monk" Lewis and the Marquis de Sade significantly refuse to make, it may be that her instincts as a popular novelist parallel her awareness of how linked to fictive self-delusion are society's acts of self-preservation. One can, of course, read in the formulaic titillating and debunking by which she both has and eats her cake her own representation of the tensions within which society binds the woman author. What is important not to lose sight of, however, is why women novelists like Ann Radcliffe and Charlotte Dacre could venture with virtual impunity into such unladylike regions. The close association between a presumptive essential female nature and the social and psychological ramifications of the Gothic is of ancient standing. It was little over a century before Radcliffe wrote that witches were still being tried and executed in both Old and New England: the basic type is still discernible in such borrowings from folk tradition as Madge Wildfire and her deranged mother in Scott's *Heart of Midlothian*. Moreover, the Gothic is the Roman Catholic cousin of the pagan fairy tale, and in the realm of fairy the landholders were mainly women. James Hogg's mother is purported to have complained that if Scott kept up with his antiquarian gatherings of songs and legends he would drive the fairies out of Scotland. Both Hogg (*Queen Hynde*) and his countryman William Tennant (*Anster Fair*) during the Regency published major works exploiting Scottish fairy lore. But a recuperative scholarship will find that, both first and last, women had sanction as guides to this realm where the forbidden and the natural are so troublingly intertwined.[6]

To concentrate attention thus on the innovations marking women's writing in the 1790s should not obscure the extent to which women authors were competing ably on the same turf as men. The sonnet revival marking this decade, for instance, and which we normally associate with Coleridge and Southey, and then after the turn of the century most notably with Wordsworth, was impelled all along by the multiple and expanding editions of Charlotte Smith's *Elegiac Sonnets*. In her wake came other women poets: her rival Anna Seward was in the forefront, but others like Ann Bannerman (1800, 1807), Mrs. B. Finch (1805), Martha Hanson (1809), and Mary Johnson (1810), whose names have survived less well, also produced volumes largely or wholly composed of sonnets, the latter three explicitly acknowledging Smith as an inspiration. Although in fiction an Ann Radcliffe might get most of her local color by elaborating what she could extract from travel books, both Mary Robinson and Charlotte Smith were fluent in French and had lived on the Continent: their novels indicate that they too are citizens of the world. Anna Barbauld published her "Epistle to William Wilberforce," on the evils of the Slave Trade, under her own name in 1791; but she also anonymously published three political orations in a style of such commanding vigor that, when the word leaked out that they were written by a woman, it seemed incredible to all. The second of these, "Sins of Government, Sins of the Nation" (1793), a work whose anti-war sentiments and stirring rhetoric resonate with timeless power, was printed under the signature of "A Volunteer." That *nom de plume* may stand appropriately as a collective signature for the women in the 1790s who volunteered to enter every list previously reserved for male authors and to speak with equal authority.

## III

The problem, of course, is that they lacked real authority. Outspoken women did not force Pitt's government rightward into its fanatical anti-Jacobin reaction, but they certainly fell victim to its excesses. The pressure was less open than for men – there were no women indicted in the treason trials of 1794–5 – but it was no less sure for being cast largely in symbolic terms. Williams was flayed by the conservative press for remaining in France. Wollstonecraft was transformed, particularly after Godwin's publication of his *Memoirs* in 1798 revealed her affair with Gilbert Imlay and her attempt at suicide after being abandoned, into an exemplary caricature regularly held up for public reproof. Godwin's indiscretion was of enormous consequence for the feminist cause in the nineteenth century, though it is probable that even without the ready spectre of Wollstonecraft other means would have been found to stifle the liberationist impulse of the 1790s. Yet, whatever the insistence on female propriety, or the constant reiteration of the appointed role of women in family life, the obvious truth is that women kept on writing, continuing a professional career by which many secured their independence. As might be expected in this age, the more conservative the viewpoint, the more likelihood that the writer would be lavishly praised, widely read, and therefore paradoxically all the more capable of attaining such independence. Hannah More was a force to be reckoned with in the last four decades of her life, even as she argued that women did not need such power for their happiness. No one has determined what her publisher paid for Jane West's book-length paean in verse to traditional values, *The Mother* (1809), but Mrs. West (as she was called by all) sustained a very public presence in the debate on woman's role, and she earned a good living from her novels.

Rather than see inconsistency or, worse, hypocrisy in such attitudes, we should perhaps recognize the priority of the enveloping cultural contradictions within which these figures labored. The interiorizing of conflict and resolution that marks so much male poetry of the Romantic period thus manifests itself in the writing of women as well. But in a very real way the role to which they turned was ready-made and tested: in the early years of the nineteenth century it would become a mode of being. Felicia Hemans neatly encapsulates its nature in titling her first full volume of mature verses *Domestic Affections, and Other Poems* (1812). As men turned inward to reflect on reflection and to imagine the nature of imaginative activity (patterns of thought perhaps most fully instanced in Wordsworth's *Prelude*), women turned in upon their essential sensibility to celebrate exquisite feeling as a value unto itself. The passions that had led Mary Wollstonecraft into a self-destructive morass were firmly kept at bay, and the softer affections, particularly as elicited and exemplified in family life, were defined as woman's distinctive province. Hemans herself became, above all, the creator and enforcer of this ideological control masking itself as praise for feminine instinct and female duty. And yet, she, too, writes from a trap of cultural contradiction, her particular form of female duty being to earn enough money to be able, as a deserted wife, to raise her children by her own means. That obligation Hemans fulfilled to the highest standard of success, since she became, it should never be forgotten, the best-selling English poet of the nineteenth century. Self-sacrifice, appropriately enough, is her abiding theme.

The means Hemans used to attain her considerable success deserve analysis, since they delineate so directly the characteristic literary bent of women writers in the early decades of the nineteenth century. First, Hemans is broadly eclectic in the range of her subject-matter, more so in fact than any contemporary except Southey. She mined, as she represented, the new cosmopolitanism of the age; which is to say, she read and wrote with equal amplitude on virtually any subject. Her mother, Felicity Wagner, was daughter of an Italian mother and a German father who acted as Imperial (German) and Tuscan Consul in Liverpool, and she directed her daughter's early education in multilingual paths, so that from an early age she was fluent in German, French, and Italian. By 1818 when she published her *Translations from Camoens and Other Poets*, Hemans had added Portuguese and Spanish to her repertory. Her poems are sprinkled with epigraphs from these languages, visible testimony of an erudition suited to an age of imperial expansion for which traditional classical training was unnecessary. What had been since the Renaissance the mark of a woman's cultural inferiority is in Hemans strikingly the manifestation of her modernity and freedom from irrelevance. Accompanying Hemans's linguistic fluency is her easy familiarity with European literatures and histories, and it did not take long for her to enlarge her horizons even further. Her *Lays of Many Lands* (1826) spans centuries and continents, and her *Records of Woman* (1828), a collection meant to universalize the values of sacrifice and endurance evidenced in her life, also pointedly does so across time and geography. The title of the latter volume, in turn, leads us to the second characteristic that dominates so much writing by women in the early decades of the nineteenth century, its engagement with history. It takes the form not of grand designs and philosophical principles, the *métier* of Gibbon, but of individuals in the specificity of their lives, whose daily acts bear the burden of historical force. Often, in both the many lengthy metrical epic romances – distinguished examples include Joanna Baillie's *Metrical Legends of Exalted Characters* (1821), Margaret

Holford's *Margaret of Anjou* (1816), Mary Russell Mitford's *Narrative Poems on the Female Character in the Various Relations of Life* (1813), Eliza Erskine Norton's *Alcon Malanzore* (1815) – and the novels that left so decided an imprint on the productions of the age, women characters assume a prominent, sometimes commanding, role. Whether in verse or prose, the emphasis on the quotidian record, as expected as it might be, is striking, and it has consequences for the chronicle of literary history that have yet to be fully elaborated.

The historical novel in England came directly from this ferment, and it can be documented that, though Scott received the credit, women charted the course he followed to his success. There were three in particular: Maria Edgeworth, Jane Porter, and Sydney Owenson. Edgeworth's satiric rendering of rural Irish local color in *Castle Rackrent* (1800) had the unforeseen result of indicating the rich stores for literary creation to be had by tapping the backwaters of the British Isles. Her attention to realistic dialect and speech patterns was unprecedented, and the sense of stylistic authenticity she realized reverberates through all subsequent fiction in English. Jane Porter's *Scottish Chiefs* (1810), centering on the Scots patriot William Wallace, is of particular import for working out the formulas by which the nineteenth-century historical novel would people crucial events with fictional characters. Sydney Owenson began by creating a romanticized Ireland – of the past in *St. Clair* (1803), of the present in *The Wild Irish Girl* (1806). Then, contemporaneous with Scott, in *O'Donnel* (1814) and *Florence Macarthy* (1818), she established a forceful Irish-based historical fiction with strong nationalistic political overtones.[7] To these works should be added two others, which tap deep roots in Scottish and Irish rural communities, Elizabeth Hamilton's *Cottagers of Glenburnie* (1808) and Mary Leadbeater's *Cottage Dialogues among the Irish Peasantry* (1811). When focused upon in such a concentrated way, these works of provincial fiction testify to how close is the link between the quotidian and the localized as instruments of women's representation. But the additional and natural link to the rendering of history is suggested by the way in which Mary Russell Mitford wrote seemingly simultaneously the sketches for her highly popular and influential *Our Village* (1824–32) and her historical tragedies from Italian history, *Julian* (1822), *Foscari* (1826), and *Rienzi* (1828).

Of the authors just cited, only Sydney Owenson writes about her contemporary world with an openly political perspective, and then only after her marriage and the title "Lady Morgan" gave her a measure of freedom from the financial and personal inhibitions on other women writers. It might be the case that, if this entire complex were adequately explored, it would be found that resonant political tensions lurk beneath the surface of many texts that deflect their attention from stresses of the contemporary world to invent the quotidian realities of an earlier culture. But the privileging of historical recording probably itself indicates the extent to which it was veritably so, in the daily bulletins from the Napoleonic Wars read in every newspaper. The sense that history was being made, or remade, on a world scale was universal; so was the recognition that it did not actually occur until it happened in print. As always in this period, the implicit interdependence of reader and writer suggests that if women writers were deliberately venturing into innovative paths, there were women consumers to whose concerns they were responding.

But there appears an odd and troubling paradox involved in this dynamic. As bourgeois culture narrowed the range of activity deemed respectable for women and the domestic circle became increasingly a circumscription, the imaginative literature enlarged its scope, roaming geographical outposts from which its readers were excluded, opening up a historical past for women as a specious correlative to the frontiers of the empire opening for men. But the two are not commensurate. The utilitarian texts of the 1820s, beginning with Thomas Love Peacock's "Four Ages of Poetry," without consciousness of the gender divisions they are creating, separate the public world of empire building and social improvement from the useless, because private, refinements of literary culture. By 1833, if John Stuart Mill's "What Is Poetry?" can be taken as an accurate index of cultural shifts, some literary ground is reclaimed by ceding to poetry the interiorized and lyric moment, while claiming for the novel, but a generation earlier wholly dominated by women, the right to speak for the large social realm of masculinist power. The region allotted to women is once again blocked off from the male preserve. It is certainly not an attic inhabited only by madwomen, but it is indubitably an interior space. Its presiding genius in the late 1830s, indeed, in a remarkably symbolic act retreats from almost all contact with the outside world, earning a universal fame from the confines of her bedroom. At least, that is one way to construe the long invalidism of Elizabeth Barrett.

That the "Angel in the House" was its presiding genius was part of the bourgeois domestic myth the nineteenth century hallowed for its ethos. But as the case of Elizabeth Barrett exemplifies, the major women writers themselves went far to create and authenticate this privileged position. Mary Russell Mitford, virtually incapacitated by rheumatism in her father's dilapidated cottage at Three Mile Cross, recreated in her detailed sketches the humble village life outside. Hemans remained in seclusion in North Wales, though her poetry appeared to roam the world. L.E.L. wrote her romantic tales of exotic times and places from the humble room she rented in a girl's school in Knightsbridge. In each case the author as person is engulfed by the creator as genius, a concept derived from Madame de Staël's *Corinne* (1807) and by the 1820s, particularly through the self-representations of the poetess popularized by Hemans and Landon, one that had attained the level of totally realized myth. But the myth can swallow more than its propagators, remaining in place long after its age to hold the historical record hostage to its inventions. It is probably true that the role of the poetess was a trap enforced by masculine disdain for cultural refinement and that just as women became known as the principal poets of England the novel was reappropriated by men and made the dominant genre. Yet, rather than reproduce that dismissive behavior, we should underscore what the prominence and achievements of the poetess actually signified for the development of English literary culture.

That requires a very long view. In essence, we might agree that the tensions of the 1790s are shared by male and female writers alike, that, if one can pinpoint various genres or literary situations where a shading by gender occurs, it is still relatively easy to speak of early Romanticism as a cohesive phenomenon. But the problem with the younger generation is that there are essentially two of them. The Younger Romantics – Byron, Keats, and Shelley – retain the radicalism, the interiorized dialogism, and the self-reflexive artistry of their now-lost leaders, and they add to these traits a more pervasive sense of isolation, even of self-exile. However great as poets and minds are the Younger Romantics, when they suddenly disappeared from the scene within four years they left a conspicuous dead end behind them. What took over in 1824 after Byron's death was a bourgeois literary culture that had been gathering force for the previous two decades. Its outlook was expansionist, materialistic in its observance of cultural diversity – in varieties of people, things, ages, histories – essentially liberal in the relatively conservative sense later pervasive in nineteenth-century England, sentimental rather than sublime in aesthetics, pious but generally latitudinarian in respect to belief, and convinced by the long conflict with France that its values were a singular model for the world. In its political dimensions this perspective, once it outlived the diehards of another age (which included two kings and a number of their ministers), moved in the 1820s to broaden the franchise to include all Christian sects and in the early 1830s the large middle class. In its commercial aspect it invented modern technology at home and the British empire abroad. It had two faces, one enlightened and just, the other vulgar and smug. Among male authors with some claim to attention as Romantics, Hazlitt and Scott are intermittently among its adherents, Thomas Campbell and Charles Lamb more directly so, the Wordsworth of *The Excursion* a voice for its ethos but from within a removed parochialism, Barry Cornwall and Leigh Hunt and the novelists

Bulwer Lytton and Disraeli among its guiding voices. From the very first and to his end, was Robert Southey – though for a dozen years in the middle he was distracted by a felt duty to kick the Satanic School around.[8] But the major figure who tried out these values in a variety of literary forms and in gaining popularity showed the middle way to others who followed within the broadly cosmopolitan, democratic, and liberal consensus she exemplified and may in some sense be said to have forged was Felicia Hemans. For most of the twentieth century she was ignored, as were almost all the figures who composed this other, second generation of Romantics and whose fate, even when attracting a modicum of attention, was condescension. But this is unquestionably the group that provides the strongest line of continuity between the Romantic and Victorian periods, and central to it is a major female literary presence. Some will argue that this female bourgeois literary culture did not truly come of age before the 1840s and the combined literary power of Barrett Browning and the Brontë sisters. Yet, we might counter so constrictive a judgment with the acknowledgment that it had been coming steadily of age, generation after generation, for a full century in a steady progress from the Bluestockings through the innovators of the 1790s, to Austen and Edgeworth's culmination of the novel of feminine manners in the Regency, to the reimagining in history of the "records of woman" undertaken by the poetesses. In the aggregate these too are records of woman, and our own reimagining of them will continue to have a profound effect on our conception of the Romantic age.

## NOTES

1. *The Sign of Angellica: Women, Writing and Fiction, 1660–1800* (New York: Columbia University Press, 1989), p. 33. Although focused on the line of fiction written by women in England during the Restoration and eighteenth century, this study in its breadth and sense of continuity provides a basic grounding for any exploration of the role of women writers in Romanticism.
2. Todd claims that for the 1790s alone, "at least three to four hundred women published during the decade" (*Sign of Angellica*, p. 218). If one takes into account the opportunities opened up outside the customary London press, by the proliferation of provincial journals, for instance, or by developments within the growing evangelical Christian movement, the numbers of women who saw some work in print, however ephemeral or topical, must have been higher than this estimate. By the 1820s, with the growth of annuals and other such literary publications dominated by women authors and a female market, the numbers must necessarily be increased. For just the numbers of poetic volumes published, consult J. R. de J. Jackson, *Romantic Poetry by Women: A Bibliography, 1770–1835* (Oxford: Clarendon Press, 1993).
3. Katherine Green, in *The Courtship Novel, 1740–1820: A Feminized Genre* (Lexington: University Press of Kentucky, 1991), pp. 110–12, offers a catalogue

of such characters drawn by Frances Burney, Mary Brunton, Maria Edgeworth, Charlotte Lennox, and Charlotte Smith, and underscores the paradox of how regularly the most successful women novelists inveighed against novel-reading.

4. Nancy Armstrong (*Desire and Domestic Fiction: A Political History of the Novel* [New York and Oxford: Oxford University Press, 1987]) provocatively argues that the rise of the novel is commensurate with the rise of middle-class political power and that thus the contention between poetry and fiction during the late eighteenth and early nineteenth centuries has a strongly ideological subtext.

5. The best exponent of a fresh understanding of Hannah More's importance for British culture is Mitzi Myers, in her acclaimed essay, "Hannah More's Tracts for the Times: Social Fiction and Female Ideology," in *Fetter'd or Free? British Women Novelists, 1670–1815*, eds. Mary Anne Schofield and Cecilia Macheski (Athens and London: Ohio University Press, 1986), pp. 264–84.

6. Examples of the transgressive potentiality of the realm of fairy for women writers can be found in the sensuality of Mary Robinson's exchange of poems between Oberon and Titania, published in the *Morning Post* for August 28–29, 1800, and reprinted by her daughter in the third volume of the *Poetical Works* (1806); the sexual fears and freedoms expressed in Charlotte Dacre's verses "The Elfin King" and "Queen Mab and Her Fays" (in *Hours of Idleness* [1805], I, 92–7; II, 56–8); and legendary materials of the Shetland Islands projecting both rapacity ("The Spirits of the Hill") and rapture ("The Fairy of the Wood") for women in fairy-land included by Dorothea Primrose Campbell in *Poems* (2nd edn., 1816).

7. Owenson's achievement is ably analyzed by Ina Ferris in *The Romantic National Tale and the Question of Ireland* (Cambridge University Press, 2002).

8. Marilyn Butler has argued Southey's centrality to a historicized view of the culture of Romanticism, invoking somewhat different grounds, in "Repossessing the Past: The Case for an Open Literary History": see *Rethinking Historicism: Critical Readings in Romantic History* (Oxford and New York: Basil Blackwood, 1989), pp. 64–84.

# 9

GARY KELLY

# Romantic fiction

During the Romantic period, from the last decade or so of the eighteenth century to the 1830s, most prose fiction was considered subliterary, suitable mainly for children, women, and the lower classes. A few works were cherished by readers in all classes as childhood reading or "popular classics," including generations-old chapbooks, such as *Jack and the Giants*, *Valentine and Orson*, and *The Fair Rosamund*, and longer works such as *The Pilgrim's Progress*, *Robinson Crusoe*, and *The English Hermit*. *Don Quixote* and the novels of Richardson, Fielding, Sterne, and Smollett were regarded as important works of literature. These and other earlier novelists were commercialized as "classics," along with certain poets, dramatists, and belletrists, by publishers such as Harrison and Cooke after the ending of perpetual copyright in 1774. The spread of stereotype printing and sale of books in sixpenny "numbers" (or parts) from around 1800 gave a new plebeian and middle-class readership to earlier sentimental and pious novels such as *The Pilgrim's Progress*, *Robinson Crusoe*, *Pamela*, and *The Vicar of Wakefield*, and to picaresque identity-mystery romances such as *Tom Jones*. Most novels published during the period itself were dismissed by critics and readers as "the trash of the circulating library," to be rented and read quickly rather than purchased and kept. Those "novels of the day" that did cause a stir were quickly cut down to sixpenny chapbooks for the new lower-class market in cheap fashionable novelties, founding the modern market for "romances" of all kinds. Some novels of the day, such as Roche's *The Children of the Abbey*, Helme's *The Farmer of Inglewood Forest* and *St. Clair of the Isles*, and novels by Catherine Ward, Hannah Maria Jones Lowndes, and Sarah Green, were recycled in stereotype sixpenny numbers from the 1810s to the 1830s. A few Romantic novels held a popular readership through the nineteenth century – Gothic "romances" by Reeve, Radcliffe, and Bennett; Minerva Press novels of social criticism such as *The Children of the Abbey* and *The Farmer of Inglewood Forest*; historical romances such as *St. Clair of the Isles*, *Fatherless Fanny* (uncertain authorhip), and Porter's *The Scottish*

*Chiefs*; Scott's novels; "orientalist" novels such as Morier's *Hajji Baba*; Bible historical romances such as Croly's *Salathiel*; and Bulwer-Lytton's novels. But most of these sustained their popularity in cheap, downmarket editions, and were considered by Victorian literary critics, "serious" novelists, and intellectuals to be inartistic and dated in theme and technique, and they lost continuing wide appeal in the early twentieth century, along with Romantic poets such as Thomas Moore, Walter Scott, and Felicia Hemans.

The past three decades have seen a revival of academic critical interest in certain novels of the period, such as Godwin's *Caleb Williams* and his daughter Mary Shelley's *Frankenstein*; Gothic romances by Charlotte Smith, Ann Radcliffe, "Monk" Lewis, and C. R. Maturin; Scott's and Galt's "Scottish" novels and James Hogg's *Private Memoirs and Confessions of a Justified Sinner*; and Irish novels by Maria Edgeworth, Sydney Owenson (Lady Morgan), and others; this is thanks mainly to historicist, Marxist, feminist, post-colonialist, and other forms of anticanonical criticism. Some Romantic novels, such as the best of the "fashionable" or "silver-fork" novels of the 1820s and 1830s, were seen at the time as engaged in the same public, literary and moral educative work as the verse epics of Southey, Montgomery, Byron (controversially), and others, and found their way into the libraries of the rich, powerful, and socioculturally aspiring of the day; but these novels were long forgotten, only a few being recently republished in scholarly editions. Psychoanalytical criticism and theory, especially when allied with feminism, have retrieved some otherwise forgotten Romantic novels by women, such as the "female Gothic" of Radcliffe and Charlotte Dacre, and the political novels of Smith, Robinson, Wollstonecraft, Hays, and others. Scholarly editions of many hitherto forgotten Romantic novels have appeared from Oxford University Press, Broadview Press, Pickering and Chatto, and other publishers in the academic education industries, with complementary academic monographs on a wide range of themes, with various approaches. Jane Austen has of course become a major academic and popular-culture industry, and has been reclaimed by a global popular readership and re-writership.

From today's perspective almost all Romantic fiction seems confined to the historical issues and commercialized culture of its own time. Yet prose fiction was one of the most widely consumed forms of print during the period, equalled or surpassed only by newspapers, closely associated with a social and cultural phenomenon known as "the rise of the reading public," and recognized as a major form of ideological communication, for better or worse, central to cultural politics. Cheap fiction served an independent urban working-class culture of novelty and commercialized consumption and enabled its readers to engage with modernity; evangelical fiction disseminated a diminutive version of bourgeois culture and values, though most remained unread by its target plebeian audience; moralistic novels old and new issued in sixpenny numbers converged with a lower middle-class Romantic puritanism; and the "modern novel" was used in the struggle for ideological self-definition within the professional or upper middle class and to project their domination of other classes. The most widely read form of imaginative writing, prose fiction could be made to address various classes comprising the "nation," as other genres could not. This influence was steadily increased towards a mass print culture by exploitation of a succession of commercial and technological innovations including the iron press, the Stanhope press, stereotyping, engraving on wood and steel (for illustrations), mechanical paper-making, the number trade, and cloth binding.

Accordingly, prose fiction of all kinds was reformed and reformulated for the unfolding political and social conflicts of the time. Outside the domain of print, the lower-class oral fiction of folktale was regarded by social reformers of all classes as a vestige of superstition and pre-modern consciousness. Yet middle-class inventors of tradition such as Walter Scott collected it and later incorporated it into novels of national origins, history, and culture. Traditional chapbook street literature was relegated to the middle-class nursery and discarded even by lower-class readers, who wanted cheap versions of the fashionable novelties being read by their "betters."[1] Middle-class moral reformers such as Hannah More saw traditional chapbook literature as a seedbed of popular culture and thus of lower-class political disaffection during the 1790s. Accordingly, she, and later the Religious Tract Society, tried to supplant this "*sans-culotte* library" with fiction "of the right sort." Later still, the Society for the Diffusion of Useful Knowledge, artisans' educational institutes and magazines, lower-class religious sects such as Methodists, and working-class radicals tried to eradicate the people's appetite for both the old chapbook fiction and the fashionable novelties. Meanwhile, most fiction formed a thematic and formal coalition and dialogue with melodrama, the form that dominated theatre during the Romantic period and that dominates live and recorded performance globally to this day.

Even fiction for children was reconstructed and, like pseudopopular chapbook fiction, used to intervene in social conflict. Children, like women, plebeians, and "primitive" peoples, were widely considered to have a "natural" love of fictitious narrative. Educationists treated this love as both a danger and an opportunity. Social reformers like Sarah Trimmer argued that if middle-class children were not carefully supervised and segregated from lower-class servants they would be seduced by the false consciousness embodied in the common folk's ghost stories, fairy tales, and adventure stories. A taste for such "fables" would also unfit these children for "solid" and "useful" reading. Thus, many writers turned to fiction, though reluctantly, both to preserve the middle-class child from the wrong kinds of fiction and to sweeten the pill of instruction. Many of these writers were women, including Trimmer, Lady Eleanor Fenn, Dorothy Kilner, Mary Wollstonecraft, Maria Edgeworth, Mary Lamb, "Arabella Argus," Alicia Catherine Mant, Mary Robson Hughes, Mary Sherwood, her sister Martha Mary Butt, Mary Pilkington, Barbara Hofland, and Mary Belson Elliott. They capitalized on the supposed expertise of their sex in child rearing so as to enter a profession and to discourse on issues of the day and knowledges otherwise closed to them, on behalf of their class but also to feminize culture and society.

Fiction for the middle and upper classes – called the "modern novel," "novels of the day," or "fashionable novels" – was as widely read and widely condemned as the fiction of the lower orders. In 1779 the Rev. Vicesimus Knox declared, "If it is true, that the present age is more corrupt than the preceding, the great multiplication of Novels probably contributes to its degeneracy." As late as 1826 a writer in the *Monthly Magazine* attributed the French Revolution to the influence of novels by Rousseau, Voltaire, Diderot, and d'Alembert, noting that a similar attempt had failed in Britain. Novels were supposed to distract young middle-class readers from the solid and useful reading necessary to accumulate moral and intellectual capital for later life, especially in the professions. Women were supposed to be rendered unfit by novel reading for domesticity. As the *New Lady's Magazine* put it in 1790, novels "not only poison the mind from relishing well-written authors, but render it less firm to resist those temptations they themselves inculcate." These temptations were supposed to stem from decadent court culture, for modern novels were seen as descendants of seventeenth-century courtly fiction and as cousins of contemporary French libertine novels.

Novels were the major reading-matter of the middle and upper classes, along with newspapers and magazines, and thus all three were sources of continuing anxiety as threats to social order and stability. Newspapers and magazines were taxed to restrict their circulation and prosecuted to intimidate their owners and editors; novels were attacked by moralists, critics, reformers, and artistic innovators. Most such attacks were based on moral more than aesthetic grounds, but the power of the novel to disseminate ideology through a wide and national readership among the political classes made it a focus for both moral and artistic reform. The novel had to be raised from its subliterary status in order to validate with the transcendent power of art whatever ideological burden it had to bear. Distinctions between art and entertainment were already deeply inscribed in culture and being refashioned to serve emergent social differences. The aesthetic was being remade in a form of knowledge as power that could be controlled by professional writers, critics, and other middle-class gatekeepers. Yet this fact introduced new anxieties about commercialization, mere popularity, and undisciplined and untrained readers; these anxieties in turn produced new or newly strengthened institutions of cultural surveillance and policing, such as literary criticism and a canon of the national literature, in which, significantly, the novel was installed during the Romantic period.

This process is seen in the development of the novel's two dominant and related forms during the period – the identity-mystery romance and the novel of manners, sentiment, and emulation. The identity-mystery romance was typified by one of its continuingly popular classics, Fielding's *Tom Jones*. The form concerns a protagonist mistakenly or criminally deprived of his or her "true" identity at birth, precipitated from "home" and down the social scale and into a series of adventures testing character and exemplifying moral identity, closing with restitution of true name, social status, and property, and the reward of a marriage of true minds. This is a myth for the socially subaltern lower and middle classes liable to feel that gentry and nobility had usurped their rightful place in society. Rooted in early modern European picaresque fiction, where the protagonist's abject origins are simply a fact, the form was transformed by Fielding, Smollett, and other eighteenth-century novelists into a myth of the conflict between subjective merit and ascribed social status, and developed in the Romantic period as a myth of class injustice and usurpation in various ways, from Minerva Press novels of the 1780s and 1790s through "English Jacobin" novels of the 1790s and Gothic novels of the 1790s to 1820s to "silver-fork" and "Newgate" novels of the 1830s, and on to Dickens.

This form shared traits and often merged with the novel of manners, sentiment, and emulation. "Manners" here encompassed social conduct as codes of social differentiation and power with moral and ethical overtones, which were applied to the culture and conduct of the nation as a whole and treated novelistically in terms of the moral, ethical, cultural, and social options (sentiment and emulation) exercised in private life by individuals. Earlier novels of manners represent upper-class life for the instruction and emulation of readers lower down the social scale, but after the "Richardsonian revolution" of mid-century, novels incorporated Enlightenment and sentimental social critiques of this relationship, representing subjectivity or inward merit oppressed by a society dominated by mere manners, or courtly conduct. Yet the same novels continue to depict the manners of the dominant classes as vital interests to middle-class readers who had increasing expectations of upward social mobility but were increasingly conscious of separate identity and power. This form of the novel was inspired by Richardson's novels, Rousseau's *La Nouvelle Héloïse*, and the sentimental novels of

Goldsmith, Mackenzie, Goethe, and others. But women novelists such as Frances Burney, Frances Sheridan, Clara Reeve, Sophia Lee, Ann Radcliffe, and Charlotte Smith exploited their sex's conventionally accepted expertise in silent suffering to advance bourgeois values and practices by representing the inward self as authentic and the external social world, controlled by aristocracy and gentry, as divided, relative, and hostile to authentic selfhood. In many novels of manners, of course, the heroine's or hero's social identity – name, family, rank – is hidden or misrepresented until the closure, as in the identity-mystery romance. Many other novels of manners, however, disclose the real name and rank of the protagonist from the outset but conceal the protagonist's "true," subjective identity or merit from other characters or even the protagonist her- or himself. By the novel's closure, subjective merit and social status have become congruent, for example in the novels of Jane Austen.

Both major forms could be said to constitute manuals for the formation of self-identity within the accelerating processes and conditions of modernity as described by Anthony Giddens in *Modernity and Self-Identity* (1991). This social process acquires the character of myth, as envisaged by Ernst Bloch in *The Spirit of Utopia* (1918) and Hans Blumenberg, *Work on Myth* (1985), enacted, however, through a purportedly "realistic" plot and characterization rather than through the allegorical, ceremonial action characteristic of earlier courtly romance.

Structures of language and narrative mode reinforce this emergent myth. The late eighteenth century saw consolidation of a national dialect, spoken and written, based on the writing culture of the elite professions.[2] Identity-mystery romances and novels of manners, sentiment, and emulation contain a linguistic universe centered by standard written English as the language of thought or the asocial and (therefore) authentic subjective self, whereas the social self, like speech, is artificial and merely relative. Thus protagonists speak and think in standard written English whereas merely social characters, of any class, speak in sociolect, dialect, and idiolect and usually have little if any subjectivity.

This linguistic structure is supported by the handling of first-person and third-person narrative modes, with a significant innovation merging the two, now known as "free indirect discourse" or reported inward speech and thought, effected especially by women novelists from Burney through Inchbald, Smith, and Edgeworth to Austen, and beyond to Gaskell, Charlotte Brontë, Eliot, Mansfield, and Woolf. The Romantic mystery-identity romance that was built on Fielding's example, from the Minerva Press through the Bentley and Colburn "silver-fork" and "Newgate" novels, used third-person narration to convey characters' subjectivity to readers and to create the narrator as a central character – a model consciousness for the reader and a goal for the fictional protagonists. Nuances of style and narration cued readers to variations of subjective response. Romantic first-person narrative, built on the intensities of reader-protagonist identification from Richardson to Rousseau, was often adapted for social-protest fiction, notably by the English Jacobin novelists, but also by late picaresque social-satire fiction. The implication of narrative form in public political contest during the revolutionary period impelled development of a fused form, free indirect discourse, in the revolutionary aftermath. The democratic polyvocalism of the novel in letters or the personal immediacy of the confessional tale was displaced by the hierarchical structure of authoritative narration in standard written English, subordinating all other forms of English in the text, often reinforced by a genteel irony, allusiveness, wide-ranging referentiality, and literariness that embodied a transcendental perspective ostensibly above the social and subjective experience represented in the text. This is implicitly the reader's viewpoint.

Through use of free indirect discourse novelists from Burney on constructed protagonists resembling the author's master-consciousness in the text. The reader may also identify with this viewpoint and thereby live the novel's world doubly from within. The protagonist is uncertain how to traverse the social world but is seen by the reader, who has access through the narrator to the character's inner condition, to be on a course towards the moral and intellectual plane on which the narrator is situated from the outset, above or beyond the social world of the story. Through this narrative irony the reader vicariously experiences both the movement or transformation of the central moral-intellectual self and that transformation's goal. Both narrative voice and plot closure are figures for harmonization of social conflict enacted on the level of local, quotidian, domestic relations and internalized in the subjective self. Within Britain this is a conflict between gentry and upper middle classes; and within the upper middle classes the conflict is an ambivalence towards the hegemonic classes, the desired and feared social "other." The larger question is whether this formalized resolution of social conflict was meant to be carried from reading to real life or become an end in itself – reading rather than revolution. Such escape or relief from reality was and is often assigned, disparagingly, to prose fiction, whether the Romantic circulating-library novel or the twentieth-century Harlequin and Mills and Boon romances, the literary heirs of the Romantic form.

The political character of this mediated subjectivity in Romantic fiction intertwines rather than merges gender difference with class conflict. The widely held (though mistaken) opinion that novels were mainly read and written by women was enforced by the conventional view of women as more subjective and less public beings than men, by the limited education and range of domestic and social duties allowed to women, and by conventional and practical restrictions on women as professionals, intellectuals, and writers. This image of woman was itself an appropriation of the upper-class lady, designed to contrast with woman in the courtly "mistress system" of intertwined sexual and political intrigue and with woman corrupted morally and emotionally by courtly manners, luxury, and power and seduced sexually by the courtly gallant, to the ruin of herself, her family, or her husband and his estate. In a society already patriarchal and antifeminist at all levels, woman was seen as the weak link in every class, confronting a superior male-dominated group. Woman is doubly the potential enemy within when she is the exclusively domestic creature of idealized gentry and upper-middle-class culture. Thus male readers could find the vicissitudes of novel heroines as interesting as the adventures of novel heroes because the woman tempted or threatened by a more powerful man could be read as the professional man or any subordinate group tempted and threatened by social superiors.

These politics inform most Romantic fiction, but a salient instance is the Gothic romance as developed by Charlotte Smith, Ann Radcliffe, Matthew G. Lewis, and others in the 1790s, followed by Francis Lathom, Charlotte Dacre, Regina Maria Roche, C. R. Maturin, and many others in the next two decades. The form was quickly appropriated by the popular market to become cheap sixpenny shockers by writers such as Sarah Wilkinson and Isaac Crookenden. Significantly, these chapbook Gothics tend to cut representation of oppressed subjectivity and retain action and incident. For like the novel of manners, sentiment, and emulation from which it sprang, the triple-decker, circulating-library Gothic romance celebrates subjectivity in the face of social conventions, institutions, values, and individuals threatening to overwhelm the virtuous individual self, and this plot was of interest mainly to the novel-reading classes rather than the chapbook-reading classes. The woman lacking worldly experience, unmarried, orphaned, or otherwise unprotected by a man enables a display of subjectivity afflicted by the evils of the paternalist, patriarchal, merely social, and above all courtly values and practices of the dominant classes, figured as an older male villain.

Gothic romance also aimed to demystify the sublime obscurity by which, according to Enlightenment sociology, court culture overawes the whole of society, thereby maintaining the power of court government. In order to do this Gothic romances often describe historical and social settings in terms of Enlightenment philosophical history and use novelistic devices and figures to constitute a critical sociology of power operating in several ways: through institutions founded in the past and now outmoded (in ruins), but nevertheless difficult or dangerous for the outsider to understand, penetrate, or master (secret entrances, passages, labyrinths, pitfalls); through social conventions (conspiracies, secret orders) unrecognized or not understood by their victims; through application of hidden laws and instruments of force (the Inquisition); through an unsuspected, inward-working transformation (by drugs, magic) of the victim's perceptions, values, ideology, or being; and through alien, not truly English values and practices (Mediterranean, oriental, Catholic). These forms of power may be accompanied by obliteration of the familiar and domestic (by savage nature, storms), and be exercised with the willing or unwilling aid of those (relatives and servants, especially females) who are socially close to the victims and should be protectors or supporters, while the victim's own father, significantly, is often absent, ineffectual, or dead.

As in novels of manners, sentiment, and emulation, these threats, harassments, or obstacles affect the protagonist's subjective self. The Gothic novel was and is known for its effects of terror, supposedly operating vicariously in the mind of the reader through the representation of terror in the mind of the protagonist. The important point is that this representation foregrounds the mind (reason and emotion) at the expense of physical action and social conduct. Furthermore, terror is depicted less often than perplexity, or being of two minds – usually fear, repulsion, or pain on the one hand and desire, curiosity, or pleasure on the other. This psychomachia is a figure for the ambivalence of the novel-reading classes toward their "betters," a conflict of fear and desire resulting in paralysis of will and action. Significantly, paralyzing perplexity often occurs when the character is passive rather than active, alone rather than in society. Such inward, passive, moral and intellectual qualities as self-control, fortitude, and endurance, rather than active resistance, see the protagonist through to the tranquillity that transcends rather than confronts or avoids social conflict and ambivalence. In fact, the male hero's resistance to oppression often proves to be futile swashbuckling – a legacy to the Gothic from seventeenth-century prose romance and heroic drama (which were still widely read and performed). Furthermore, the most self-divided and tormented characters in Gothic novels are also those who seek power over others. As psycho-drama, this structure has made Gothic fiction amenable to twentieth-century psychoanalytic and neo-Hegelian readings, but the structure is also informed by the deontology, ethics, theodicy, and politics of the period, if not of today. The self-mastery of the virtuous protagonist is its own reward; ambition, desire, and lust for power are their own punishment. Yet the socially and morally transgressive individualism of the Gothic villain continued to fascinate, offering political lessons to an age of middle-class participation in violent revolution in France and flirtation with lower-class political militancy in Britain.

Not surprisingly, then, Gothic elements turn up in overtly political novels, or philosophical romances as they were called. "Philosophical" here signifies Enlightenment social, political, and cultural critique as applied by French revolutionaries and British reformers in the 1790s. Such philosophical romances range from English Jacobin and anti-Jacobin novels of the 1790s to "silver-fork" and "Newgate" novels of the 1820s and 1830s, but elements are also found in Minerva Press and other kinds of popular novels and in sixpenny chapbook novelettes. These often follow earlier philosophical dialogues, oriental tales, fables, and allegories in which social criticism is framed by fiction to achieve a wider readership. English Jacobin novelists develop an Enlightenment sociology of knowledge to argue that individuals and social groups are constructed by the political and cultural system under which they live. Accordingly, the English Jacobin rhetoric of fiction requires detailed representation of social conventions, institutions, and structures of power and a new particularity and authenticity in representing individual psychology. Yet this particularity also has to seem socially typical, the consequence of systemic injustice rather than the accidents of individual destiny or moral character. Although several English Jacobin novelists adapted the picaresque form, they give it and other appropriated forms a rigorous connection between character, plot, and setting in order to show how the individual is first constructed by social conditions and then necessarily responds to these conditions by ethical action of certain kinds.

To serve this "necessitarian" plot, English Jacobin novelists prefer first-person confessional narration showing how self-reflection and its resultant political consciousness can break the cycle of institutional reproduction of evil or error. The individual internalizes false consciousness and social difference, thereby becomes self-divided, searches for reunifying self-understanding, and discovers the cause of his or her self-conflict and social alienation in the actual injustice and oppression of society. But this new consciousness must then be expressed socially, as a confessional self-vindication or warning to others – the text of the novel itself or an inset narrative within it. This complex of philosophically motivated techniques embracing political autobiography is reinforced by historical allusions and contemporary parallels that generalize the condition of the novel's protagonist to other people, entire classes, and other societies, either in the past or in contemporary but foreign locations. This is the structure of novels such as Thomas Holcroft's *Anna St. Ives* (1792), William Godwin's *Things As They Are; or, The Adventures of Caleb Williams* (1794), Mary Hays's *The Memoirs of Emma Courtney* (1796), and Mary Wollstonecraft's *The Wrongs of Woman;*

*or, Maria* (1798). Some English Jacobin novelists adapted the picaresque and the identity-mystery romance as in Robert Bage's *Man As He Is* (1792) and *Hermsprong; or, Man As He Is Not* (1796), and the sentimental tale as in Elizabeth Inchbald's *Nature and Art* (1796) and Amelia Opie's *The Father and Daughter* (1801) and *Adeline Mowbray* (1805).

Anti-Jacobin fiction became prominent in the second half of the 1790s with such novels as Elizabeth Hamilton's *Letters of a Hindoo Rajah* (1796), Isaac D'Israeli's *Vaurien* (1797), Charles Lloyd's *Edmund Oliver* (1798), Jane West's *A Tale of the Times* (1799), and Elizabeth Hamilton's *Memoirs of Modern Philosophers* (1800). After the revolutionary violence of 1792 and Jacobin Terror of 1793–4 in France and the plebeian political protests of 1792–5 in Britain, many middle-class writers and readers began to fear the effects of their own reformist zeal. Anti-Jacobin novelists came from the same social backgrounds as their literary foes and shared their criticism of court politics and plebeian unreason and insubordination, but they sought coalition rather than conflict with the dominant classes. Accordingly, they draw on more genteel and learned, less "democratic" literary traditions than their rivals and rely on parody and burlesque. Like satirists going back through Cervantes to Lucian and Aristophanes, they purport to expose a gap between theory and practice, speculation and experience, "philosophy" and "reality." They often use bathos to show the comic consequences of theory in practice. They base characters on figures such as Godwin, Wollstonecraft, and Hays and use footnotes to link certain characters' absurd utterances to English Jacobin writings, thus countering the English Jacobins' fictionalized autobiography and use of footnotes to document systemic and historical injustice. They adapt the novel of education to show how a protagonist infatuated with "philosophy" or seduced by a "new philosopher" is either ruined or reeducated to social "reality." Significantly, the Jacobin villain is either an amoral aristocrat or a plebeian masquerading as one and using revolutionary politics to serve his own greed and ambition; his victim is often a naive young woman, representing the element in middle-class individuals (men or women) and in the class as a whole that is susceptible to seduction by the upper class or contamination by the lower class, especially when it is disguised as middle-class revolutionary principle.

For literary political reasons anti-Jacobin novels often lack a central interest in subjectivity and avoid first-person expressive or confessional narration. During the 1790s the culture of sensibility became associated in the opinion of many with the French Revolution, partly through the revolutionary appropriation of Rousseau and partly through English Jacobin interest in subjectivity as the site of ideological struggle. In reaction, anti-Jacobin novelists emphasize sociability and the individual's duty to social convention and laws, satirize sensibility, avoid identification of reader with protagonist through immediate first-person narration, and prefer the detached, intrusive, authoritative, witty, learned, worldly-wise narrator – a model professional-genteel consciousness representing a dialectic between the professional middle class and the landed gentry, rather than the overthrow of the latter by the former. This fictional structure, which thus formalizes the modified paternalist social order advocated in the novels' thematic material, left an important legacy for Jane Austen, Walter Scott, and their Victorian successors in the "great tradition," who developed the form into a major vehicle for imagining and promoting a coalition of gentry and professionals to dominate Britain and its empire.

In the aftermath of the 1790s Britain faced increasing class conflict at home and military challenge abroad. In response, middle-class writers intensified their attacks on the moral and political failings of the ruling class, increased their efforts to replace the lower ranks' lottery mentality with a form of bourgeois investment mentality, and aimed to reconcile the differences created within the nation and their own class by the Revolution debate. Continuing concern over lower-class rebelliousness led to increased production of pseudopopular fiction for the common people, modeled on Hannah More's "Cheap Repository" (1795–8, reprinted in the 1810s and 1820s) and extended by the Religious Tract Society (1799 on) and other local, national, and imperial agencies. But this concern also produced new ways of depicting the common people in fiction for middle-class readers, merging with concern to represent a dialectic and coalition between the hegemonic classes and the professional middle class. Novelists represented a new social diversity-in-unity by inventing a national history, culture, literature, and destiny for Britain. This task required new social-descriptive matter, which in turn required new formal practices that were developed from the early 1800s to the 1830s by novelists of Britain's margins such as Maria Edgeworth, Jane and Anna Maria Porter, Sydney Owenson (Lady Morgan), and Walter Scott; by orientalist novelists such as Thomas Hope and James Morier; and (for England itself) by "silver-fork" and "Newgate" novelists such as Catherine G. Ward, Constantine Normanby, Thomas Henry Lister, Mrs. (Catherine) Gore, Lady Blessington, Edward Bulwer Lytton, and others.

Edgeworth was the first of many novelists to model a "British" ruling class of professionalized gentry and gentrified professionals for the post-revolutionary age. In her Burneyesque novels such as *Belinda* (1801) and *Patronage* (1814) and tales such as *Castle Rackrent* (1800), *Moral Tales* (1801), *Popular Tales* (1804), *Tales of Fashionable Life* (1809–12), and *Harrington* and *Ormond* (1817) Edgeworth portrays this ruling coalition as both local and national in a way neither the solely local common people and petty bourgeoisie nor the urbanized and cosmopolitan court aristocracy could be. Edgeworth was the most widely respected novelist between the revolutionary 1790s and the 1814 success of Scott's *Waverley,* and her novels portray heroes with gentry status and professional middle-class subjectivity, supported by women practicing a domestic version of this discourse of merit, and followed by a populace that is naturally loyal and docile, needing only proper leadership and replacement of their "traditional" culture and customary moral economy. Yet in Edgeworth's "Irish tales" as in Porter's and Morgan's "national tales" and Scott's "Waverley Novels" the common people and certain women characters remain the wellspring of the national culture of folksong, folksay, folktale, and the mother tongue against the alien and "not British." But once inscribed in writing, this largely oral culture of the people became the cultural property and ideological instrument of those who commanded the culture of print.

Regional and historical novels, as further variants of the identity-mystery romance and the novel of manners, sentiment, and emulation, became the major forms of this instrument, using a particular representation of the national language. In both her regional tales and Burneyesque novels Edgeworth uses dialect or idiolect and sociolect in a hierarchy dominated by standard written English, the dialect of the professional middle class, implicitly national and British because it belongs to no particular place. This linguistic structure is reinforced by an authoritative third-person narrative voice using standard English, by morally correct and intellectually developed characters using the same dialect, and by detailed and energetic description of regional and class-based social life and customs. As standard languages were being developed from written vernaculars used by professionals into the model for correct written and spoken language, the novel representing the linguistically differentiated yet ordered nation became a major vehicle for Romantic nationalism in Europe and elsewhere, into the twentieth century. Edgeworth may be said to have invented it.

The fact that women led the way in developing this form is significant. For most contemporary critics, the novel was gendered feminine and therefore ranked low in the cultural and literary hierarchy; yet because of this fact women writers could use the novel to participate in national issues, otherwise conducted by men. But while Edgeworth, the Porter sisters, and Owenson addressed issues of nation formation, other women novelists such as Amelia Opie, Elizabeth LeNoir, and Mary Brunton specialized in conventionally feminine domains of sentiment, the domestic affections, and local, quotidian life. These subjects, too, were political, however, and such novelists tried to avoid the political implications given to the culture of sensibility by English Jacobin novelists. Edgeworth and Austen represented women's subjectivity in moral, intellectual, and socially integrative terms, rather than as emotional excess, cultural transgression, and social alienation, unlike more "liberal" sentimental, Gothic, and "silver-fork" novelists. In the revolutionary aftermath, transgressive subjectivity, including erotic desire, became an increasingly complex theme, associated with "*avant-garde*" Romantic culture and liberal politics yet rooted in Enlightenment and English Jacobin materialist epistemology and taken up by Romantic poets such as Shelley and Byron, the utilitarians, and early empirical psychologists. Transgressive selfhood could be a powerful if ambiguous figure for transcendence of the "merely" social and political sphere in a variety of novels by women and men, including Germaine de Staël's *Corinne* (1807), widely read and influential in Britain, Percy Shelley's *Zastrozzi* (1810), Opie's *Temper* (1812), Lady Caroline Lamb's *Glenarvon* (1816), Mary Shelley's *Frankenstein* (1818), C. R. Maturin's *Melmoth the Wanderer* (1820), J. G. Lockhart's *Adam Blair* (1822), Hazlitt's *Liber Amoris* (1823), James Hogg's *Private Memoirs and Confessions of a Justified Sinner* (1824), Benjamin Disraeli's *Vivian Grey* (1826–7), and Bulwer-Lytton's *Pelham* (1828). Central to these texts is a Romantic irony of excessive selfhood thwarted by social convention, oppressive institutions, or cosmic indifference.

Thus, representation of excessive selfhood was a major way of redefining the social, often converging with representation of the social in regional and historical novels so as to redefine the nation in terms of the values held by readers of such fiction. Edgeworth's tales created a politically influential image of Ireland; Scott's novels invented Scotland as our culture (or the tourist industry) still knows it; and in *Our Village* (1824–32), one of the few surviving popular classics from the period, Mary Mitford invokes Gilbert White of Selborne and Jane Austen to recreate rural England in the image of the leisured intellectual middle class. Together these novels created a powerful and lasting cultural myth that the real Britain was to be found in a rural middle-class cottage culture. Meanwhile the urban scene, with its politically volatile lower classes, places of fashionable but immoral resort, criminal haunts, and increasingly separate working-class cultural life, was accommodated in the imaginary topography of the nation by being treated as alien ground, in Pierce Egan's *Life in London* (1820–1); "Newgate" novels such as *Richmond; or, Scenes in the Life of a Bow Street Runner* (1827, possibly by Thomas Gaspey), Bulwer-Lytton's *Paul Clifford* (1830), Charles Whitehead's *Autobiography of Jack Ketch* (1834, dated 1835), and Dickens's *Oliver Twist* (1837–8); and popular American imports by Irving and Cooper. Such novels did direct criticism of the "old order" towards criminal law reform, the Reform Bill of 1832, the Poor Law reform of 1834, and improvement of urban administration and policing. Yet these novels also depict urban lower-class life as exotic and glamorous but beyond reform and redemption, except in the individual case or by middle-class philanthropic societies.

This vision of national reconstruction was extended to the empire by orientalists, missionary organizations, utilitarians, and administrative reformers. Dr John Moore's *Zeluco* (1786) traced the career of a despot from child bully to adult plantation slave-driver. Elizabeth Hamilton, sister of an orientalist, novelized the group's cultural and political interests in *Memoirs of a Hindoo Rajah* (1796), published in the midst of the Revolution debate. Mary Sherwood fictionalized the missionary campaign in such stories as *Little Henry and His Bearer* (1814). Charlotte Dacre's Gothic novel *Zofloya; or, The Moor* (1806) defined the "not British" as Catholic and Mediterranean or Islamic and Moorish – in either case autocratic, courtly, and sublimely mysterious, implying that such elements within Britain were alien. The threat from French revolutionary and Napoleonic imperialism gave new energy to these themes, especially during the Peninsular War, in poems by Southey, Byron, Moore, and Felicia Hemans and novels such as Thomas Hope's *Anastasius; or, Memoirs of a Greek* (1819), James Morier's *The Adventures of Hajji Baba* (1824), and Scott's *The Talisman* (1825). These texts develop the Enlightenment critique of court culture into criticism of Britain's governing classes at a time of national crisis and link Britain's imperial mission to modernize the empire from Ireland to the East with a domestic mission to purge Britain of supposedly oriental elements.

Engagement with these major cultural and political issues of the revolutionary aftermath gained increasing respect for the modern novel, but intellectuals, *avant-garde* writers, evangelicals, and political radicals – most of them men – continued to associate most prose fiction with subcultures of unenlightened plebeians, under-educated women, and uneducated children. Nevertheless, some of these critics attempted to disseminate their ideas by appropriating prose fiction in experimental hybrid texts, or quasi-novels, including John Thelwall's *The Peripatetic* (1793), Elizabeth Hamilton's *Memoirs of Agrippina, Wife of Germanicus* (1804), Thomas Frognall Dibdin's *Bibliomania* (1809), Moore's *Lalla Rookh* (1817), Thomas Love Peacock's *Nightmare Abbey* (1818), "Noctes Ambrosianae" in *Blackwood's Magazine* (1822–35), Hazlitt's *Liber Amoris* (1823), and Southey's *The Doctor, &c.* (1834–47). These texts combine fictional narrative with some other genre or discourse, such as philosophy, poetry, social criticism, history, topical commentary, criticism, or autobiography, to which the fiction is subordinate.

A similar critical relation to the "mere" novel also characterizes the fiction of Austen and Scott, thought by contemporary readers (in the case of Scott) or modern critics (Austen) to have transcended the ephemeral "novel of the day" and become literary classics, or rereadable texts. Yet Austen is centrally a novelist of her time in dealing with the major concern of the novel-reading classes during her lifetime – the relation of the professional middle class and landed gentry. She focuses this concern around familiar themes in late eighteenth-century fiction of social criticism. First there is the problem of passing on the landed estate and the culture it sustains, seen most critically in *Mansfield Park*; Austen's readers would readily see this problem as a metonymy for survival of the larger state. The dangers to estate and state are seduction of county gentry by court culture (in *Sense and Sensibility* and *Persuasion*), local gentry remaining untouched by wider cultural progress and social responsibilities (in *Northanger Abbey* and *Emma*), and excessive social emulation, subservience, or independence of members of the gentry and elite professions (in *Pride and Prejudice*). Finally, in all Austen's novels there is the important role of women as catalysts in the survival or decline of families in the upper and middle classes and thus in society at large.

Austen began writing novels in the 1790s but published them during the Regency, when these familiar issues from prerevolutionary social criticism had renewed relevance. Like a prerevolutionary novelist of manners, sentiment, and emulation, she uses the courtship story, settings in genteel domestic and social life, and the plot of romantic comedy to show the interaction of landed gentry and their professional middle-class dependents and allies as they negotiate through temptations of courtliness, contamination by vulgarity, or socially destructive independence. More important, Austen also uses a metaphor of reading-as-cognition to show both the priority of the moral-intellectual self and the necessity of integrating that self into landed society and culture. Here she merges the prerevolutionary conduct-book ideology of domestic women with the revolutionary feminist protest that women deprived of intellectual development would be unable to exercise free will correctly in personal and family life and thus would fail to sustain the major ideological and cultural role in state formation that was expected of them in the revolutionary aftermath.

Here too Austen reverses the familiar criticism of the novel as disseminator of court culture and emulation, especially for women. For she both depicts her heroines' problems in "reading" the world and presents her readers with the problem of novel-reading. An instance is the heroine of *Emma* almost disastrously misreading her protégée Harriet Smith's life as an identity-mystery romance. More broadly, Austen shows heroines negotiating between social convention and subjective authenticity just as she forces her readers to negotiate between literary convention and originality. The young Austen burlesqued the conventions of various genres and discourses, including the novel, but as an adult she went further, taking familiar elements of the novel of manners, sentiment, and emulation, inviting a conventional reading of them, but repeatedly refusing to meet conventional expectations and thus presenting her reader with the same challenge to correct reading that is faced by her heroine, but in literary discourse rather than "real life." The consequences of misreading novel and world are different but analogous, making novel-reading a central cultural and social practice in construction of the individual and thus the family and the nation. Rather than deny she was writing novels, as many contemporaries did, Austen subjoined "A Novel" to each of her titles: what, she implies, could be of more interest to the novel-reading classes than the problem of reading posed in and by her novels?

Accordingly, these novels aim to be "literature" in a specific, emergent sense: rereadable texts transcending their particular historical, social, and cultural conditions of production. Novels of the day exploited fashionable novelty, were rented from circulating libraries rather than owned by their readers, and were thus unrereadable texts in several senses. By contrast, rereadable texts supposedly had more intrinsic and lasting value, required critical reflection on the literary conventions they exploit, and so were worth owning, especially when marketed, as Austen's were from the 1830s, in series of five-shilling monthly volumes of "classic" and "standard" works. The kind of critical reflection required in reading such works may be considered similar to that required by men, such as those in the Austen family, in their professional work and, in Austen's novels, is required by the novels' heroines in order to negotiate through social conventions and gain an "establishment" in life, thereby contributing to social stability. Thus the aims of Austen's novels may seem to resemble those of both feminists in the 1790s and women writers of national reconstruction in the revolutionary aftermath, whatever their ideological and political differences.

This resemblance is misleading. Austen's novels not only reworked the commercialized "trash of the circulating library" but also excluded thematic and formal topicalities of much writing in the revolutionary decade and its aftermath. In this way Austen pretended to deal with central and universal human "nature" rather than the partial "realities" of one party or another of political and cultural revolutionaries. Yet Austen is political. As a clergyman's daughter and sister of professional men, she affirms the relevance of Anglican values, culture, and institutions in a long and successful coalition of gentry and professions leading local society and thus the nation from the past through the present crisis and into the future. Contemporary challenges to this culture were intertwined with religious Dissent and *avant-garde* Romanticism; to refute them and bring about the hegemonic coalition she represented and advocated, Austen deliberately made her novels seem old-fashioned in form and technique. Paradoxically, one of Austen's early admirers was the Prince Regent, leader of the commercialized culture of emulation that she and most writers of her time, Jacobin or anti-Jacobin, Romantic or anti-Romantic, attacked. Appropriately, Austen's novels were not widely recognized as classics, or as literature, until near the end of the Romantic period, when they were republished in Bentley's Standard Novels.

The writer who did most to establish the novel as literature during the period itself was Walter Scott. Austen and Scott seem very different, as each noted.[3] She wrote novels of generalized contemporary life; he wrote historical romances. She converted the "trash of the circulating library" into literature; he used his extensive legal, historical, literary, and folkloristic knowledge and his mastery of narrative poetry to convert mere romance into literature. She transformed a genre closely associated with women, and thus subliterary, into art; he elevated the status of the novel by adding elements of men's learned culture. She limited herself by design to the decorously feminine local and domestic, implying their centrality to public and national life; he treated the local and domestic in terms of the national and the public. Both largely avoided the kind of representation of erotic subjectivity found, politicized, in novels of their more liberal contemporaries. Yet both wrote about the social issues and crises of their present by indirection, displacement, or generalization, and both argue for a coalition of gentry and professionals to lead Britain through immediate domestic and international crises while leaving the paternalist social structure in place.

Scott himself rose from urban professional to landed gentleman thanks to his literary success. In Scotland such a dialectic of gentry and professionals was well established by 1800, centered on the legal profession to which Scott was bred and legitimated by the Scottish Enlightenment from which he drew his critique of court culture and belief in modernization, or the eradication of feudalism, the precapitalist customary economy, superstition, and provincialism. Scott was an anti-Jacobin who organized a troop of citizen-cavalry to resist French invasion and intimidate rebellious laborers, and he hobnobbed with leading men of power and patronage. He was also widely read in "street literature," early verse romance, Shakespeare and other dramatists, classic English poets and essayists, and Enlightenment philosophical historians: these materials enriched his novels with a wide range of literary and learned allusion. His masters in novel form were his eighteenth-century predecessors – Le Sage, Fielding, Smollett, Mackenzie, and Defoe – from whom he took the loose, romance-journey, social-survey story; elements of the identity-mystery romance; the errant, impressionable hero; the vivid minor characters equipped with characteristic speech, often in dialect; and the striking description and incident at once realistic and symbolic (as in his narrative poems). Yet he also knew contemporary women novelists, taking from Edgeworth the theme of British consciousness and professionalization of the gentry and peasantry, from the Porter sisters elements of the historical romance, and from Radcliffe topographical and other kinds of description. His Scottish novels in particular may be seen as a conscious reformulation of those of his immediate women predecessors, particularly Elizabeth Helme's *St. Clair of the Isles* (1803) and Jane Porter's *The Scottish Chiefs* (1810). Scott's construction of the novel was later criticized by some self-consciously artistic Victorian novelists (who were nevertheless in his debt), yet it became the major vehicle for the invention of national identity, history, and destiny, used to disseminate Romantic nationalism in many cultures and countries.

Scott's preoccupation as a novelist of the 1810s and 1820s was that of the 1790s during which he was a young man – revolution – but viewed through a Scottish Enlightenment philosophical history of the progress of civilization. His Scottish novels, now widely considered his best, deal with points of revolutionary change in Scotland's emergence from feudalism to modernity: the "killing time" of the religious persecutions of the 1680s (*Old Mortality*, 1817), the Union of England and Scotland in 1707 (*The Bride of Lammermoor*, 1819), the 1715 Jacobite uprising (*Rob Roy*, 1817), the Porteous Riots of 1736 (*The Heart of Midlothian*, 1818), the Jacobite rising of 1745 (*Waverley*, 1814), the period of modernization (*Redgauntlet*, 1824; *Guy Mannering*, 1815), and the threat to stability of the 1790s (*The Antiquary*, 1816). In this sequence of novels Scotland is a figure for Europe at large. In other novels, many of which equal the best of the Scottish novels in artistry and political edge, Scott deals with revolutionary crises or transformations of other kinds: the coalescence of Norman and Anglo-Saxon into English identity (*Ivanhoe*, 1819), the merging of feudal and commercial social orders (*The Fair Maid of Perth*, 1828), the medieval confrontation of courtly and democratic cultures (*Anne of Geierstein*, 1829), the collision of East and West (*The Talisman*, 1825; *Count Robert of Paris*, 1831), and the building of a new political consensus in the aftermath of the English Civil War (*Woodstock*, 1826).[4] It is not so much these themes, however, as Scott's handling of them in novel form that made the Waverley Novels so interesting to contemporaries and so stimulating to readers and followers for the rest of the century.

Like Enlightenment historians and anti-Jacobin novelists, Scott adopted an authoritative third-person narration to constitute a model consciousness with a transhistorical perspective, confidently recreating the past and comparing or contrasting it with the present, thereby reinforcing the Waverley Novels' sense of history as loss and gain. The narrator's gravity of tone and formality of style represent the voice of historiography, the master-discourse of professional intellectuals, and dominate the voices of the novel's speakers of dialect, sociolect, and idiolect. This narratorial authority is only emphasized by Scott's use of various comic narrative personae to register fiction's rhetorical, constructed nature. Thus figural description and authoritative narration together give cogency to the Waverley Novels' critique of both court government and fanatical opposition to it. For Scott's novels, written across the period from the end of the Napoleonic Wars to the threshold of the Great Reform Bill, are preoccupied with the situation of the middle classes faced with inadequate leadership from above, political rebellion from below, and dissension within. The Waverley Novels are not only an encyclopedia of the forms and themes of prose fiction up to the early nineteenth century but the Romantic period's most comprehensive fictional meditation on the social divisions and changes revealed in the 1790s and exacerbated in the revolutionary aftermath.

Thus it is in being novelists of their time that Austen and Scott helped to make the novel into literature and to refound literature as class property, the new national institution of verbal art, which became the defining center for the evolving practices of writing controlled by the professional class and used to dominate society and remake it in their own image. That Austen and Scott, however different, are central to Romantic novel readers' interests, artistic and political, is seen in the fate of a novel only now becoming a classic – James Hogg's *Private Memoirs and Confessions of a Justified Sinner, Written by Himself* (1824). It takes on the social-historical novel, the novel of passion and intense subjectivity, and a variety of other emergent modes of Romantic fiction and writing, and by representing social divisions of self, class, gender, language, culture, and history in an irremediably divided text, it exposes the assumptions underlying Romantic literature's imagined community of the nation.

Hogg's novel contains two texts – the autobiography of an early eighteenth-century Scottish antinomian and "The Editor's Narrative" of the same events. These texts, one confessional and self-justifying, the other authoritative, seem to present the story of a Scottish landed gentleman's second son, who grows up in a divided house, quarrels with his older brother at the time of the Union of England and Scotland – conventionally the origin of modern Scotland – is encouraged by his double, Gil-Martin, who may be the devil, to commit various crimes out of self-righteousness, tries to publish his self-vindicating autobiography, becomes a social outcast, and commits suicide. But the Editor confesses that he doesn't understand the Sinner's narrative. There is no final explanation of the Sinner's life, no closing of the book on the past, only an unbridgeable abyss between Sinner and Editor, past and present, pre-modern and modern consciousness, superstition and Enlightenment, speech and writing. The present cannot accommodate or domesticate the past; the Sinner's confessions, his self-writing, do not "justify" himself, but lapse into a narrative irony as the reader understands him and his actions more fully than he (or the Editor) does, through a sociology of fanaticism, or self-obsession, familiar enough in Romantic fiction and part of a widely understood sociology of rebellion and revolution at the time. Furthermore, the only truth apparent to the reader is offered by dialect speakers, not the two principal narrators who use standard written English. In this novel, speech, not writing, bears truth. Significantly, the contradictors are social outcasts – women or working people – whose speech undoes the writing of the professional middle-class men who weave a web of words to encompass reality. Hogg subverts the new discourse of combined history and romance being used to invent the Romantic nation and thereby to reconcile social divisions of class, gender, and region under the aegis of the professional middle class.

Not surprisingly, Hogg's novel was greeted with incomprehension, anger, and derision in its time, mutilated in later editions, forgotten, and only rediscovered in the twentieth century. Most Romantic fiction fared as ill, or worse – soon forgotten, appropriated by "street literature" or cut down for the nursery or schoolroom, barely canonical now, and only canonized at the cost of being stripped of its politics. It is often assumed (and occasionally argued) that, while Romantic fiction deals with the merely social, Romantic poetry best embodies the period's "discoveries" about the self and nature, and even that it had more influence on the Victorian and modern novel. Yet Romantic novelists attempted as much or more than the poets in writing about the self, celebrating the domestic affections and local quotidian life, creating a national imagined community, and establishing a national language and literature commanded by the classes who read and wrote this literature and fiction and whose interests they served – and still serve. Meanwhile, the dialogue initiated during the Romantic period between prose fiction and melodrama produced those genres that would dominate the popular fiction, theatre, cinema, and television that most people use to understand and negotiate their everyday lives.

## NOTES

1. See Richard Carlile's remarks in *The Gauntlet: A Sound Republican Weekly Newspaper*, February 10, 1833: 2–3.

2. See Dick Leith, *A Social History of English* (London: Routledge, 1983), pp. 32–57.
3. *Jane Austen's Letters to Her Sister Cassandra and Others*, ed. R. W. Chapman, 2nd edn. corr. (1959; reprinted, Oxford University Press, 1979), p. 404; *The Journal of Sir Walter Scott*, ed. W. E. K. Anderson (Oxford: Clarendon Press, 1972), p. 114 (March 14, 1826).
4. Dates of publication are those when the novels actually appeared, rather than the dates on title pages.

# 10

STUART CURRAN

# Romantic poetry: why and wherefore?

AGES are marked by literary fashion as much as by their political settlements or upheavals. We speak commonly of Elizabethan drama or of Enlightenment prose, thereby defining the epoch generically and even temperamentally. The continuing preoccupation with "Renaissance self-fashioning" only puts a modern gloss on the conventional notion that it was an age for drama. The eighteenth century has long been conceived as inseparable from its monumental achievements in prose, works reflecting the massive organization and integration of European civilization – the French *Encyclopédie*, Johnson's *Dictionary*, even, seemingly almost as long, Richardson's *Clarissa*. What is it, then, that makes us commonly associate British Romanticism with poetry? Why, indeed, until recently did we generally separate the writers of prose – except for literary theorists like Coleridge and Hazlitt – from the poets, pretending, for instance, that Jane Austen inhabited a world fundamentally different from that of Shelley rather than living at the same time and, indeed, about twenty-five miles from his birthplace, and writing constantly about families that easily could pass for Shelley's own? The Victorians started this conventional association almost as a way of distinguishing their epoch, another age of prose or at least to their minds of robust narrative, from that softer, more emotional, more lyrical world that preceded theirs, an irrecoverable infancy to which they longed to retreat. But that is a manifest caricature of an age in which all the major poets (and a multitude of minor ones too) planned and, except for Coleridge, executed epic poems. That very fact, however, indicates that part of the answer lies simply in numbers. Let us, then, begin on the level of statistics.

In the thirty-five years between 1789, the inception of the French Revolution, and 1824, when Byron died, a generation that may be said to encompass British Romanticism, some five thousand books of original verse were published in Britain.[1] The sheer numbers, from the start, point to an intractable problem for later readers. The average student of Romantic poetry reads selectively in three publications of Wordsworth's, two of Coleridge's, at best two of Keats's, perhaps as many as four each of the books published by Byron and Shelley, a sprinkling of verse from fewer than a half-dozen women's volumes, and a few works of Blake's that, strictly speaking, were hand-printed, never actually published at all. Less than twenty-five books out of five thousand is a minuscule number on which to base generalizations about the literature of a period, especially of the sweeping kind that often characterize critical statements about Romantic poetry.

Perhaps we are right to regard the great poems of the period as modern critics tend to, as embodying a bridge between the old and the new, leading with an undeviating aim in the direction of ourselves and our modern pre-occupations with inner growth, the psychology of creativity, the aspiration for a simple, organic engagement with the natural or, less optimistically, with our fundamental uncertainties, divided allegiances, and desires beyond fulfillment. But it is likewise possible that we are holding up a mirror to ourselves and calling the reflection Romanticism and thus wrong the spe-cial historical configuration of a time with very different values, political and cultural stresses, economic exigencies, discoveries about the self and the world. In England, to list a few examples, except for the first few years after the fall of the Bastille, the word democrat was a term of opprobrium; the constant if sometimes muffled thunders of war, and for the first time on a world scale, reverberated for the twenty-two years separating the beheading of Louis XVI and the armageddon of Waterloo; simultaneously, an Asian and African empire was silently attached to notions of British destiny, all in the name of averting French anarchy; and, with factory riots, a periodic threat of famine, the dislocation into the army and navy of an enormous number of young males, and widespread political agitation posing increasing chal-lenges to an outdated, inept political establishment, England emerged from the Napoleonic Wars paradoxically the richest nation on earth and to prove it rebuilt the west end of London in the grand, public manner that still sur-vives as a wonder of monumental architecture and urban planning. If one mulls over such a disjointed, perhaps contradictory record, none of its con-stituents (except warfare) really sounds modern at all. Least of all, according to our normal scale of literary expectations, should be the connection of such a turbulent, even chaotic, time with the artistic craft and dependence on traditional refinements associated with poetry.

In 1820, which was the highwater mark for verse in the Romantic period, at least 323 volumes or collections of verse were published in Great Britain, 204 of these at a minimum being original. Among the latter were the book on which Keats's fame rests, Shelley's *Cenci* and *Prometheus Unbound, and Other Poems* (which contained as well the "Ode to the West Wind," "The Cloud," and "To a Sky-Lark"), some cantos of *Don Juan* and Byron's first historical drama, *Marino Faliero*, Wordsworth's *River Duddon* sonnet sequence and a four-volume collection of his *Miscellaneous Poems*, and the first publication by John Clare. These are themselves monuments in the history of English poetry; yet they form a modest component of the greater monument constituted by all this verse in the aggregate. Poetry mattered to this age in a way that it has never mattered since – neither in Britain, in other English-speaking countries, nor in Europe. Although Shelley in Italy was hardly in a position to count the numbers for 1820, it is almost as if his *Defence of Poetry*, which he began in February 1821 and which for many is the most exalted celebration of poetry ever written, was impelled to existence by this unparalleled personal faith in and public outpouring of verse.

It is tempting to ascertain submerged reasons for such a phenomenon. Perhaps the fittest way to survive the longest war in modern history was to retreat into a mental sanctuary, presiding over it as its priest, which is how Keats characterized his role as poet in the "Ode to Psyche" he published in 1820. But had the Napoleonic Wars, five years past, driven two hundred poets in one twelve-month period into such hermitages of obsessive versifying? Perhaps it was the death of the old order in George III that same year and the necessary accession of another unreconstructed old order in the gouty, pleasure-loving George IV? It is hard to imagine either such possibility as the impulse, and harder still, if either were at all near the case, not to think it the symptom of a profoundly disturbed civilization. Against the enormous dislocations of that war, or the girth of the new monarch, what good were a few dozen sonnets? Crude social formulations of this sort can only throw into relief the kind of verse able to respond to them. And there was much of that among this outpouring of verse in 1820: the plentitude of satires and books of political doggerel serve to remind us that if we robe all Romanticism in the priestly vestments in which Keats imagined himself garbed in one poem, judging the period uniformly as characterized by a profound isolation or interiority, we do so only by blinding ourselves to the social and political manifestations of literature during the age.

But even to acknowledge that dimension is to underscore the otherness of the culture. Poetry mattered in a political, a social realm. Shelley's *Mask of Anarchy* ought to have been one of those volumes of original verse published in 1820; but his friend Leigh Hunt, to whom the poet consigned it for publication, fearing the consequences, held it back until the atmosphere surrounding the debate of the Reform Bill of 1832 allowed safe passage to its radical ideas and language and to their disseminator. Hunt's temerity was well founded. He had himself as a journalist been imprisoned for writing an unflattering portrait of the Prince Regent, the future George IV; his brother John, who published the joint periodical of Byron, Shelley, and

Hunt, *The Liberal*, during their absence in Italy, was indicted in 1823 and convicted of libel for printing Byron's satire on George III and the laureate Robert Southey, *The Vision of Judgement*. This was the same year that George Canning, installed as leader of the Tory House of Commons and as Foreign Secretary of the government after years on the back bench, attended to a major consolidation of his public career by publishing his collected poems. Poetry mattered.

It is no surprise that literature should be seen to threaten temporal establishments, as we verify in the record of dispossessed, exiled, or imprisoned writers in our own times. Still, it takes a leap of the historical imagination to place ourselves within a culture in which so much stock was placed not merely in writing, but specifically in poetry.

> In spite of difference of soil and climate, of language and manners, of laws and customs: in spite of things silently gone out of mind, and things violently destroyed; the Poet binds together by passion and knowledge the vast empire of human society, as it is spread over the whole earth, and over all time.
>
> (*Prose*, I, 141)

So wrote Wordsworth in the preface to *Lyrical Ballads*.

> Poets are the hierophants of an unapprehended inspiration, the mirrors of the gigantic shadows which futurity casts upon the present, the words which express what they understand not; the trumpets which sing to battle, and feel not what they inspire: the influence which is moved not, but moves. Poets are the unacknowledged legislators of the world. (*Poetry and Prose*, p. 508)

That, of course, is the famous end of Shelley's *Defence of Poetry*. Can anyone today, at least anyone residing in the First World, read either of those two statements without a sense of meager embarrassment in the presence of such embracing, majestic rhetoric? And who in modern cultures would stake existence itself on the ambition of the 22-year-old Keats: "I think I shall be among the English Poets after my death" (*Letters*, p. 161: October 14, 1818)? Why, in other words, should poetry have so mattered to the culture of English Romanticism?

In Keats's case, we have come to see, and without diminishing by a mite the nobility of the ambition or the rare talent in which he embedded it, that the pretensions of class and poetry were closely intertwined.[2] In the age of Enlightenment no less than the Renaissance England observed the peculiar fiction that a gentleman wrote verse. There is a strain in Byron that goes back to the cavalier aristocrats, even a deeper, less open because truly pretentious, strain in him that reminds one of the range and *sprezzatura* of a Sidney, which is to say, of a true nobleman. With Shelley, heir to a baronetcy and fluent in six languages besides English, we observe the mutual fertilization of learning and literature so characteristic of Enlightenment intellectuals in France. But for Keats there is no such natural model. He is unable to fit into the mold of rural proletarian discovery that, starting with Burns and running through a succession of poets like Robert Bloomfield and John Clare (the last of whom was promoted by Taylor and Hessey, Keats's publishers), testified directly to the social mobility offered by poetry. Nor could he easily assume the superficial nonchalance of the journalist poet Leigh Hunt, who was for a time his mentor and whose style of studied suburban comfort in both life and verse, though assuredly attractive to the son of a livery stable owner, rang false to Keats's own experience. The place of poetry in English culture, precisely because it was so deeply based in class distinctions, promised liberation from those very distinctions if only Keats could succeed in "becom[ing] one of the English Poets."

Even stronger than the conventional ties between poetry and an educated leisure class were those that restricted it in terms of gender. Of the traditional "English Poets" to which Keats refers, either in the multi-volume collections of Samuel Johnson (1779–81), John Bell (1789–94), Robert Anderson (1792–5), or Alexander Chalmers (1810), or in the "Select Beauties" anthologized by Henry Headley (1787), the "Specimens" of George Ellis (1790), or other such smaller compilations, only one woman appears: Queen Elizabeth. The reaction of women to such ingrained exclusionary biases is analyzed separately in this volume, but the biases themselves firmly linked gender to genre. As long as fiction could be conceived to be a woman's genre, it could be attacked as morally pernicious, anti-intellectual, an affront to civilized values, and therefore subversive of the state. These terms were in some sense universally accepted until midway through the second decade of the nineteenth century, when Austen's genius was recognized just before her death and the early novels of Scott's *Waverley* series took Britain by storm, simply settling the question for good. But even then, one observes that Lord Byron did not turn to writing novels; by no means – his snobbish answer to Scott's rivalry was an intentionally unending epic poem. Nor did John Keats, who needed money desperately, turn to prose to get it. If poetry had the capacity to declassify him, fiction would stamp his lower-bourgeois educational and family credentials indelibly upon him. Instead, with the consumption setting in, he projected a series of neo-Shakespearean tragedies as the never-to-be-completed fulfillments of his genius. There would have been no money in them either, nor any sense at all from the perspective of the timely or the relevant.

To be "among the English Poets" was a just ambition for the *declassé* and the marginalized, who found themselves excluded beyond any seeming desert from the centers of power and privilege in British society. Poetry, though celebrated as surpassing national and even temporal boundaries in the encomia of Wordsworth and Shelley, could be characterized as a distinctly British passion, or resource. Not that other countries lacked their poets, but no nation in modern Europe had the sustained tradition of greatness, generation by generation, over several centuries that the English language could boast. Until the last decades of the eighteenth century Britain had liberally borrowed its artists (Holbein, Kneller, Van Dyke), as it did its musicians (Bononcini, Handel, Haydn), from the rest of Europe. In poetry only did the country express its heart and soul, preserve a unique national heritage. It was the symbolic center of the nation's spirit both to those who never had a chance to breathe the actual atmosphere at that center or to young intellectuals like Coleridge and Wordsworth who, having had it, retreated in disaffection from its tainted odour. It is not an accident that against "the fen / Of stagnant waters" Wordsworth saw in contemporary England in "London, 1802" he should pose the historical presence of one of the nation's greatest poets ("Milton! thou should'st be living at this hour"), nor indeed that he should attribute to poetry vatic, almost messianic, properties in the higher planes of his preface to the *Lyrical Ballads*. The poetry apostrophized by Wordsworth is beyond mere versification: it is the essential character of the British people as expressed through the English language, "the real language of men." To tap it at its source, he promises himself in the final books of *The Prelude*, is in some unexplained sense to begin a process of national redemption. Surely, this is mystification on a grand scale; and yet it is not laughable, and it is much more innocent and probably nobler than the similar mystification that made the English language the measure by which civilization was spread through nineteenth-century territorial or twentieth-century commercial imperialism, by Britain and then America. Thus, what begins as a center of privileged discourse restricted by class, education, and gender is raised from its original value of the merely prestigious to a plane transcending its restrictive elements and at last becomes expressive of the very nature of British culture.

If we return to the movement of women into the literary marketplace, we may be able to place this entire complex in focused perspective. Mary Robinson, Charlotte Smith, and Helen Maria Williams (to name three of the better-known women authors of the 1780s and 1790s) all made money, indeed to some extent a living, from their prose; yet each seems to have invested greater care, from insuring the elegance of the book as artifact to oversight of multiple editions, in their poetic productions. We could understand the difference as being wholly contained by that sense of the prestigious residing in the poetic and, as with Keats, the desire to be known as a poet would then be expressive of a social mobility ambitiously grasped in order to move up the scale. We might likewise wish to observe in this endeavor a deliberate invasion of a male realm by writers refusing simply to be relegated to spinning fantasies for ladies of leisure who needed something to occupy their time until the husband came home. So Helen Maria Williams underpins her early career with a long, quasi-epic poem about that exotic country for male exploration and exploitation, Peru; or Charlotte Smith annotates her generically different *Elegiac Sonnets* with knowing citations of Petrarch as a shorthand substitute for the learned disquisition she implies she could write on the subject; or Mary Robinson publishes her final volume of verse, *Lyrical Tales*, with the same firm that produced *Lyrical Ballads*, claiming her intellectual and creative kinship with the *avant-garde* and complexly reconceiving the dynamics of the Wordsworth–Coleridge collaboration. In some sense each of those patterns conforms to the dynamics of class, gender, and literary value that mark the age; and we would be wrong to rule them completely out. Yet finally, the motive could be purer and the recompense more refined than such models might suggest. It could be, however expressive of fantasy or wishful thinking, that these English women wrote for fame in verse not out of a sense of disadvantage nor even of asserting rightful equality, but simply to align themselves with that mystified national spirit that through poetry transcended all the barriers into which they were introduced at birth. "There is / One great society alone on earth," Wordsworth avers, "the noble Living and the noble Dead" (*Prelude*, XI.393–5). Its voice is poetry. "Poetry is the breath and finer spirit ... Poetry is the first and last[,] of all knowledge – it is as immortal as the heart of man," is his expression in the preface to *Lyrical Ballads* (*Prose*, I, 141). These are sentiments just short of religious.

Should a later time choose to shake its collective head in disbelief before such enthusiasm, we can be sure that earlier ones would have too. Nowhere in Johnson's *Lives* would we find any language approaching this kind of mystification, nor does Dryden ever elevate the value of poetry very far above an actual text on the page or stage. If Wordsworth's high rhetoric reminds us of the claims Shakespeare makes for the immortality of his sonnets or the transubstantiation by which, in Sidney's *Apology*, poets replace Nature's "brazen" world with one "golden," it may be no accident. Wordsworth thought Johnson's *Lives of the Poets* thrown away on mere "metrical writers utterly worthless and useless" (*Prose*, III, 79), as he put it in the "Essay, supplementary to the Preface" adjoined to his 1815 edition, celebrating in their place Chaucer, Spenser, Sidney, and Shakespeare. The shift in taste between Johnson and Wordsworth we may feel represents a fundamental index of differences between their cultures. But it actually does so in very specific terms that go far to explaining why this sudden veneration for poetry and exaltation of the place of the poet should have occurred at this time and in this culture. The political rationales earlier posed for the outpouring of verse in 1820 were not wholly facetious. It could be justly argued that the long war with France did, indeed, and with particular force, give a nationalist coherence to Britain's sense of a distinctive mission; and it is probably true that the national stress occasioned by George III's long madness had its indirect effects in the arts, if only by way of impelling proof that the spirit of the people transcended an all-but-vacant throne. But an even more elemental impetus came from the collections of English poetry also noted earlier. These are, like its encyclopedias, a publishing phenomenon of the age, and just as indicative of its scientific organization of new knowledge. Johnson's collection of poets from Milton to his own time was not his own idea, but the commission of a publisher; and in an ironic way the inadequacy of the edition was of essential importance to radically recasting the accepted tradition of English literature. This revision was spurred as well by two major efforts of antiquarian research in the second half of the eighteenth century, Thomas Percy's *Reliques of Ancient English Poetry* (1765) and Thomas Warton's *History of English Poetry* (1774–81), which between them established texts and interconnected their authors within a historical progression reaching into the seventeenth century. It is hard to imagine a time when medieval poetry beyond Chaucer was not known, when figures such as Wyatt or Marlowe, Donne or Herrick, were almost as legendary as the lost Homer was for the Middle Ages, but, except for the diligent and scholarly among poets, a Pope or a Gray, no less than among their readers, this was the general case of the early eighteenth century in Britain. Warton's *History of English Poetry* and Johnson's *Works of the English Poets* were completed the same year, and their volumes stood in total contradiction in their representation of the centuries and the canon they inscribed. Johnson elaborated a world of poetry with which his contemporaries were comfortable, a world they recognized and in which they recognized themselves. Its inclusive title notwithstanding, his *Works* scarcely went back more than a century. Warton, whose huge second volume, incredible as it seems, was entirely devoted to the literature of the fifteenth century, offered his readers a *terra incognita* as strange and wonderful as the new world. And, on the British imperial model, it was immediately colonized and exploited.

Thus we find Charlotte Smith's *Elegiac Sonnets* of 1784, as noted before, pointedly citing Petrarch and other sonnet writers of earlier centuries in their annotations. Her miniatures drew a host of other poets to rival her for honors, spawning a veritable craze for the sonnet in the 1790s, which led in turn with the new century to major scholarly resuscitations of Elizabethan and early Italian examples and, at the crest of the renewed interest, to the sonnets of Wordsworth and Keats, which together constitute the finest sustained exploration of the form since Milton. It is easy enough to see the effect of the revival of Renaissance forms on Keats, in his Shakespearean sonnets, his neo-Elizabethan romances like "Lamia," the perfect odes, the Miltonic or Dantean versions of the Hyperion legend. But let us, for a less obvious instance, trace how Wordsworth's disdain for the generality of Johnson's poets and veneration for an earlier canon of verse affected his work. The collaboration of Wordsworth and Coleridge in *Lyrical Ballads* is of such revolutionary impact for the future of poetry in English on ideological, psychological, and stylistic grounds that it is easy to overlook the extraordinary dexterity with which both poets employ the ballad stanza, deliberately recreating the range to be found in Percy's extended collection, making the ballad a fit vehicle for the sublime, as in "The Rime of the Ancient Mariner," or the ridiculous, which Wordsworth attempts to encompass in "The Idiot Boy," and for numerous shades between. Included in the single volume edition of 1798 were likewise masterful variations on the blank-verse meditation, in the vernacular conversation of Coleridge's "Nightingale" and the high sonorities of Wordsworth's "Lines Written a Few Miles Above Tintern Abbey"; and in "The Female Vagrant" a poem of harsh reality was rendered for contrasting effect in the Spenserian stanzas conventional to romance. From this point on, Wordsworth continually experimented to determine how his inimitable voice, with simple monosyllables and deliberately flat tones, might accommodate a panoply of different forms and genres. The second volume of *Lyrical Ballads*, added in 1800, embodies one of the greatest elaborations of a distinctly English pastoral ever written, from the high plane of "The Brothers" and "Michael," through the touching vernacular of the Matthew poems, down to the sentimental reduction, which is yet an aspect of the pastoral tradition, exemplified in "The Pet Lamb." In his next collection of poetry, *Poems, in Two Volumes* (1807), Wordsworth extended his range further, ending the first section with a Horatian "Ode to Duty" and the second volume with the last great Pindaric ode in English, "Intimations of Immortality," including as well two different, equally brilliant sonnet sequences in private and public modes, and almost ostentatiously showing off his learning and craft in the unlikeliest of places: "Resolution and Independence," the story of his encounter with the Leech-Gatherer, is set in rhyme royal, which is named after the meter of *The Kingis Quair* written by King James I of Scotland in 1423. You will look very far in the eighteenth century for examples of rhyme royal and not find one – unless, that is, like Wordsworth you were to consult Warton's *History of English Poetry*.

The merest tyro in the development of English poetry could, without needing complex critical formulations, or much history, or any philosophy, explain the most marked difference between the poetry at the end of the eighteenth century and that of the beginning. A landscape flooded with couplets was drained to reveal a remarkable topography of forms and, with them, opportunities for formal experiment, testing, arrangement, revisionism. That happened because of Percy's and Warton's antiquarian researches and the embodiment of the results on all sides and even with concentrated passion, both in massive collections and selective anthologies. The history of English poetry, considered a newly discovered heritage by the poets of the Romantic period, bore something like its present canonical form, though with some minor poets – Drummond of Hawthornden, say, or Edmund Waller – there was a much more detailed knowledge than survives today except among specialists. It cannot be overemphasized how significant an event the renaissance of the Renaissance was. For the first time there was an actual *history* not of literature *per se*, but of poetry in English. The generation beginning in the 1780s and truly emerging into artistic leadership in the 1790s was the first ever to know that history. The effect of its knowledge, coinciding as it did with a declaration of warfare, was, as we have seen, profoundly nationalistic. But it was also explosive. The numbers of volumes with which this consideration began and to which the subject must continually revert as a cultural phenomenon, if studied through a cross-section, would reveal not just a record of isolated ambitions and fantasies of prestige, but the result of the sudden opening-up of centuries of the past, a result at once embedded in tradition and expressed through experimentation, the testing of possibilities, even the mixing of what might have seemed unnatural colors. Making allowance for differences in century and artistic mode, is there not something very like the effect of a Matisse still-life in the deliberate crossing of antithetical forms, colors, and patterns of expectation attempted in the *Lyrical Ballads*? Lyrics are personal, private, emotive; ballads are communal, public, narrative. The critic Francis Jeffrey and even Coleridge himself in his lengthy critique of Wordsworth in the *Biographia Literaria* look at Wordsworth's experimentation as akin to a mixed metaphor whose meaning is vitiated by contradiction. But the real experiment was to create the poetic equivalent of an oxymoron, an impossible combination yet one that is ultimately true to the conditions of life. Today, perhaps we take Wordsworth's success too easily for granted. It was hard to do. And it was even harder to conceive in the first place.

There was a time when commentators on Romantic poetry mistook the atmosphere of artistic experimentation in the period, which is normal to all art, for an abandonment of tradition, which is not. The profusion of sonnets, odes, even epics, however, testifies to the opposite of that abandonment, an intense engagement with the possibilities of form opened up by, contained within, the new history of poetry in English. Along with that exploration within forms, and perhaps as expected (so at least the example of *Lyrical Ballads* would intimate), poets frequently experimented across traditional genres, trying out new combinations, mixed forms, what Wordsworth, in his own taxonomy of kinds of verse in the "Preface" of 1815, called "composite order[s]" (*Prose*, III, 28). Some of the major works of the period – Wordsworth's *Prelude*, Byron's *Don Juan*, Shelley's *Prometheus Unbound* are prime examples – bear strong evidence of generic intermixture on a grand scale. That generic mixture extends as well into gender, though it is a subject that has only just been broached by criticism of the period. For instance, Wordsworth's "lyrical romance," *The White Doe of Rylstone*, subjects the entire ethos of heroic endeavor conventionally celebrated by the romance to a feminine perspective, as the male contingent of a family in the late Middle Ages goes to its death in war on a point of masculinist honor, leaving the young Emily to suffer and endure. Needless to say, the newly arrived women poets are even more sensitive to the implicit links between gender and genre and exploit them continually. The female sonnet writer who invokes Petrarch – and Charlotte Smith set a pattern many followed – is supremely conscious that Laura has now taken up the pen and is no longer simply a silent, worshiped object whose purpose is to define the masculine ego.

There is an implicit protest in this poetry, as an earlier essay in this volume documents. But the element of protest in the more canonical poets is muted, with the exception of Blake who was operating outside the system or of Shelley who tended to speak his mind and suffer the consequences. Part of this occurs as the effect of time. It requires not just sensitivity to, but also actual knowledge of, the conditions of the age to see in Wordsworth's continual representation of marginalized figures in the *Lyrical Ballads* an active social conscience questioning both means and ends in society's creation of outcasts. Yet, for today's student of this poetry even the combination of sensitivity and knowledge may prepare one inadequately, because one of the veritable conditions of the age was censorship.[3] It was first deployed against Jacobin sympathizers with the Revolution in France; but it increasingly became used to control political agitation and to threaten any organized effort to alter the *status quo*. Such censorship took many forms. There was the overt sort used for the stage, which, for instance, banned production of Shelley's *Cenci* and virtually disallowed any political theme outside a numbing jingoism. There was likewise a direct threat from the law. Byron's *Vision of Judgement* was by no means the only work to fall foul of government prosecution, for the statutes covering libel against the monarch and blasphemy against the deity, not to ignore strong sanctions against sedition, were used to disguise political indictments throughout the age. Then, there were subtler pressures exerted on publishers by various agencies of government, from lucrative contracts for printing government publications to honorific annuities provided to cooperative writers (both Southey and Wordsworth succumbed to that temptation), to straightforward, if under-the-table, graft to hirelings. In circumstances like these, where an author cannot be certain where the line of legality lies or when the threat of reprisal may be invoked, an atmosphere is created forcefully conducive to self-censorship.

The surprise, given this state of active and passive repression, is that there should be any political content at all to Romantic poetry. Where it occurs not openly, in the form of a direct moral or political challenge to the established order, but rather obliquely, as with the trail of the dispossessed in *Lyrical Ballads*, we may be sure that contemporary readers could decipher the intent and register its political implications. At times the coding is fairly obvious. Byron's diatribe against the misuse of genius by a venal, hypocritical Italian culture in his *Prophecy of Dante* easily transposes into a personal attack on British society. Marino Faliero's great final speech predicting the downfall of the Venetian oligarchy could have been delivered by Byron, with but a few changes of phrase, in the House of Lords. Shelley's reputation for outspokenness notwithstanding, there are sentiments that he cannot express directly and see in print. Review after review of *Prometheus Unbound* arraigned him for the first-act vision of Christ crucified by the Church, which, since it is mentioned briefly in a dream sequence within a drama where all the characters were classical, Shelley clearly thought could slip by without problems. He is far subtler in *The Cenci*, where his representation of the Roman Catholic hierarchy, playing openly on age-old, English anti-Catholic prejudices, drew no fire on that score; but needless to say the Church of England preserved the same hierarchical order, also owned vast tracts of land, and, with its dependable block of conservative votes in the House of Lords, illustrated the abuses of temporal power. *The Cenci* is a profoundly antireligious work that within its Italian Catholic setting knowingly taunts the law of blasphemous libel from end to end. The different taunt of *Prometheus Unbound*, however, should alert us to a feature of this landscape that is easily overlooked.

However strong an aesthetic force neo-Hellenism exerted on the arts in the Romantic period, it also represented an officially sanctioned counterculture, and the codes were universally understood. All the Younger Romantics, both the major poets – Byron, Keats, and Shelley – and more minor figures like Leigh Hunt and Thomas Love Peacock, use classical settings to sanction a sexual permissiveness that in a modern dress would be roundly condemned.[4] That may not seem to threaten revolution, but the effect is compounded by the political implications that can be derived from such a setting. The overthrow of Jupiter in *Prometheus Unbound*, after all, is a toppling of the tyrannical king of the gods, who keeps dissidents in chains and surrounds himself with unctuous lackeys. When in the sublime curtain calls of the fourth act Demogorgon calls on the stars and planets of the universe, they respond in one voice, "Our great Republic hears" (IV.533) – not constitutional monarchy, but republic. Keats is generally thought the least openly political of the Younger Romantics, and that may well be the case, since he has everything to lose. Yet, the essential point of the Hyperion poems is a dynastic shift, and to conceive its terms solely as an aesthetic formulation is to exclude connotations that could not but be in the mind of a contemporary reader. Let us, for instance, read Oceanus's justification of the fall of the titans within the context of Keats's own time:

> So on our heels a fresh perfection treads,
> A power more strong in beauty, born of us
> And fated to excel us, as we pass
> In glory that old Darkness.　　("Hyperion," II.212–15)

At the very least, this is a calm recognition that political revolutions are inevitable and even welcome. In more specific terms, although Napoleon may be exiled to St. Helena and the old order replaced on the thrones of Europe, still that "fresh perfection" is "fated to excel us"; which is to say, the revolution of the European system promised by France cannot be forestalled. The "us" has a dramatic focus, referring to the titans whom Oceanus addresses, but it is written on an actual piece of paper by a young Englishman around the beginning of 1819, a year of enormous political stress and agitation across the breadth of Great Britain.

There is another network of codes that operates through all literature but that, because of the combined force of the revival of literature and the political repression accompanying the war, has a particularly intense impact on the nature of Romantic poetry. This is the coding of intertextuality, incorporating through allusion or similarity of situation the dynamics of one or more works by another. If any of us were to read at length in the *oeuvre* of one of the near-contemporaries whom Johnson included in his version of the English poets, the range of allusiveness would be predictable. The lineaments of the earlier neo-Augustan style would remain, with an obligatory allusion to the common stock of Latin verse read at school or college. Shakespeare, and less often Milton, could be expected to resonate now and again through the verse. But for the rest, perhaps surprisingly, the allusiveness would be largely confined to the previous two generations of English poets, beginning with Pope and continuing through James Thomson, Edward Young, William Collins, and Thomas Gray. Those voices continue to be heard, though more faintly, among the poets of Romanticism, but they are joined and rather drowned out by a chorus of others, Milton and Spenser on the grand scale, but also the newly recovered sixteenth- and seventeenth-century poets, dramatists contemporary with Shakespeare, the Greek dramatists, and major European poets such as Dante. To stand back and observe this phenomenon objectively is to recognize once again how intensely privileged the status of poetry has become, how almost professionalized is the role of the contemporary poet, and how well educated – whatever down-to-earth and democratic allegiances Wordsworth may assert – the common reader is expected to be.

Milton is a favorite among Romantic poets and readers alike, partly the result of a massive investment in editions and biography in the 1790s and 1800s, and he exerts a particularly complex force on the poetic scene. Some of the critical engagement with Milton during the 1790s has a distinctly political edge to it: this is particularly the case with William Hayley's life and works of 1794–6. Shelley stops to make the political issue clear in a brief reference to Milton in his preface to *Prometheus Unbound*: "the sacred Milton was, let it ever be remembered, a Republican, and a bold enquirer into morals and religion" (*Poetry and Prose*, p. 134). Wherever one senses the presence of Milton in Shelley's poetry, this is what it constitutes. Blake generally is of a like mind, though his veneration is tempered by probing theological interrogation. Byron depends on the model as well, but he draws back from what he took to be an exceedingly stern personality. Yet if it was the "bold enquirer" whom Byron invoked in wrapping his drama *Cain* within the cloak of Miltonic language and situation, he provoked a virulent reaction from the defenders of orthodoxy, so much so that throughout the nineteenth century he was denied a monument in Westminster Abbey on the grounds of his alleged blasphemy. No other poet tried so direct an appropriation of Milton's spirit. Instead, he too enters the discourse under the shadow of censorship, through oblique and cryptic allusion. Given the fact, as the reception of *Cain* all too sharply indicates, that *Paradise Lost* had been assimilated to orthodox Christianity, its elements could not easily be recast, revised, or criticized without a poet's treading on forbidden ground. The alternative was to recall the work by derivative language or situation, thereby safely assimilating its example. This is essentially the ploy of both Keats and Shelley in "Hyperion" and *Prometheus Unbound*, works centrally concerned with the justification of evil and continually foregrounding Milton's solution, or attempted solution, to the problem as a means of distinguishing their own. The fact that Prometheus's curse, repeated by the Phantasm of Jupiter in act 1, prominently assimilates Satan, God, and Jesus through echo or icon, suggests how complicated, how deliberately "literary," this process can become. Unquestionably, Shelley's erudition and love for Milton influence his drawing so heavily on him; but the example indicates as well the extent to which an age of repression, censorship, and legal threat enforced a cryptic, allusive, richly layered style. All of this is suggestive, perhaps, of Milton's methods as well: one reason he must have appealed to poets of the Romantic age was that he wrote his last works under similar political pressures and in even direr political circumstances than those confronting them.

This link between the mechanics of censorship and the refinements of intertextuality indicates a further extension within characteristic patterns of Romantic poetry that, in recent years, have drawn considerable attention and even sparked some debate. These might be grouped together under the notion of a poetic of disengagement, or of deliberate, subtle deconstruction. Although the extent of Shelley's radicalism he made plain from the first in *Queen Mab*, it is not always certain how far to read a political or social agenda into his writings, particularly after he moved to Italy in 1818. Byron wavers in his revolutionary sympathies, as most aristocrats would, and in the fragmentary last canto of *Don Juan*, left unfinished by his death, he celebrates the consistency of his inconsistency. Keats's liberalism interlaces his correspondence but in the poetry surfaces, it would seem, only in the allegorized form already noted in the Hyperion poems. The early generation of Romantic poets represents an even more complicated picture, since Coleridge, Southey, and Wordsworth traversed the entire political spectrum from disaffection and dismay in the 1790s to becoming upholders of established order by the Regency two decades later. Where political allegiances of the latter kind surface in their poems – in Southey's laureate odes celebrating bloody battles or the Russian Czar, or in Wordsworth's "Sonnets on the Punishment of Death" – we prudently shut our eyes. As for Coleridge's reactionary advocacy of government by clerisy, like many another quaint expression of British eccentricity, it did no harm.

The picture is complicated even more by the persistence throughout the entire Romantic period of characteristic modes of Enlightenment poetry. There are, however mixed their quality, dozens of satires published every year, some of them clearly sanctioned by the government since until Waterloo settled the threat of foreign Jacobins the satiric impulse is almost entirely of a reactionary kind.[5] Didactic and prescriptive poetry is still written well into the nineteenth century. There are numerous versified histories and travelogues, even textbooks in verse that would make it mnemonically easier to keep Linnean classifications in the head, along with celebrations of the progress of various illustrious institutions, and anatomies of the emotions, as exemplified by a popular poem like Samuel Rogers's *Pleasures of Memory*. It should not be forgotten, although almost all the examples are, that a multitude of poems during the period rewrote Scripture or gave pious admonition to the faithful or threatened damnation to atheists and democrats. The generals were regularly feted for their victories and sometimes mourned in their deaths. The royal family was honored. Napoleon was regularly excoriated. All in all, there was sufficient poetry of statement during this period to give poetry a bad name.

Still, this only makes all the more anomalous the extent to which Romantic poetry, at least what we consider the best of it, resists being reduced to statement or to paraphrase, so much so, indeed, that at one time, holding the mirror up once again to nature, we could discern the course of modernism within Romanticism and today, after another glance at the glass, we find it is post-modernism whose strategies came to the fore in this body of literature. The days in which Shelley could be tapped for a realized political program, whether by Chartists or Fabian Socialists, or in which the venerable Wordsworth could be consulted on his "philosophy" of nature or queried about his beliefs in reincarnation in the "Intimations Ode" are long gone, with all their nostalgic innocence. Now Shelley's brilliant political analyses transmogrify into just further traps of the metaphoricity by which life will enact its triumph over us, and Wordsworth's veneration for Nature issues in the savage rape of "Nutting." As for the "Intimations Ode," even Wordsworth late in life acknowledged that the "clouds of glory" were wisps of metaphor. Although Coleridge asserted that the symbol did, indeed, guarantee access to what it symbolized and that the imaginative powers of the mind were replications of the attributes of God, everywhere in his poetry, from the alienation of the Ancient Mariner to the conditional clause that concludes "Kubla Khan," we confront a record of divorce between the signifier and signified, one all the more fearsome because their correspondence is conceived so essential for the meaning of human life. Poststructuralist theoretical formulations did not write these poems; they simply make us highly conscious of the care with which they come to conclusions in which, as Dr. Johnson entitled the last chapter of *Rasselas*, nothing is concluded. That convenient rubric of 1759, in turn, may remind us that deconstructive strategies are not confined to English Romanticism but tend to arise whenever high ambition and frustration go hand in hand, which is to say, through most human endeavors.

The Romantic period had before it, indeed was engaged actively in living through, perhaps the most exemplary instance of the frustration of high ambitions in modern times. From an Olympian perspective even the various modes of censorship adopted in Britain and the repressive legislation promulgated by Pitt and later by Lord Liverpool simply repeated on a mundane level the dynamics of that frustration, reminding any so inclined that there were material consequences to be suffered for venturing too high. What gives the major Romantic poets their lasting significance and compelling immediacy, therefore, is not a program or a consistent philosophy, but rather their force as embodiments of the intense doubleness of the age. Blake, who would "not cease from Mental Fight / ... Till we have built Jerusalem, / In England's green & pleasant Land" (*Milton*, 1.13–16) writes in his notebook for January 20, 1807, the cryptic memorandum "between Two and Seven in the Evening – Despair." The epic *Jerusalem*, which was the record of that struggle for apocalyptic victory Blake was writing at this time, is bloody beyond belief. It is doubtless the case that Wordsworth's "Nutting" enacts a process of natural ravishment, but on the other hand his prospectus to *The Recluse*, in which he sets out the design of his life's work, claims that he "would chant ... the spousal verse / Of this great consummation" (*Recluse*, 810–11), which is conceived as a true marriage of the mind and nature. The rhetorical figure of the oxymoron, the enjambement of opposites, which was invoked earlier to suggest the nature of *Lyrical Ballads*, is, in truth, the abiding figure of British Romanticism. Byron's "unreached Paradise of our despair" (*Childe Harold's Pilgrimage*, IV.1096) compresses the polar dynamics of acute desire and palpable frustration surveyed twice-over on Keats's urn where the images coexist ever and never, both in and out of existence. Keats is *the* poet of the oxymoron; there is no serious poem from his pen that does not enact some version of a creation out of the vacuum of its contradictory elements. It may seem pat, but nonetheless it is almost unavoidable that a *déclassé* genius who created for himself bowers of imagined pleasure in the midst of the wreckage of a war-torn world should immerse himself rhetorically in the authentic condition of his life.

Creation *ex nihilo* and for its own sake is, of course, an image of the purest poetic process, and at one point or another all the canonical British Romantics invoke such a notion of their art. Yet, each of them also conceives himself engaged in "Mental Fight" on the side of the future. Shelley, in the conclusion of *A Defence of Poetry*, goes so far as to equate the two, suggesting that the purest creativity, or even that entertained from reactionary motives, leads inevitably to future good because the exercise of the imagination is in its essence an ethical act of identification with what we admire. Without detracting from the value of that insight, or the honesty of its utterance, however, we can underscore how much it is engaged in snatching victory from the jaws of defeat, as Shelley's entire document brilliantly defines the centrality of the poetic voice marginalized by modern utilitarian impulses. The oxymoronic space is created out of the dialectic of contrary forces that, in Blake's terms, can contradict without thereby negating each other: "Without Contraries is no progression" (*Marriage of Heaven and Hell*, plate 3). By the time of Waterloo, it might be said that the attrition of contrary forces had virtually negated Europe; but still, Blake's axiom stands almost as a defining concept for the Romantic impulse in poetry. It even justifies self-contradictory or ambivalent stances as being stations in a progression yet to be worked out, expressions of experience not yet codified or reduced to the prescriptive.

To turn this complex around and characterize its positive obverse is to recognize how thoroughly the events of this time of clashing ideologies and armies, and even of forces within British society independently transforming an agricultural into an industrial base, conspired to enfranchise a poetry not of statement but of exploration, a poetry of and in process. Wordsworth's philosophy of nature is not an abstraction from nature *per se* as much as it is an engagement with natural process which is at once destructive and creative. The outcome of this engagement will naturally be something on the order of the "Lucy poems," which stand so wholly on their ambivalence that they cannot be read by paraphrase, because any critical paraphrase will be a translation of their terms, poised on a knife edge of double meanings, into a reduction. So in the shortest great poem of Romanticism in English, the eight-line ballad "A slumber did my spirit seal," any consideration of that opening phrase must stumble over the multiple and opposite possibilities for reading each of its terms. Why "A" rather than simply the abstraction "slumber"? What is the difference between "slumber" and sleep? Why this euphemism if death is meant? But is death involved if it is the poet's slumber; and if so, does slumber entail or preclude dreams? The emphatic "did" forces planes of time, as "slumber" introduces planes of consciousness, on the poem: but to what end? And from what is "spirit" being differentiated, and in what way is the possessive force of "my" exerted upon it? Is this too a euphemism for "better self," or for Lucy, or by the assertion of separate identities is it meant to distinguish both? And, with the ambiguities tumbling out of this simple line, we finally confront the verb held back to its end: is this the "seal" on the grave or on the heart, a mark of divorce or of an eternal contract? There are further and multiple shades of meaning possible through this interpretive process, as the terms of the remaining seven lines are brought to bear. And the compressed, enigmatic nature of the poem virtually invites that process to continue. Indeed, it is so active a process that one finds the poem formally read to demonstrate hermeneutic skills by a host of distinguished critics, from F. W. Bateson and Cleanth Brooks to Paul de Man and J. Hillis Miller, each treatment differentiating its present interpretation from those taken by others in the past, each functioning under the pretense of making a definitive statement while actually inviting another reader to come along and in this seemingly unending critical process presume to play a trump card. But there are no trump cards; to pursue the metaphor, however initially distinct their faces seem, with a second glance all the cards appear to be the same and to exist without hierarchy.[6]

How, then, can one "read" this poem? The answer is obvious but requires that we discipline our minds to an exploration of terms rather than a reductive interpretation of them. The questions listed above, and any others that any reader from any culture or epoch wishes to add to them, constitute the actual process of reading, which is the re-creation in the reader's mind of an experience of loss as fulfillment and of fulfillment as loss, which in turn is Wordsworth's profound understanding of the nature of death as it continues to live in the mind. And why should not poetry, as Wordsworth characterizes its transcendence of time and space, transcend as well a fixed and finite meaning? That is only to replicate the nature of the other arts, reinterpreted through being replayed or reseen, whose value is in the experience of them.

As other essays in this volume suggest, there are other, indeed many and mighty, forces in philosophy and linguistics coalescing behind a poetics of skepticism and of active dialectical balancing in the Romantic age. The analysis undertaken here is meant by no means to exclude those considerations, but rather to refocus them within the perspective of a British literary history that had privileged poetry as the authentic voice of the national culture and through its rediscoveries in the preceding generation had remarkably intensified that sense of special value. Against this reservoir of meaning and potentiality, a pure source of nourishment removed from temporal threat, was juxtaposed a clash of empires and ideologies, political repression that seemed at times to vie with that to be encountered on the Continent, and a new economic order, whose full dimensions could be seen only after the war but whose utilitarian terms of opposition to the poetic, beginning with its indelible ties with prose, could be glimpsed on every hand. This world of contradictions empowers Romanticism to undertake a poetics that could subsume their stresses, and it is that conception of poetry as enacting the process it contains that has been the enduring legacy of its art.

## NOTES

1. The exact number of new publications in verse during these years, according to J. R. de J. Jackson's *Annals of English Verse, 1770–1835: A Preliminary Survey of the Volumes Published* (New York and London: Garland, 1985) is 4,884. But as his subtitle indicates and further bibliographical search has documented, these numbers should be augmented: by perhaps as much as 20 percent.

2. This is an aspect never far from the view of those English critics, notably John Bailey, Christopher Ricks, Andrew Motion, and Nicholas Roe, who have brought

a sensitive understanding of the class dynamics of British culture to their appraisal of Keats. It has been strongly focused by Marjorie Levinson's full-length study, *Keats's Life of Allegory: The Origins of a Style* (Oxford: Basil Blackwell, 1988).

3. The attempt to center attention on the effects of censorship on all modes of writing in sixteenth- and seventeenth-century England has posed startling caveats for modern literary interpretation, ranging from restoring a sense of the precise political tensions of the period in which a work is written or published (or even republished) to discerning the many ways in which strategies of allusion, generic expectation, and even title page format can encode unstated meaning. See Christopher Hill, "Censorship and English Literature," in the first volume of his *Collected Essays: Writing and Revolution in 17th-Century England* (Amherst: University of Massachusetts Press, 1985), pp. 32–71; and Annabel Patterson, *Censorship and Interpretation: The Conditions of Writing and Reading in Early Modern England* (Madison: University of Wisconsin Press, 1984). The awareness of these two major Renaissance scholars is one that needs to be transposed to the study of the Romantic age, which saw a revival of something approaching the political instability and the arbitrary power of the establishment characteristic of the seventeenth century.

4. On the intellectual and political resonances of this new paganism, consult Marilyn Butler, *Peacock Displayed: A Satirist in His Context* (London: Routledge and Kegan Paul, 1979), pp. 102–10.

5. This genre has finally been given the attention it deserves in Gary Dyer, *British Satire and the Politics of Style, 1789–1832* (Cambridge University Press, 1997), and Steven E. Jones, *Satire and Romanticism* (New York: St. Martin's, 2000); see also Jones's edited volume, *The Satiric Eye: Forms of Satire in the Romantic Period* (New York: Palgrave, 2003).

6. M. H. Abrams, focusing on contemporary deconstructive readings of the poem in order to suggest their limitations, gives a valuable sense of the range of these interpretations from the New Critics on. See "Construing and Deconstructing," in *Romanticism and Contemporary Criticism*, eds. Morris Eaves and Michael Fischer (Ithaca: Cornell University Press, 1986), reprinted in Abrams's *Doing Things with Texts: Essays in Criticism and Critical Theory*, ed. Michael Fischer (New York and London: Norton, 1989).

# II

MORRIS EAVES

# The sister arts in
# British Romanticism

Which first, the good news or the bad news? In honor of optimists who test their commitments by rising above the worst, I submit a three-part package of disheartening wisdom. W. J. T. Mitchell on pictures and words: "The history of culture is in part the story of a protracted struggle for dominance between pictorial and linguistic signs, each claiming for itself certain proprietary rights on a 'nature' to which only it has access." John Barrell on efforts to shelter the two arts of picturemaking and wordmaking under one critical label: " 'Romanticism' has never become a well-established term in the discussion of English painting, and art historians do not seem, on the whole, to have found the term of great explanatory power even when applied to such obvious subjects as Turner, Palmer, or Blake himself." And finally, the most quotable line ever written about all relations among all arts, Susanne Langer's heartstopping proclamation that "there are no happy marriages in art – only successful rape."[1] These warnings open suitably dark themes that we would be mistaken to bypass, because they are fundamentally true to life. Awesome combinations of failure, difference, distance, lag, divergence, and conflict establish the relations of texts and images in the Romantic period to such a degree that we cannot hope to understand those relations without them. Any elevation of spirits about the future of scholarship in "literature and the visual arts," as it has come to be standardized in a phrase, can only be achieved by climbing a mountainous collection of depressing realities.

I say so outright, at some risk of stating the obvious, because the verbal copulation of literature and the visual arts summons likeness and comparison and positive augmentation. These are, after all, the "sister arts," as the eighteenth and some of the nineteenth century knew them, and were they not supposed to be a naturally compatible pair? The pairing has had, on occasion, and especially when the subject is Romanticism, the power to return us to nineteenth-century dreams not of arts but of Art as the single revelation that singleminded, multitalented creative personalities seek in complementary modes, some with a talent for words, others for music or pictures, all epitomized by an impossibly rare double or triple Romantic Genius such as William Blake, poet, painter, engraver, and, it was said, a natural musician.

Given the encouragement to cross-fertilization provided by the metaphors of Romantic aesthetics, which names "Vision" in poetry and "Poetry" (in painting) among its highest ideals, it is unsurprising that students working under the literature-and-visual-arts authorization have launched searches for philosophical, theological, psychological, aesthetic, and political bases for comparing Romantic verbalizations and visualizations. This is bound to be an attractive procedure because almost every Romantic issue, theme, or aspect can be formulated, in some sense at some level, in both words and pictures, and doubly attractive because the double formulation allows us to tie great writers like Wordsworth, Coleridge, and Shelley to great artists like William Blake, John Constable, Samuel Palmer, and J. M. W. Turner, not to mention the lures of a European Romanticism that frequently extends the field of possibilities.

In studies of British Romanticism authoritative themes for students of the sister arts have included the pictorialism of Keats's poetry, informed and reinforced by his experience of painting and sculpture; "nature" as a common focus of literary and pictorial attention; the "visionary" theories of knowledge, perception, and self, expressed and exemplified in both Romantic poems and pictures; the influence of certain aesthetic categories, principally the sublime, the picturesque, and the organic, on literature and painting alike; and literary and visual responses to crucial historical events such as the French Revolution. I would deny neither the abiding importance of these topics nor their fascination, not even the still-fertile promise of the time-honored favorites – such overplowed fields of comparison and contrast as the Nature verbalized in Wordsworth's poetry and visualized in John Constable's Suffolk landscapes, the sublime of indefinity that supposedly links poet Shelley and painter J. M. W. Turner, or the sublime of vision that makes Samuel Palmer a successor to Blake.

The problem is that the studies themselves have typically taken top-down approaches to subjects that need to be researched from the bottom up to protect them from glibness and forgettability. Certainly, as Barrell says, attempts to explain British wordmaking and picturemaking with the single term "Romanticism" have met with (occasionally entertaining, usually insipid) failure regularly, success rarely. Although one might reasonably expect adding arts to add intellectual excitement, the most useful lessons, even of much of the latest criticism, have been about the artificiality and superficiality required to hide the dangerous unreliability of flawed approaches.

The signs of stress have often been all too visible right on the surface: at its most obvious, the uninhibited reaching across strong and significant geographical, linguistic, cultural, and chronological borders in search of comparisons; at its most egregious, the implicit or explicit use of implausible, anachronistic models of intellectual association (from Delacroix, Sand, and Chopin, through Baudelaire, Ruskin, the Impressionists, and the Bloomsbury Group, to Stein and Picasso). Is it insignificant that Wordsworth did not learn how to look at paintings from (even) Constable, or Coleridge from Caspar David Friedrich, but from the aristocratic amateur George Beaumont and the American fundamentalist Washington Allston respectively, two very conservative and yet also very different sources?

The blame for questionable procedures does not rest entirely on the shoulders of the scholars who have adopted them. What has been missing are the adequate histories that allow one to assess the complexities of the cultural situation. Often the fundamental weaknesses of art history and literary criticism, instead of cancelling each other out, have combined to defeat heroic efforts that have tried to fly before they could walk. In any case, at least for the foreseeable future, the best work will continue to be about problems not solutions, and in moods to match. In literature and the visual arts, this is a Jacobean not an Elizabethan age.

But the thrill of adventure remains. Despite a handful of recent works that have risen considerably above the previous norm, the study of British Romantic literature and the visual arts is a vast underexplored critical wilderness approached by many promising but mostly untried roads. Even the big, obvious subjects have not received sustained or sophisticated attention. We could profitably hear more than we have about Wordsworth's association with his painter-patron George Beaumont; about the relevance of Hazlitt's experience as a trained portrait painter to his literary work or the influence of Benjamin Robert Haydon's ideals of history painting in the circle of the Romantic poets; about the bizarre continuities and discontinuities of visual neoclassicism that connected the elder Josiah Wedgwood with the artist and sculptor John Flaxman and painter Benjamin West, and the literary neo-Hellenism associated chiefly with writers of a later generation like Shelley – widely separated phenomena joined by strong filaments.

The exception to the rule of neglect would seem to be William Blake, the object of almost overwhelming critical efforts for the better part of the past century. And indeed, to learn about literature and the visual arts in the Romantic period, one must always circle back to confront Blake as the central figure or the central enigma. In some accounts he is not a Romantic at all but a cultural souvenir lost in time from an earlier era of Enlightenment, and yet in other accounts he is the futuristic prototype of "visionary" Romanticism. He has often been made to seem the harbinger of the post-Romantic modern world, the point at which Romanticism predicts the coming of Marx and Freud. In that version of the story of British Romanticism Blake's "illuminated books" in "illuminated printing" as he called them, or his "prophecies" as they are often called, become the prototypes of Romantic poetry in its most ambitious epic reaches. Extracted from the range of his other work, these illuminated books have frequently been treated as a master canon of Romantic artistic ambition, unified by medium because they are (most of them) watercolored relief etchings; by biography because they are (more or less) the output of a productive lifetime; and by theme and manner because they (sometimes) repeat characters and incidents and display a (rough) pattern of evolution from the more fragmentary efforts of the 1790s to the more comprehensive mythical structures of *Milton a Poem* and *Jerusalem: The Emanation of the Giant Albion* from the years after 1800. Finally, to the extent that these prodigiously complex structures threaten to unread themselves into a tantalizing illegibility – which is to a very significant extent – Blake has even gained some currency as the most eligible Romantic liaison with the postmodern, an alliance further encouraged by the realization that his "poems" are not just printed lines but media events.

Of course, there are significant issues that cannot be raised through Blake, who as an artist sits uncomfortably in our art histories and as a poet was tangential to his written culture. But in major respects, having bequeathed to posterity a stock of work that concretely and intricately consolidates or at least splices elements of written language and graphic design from his own hands, Blake would seem to be the Romantic literature-and-visual-arts subject *par excellence*. If that is true, as it may be, it is equally true that Blake, even as he tempts us to put faith in the viability of these interdisciplinary approaches, also provides the paradigm *par excellence* of the array of obstacles that frustrate the literature-and-visual-arts project.

## I Words and pictures

Blake's illuminated printing gives us an opportunity to reassess the problem that some commentators have identified as the root of those frustrations, the vexing relation between words and images. Asking when a word is a word or an art an art is a bit like asking when a male is male or sex is sex. Langer's malicious claim that the intimate relations of texts and images can only be characterized as acts of criminal violence inflicted by one gender on another is a hysterical exaggeration of some conventional observations: words are different from images; the difference can be dangerous; and the most satisfactory resolution of the crisis of relationship is no relationship. The conclusion that the difference between texts and images is one that divides, and even threatens conflict and dominance, may seem most powerful when the opposing parties are located differently on the body. When words are oral and aural and images are tactile and visual, they are perhaps as different as they ever get to be. But a closely related set of observations – of two senses contributing, as it were, to a single human body's task of perceiving the world – motivates the opposite conclusion, that the difference between the two senses is complementary.

The way to avoid such petrified oppositions is to notice how the differences are not fixed. They are sensitive to context – technologically sensitive, for instance. They threaten to collapse when words are not primarily sounds but sights (see figure 11.1). The words in plate 81 of Blake's *Jerusalem* are produced by the same technology, relief etching, that produces the pictures. Hence the distance between the two is one of the factors subject to the producer's control, as here, where the fairly regular lines at the top of the plate seem least like the images of human bodies in the middle, while the words left of the central human figures seem well on their way to becoming images: rotated ninety degrees from horizontal lines and reversed to obstruct legibility, curved to conform to surrounding image structures (clouds, bodies, black graphic envelope) – to yield to them, hence acknowledging their priority at this point – and arranged on the left symmetrically opposite the graphic elements on the right to complete the bifurcated global shape. We would be remiss to overlook the powerful element of choice left to the reader/spectator, who *may* look at these words for image-form before reading them for lexical-content – but may not, and may even ignore one or the other altogether.

We now know that the ways Blake prepared plates for illuminated printing depended heavily upon the technologies of handwriting and freehand drawing adapted to the requirements of relief etching.[2] Without minimizing these technical requirements or their effects – such as writing/drawing on copper rather than paper, and writing/drawing in reverse (thus the backward writing on plate 81, the hardest for us to read, was the only writing on that plate executed in the easiest way, conventionally forward) – we can see that, as Blake used them, the handicrafts of writing and drawing overlap: same hand, same surface, similar tools. So used, they blur the differences between words and images that human physiology may seem to reinforce. A circle on one of Blake's plates may be the outline of an eye or the letter O or both – if an eye, then "drawn," if a letter, then "written." We generally maintain the distinction between "writing" and "drawing" anyway for purposes of cultural organization, as any schoolchild knows who is waiting for "writing" class to end and "drawing" class to begin, and regard one as indispensable basic education and the other as play, but at that level

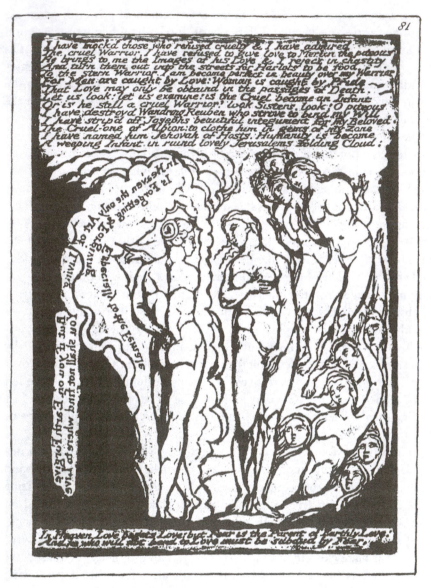

11.1 William Blake, *Jerusalem*, plate 81 (copy D), relief etching, c. 1804–20.

the distinction becomes much more a matter of how we use and value what we see than of how we make it.

In any event, the dominant reproductive technology of Blake's time was not relief etching. It was letterpress printing with movable type, which, though a visual means of reproduction, to a certain extent reinstates the difference between words and pictures by establishing a visual context resistant to nonalphanumeric images (see figures 11.2 a and b). To incorporate images into the alphanumeric regimen of printing technology, other media – woodcuts, engravings (or in this reproduction of pages from a modern edition, photolithographic halftone) – had to be accommodated in roundabout ways, leading to the rigid segregation, by medium, of pictures from texts. The segregation did not follow directly from any difference between words and pictures but indirectly from the particular technological means by which movable type made the reproduction of words so efficient – leaving, as it were, images in its economic wake. We can see this most easily by comparing letterpress printing with other reproductive media. Engraving and photography, for example, "see" words as images; it is as easy to engrave words on copper as to engrave pictures and as easy to photograph the word "tree" as to photograph a tree. Likewise, computer designers exploit the enormous flexibilities of the electronic digitization that allows letters to be "written" and "read" *as* pictures, and all to be reproduced indiscriminately by pixels. The word-picture distinction does not disappear – as long as users come to the technology wanting letters and words, the technology will have to include that category in its *modus operandi* – but it seems fair to say that "graphically oriented" computer environments treat words as a special case of pictures.

Thus the segregation of two overlapping cultural categories, words and pictures, was powerfully influenced by letterpress printing, which made pictures hard to deal with because movable type could not reproduce them and image-reproducing technologies like engraving were inefficient and expensive by comparison. Letterpress printing was the dominant technology of a particular historical moment that happens to have been Blake's moment, and the Romantic moment. Conversely, since that time, photographic, cinematographic, videographic, and digital technologies have given pictures a new lease on reproductive life and hence a new hold on cultural life, although their content is not well served by existing search technologies, in stark contrast to the searchability of texts.

Even so, it is important not to be hypnotized by "words" and "pictures" into imagining these convenient names as stable, discrete categories that are promoted and demoted in a simple reproductive ratio regulated by available technology. Rather, "audio" and "video," "texts" and "images," "literature"

(a)   She hid them in his loins; raving he ran among the rocks,
Compelld into a shape of Moral Virtue against the Lamb.
The invisible lovely one giving him a form according to
His Law a form against the Lamb of God opposd to Mercy
And playing in the thunderous Loom in sweet intoxication       80
Filling cups of silver & crystal with shrieks & cries, with groans
And dolorous sobs: the wine of lovers in the Wine-press of Luvah

O sister Cambel said Gwendolen, as their long beaming light      c
Mingled above the Mountain[:] what shall we do to keep
These awful forms in our soft bands: distracted with trembling     85
PLATE 81
I have mockd those who refused cruelty & I have admired
The cruel Warrior. I have refused to give love to Merlin the piteous.
He brings to me the Images of his Love & I reject in chastity
And turn them out into the streets for Harlots to be food
To the stern Warrior. I am become perfect in beauty over my Warrior   5
For Men are caught by Love: Woman is caught by Pride
That Love may only be obtaind in the passages of Death.

t

11.2 a and b William Blake, *Jerusalem*, plate 81 (copy D), and corresponding text from David V. Erdman, ed., *The Complete Poetry and Prose of William Blake*, revised edn. (Berkeley and Los Angeles: University of California Press, 1982), pp. 238–9.

(b) Let us look! let us examine! is the Cruel become an Infant
  Or is he still a cruel Warrior? look Sisters, look! O piteous
  I have destroyd Wandring Reuben who strove to bind my Will    10
  I have stripd off Josephs beautiful integument for my Beloved,
  The Cruel-one of Albion: to clothe him in gems of my Zone
  I have named him Jehovah of Hosts. Humanity is become
  A weeping Infant in ruind lovely Jerusalems folding Cloud:
  In Heaven Love begets Love! but Fear is the Parent of Earthly Love!  '15
  And he who will not bend to Love must be subdud by Fear,

PLATE 82

  I have heard Jerusalems groans; from Vala's cries & lamentations
  I gather our eternal fate: Outcasts from life and love:
  Unless we find a way to bind these awful Forms to our
  Embrace we shall perish annihilate, discoverd our Delusions.
  Look I have wrought without delusion: Look! I have wept!    5
  And given soft milk mingled together with the spirits of flocks
  Of lambs and doves, mingled together in cups and dishes
  Of painted clay; the mighty Hyle is become a weeping infant;
  Soon shall the Spectres of the Dead follow my weaving threads.

  The Twelve Daughters of Albion attentive listen in secret shades  10
  On Cambridge and Oxford beaming soft uniting with Rahabs cloud
  While Gwendolen spoke to Cambel turning soft the spinning reel:
  Or throwing the wingd shuttle; or drawing the cords with softest songs
  The golden cords of the Looms animate beneath their touches soft,
  Along the Island white, among the Druid Temples, while Gwendolen  15
  Spoke to the Daughters of Albion standing on Skiddaws top.

  So saying she took a Falshood & hid it in her left hand:
  To entice her Sisters away to Babylon on Euphrates.
  And thus she closed her left hand and utterd her Falshood:
  Forgetting that Falshood is prophetic, she hid her hand behind her,  20
  Upon her back behind her loins & thus utterd her Deceit.

  I heard Enitharmon say to Los: Let the Daughters of Albion
  Be scatterd abroad and let the name of Albion be forgotten:
  Divide them into three; name them Amalek Canaan & Moab:
  Let Albion remain a desolation without an inhabitant:    25
  And let the Looms of Enitharmon & the Furnaces of Los
  Create Jerusalem, & Babylon & Egypt & Moab & Amalek,
  And Helle & Hesperia & Hindostan & China & Japan.
  But hide America, for a Curse an Altar of Victims & a Holy Place.
  See Sisters Canaan is pleasant, Egypt is as the Garden of Eden:  30
  Babylon is our chief desire, Moab our bath in summer:
  Let us lead the stems of this Tree let us plant it before Jerusalem
  To judge the Friend of Sinners to death without the Veil:
  To cut her off from America, to close up her secret Ark:
  And the fury of Man exhaust in War! Woman permanent remain  35

and the "visual arts" are unstable entities that slip and slide this way and that under the complex pressures of history, among which are the pressures of technology. "Words" and "pictures" are not things-in-themselves but ways of understanding things. Put philosophical pressure on any conceivable definition of the terms, and they yield. Even in movable type, after all, an L or P "is" an image if seen as one, and, indeed, type- and book-designers have made a business of seeing and understanding type, pages, and books as two- and three-dimensional images, with all the help from visual aesthetic categories that "design" suggests.

## II   Social hierarchy

If the distance between literature and the visual arts in the Romantic period is in part the technological distance between words and pictures, that distance is both cause and consequence: it depends on available technologies, but the availability of technologies also depends on social and historical negotiations at many levels. One set of such broader cause-effects involves the distribution of social privileges and rewards. Words and images are assigned to divergent patterns of distribution, Blake again being a usefully indicative case. Readers often notice his marked difference from the other Romantic poets. Positively, they may say that he is the most original or imaginative; negatively, that he seems insane. In some respects a more satisfactory translation of these readerly reactions would be simply "he is a London engraver of the period 1757–1827," which is very far from saying, "he is one of the six major British Romantic poets." As an engraver, his social, intellectual, political, religious, and professional affiliations were not utterly different from the other five but very, very different. Wordsworth and Shelley were from different places, generations, classes, and universities; but by comparison Blake was as from a different world. I am not rescuing him from the charge of insanity but saying that the best social vantage point from which to view his mental condition is not the same as the one from which to view Coleridge's. As Blake and Coleridge go as producers, so go their products: it is a heady challenge to find one social vantage point from which to view both images and words.

Blake lived and died in a socio-economic network of painters and paintings, line engravers, stipple engravers, mezzotinters, and prints. In such an environment, dedicated to making and marketing images, words were things to illustrate. He is the only one of the six canonical poets to have completed an apprenticeship (Keats cancelled his) and the only one to have spent a lifetime doing what he learned. He is the only one except Keats without university education and the only one to have had no formal education in the usual sense. Instead of "education" he had "training," all in the visual arts – drawing lessons, apprenticeship, the Royal Academy schools. In these respects Blake's situation was typical of the picturemakers in relation to the wordmakers of his time and place.

As an engraver Blake's life ran on the lower social track of the visual arts, with the reproducers not the producers of pictures. Whenever he painted rather than engraved, as he often did, he was not just changing media but trying to climb a slippery social ladder. Engravers were artisans working at a trade, while painters and sculptors were "artists" in a newly elevated sense. Ever anxious to preserve the social gains that painting and sculpture had lately won as "fine" arts, the Royal Academy, founded in 1768, regularly refused to admit engravers as equals until the twentieth century, always on the grounds that engravers had manual skill but lacked invention, the intellectual ability that raised artisanry to an art and painters to poets.

In what we might call their assigned levels of intellectual responsibility, engravers were closer to printers, painters to poets, but even painters remained socially handicapped by the conditions of their craft. They required a separate course of training outside the grammar schools and universities, and they had to work in messy studios with materials in various degrees of wetness. British painters had only very recently exploited the logic of specialization to set themselves above a rather undifferentiated group that included house painters, coach painters, and heraldic painters. The engravers, who traced the origins of engraving to sculpture but usually worked for painters, tied their social aspirations to the ascendant group by presenting themselves as painters *manqués* both in word (as when they demanded admission to the Academy) and deed (as when they demanded exhibition space with the painters, or when they themselves took up painting). The painters' own cloudy status made them resist such claims to equality, leaving engravers and their allies to organize separate groups to promote their well-being, which they did repeatedly without much success.

In terms of social distance, what were the consequences? When writer Robert Southey looked in on Blake's one-artist exhibition (at his brother's house in 1809–10), his "melancholy impression" of what he saw should raise profound social as well as aesthetic questions (*Blake Records*, p. 531). So should his subsequent declaration, despite a level of disapproval close to revulsion, that "nothing but madness" kept Blake from "being the sublimest painter" in the world – this from a man who had earlier confessed to Haydon that "In matters of Art I am entirely ignorant" (*Blake Records*, p. 531). Could he under any imaginable circumstances have thought, "Ah, here is one of the three major Romantic poets of the first generation. I should introduce him to my brother-in-law Coleridge and my Cumberland neighbor Wordsworth?"

Much of this distance is social and vocational and could only be closed by the historical amnesia that time can induce over several decades. It is of course not surprising that Blake knew none of his Romantic literary peers. But they probably knew no other engravers either. When Bernard Barton asked Charles Lamb about Blake in 1824, Lamb answered as vaguely about this citizen of London as if he were in India: "Blake is a real name, I assure you, and a most extraordinary man, if he be still living" (*Blake Records*, p. 393). He was, but Lamb was satisfied to leave the personal contact to the ever-curious Henry Crabb Robinson, the only one of this literary crowd ever to converse with Blake.

A very few painters, such as Henry Fuseli of Blake's generation and Haydon of Keats's, managed to be simultaneously middle-class literati and painters, but most chose the comfort of a more segregated social circle. To my knowledge, no engraver of the period, and certainly none with Blake's (not uncommon) combination of radical religious and political opinions, offended this boundary between wordmakers and imagemakers for any length of time. Instead, intrepid agents of the literati such as Crabb Robinson ventured across the line to fetch exotic anthropology from the dark side.

## III   Histories

Across this social divide emerged distinct histories in the service of disparate issues. The separated lives of word and image took numerous forms, virtually all of which reinforced a hierarchy that put writers in the superior position. That was true both in a very general sense – this was a culture in which words were granted various kinds of superiority over pictures – and in a more particular sense, such that, while British poets were cast as world-class competitors for poetic fame, the painters were cast as latecomers of undemonstrated merit. The abiding question on the literary side was whether the writers could become the worthy inheritors of a relatively recent but highly esteemed history of British accomplishment by reaching the mark set by past successes. The question on the visual side was whether the artists could overcome a history of British failure and neglect.

By the generation of Wordsworth and Coleridge the literary gold standards were Shakespeare and Milton, though one could extend and deepen the history, and enlarge the stock of poetic possibilities, by adding primitives such as Chaucer and the ancient bards of Scotland. Shakespeare's plays were taken as a demonstration that the British could compete for literary laurels with the greatest of any period or nation, and Milton's poems proved that Shakespeare's success had been only one manifestation of a British way with words that deserved a place in the history of European letters beginning with Homer. Some literary critics have emphasized the anxiety induced in British poets by this daunting history. An intimidating question for late-arriving poets like Wordsworth and Keats was whether they had any hope of becoming anything larger than a footnote. Then there was the question of sufficiency – whether the plethora of great poems from Homer to Milton had left room for any more – and the potentially devastating "modern" question addressed by Peacock's "Four Ages of Poetry" and Shelley's *Defence of Poetry* – whether the course of history was eliminating the function of poetry. But as they studied intently the competition across generations and nations, British writers virtually ignored the possibility for competition across arts. They wasted none of their anxiety on the painters and musicians to whom we look whenever we are tempted to broaden Romanticism to take in Constable's landscapes and Beethoven's symphonies.

On the other side, the producers of British imagery found themselves in a historical predicament marked not by what they had had but by what they had lacked. Shakespeare's visual counterpart was stunningly absent. For decades Continental critics – Montesquieu, Du Bos, Winckelmann, and others – had pointed to the uneven distribution of verbal and visual accomplishments in Britain and attributed it to fixed conditions of climate (cold) and temperament (calculating) that produced good merchants but bad pictures. The most mercantile of the visual genres was portrait painting, and naturally the British had done best in that.

For British artists the legal tender was not British but Italian, and the touchstones were Raphael and Michelangelo, which did not increase the allure of Joshua Reynolds and Thomas Gainsborough, not to mention William Hogarth. By comparison with the rich, layered literary culture to which writers like Dryden, Pope, and Swift had (various kinds of) access, the culture of British imagery was meager indeed. After all, while Shakespeare was vying for position in a pack of fiercely competitive native writers, "British painting" would have been only a laughable contradiction in terms. The court painter to Henry VIII was the German Hans Holbein the Younger (c. 1497–1543), who settled in England for the last few years of his life, and the painter to Charles I, one of the most avid and ambitious art collectors ever, was the Flemish Anthony Van Dyck (1599–1641). When Virginia Woolf inquired as to the whereabouts of Shakespeare's sister, it did not occur to her that she might have been an Elizabethan painter.

Hence painters and their cultural allies spent much of their intellectual capital defending themselves against charges of chronic inferiority, putting their belated arrival in the best light, and designing remedial programs for themselves and their spectators. These polemical, critical, and instructional bids for status began as early as the late seventeenth century, perhaps with

William Aglionby's translation of some of Vasari's *Lives of the Painters* into English (1685); continued in the early eighteenth century with Jonathan Richardson's extensive efforts to outline – in *The Theory of Painting* (1715), *Essay on the Art of Criticism*, and *The Science of a Connoisseur* (1719) – a theory of painting suited to the British situation, including instructions for becoming a proper judge of painting; and then entered a far more programmatic phase of development with the establishment of the Royal Academy in 1768 (see figure 11.3), just in time to run parallel with the two generations of British Romantic writers who are the main concern of this volume. As its noisy critics proclaimed, the Royal Academy was never a disinterested body. In a state-sponsored institution it consolidated aesthetic, pedagogical, and commercial initiatives to improve the lot of British painters (especially of its self-selected membership). It contacted the public most effectively at its annual exhibitions, where potential customers could see in a single visit the current work of British painters, thus giving weight and substance to the notion that there indeed existed a British School of Painting. Writers were not perceived to need anything comparable to the economic development plan that made the Royal Academy seem so necessary and so late in arriving on the shores of Britain.

Although in our retrospective eyes the period from Reynolds and Gainsborough through Flaxman, Blake, Constable, Turner, and Palmer may appear to have been a great age of British art, throughout the last quarter of the eighteenth century and well into the nineteenth, inferiority, failure, and neglect remain the prime generative topics of British art writing, spawning a standard gloomy vocabulary of urgencies, inquiries, trials, perils, and crises that keeps the rhetorical temperature high: "The present moment is considered by artists as teeming with the crisis ... of the destiny of their Art in England," proclaims Prince Hoare on p. 211 of his *Inquiry into the Requisite Cultivation and Present State of the Arts of Design in England* (1806), refurbishing a title already employed a quarter of a century earlier in James Barry's *Inquiry into the Real and Imaginary Obstructions to the Acquisition of the Arts in England* (1775) and dusted off yet again nearly a quarter of a century later in Benjamin Robert Haydon's *Some Enquiry into the Causes Which Have Obstructed the Advance of Historical Painting for the Last Seventy Years in England* (1829).

They reported a history of "obstructions" – the Reformation, the Civil War, occupation by an army of foreign artists – that had unnaturally blocked the course of a natural "advance" that would have occurred in Britain as it had in other European nations, especially Italy and France. Most of the proposed remedies involved notions of "cultivation" and "acquisition" through public and professional education: systematic training in theory and practice to

11.3 Pietro Martini after J. H. Ramberg, *The Exhibition of the Royal Academy*, 1787, engraving, 1787.

educate the artists, exhibitions to educate the artists and the audience, and official support for public projects to "encourage" (employ) British artists and make their work as visible as the work of artists in other countries. The kind of art most congenial to such proposals is an international one that can be measured by rational standards such as those laid out in the most formidable of British art theories of the period, Joshua Reynolds's fifteen *Discourses on Art* delivered at the Royal Academy from 1769 to 1790. This standard does not appeal to British uniqueness: although it may accept British history or British landscape as content, it does so on equal terms with any other national history or geography. All local content competes on an international market by moving beyond locality and singularity, by generalizing its particulars and by delivering that generalization in internationally sanctioned techniques and forms. To "acquire" that standard repertory of content, form, and technique, most painters spent at least months and preferably years in Italy copying from the verified (foreign) old masters. To gauge meaningfully the possibilities for literature and the visual arts in Romantic Britain, one must study the calculus of differences between the academy-less education of native poetic genius that Wordsworth and Keats designed to elevate themselves to positions in the British literary record, and the programmatic training, in the service of internationalism and eclecticism, by which British artists aimed to move their art into the European mainstream.

## IV  Markets

The formulation of the crisis-ridden narratives of British art in the eighteenth and early nineteenth century cannot be understood as a merely historical activity. It was an exercise in self-understanding and self-justification, certainly, but it was, and perhaps was more significantly, also an element in a marketing strategy. The dissimilar histories of British literature and visual arts were, among other things, responses to dissimilar markets. The literary market was broader, more settled and mature, but also more parochial and less innovative. The art market was immature, and very much in flux. It had international aspirations, not simply because the British art market was small – although it was – but because images promise more portability than words. On the market, British painters and their commercial allies often display the mentality of the oppressed, sometimes self-defeatingly compliant and/or stubborn and inclined to copy the standards of others rather than to create their own, at other times devilishly clever, inventive, and resourceful in finding ways to show and sell their work (see figure 11.4). For British writers of the period, the familiar four-way alliance of author, publisher,

11.4 Francesco Bartolozzi, engraved ticket of admission to the 1791 exhibition of Copley's *Siege of Gibraltar* (facsimile of ticket by unidentified artist).

printer, and bookseller, though it could be adjusted to suit the situation, was firmly established as the dominant commercial arrangement and relatively well integrated with the educational institutions that served as the training ground for writers. In the visual arts the mechanisms of training, production, and marketing were far less sure and successful, and far more open to, as well as desperately in need of, innovation. This engraved ticket of admission illustrates a marketing concept with which several painters had great success. Exploring the boundary that painting shared with the theatre, the raree show, and other spectacles for public amusement, it called for the public display of a huge history painting with contemporary interest – here John Singleton Copley's *Siege of Gibraltar*, a patriotic spectacle that drew thousands of visitors to a tent in Green Park in 1791. Profit came from the price of admission and the sale of subscriptions to a forthcoming engraving (often with a key to the faces in the painting). Throughout the period (and well beyond), other painters with a knack for history painting as spectacle, most memorably John Martin (1789–1854), continued to exploit the effects of sheer immensity. Like his predecessors, he understood the advantage of marketing a single image in multiple formats. With a bit of modification, Martin's large images were easily converted to stage sets. Reduced, they could be turned into prints and sold as private souvenirs of the stupendous public originals, either separately or as illustrations to the text that had provided the occasion for the painting to begin with.

*The Portland Vase.*

11.5 William Blake, *The Portland Vase*, engraving for Erasmus Darwin's *The Botanic Garden* part I, *The Economy of Vegetation*, 1791.

Marketing brings us back to some fundamental influences on the circulation of words and images in this period. The market for words is dominated by the commodity in its second-order, reproduced rather than produced, form – newspapers, magazines, and books rather than manuscripts. But in images the market is still dominated by the art object, the first-order, the produced, form of the commodity – the watercolor, the painting – even as efforts were being made to find cheaper, more efficient modes of reproduction. Old-line "great-man" patronage, which rested largely on the production of unique art objects, remained more influential in painting than in literature, both in fact – as Benjamin West was patronized by George III for several good years in West's prime – but perhaps even more significantly in the artists' polemics: they dwelled on the dearth of aristocratic and state patronage (contrasted to the supposed abundance of "opportunity" and "encouragement" in foreign climes) even to the point of distraction from the primary business at hand.

And indeed there emerged new ventures that did not depend upon traditional patronage, such as Josiah Wedgwood's heavy investment in neoclassicism – not, of course, the neoclassicism that literary historians associate with Dryden, Pope, and Swift, but a late eighteenth-century visual fashion with no significant stylistic counterpart in the mainstream of British Romantic writing of that period. (The neo-Hellenism of the younger generation of Romantic writers is a good deal later and very differently formulated.) In employing artist and sculptor John Flaxman to create spare and elegant neoclassical designs for his pottery, Wedgwood cleverly capitalized on the commercial advantages of an international style. It was radically simple and adaptable, it leveraged the prestige and authority of the Greek-centered (and anti-British) histories of art developed by Continental critics such as Winckelmann, and hence it traveled extraordinarily well (see figure 11.5). In such a project as Wedgwood's copy of the Portland (or Barbarini) vase – here engraved by Blake for Wedgwood's friend Erasmus Darwin's *Economy of Vegetation* (1791) – we can glimpse something of the complex intersection and divergence of literary and visual cultures that a term such as "neoclassicism" can cover. Wedgwood's immensely successful merchandizing of visual neoclassicism through Flaxman's designs for Wedgwood ware is one interesting strand; it was Flaxman who first urged Wedgwood to come to London to see the Portland vase. The double appropriation of neoclassicism by reactionary and radical politics is another; the radical side is represented here by the implicit proximity of the radical intellectuals Darwin, Wedgwood, Priestley, *et al.*, but the circle of evidence stretches much further, from George III's employment of Benjamin West to the Revolution's employment of Jacques-Louis David. The British literary background is quite different: there "neoclassic" is conventionally treated as the opposite of "Romantic" and calls to mind Dryden and Pope, not Wordsworth. And yet one only has to name the Elgin (Parthenon) marbles for which painter Benjamin Haydon lobbied so intensely, Keatsian Grecian urns, Shelleyan Grecophilia, and Byron's sponsorship of Dryden and Pope to see that the mutual infiltration of visual and literary neoclassicisms is one of the most tantalizing, least exhausted sister-arts topics in all of British Romanticism.

Far more often than they collaborated with potters and other artisans, however, visual artists attempted to join forces with writers. Earlier I made the point that the technological basis of word-production and image-pro-duction caused a lack of coordination that made intimate relations difficult. It also had serious consequences in marketing. The relative efficiency of let-terpress printing and the inefficiency of engraving defeated one of the most promising marketing gambits of the era – the attempt to tie the fortunes of British images to the prestige of British words. This is clearest in the 1790s, in British imagemaking the decade of the "gallery," a marketing experiment constructed from more or less familiar components.

"Alderman" John Boydell's Shakespeare Gallery, conceived in the mid 1780s and opened with great fanfare in 1789, was the most important of several gallery projects of the decade, including Macklin's Poets' Gallery, inaugurated in 1788 and followed by Macklin's Bible project in 1790, painter Henry Fuseli's Milton Gallery the same year, and Bowyer's Historic Gallery in 1792. (Only Fuseli's Milton Gallery was to consist of paintings by a single artist.) Boydell's was the most elaborately planned of these ventures in artistic opportunity based on commercial speculation rather than aristo-cratic patronage and thought perhaps to be particularly well suited to the British genius for trade. Indeed, just before the opening of the Gallery and three months before the fall of the Bastille, a crowd of dignitaries including Edmund Burke, Joshua Reynolds, and the Prince of Wales toasted Boydell as the "Commercial Maecenas" (after the Roman patron of Horace and Virgil), "an English tradesman, who patronizes the art better than the Grand Monarque of France."[3]

The marketing nucleus of his project was simple and entirely conven-tional: exhibit a painting (one either commissioned for the purpose, or one to which the reproduction rights have been purchased) and take orders ("subscriptions") for engraved prints of the painting, with the printseller stationed at the commercial intersection of painter, engraver, and customer. In the 1770s and 1780s Boydell had built Britain's most successful printsell-ing business by effectively applying this formula to popular paintings. In the 1790s he elaborated it into the logic of a multidimensional "gallery" in several ways, as follows.

He sold a theme instead of a single painting, thus multiplying both the number of related products available to the consumer (in the familiar commercial form of a "set" or "series"), and he sold in multiple formats to attract buyers with a range of disposable income. He chose a theme that could sell British images by selling Shakespeare, that is, by standing them on the strong shoulders of British literature. He increased his international opportunities by choosing the British wordsmith with the best international reputation – Italy had Jesus and the saints for their paintings, Britain had Shakespeare – and by adding to Shakespeare's difficult language images that would increase his legibility, as it were, even to foreign consumers. At the same time, cautious not to allow the words to seem a mere excuse for the pictures, Boydell projected the most authoritative edition of Shakespeare ever.

On the home front he sold the crisis of British art by appealing to national shame and pride, hammering on the familiar themes of British art history – obstructed aspirations, chronic neglect, unsympathetic criticism from the Continent, etc.:

> In this progress of the fine Arts, though Foreigners have allowed our lately acquired superiority of Engraving, ... yet they have said with some severity ... that the abilities of our best Artists are chiefly employed in painting Portraits ... While the noblest part of the Art – HISTORICAL PAINTING – is much neglected. To obviate this national Reflection was, as I have already hinted, the principal cause of the present undertaking.[4]

Boydell exploited the stock opposition between portrait painting – associated with commerce, the gratification of personal vanity, and the low aims of English art – and history painting by designing a project that could produce, at one level, history paintings, theoretically the highest and most celebrated but practically the most expensive and most neglected genre, but sell them, at another level, through the popular medium of book illustration, which was, with portraiture, one of the two mature areas of the British market. The Shakespeare Gallery would thus display history paintings but sell book illustrations.

Boydell embodied in himself the promise of "this progress in the fine Arts." Claiming that his previous projects had won international recognition for the slighted English School of Engraving, he would now turn his attention to the English School of Painting. The number of painters and engravers he could involve allowed him to speak as the collective voice of the English School and to sell his project as a public service rather than a private speculation. Hence he decorated and furnished the Shakespeare Gallery as a mock-public institution, complete with dignified facade and commissioned sculpture in Pall Mall, entirely apart from his own printshop in Cheapside (see figure 11.6). As the Royal Academy lent reality to the British School

11.6 S. Rawle, *View of the Shakespeare Gallery*, etched frontispiece to the *European Magazine* vol. 46, 1804.

in one way, Boydell's Shakespeare Gallery attempted to lend it reality in another, by presenting itself architecturally in quasi-institutional form – and indeed, after the Boydell collapse and lottery in 1805, the Gallery building was immediately taken over by the new British Institution, which built a collection and sponsored thematically organized exhibitions and competitions. (To the extent that the Institution's activities overlapped the Academy's, it was a competitor, despite its own declarations to the contrary.) Cultivating the role of public benefactor, Boydell declared that he would eventually give the Gallery to the nation.

After more than a decade, Boydell's exciting venture reached the beginning of the end by 1800, the year of the second edition of Wordsworth and Coleridge's *Lyrical Ballads* – the end of an era for the visual arts, the beginning of one for literature. In maximizing the economic advantages of his project to so many groups, Boydell necessarily maximized the areas in which failure could occur and the span of time over which it might occur. He died in December 1804, and the next month, January 1805, with Parliament's permission, the Gallery and all its contents were sold off by lottery, a total commercial failure. (None of the other gallery projects fared any better.) Boydell publicly blamed the French Revolution and Jacobin politics for vandalizing, as he said, his markets. No doubt there was something to that, and certainly the advantages of art as an international commodity had turned into temporary disadvantages during the Revolution and its aftermath.

But the Achilles' heel of the Shakespeare Gallery lay in the rift between its images and its words. Boydell had to allow the slowest component in the technological mix, the engraved reproductions, to set the pace for the whole. The more he tried to speed up the copying by using efficient methods, such as "dotting" (stipple engraving), the more his project took on the look of a cheap commercial job and retreated from its claim to being a dignified exercise in national artistic prestige. But the slowness of more prestigious "line" engraving was legendary. Fancy line engravings could take years – to the despair of painters who pinned their hopes on the sale of reproductions. In earlier years and simpler circumstances, most famously in publishing the print of West's *Death of Wolfe*, Boydell had exploited line engraving as well as anyone could (see figure 11.7). Behind both painting and engraving lie strong workshop traditions of dividing labor among a master and assistants, unlike anything in the customary production of poems and novels. The only reason Woollett's engraving of West's painting took *merely* five years was that assistants did the preliminary work; if Woollett had engraved the *Wolfe* from start to finish, West and Boydell might have waited much longer. As it was, the very profitable engraving boosted the reputations of all three men considerably. For Boydell it was an important step along the way to the

11.7 William Woollett after Benjamin West, *The Death of General Wolfe*, engraving, 1776.

Shakespeare Gallery. But on a far larger scale and in a bad market, Boydell simply could not coordinate the key elements of his project. It spun out of control and fell into the abyss between literature and the visual arts.

The Shakespeare Gallery building in Pall Mall was quickly refurbished and reopened in a matter of months as the new British Institution, a self-proclaimed supplement to the Royal Academy in the durable crisis of British picturemaking. A new wave of lament and analysis began: "the Arts of Design in England … are declared to be in danger of perishing for ever. They stand therefore on the brink of splendour or annihilation; they plead before a profoundly reflecting nation; they demand a trial."[5] Immediately Boydell began to acquire his mythical status as a merchant-hero vanquished by French radicals – following the familiar narrative of achievement thwarted by foreign intervention – and the last quarter of the eighteenth century began to be seen nostalgically as an era of superlative promise. Engraver John Landseer was stopped from lecturing on the history of British engraving when it became clear that he was going to blame its problems on Boydell. New cries for government support went up, old proposals for public art projects were dusted off and new ones put forward, usually in the familiar language of inferiority, announcing projects that promise to "save every true Englishman the painful feeling of being surpassed by our active rival France."[6]

In his *Inquiry* of 1806 – the year after the Boydell lottery, but also the year after a rousing demonstration of British naval power at Trafalgar – Prince Hoare in a letter to the *True Briton* called for reconsideration of a Royal Academy scheme that painter John Opie had first presented in 1800: the Gallery of British Honour, a great circular naval monument modeled on the "Pantheon at Rome." Large pieces of sculpture – Neptune paying homage to Britannia, a statue of George III – would set the mytho-political tone, while in a series of compartments around the circle statues of naval heroes would alternate with paintings of victories. The monument would inculcate patriotism with a visceral sublimity, giving "pleasure" through the "terror and admiration" of "Britain's thunder" – "fire, water, wind, and smoke, mingled in terrific confusion": "In the midst, British valour triumphantly bearing down all opposition, accompanied by humanity … ready to succour the vanquished foe!"[7]

The Gallery of British Honour was no isolated proposal but one episode in the continuing effort to locate the polite arts advantageously in the economy, and more particularly in the effort to create viable formats for public art education, government patronage, and commercial display, three aims that had always been closely linked in the history of efforts to establish a British School. The direction changed somewhat, swerving away from Enlightenment-style internationalism and eclecticism. In these years

British art tried hitching its fortunes to the British lion of military adventure, Nelson, Wellington, and all that, with exhibitions organized on military and imperial themes, and government-sponsored contests to commemorate the new heroes of empire (see figure 11.8). The French Revolution and the Napoleonic Wars strengthened the motivation to find artistic work in patriotic, nationalistic, militaristic, and imperialistic subjects. In 1799 John Flaxman entered a competition to design a naval monument to commemorate British victories over the French (Blake engraved Flaxman's designs), and Gillray half-parodied, half-entered the competition himself with the design reproduced here. There were numerous other ideas developed at the intersection of artistic opportunity and affairs of empire. Flaxman designed a Trafalgar vase and a statue of Nelson. Prince Hoare revived John Opie's proposal for a Gallery of British Honour in 1806, while others urged that St. Paul's Cathedral be turned into the British Pantheon. Such programs provide a context for understanding such widely separated events as Blake's paintings of Nelson and Pitt (exhibited 1809–10), his 1809 proposal for a "portable Fresco" – "I could divide Westminster Hall, or the walls of any other great Building, into compartments and ornament them with Frescos, which would be removable at pleasure" (*Poetry and Prose*, p. 527) – and Benjamin Haydon's proposal to have British artists decorate the Houses of Parliament, rebuilt after the fire of 1834, with scenes from British history. The notion that the prosperity of the Italian and French Schools of Painting had rested substantially on a kind of state "encouragement" that had been missing in Britain is a key theme in the discourse of the British School from at least the 1760s, when a group of painters promoted, unsuccessfully, the idea of having British artists decorate Westminster Abbey. Such revealing events as the government's purchase of the Parthenon frieze sculptures – the "Elgin Marbles" – in 1816, for which Benjamin Haydon campaigned so strongly, and the founding of the National Gallery (housed in a building, constructed 1832–8, that it shared for thirty years with the Royal Academy), to which Wordsworth's friend and patron George Beaumont donated his important picture collection, were all promoted in large part through the stock discourse of the British School, adjusted to exploit the newly felt privileges and obligations of an imperial power.

And new, perhaps Romantic, theories and histories of painting begin to appear with revised hopes based on new themes amalgamating nationalism with individualism. Hazlitt, for instance, writes strongly for the genius of the individual painter and against the Royal Academy exhibitions and training programs that, he said, diffuse taste and skill without improving them.[8] The older history of art in Britain, emphasizing its successes in emulating eclectic international styles through painters such as Joshua Reynolds, begins

11.8 James Gillray, *Design for the Naval Pillar*, etching, 1800.

to give way gradually to claims for the unique national genius of British painting. In Allan Cunningham's *Lives of the Most Eminent British Painters*, Reynolds's role as father of the British School is downplayed in favor of "the truly English and intrepid spirit of Gainsborough," whose paintings have a national look.[9] In this historical climate Hogarth, previously vulnerable to criticism for a lack of skill and for isolation from Continental traditions, begins to emerge as the previously suppressed first term of an emphatically *British* art. Sometimes, as in the theorizing of John Constable, the old claims for the poetic nature of painting give way to scientific claims for painting as an applied optics that would accord better with Britain's reputation for native scientific and technical aptitude: "In such an age as this, painting should be *understood*, not ... considered only as a poetic aspiration, but as a pursuit, *legitimate, scientific, and mechanical.*"[10]

## V The institutional embrace

I have stressed how little traffic there was between Blake and the other poets at the core of British Romanticism. The only work any of the Romantic poets knew of Blake's was the *Songs of Innocence and of Experience*, which Coleridge and Wordsworth read because an acquaintance who owned a copy wanted to know what they thought. Although both were apparently alerted in advance that they were reading the poems of a probable lunatic, they responded favorably, if condescendingly. As poetry experts, both treated the (illuminated) *Songs* chiefly as occasions for reading not spectatorship, but in any case sought out no more of the work of this strange outsider. Though Blake read some Wordsworth and addressed his final illuminated book, *The Death of Abel* (1822), to Byron the author of *Cain*, if Byron, Shelley, or Keats ever heard of Blake at all they left no record of it.

Yet today, in the house of British literature, we are called upon to recognize that Blake "is" a "poet," one of the usually six "major" poets of this particular national branch of Romanticism. Meanwhile, one of the most interesting facts about the history of visual art that Blake joined is how small a part he has played in it, and what great resistance his work has faced, "an anomaly in the history of painting even though he is now rightly seen as a central figure in poetic history."[11] Given the sociointellectual distance between Blake and his literary peers, how is it that we have crossed that distance to rehouse this artist-engraver with these poets? The most important answer, for relations between literature and the visual arts, involves the key issue of specialized institutional memories. The tendency towards specialization is, verging on paradox, very often accompanied by the tendency towards imperialism by which everything, including the messages from other institutions, gets

translated into the terms of the institutional discourse. Usually this translation seems innocent enough: as a falling apple may be consulted for its
physical interest by a physicist, so a poet (like Coleridge, like Blake) may
be consulted for philosophical, psychological, or theological interest by philosophers, psychologists, or theologians. An argument over Blake's cultural
location may seem idle, then, unless we remember that the messages sent
from that location may take editorial form.

Wrote Henry Crabb Robinson of Blake in his diary: "And of his poetical & pictorial genius there is no doubt I believe in the minds of judges –
Wordsworth & Lamb like his poems & the Aders his paintings" (*Blake
Records*, p. 424). This segregation has typified efforts to send, retrieve, and
evaluate Blake's work. Earlier, in discussing the word- and image-content of
*Jerusalem*, I emphasized the powerful element of choice left to the reader-
spectator when it comes to favoring words or imagery. This choice may be
made at the level of the choosing individual but also at the level of institutions. It emerges prominently in the history of Blake's reputation, which is
the most interesting institutional history among the Romantic "poets" largely
because it involves a startling conversion across institutional borders.

Blake invested his life's work in two separate institutions, but far more
heavily *in* the visual than the verbal, and he made his investments *from* the
cultural location of the visual. This double investment paid off, I should
add, but only posthumously, over the long term through the actions of what
we sometimes call posterity. During his life and for several decades afterward, the double investment provoked a kind of cultural confusion that had
to be waited out and sorted through. As his contemporary audience was
dominated by spectators rather than readers, and as he died a minor visual
artist working in a minor art, surrounded by other artists, his vocational
position was, understandably, taken for granted. Frederick Tatham, faced
with the task of selling the only copy of *Jerusalem* that Blake ever colored
(copy E, the "Mellon" copy), advertised it the best way he knew how, as a
set of "Expressive" and "sublime" prints looking for an appreciative buyer.
He perceived the words and pictures of *Jerusalem* not as a complementary
pairing but as an "heterogeneous" embarrassment, "lofty" images drowning
in a sea of "ridiculous" words. He discouraged reading and recommended
looking because he assumed that the lookers would be his buyers.

Blake was never, as is sometimes thought, forgotten as an artist. But the
key to his twentieth-century reputation is his change of cultural venue. That
begins during his lifetime, with the anthologization of a few of the *Songs*
without designs in printed collections, but the elements to make the change
on a significant scale do not come together until the later decades of the century, when Swinburne, for instance, defines Blake as a poet whose images are

perhaps useful optical bait for novices but dispensable accessories for serious readers. As Blake becomes something of a late-century fashion, projects to publish expensive facsimiles that can recall his work in illuminated printing *as* illuminated printing affect a small circle of the well heeled and visually committed. But the kind of argument with which William Michael Rossetti reacted against a facsimile of *Jerusalem* published in 1877, that the handwritten script of the illuminated books impedes understanding, was the dominant one: "the publication in ordinary book-form, without designs, and without any attempt at facsimile of text, of the *Jerusalem* and the other Prophetic Books, is highly to be desired. Difficult under any circumstances, it would be a good deal *less* difficult to read these works in an edition of that kind, with clear print, reasonable division of lines, and the like aids to business-like perusal."[12] This is a strong rationale for printing *Jerusalem* – and for *reading* it. Hence the events to watch were happening not in the graphic-arts workshops but on the printing press, where Blake was being reprinted as a poet of poems translated into the clarity of readable type.

Succeeding generations have experienced Blake primarily in such institutional translation. His poetic reputation mounted swiftly and steadily as his sponsors piled up useful connections between Blake and twentieth-century writing – Blake and the modernists, Blake and the Beats, Blake and the critical theory of Northrop Frye. He often served as a wild card to be added to any hand, always more quotable than readable. His images, while not forgotten, were lifted clear of their context in the visual arts of his time and relegated to the secondary place of essential afterthought, the *je-ne-sais-quoi* factor that gives poets the tantalizing aura of hermeneutic promise by making them seem larger than the reader's experience of them. Meanwhile, the other Blake, the art-historical one, has lived quite a separate, and a far quieter, institutional life as an odd-man-out who makes an occasional appearance in histories of the graphic arts whose reproductive function is largely ignored, and in histories of painting as they pass through something resembling a Romantic period, or at least moment.

The strange passage of Blake from the visual to the verbal column has distorted some of the most heroic attempts to understand him. His cultural location having been misplotted, all sorts of misunderstandings have followed from using a bad map. It is not that Blake's Chaucer (the subject of an essay motivated by the need to explain a painting and an engraving on display and for sale, and by debates about the quality of British art) and Coleridge's Chaucer (the subject of notes and lectures on the history of British literature) cannot be studied together for mutual advantage. They must be studied together. Blake and Coleridge were not speaking from hermetically sealed cultural compartments, but from very different positions to think "Chaucer." The problem is too fundamental to be solved by characterizing Blake as an aberration, because in many fundamental ways he was not. The difficulties he presents for students of literature and the visual arts are typical rather than anomalous, whether the subject is Chaucer, neoclassical style, theories of artistic harmony, production practices, commercial arrangements, politics, or religion.

## VI  Some dancing lessons for the sister arts

The confidence necessary to advance literature-and-visual-arts projects may be eroded by the suspicion that all attempts to find firm footing are doomed from both sides: from the certainty that words and pictures are sometimes so different that they cannot be fruitfully combined, either for presentation (as art) or discussion (as criticism), and from the certainty that words and pictures are sometimes so much alike that they cannot be told apart. I see this as a political and historical question like those encountered in studying nation-states, where the welter of crossed and conflicted and discontinuous identities can make nonsense of any firm notion of what it means to be "German" or 'Italian" without some very exact specifications. For, despite all the obvious encouragements, like Blake's illuminated books, for attempting the broader view promised by literature and the visual arts, unfortunately it has to be regularly confessed that "We know how to connect English and French literature more precisely than we do English literature and English painting"[13] – or, for that matter, more precisely than we know how to connect just about any "literature" with any "painting," even when both are expressions of the same brain and hand on the same surface. After all, words and pictures have been separated by some of the deepest chasms, spanned by some of the least reliable bridges, in Western culture, the very ones from which Coleridge warned of the "despotism of the eye" (*Biographia Literaria*, I, 107), Byron declared repeatedly how little he knew or cared about painting, "of all the arts ... the most artificial & unnatural – & that by which the nonsense of mankind is the most imposed upon" (*Letters and Journals*, V, 213), and the old Wordsworth, in his sonnet on "Illustrated Books and Newspapers" (1846, *Works*, IV, 75), agitated gloomily over the visual fixations of a younger generation neglecting its books – "Must eyes be all in all, the tongue and ear / Nothing?" – a theme sounded many times since. Only hopeless optimists would dream of being able to study literature and the visual arts, or texts and images as we now more often say, together without risking the consequences of studying over thin air.

We began on the side of the optimist facing bad news. In the background looms a joke about the optimist who thinks this is the best of all possible worlds and the pessimist who agrees. How to avoid giving the pessimist the final say? If we start by acknowledging that "poetry" and "painting" name two specialized activities carried out under the aegis of specialized cultural institutions and understood in the tailored terms of specialized languages, and that specialization has the indispensable virtue of focusing the attention, we can nonetheless end by acknowledging as well that, because focus on one thing is always achieved at the price of distraction from others, the only kind of study that can ever do any subject justice has to be dialectical, alternating between moments of focused and unfocused attention, aspiring towards higher levels of augmented and integrated attention.

When we study literature and the visual arts, then, we look for points of contact, intersections, and even homologies, but always in a context of contrasts and differences, with an appreciation of the difficulties and an assessment of the complexities of the situation. Furthermore, the study of literature and the visual arts will not be much more satisfying than it now generally is until it more often enlarges its purview to take in the histories of institutions, including the histories of crafts, technologies, and social groupings. That would give us new hope of profitably reopening the books on some of the vast subjects – neoclassicism, the sublime, the picturesque – that have been severely stunted by a too exclusive attention to words or pictures.

Earlier I remarked that many studies of literature and the visual arts produce results that can be, and have been, largely ignored outside the small circle of scholars who do this sort of thing for a living. That is provocative but simplistic because the neglect is not altogether just. It, too, is partly the product of the very cultural divisions that keep texts and images apart, repeated in this instance in the institutions charged with remembering, studying, and teaching them. The only thing that gives us a prayer of ever capturing an augmented Romanticism that could deal fully, which is to say sympathetically but critically, with Blake, with Coleridge and Washington Allston, Wordsworth and George Beaumont, Keats and Benjamin Haydon, not to mention Wordsworth and John Constable or Shelley and J. M. W. Turner, is the ability to entertain painfully in the mind at once two incompatible propositions: the separability of words and pictures had profound consequences in the Romantic period and has them now *and* the inseparability of words and pictures had profound consequences in the Romantic period and has them now. (Which is not to suggest that the relation of words to images in the Romantic period was what it is now or meant what it does now.) The minute one begins to slip into a one-way logic towards uncritical synaesthesias, organicisms, and global villages or, the other way, towards hypercritical ruptures and discontinuities, the game, at least for the student of literature and the visual arts, is up. Unfathomable abysses and transcendent unities are both mysteries, hence both intolerable to critical intellects. What we want are not unplumbable depths or heights but bridges. They acknowledge the abyss, offer views of it, and give us somewhere to go. The only way to extract any critical energy from a deadening claim like Susanne Langer's is to allow and resist it. Against her quote Truffaut: "Neither with you, nor without you" (*The Woman Next Door, La femme d'à côté*).

## NOTES

1. Mitchell, *Iconology: Image, Text, Ideology* (University of Chicago Press, 1986), p. 43; Barrell, *The Political Theory of Painting from Reynolds to Hazlitt: "The Body of the Public"* (New Haven and London: Yale University Press, 1986), p. 223; Langer, "Deceptive Analogies: Specious and Real Relationships among the Arts," *Problems of Art* (New York: Scribner's, 1957), p. 86.
2. See Robert N. Essick, *William Blake, Printmaker* (Princeton University Press, 1980), and Joseph Viscomi, *Blake and the Idea of the Book* (Princeton University Press, 1992).
3. Quoted in Edmund Burke, *The Correspondence of Edmund Burke*, ed. Holden Furber (Cambridge University Press, 1958–78), v, 465.
4. Preface to the 1789 catalogue of the first exhibition in the Shakespeare Gallery, quoted in Sven H. A. Bruntjen, *John Boydell 1719–1804: A Study of Art Patronage and Publishing in Georgian London* (New York and London: Garland, 1985), p. 71.
5. Hoare, *Inquiry into the Requisite Cultivation and Present State of the Arts of Design in England* (London, 1806), p. 263.
6. *The Examiner*, May 13, 1810: 304; quoted in John Gage, "An Early Exhibition and the Politics of British Printmaking, 1800–1812," *Print Quarterly* 6 (1989): 134.
7. Hoare, *Inquiry*, pp. 47, 50–1.
8. "Enquiry Whether the Fine Arts Are Promoted by Academies and Public Institutions," in James Northcote, *The Life of Titian; with Anecdotes of the Distinguished Persons of His Time* (London, 1830), II, 370–83 (appendix 8).
9. *The Lives of the Most Eminent British Painters, Sculptors, and Architects* (London, 1830–46), I, 356.
10. *John Constable's Discourses*, comp. and annot. R. B. Beckett (Ipswich: Suffolk Records Society, 1970), p. 69.
11. Harold Bloom, review of Martin Butlin, *The Paintings and Drawings of William Blake*, in the *New York Times Book Review*, January 3, 1982: 4.
12. Quoted in R.W. Peattie, "William Michael Rossetti's Aldine Edition of Blake," *Blake / An Illustrated Quarterly* 12 (1978): 7.
13. Mitchell, *Iconology*, p. 44.

*Standard editions of Romantic writers cited*

Blake, William. *Blake Records.* G. E. Bentley, Jr. ed., 2nd edn. New Haven and London: Yale University Press, 2004.

*The Complete Poetry and Prose of William Blake.* David V. Erdman ed., rev. edn. Berkeley and Los Angeles: University of California Press, 1982.

Burns, Robert. *The Letters of Robert Burns.* J. deLancey Ferguson ed., G. Ross Roy rev., 2 vols. Oxford: Clarendon Press, 1985.

Byron, George Gordon, Lord. *Byron's Letters and Journals.* Leslie A. Marchand ed., 12 vols. London: John Murray; Cambridge, Massachusetts: Harvard University Press, 1970–81.

*Lord Byron: Complete Poetical Works.* Jerome J. McGann ed., 7 vols. Oxford: Clarendon Press, 1980–93.

*The Works of Lord Byron: Letters and Journals.* Rowland E. Prothero ed., 6 vols. London: John Murray, 1922–4.

Clare, John. *John Clare's Autobiographical Writings.* Eric Robinson ed. New York: Oxford University Press, 1983.

*The Letters of John Clare.* Mark Storey ed. Oxford: Clarendon Press, 1985.

Coleridge, Samuel Taylor. *Biographia Literaria.* James Engell and W. Jackson Bate eds. Princeton University Press, 1983.

*Collected Letters of Samuel Taylor Coleridge.* Earl Leslie Griggs ed., 6 vols. Oxford: Clarendon Press, 1956–71.

*The Complete Poetical Works of Samuel Taylor Coleridge.* Ernest H. Coleridge ed., 6 vols. London: John Murray, 1922–4.

De Quincey, Thomas. *Works.* Grevel Lindop gen. ed., 21 vols. London: Pickering & Chatto, 2003.

Hazlitt, William. *Complete Works of William Hazlitt.* P. P. Howe ed., 21 vols. London: J. M. Dent, 1935.

Keats, John. *Letters of John Keats.* Robert Gittings ed. Oxford University Press, 1970.

*The Poems of John Keats.* Jack Stillinger ed. Cambridge, Massachusetts: Harvard University Press, 1978.

Moore, Thomas. *The Poetical Works.* A. D. Godley ed. London: Henry Frowde, 1910.

Shelley, Percy Bysshe. *The Letters of Percy Bysshe Shelley*. Frederick L. Jones ed., 2 vols. Oxford: Clarendon Press, 1964.

   *Shelley's Poetry and Prose*. Donald H. Reiman and Neil Fraistat eds., rev. edn. New York: Norton, 2002.

Wordsworth, William. *The Letters of William and Dorothy Wordsworth: The Early Years 1787–1805*. Ernest de Selincourt ed., C. L. Shaver rev. Oxford: Clarendon Press, 1967.

   *The Letters of William and Dorothy Wordsworth: II. The Middle Years*. Ernest de Selincourt ed., Mary Moorman rev., 2 vols. Oxford: Clarendon Press, 1969.

   *The Prelude, 1799, 1805, 1850*. Jonathan Wordsworth, M. H. Abrams, Stephen Gill eds. New York: Norton, 1979.

   *The Prose Works of William Wordsworth*. W. J. B. Owen and Jane Smyser eds., 3 vols. Oxford: Clarendon Press, 1974.

### Other standard editions

Austen, Jane. *Works*. Janet Todd gen. ed., 9 vols. Cambridge University Press, 2006–8.

Blake, William. *Poetry and Designs*. Mary Lynn Johnson and John E. Grant eds., rev. edn. New York: Norton, 2008.

   *William Blake Archive*. Morris Eaves, Robert Essick and Joseph Viscomi eds. Available at www.blakearchive.org/blake [last accessed January 28, 2010].

Byron, George Gordon, Lord. *Complete Miscellaneous Prose*. Andrew Nicholson ed. New York: Oxford University Press, 1991.

Clare, John. *The Early Poems of John Clare, 1804–1822*. Eric Robinson and David Powell eds. Oxford: Clarendon Press, 1989.

   *The Later Poems of John Clare, 1837–1864*. Eric Robinson and David Powell eds., 2 vols. Oxford: Clarendon Press, 1984.

   *Poems of the Middle Period, 1822–1837*. Eric Robinson and David Powell eds., 5 vols. Oxford: Clarendon Press, 1996–2003.

Coleridge, Samuel Taylor. *Collected Works*. Kathleen Coburn *et al.* eds., 16 vols. Princeton University Press, 1969–2001.

   *Complete Poems*. William Keach ed. Harmondsworth: Penguin, 1997.

Edgeworth, Maria. *Works*. Marilyn Butler gen. ed., 12 vols. London: Pickering & Chatto, 2003.

Godwin, William. *Collected Novels and Memoirs*. Pamela Clemit, Maurice Hindle and Mark Philps eds., 8 vols. London: Pickering & Chatto, 1992.

   *Political and Philosophical Writings*. Mark Philps gen. ed., 7 vols. London: Pickering & Chatto, 1993.

Hunt, Leigh. *Selected Writings*. Robert Morrison and Michael Eberle-Sinatra gen. eds., 6 vols. London: Pickering & Chatto, 2003.

Shelley, Mary. *The Novels and Selected Works*. Nora Crook gen. ed., 8 vols. London: Pickering & Chatto, 1996.

Shelley, Percy Bysshe. *Complete Poetical Works*. Donald H. Reiman *et al.* eds., 10 vols. Baltimore: The Johns Hopkins University Press, 2000–.

   *Prose Works* [1811–18]. E. B. Murray ed. Oxford: Clarendon Press, 1993, vol. I.

Smith, Charlotte. *Works*. Stuart Curran gen. ed., 14 vols. London: Pickering & Chatto, 2005–7.

Wollstonecraft, Mary. *Works*. Janet Todd and Marilyn Butler eds., 8 vols. London: Pickering & Chatto, 1989.

Wordsworth, William. *The Cornell Wordsworth* [complete poems]. Steven Maxfield Parrish *et al.* eds. Ithaca: Cornell University Press, 1975–2007.

    *Lyrical Ballads: 1798 and 1800*. Michael Gamer and Dahlia Porter eds. Peterborough, Ontario: Broadview, 2008.

### Citations in philosophy

Berkeley, George. *The Works of George Berkeley, Bishop of Cloyne*. A. A. Luce and T. E. Jessop eds. London: Thomas Nelson, 1948–57.

Condillac, Etienne Bonnot de. *An Essay on the Origin of Human Knowledge: A Supplement to Mr. Locke's "Essay on the Human Understanding" (1756)*. Thomas Nugent trans., facsimile edn., intro. Robert G. Weyant. Gainesville, Florida: Scholars' Facsimiles & Reprints, 1971.

Fichte, Johann G. *Science of Knowledge (Wissenschaftslehre) with the First and Second Introductions*. Peter Heath and John Lachs trans., eds. New York: Appleton, Century, Crofts, 1970.

Hegel, Georg W. F. *Aesthetics: Lectures on Fine Arts*. T. M. Knox trans., 2 vols. Oxford: Clarendon Press, 1975.

    *The Phenomenology of Mind*. J. B. Baillie trans. New York: Macmillan, 1931; A. V. Miller trans. Oxford: Clarendon Press, 1977.

Kant, Immanuel. *Critique of Pure Reason*. Norman Kemp Smith trans. London: Macmillan, 1929; reprinted 1964.

Locke, John. *An Essay Concerning Human Understanding*. Peter H. Nidditch ed. Oxford: Clarendon Press, 1979.

Monboddo, James Burnett, Lord. *The Origin and Progress of Language*. 6 vols. (1774–92); facsimile edn. Menston: Scolar Press, 1967.

Schelling, Friedrich W. J. *System of Transcendental Idealism*. Peter Heath trans. Charlottesville: University of Virginia Press, 1978.

Tooke, John Horne, ἘΠΕΑ ΠΤΕΡΟΕΝΤΑ, *or, The Diversions of Purley*. 2 vols. (1786–1805); facsimile edn. Menston: Scolar Press, 1968.

### Criticism and theory

Arac, Jonathan. *Critical Genealogies: Historical Situations for Postmodern Literary Studies*. New York: Columbia University Press, 1987.

de Man, Paul. *Blindness and Insight: Essays in the Rhetoric of Contemporary Criticism*. 2nd edn., rev. Minneapolis: University of Minnesota Press, 1983.

    *The Resistance to Theory*. Minneapolis: University of Minnesota Press, 1986.

    *The Rhetoric of Romanticism*. New York: Columbia University Press, 1984.

Eaves, Morris, and Michael Fischer eds. *Romanticism and Contemporary Criticism*. Ithaca and London: Cornell University Press, 1986.

Fry, Paul. *The Reach of Criticism: Method and Perception in Literary Theory*. New Haven and London: Yale University Press, 1983.

Frye, Northrop. *A Study of English Romanticism*. New York: Random House, 1968.

Hartman, Geoffrey. *Beyond Formalism: Literary Essays, 1958–1970*. New Haven and London: Yale University Press, 1970.

*The Fate of Reading*. Chicago and London: University of Chicago Press, 1975.

Jordan, Frank ed. *The English Romantic Poets: A Review of Research and Criticism*. New York: Modern Language Association, 1985.

Levinson, Marjorie, Marilyn Butler, Jerome McGann, and Paul Hamilton. *Rethinking Historicism: Critical Readings in Romantic History*. Oxford and New York: Basil Blackwood, 1989.

Mitchell, W. J. T. ed. *Against Theory: Literary Studies and the New Pragmatism*. University of Chicago Press, 1985.

Nemoianu, Virgil. *The Taming of Romanticism: European Literature and the Age of Biedermeier*. Cambridge, Massachusetts: Harvard University Press, 1984.

Peckham, Morse. *The Triumph of Romanticism*. Columbia: University of South Carolina Press, 1970.

Rosso, G. A., and Daniel P. Watkins eds. *Spirits of Fire: English Romantic Writers and Contemporary Historical Methods*. Rutherford, New Jersey: Fairleigh Dickinson University Press, 1990.

Simpson, David. *Irony and Authority in Romantic Poetry*. London: Macmillan, 1979.

*Romanticism, Nationalism and the Revolt against Theory*. London and New York: Routledge, 1992.

Weiskel, Thomas. *The Romantic Sublime: Studies in the Structure and Psychology of Transcendence*. Baltimore and London: The Johns Hopkins University Press, 1976.

### Philosophical bearings

Adorno, Theodor, and Max Horkheimer. *Dialectic of Enlightenment*. John Cumming trans. Oxford University Press, 1953.

Ashton, Rosemary. *The German Idea: Four English Writers and the Reception of German Thought*. Cambridge University Press, 1980.

Beiser, Frederick C. *German Idealism: The Struggle against Subjectivism, 1781–1801*. Cambridge, Massachusetts: Harvard University Press, 2002.

Christensen, Jerome. *Practicing Enlightenment: Hume and the Formation of a Literary Career*. Madison: University of Wisconsin Press, 1986.

Engell, James. *The Creative Imagination: Enlightenment to Romanticism*. Cambridge, Massachusetts: Harvard University Press, 1981.

Hamilton, Paul. *Coleridge and German Philosophy: The Poet in the Land of Logic*. London: Continuum, 2007.

Harris, Wendell V. *The Omnipresent Debate: Empiricism and Transcendentalism in Nineteenth-Century Prose*. DeKalb: Northern Illinois University Press, 1981.

Kipperman, Mark. *Beyond Enchantment: German Idealism and English Romantic Poetry*. Philadelphia: University of Pennsylvania Press, 1986.

McFarland, Thomas. *Coleridge and the Pantheist Tradition*. Oxford: Clarendon Press, 1969.

*Originality and Imagination*. Baltimore: The Johns Hopkins University Press, 1985.

Mellor, Anne K. *English Romantic Irony*. Cambridge, Massachusetts: Harvard University Press, 1985.

Orsini, G. N. G. *Coleridge and German Idealism: A Study in the History of Philosophy with Unpublished Materials from Coleridge's Manuscripts*. Carbondale and Edwardsville: Southern Illinois University Press; London and Amsterdam: Feffer and Simons, 1969.

Thomas, Keith G. *Wordsworth and Philosophy: Empiricism and Transcendentalism in the Poetry*. Ann Arbor and London: UMI Research Press, 1989.

Thorslev, Peter. *Romantic Contraries: Freedom versus Destiny*. New Haven and London: Yale University Press, 1984.

Wellek, Rene. *Immanuel Kant in England*. Princeton University Press, 1931.

Yolton, John W. *Locke and the Compass of Human Understanding*. Cambridge University Press, 1970.

## Language and literature

Aarsleff, Hans. *From Locke to Saussure: Essays on the Study of Language and Intellectual History*. Minneapolis: University of Minnesota Press, 1982.

*The Study of Language in England, 1780–1860*. Princeton University Press, 1967.

Attridge, Derek. *Peculiar Language: Literature as Difference from the Renaissance to James Joyce*. Ithaca: Cornell University Press, 1988.

Barrell, John. *Poetry, Language and Politics*. Manchester University Press; New York: St. Martin's, 1988.

Brisman, Susan Hawk. "'Unsaying his high language': The Problem of Voice in Prometheus Unbound," *Studies in Romanticism* 19 (1977): 51–86.

Christensen, Jerome. *Coleridge and the Blessed Machine of Language*. Ithaca: Cornell University Press, 1981.

Cohen, Murray. *Sensible Words: Linguistic Practice in England, 1640–1785*. Baltimore: The Johns Hopkins University Press, 1977.

Cronin, Richard. *Shelley's Poetic Thoughts*. New York: St. Martin's, 1981.

Derrida, Jacques. *The Archaeology of the Frivolous: Reading Condillac*. John P. Leavey, Jr. trans. Lincoln: University of Nebraska Press, 1980.

Elfenbein, Andrew. *Romanticism and the Rise of English*. Stanford University Press, 2009.

Ferguson, Frances. *Wordsworth: Language as Counter-Spirit*. New Haven: Yale University Press, 1977.

Furniss, Tom. *Edmund Burke's Aesthetic Ideology: Language, Gender, and Political Economy in Revolution*. Cambridge University Press, 1993.

Hanley, Keith, and Raman Selden eds. *Revolution and English Romanticism: Politics and Rhetoric*. Hemel Hempstead: Harvester Wheatsheaf, 1990; New York: St. Martin's, 1990.

Hogle, Jerrold E. *Shelley's Process: Radical Transference and the Development of His Major Works*. Oxford University Press, 1988.

Keach, William. *Arbitrary Power: Romanticism, Language, Politics*. Princeton University Press, 2004.

*Shelley's Style*. London: Methuen, 1984.

Land, Stephen K. *From Signs to Propositions: The Concept of Form in Eighteenth-Century Semantic Theory*. London: Longman, 1974.

*The Philosophy of Language in Britain: Major Theories from Hobbes to Thomas Reid*. New York: AMS Press, 1986.

"The Silent Poet: An Aspect of Wordsworth's Semantic Theory," *University of Texas Quarterly* 42 (1973): 157–69.

McKusick, James C. *Coleridge's Philosophy of Language*. New Haven: Yale University Press, 1986.

Reed, Arden ed. *Romanticism and Language*. Ithaca: Cornell University Press, 1984.

Ricks, Christopher. "Wordsworth: 'A Pure Organic Pleasure from the Lines'," *Essays in Criticism* 21 (1971): 1–32.

Smith, Olivia. *The Politics of Language 1791–1819*. Oxford University Press, 1984.

## Historical backgrounds

Briggs, Asa. *The Age of Improvement 1783–1867*. London: Longman, 1959.

Bulwer-Lytton, Edward. *England and the English*. 1833; Standish Meacham ed. Chicago and London: University of Chicago Press, 1970.

Butler, Marilyn ed. *Burke, Paine, Godwin, and the Revolution Controversy*. Cambridge University Press, 1984.

Christie, Ian. *Wars and Revolutions: Britain 1760–1815*. London: Edward Arnold, 1982.

Colley, Linda. *Britons: Forging the Nation, 1707–1837*. New Haven: Yale University Press, 1992; reprinted 2005.

Crossley, Ceri, and Ian Small eds. *The French Revolution and British Culture*. Oxford University Press, 1989.

Darvall, Frank Ongley. *Popular Disturbances and Public Order in Regency England*. 1934; reprinted Oxford University Press, 1969.

Dickinson, H. T. *British Radicalism and the French Revolution 1789–1815*. Oxford: Basil Blackwell, 1985.

Dickinson, H.T. ed. *Britain and the French Revolution*. Houndmills: Macmillan, 1989.

Emsley, Clive. *British Society and the French Wars 1793–1815*. London: Macmillan, 1979.

Furniss, Tom. *Edmund Burke's Aesthetic Ideology: Language, Gender, and Political Economy in Revolution*. Cambridge University Press, 1993.

George, M. Dorothy. *English Political Caricature; A Study of Opinion and Propaganda 1793–1832*. Oxford: Clarendon Press, 1959.

Goodwin, Albert. *The Friends of Liberty: The English Democratic Movement in the Age of the French Revolution*. London: Hutchinson, 1979.

Halévy, Elie. *England in 1815*. 1913; E. I. Watkin and D. A. Barker trans. London: Ernest Benn, 1961.

*The Liberal Awakening (1815–1830)*. 1923; E. I. Watkin trans. London: Ernest Benn, 1961.

Hobsbawm, E. J. *The Age of Revolution 1789–1848*. London: Weidenfeld and Nicolson, 1962.

Rickword, Edgell ed. *Radical Squibs and Loyal Ripostes: Satirical Pamphlets of the Regency Period 1819–1821*. Bath: Adams and Dart, 1971.

Thompson, E. P. *The Making of the English Working Class*. 1963; reprinted Harmondsworth: Penguin Books, 1968.

White, R. J. *Waterloo to Peterloo*. 1957; reprinted Harmondsworth: Penguin Books, 1968.

## Literature and history

Abrams, M. H. "English Romanticism: The Spirit of the Age," in *The Correspondent Breeze: Essays on English Romanticism*. New York: Norton, 1984; and in *Romanticism Reconsidered: Selected Papers from the English Institute*. Northrop Frye ed. New York and London: Columbia University Press, 1963.

Bainbridge, Simon. *Napoleon and English Romanticism*. Cambridge University Press, 1995.

Barrell, John. *English Literature in History 1730–1780: An Equal Wide Survey*. New York: St. Martin's, 1983.

Bennett, Betty T. ed. *British War Poetry in the Age of Romanticism: 1793–1815*. New York and London: Garland, 1976; reprinted, available at www.rc.umd. edu/editions/warpoetry [last accessed January 31, 2010].

Boulton, James T. *The Language of Politics in the Age of Wilkes and Burke*. London: Routledge and Kegan Paul, 1963.

Brown, Marshall. *Preromanticism*. Stanford University Press, 1991.

Butler, Marilyn. *Romantics, Rebels and Reactionaries: English Literature and Its Background 1760–1830*. Oxford University Press, 1981.

Chandler, James. *England in 1819: The Politics of Literary Culture and the Case of Romantic Historicism*. University of Chicago Press, 1998.

Christensen, Jerome. *Romanticism at the End of History*. Baltimore: The Johns Hopkins University Press, 2000.

Dart, Gregory. *Rousseau, Robespierre, and English Romanticism*. Cambridge University Press, 1999.

Deane, Seamus. *The French Revolution and Enlightenment in England, 1789–1832*. Cambridge, Massachusetts: Harvard University Press, 1988.

Gaull, Marilyn. *English Romanticism: The Human Context*. New York: Norton, 1988.

Gilmartin, Kevin. *Writing against Revolution: Literary Conservatism in Britain, 1790–1832*. Cambridge University Press, 2007.

Harris, R. W. *Romanticism and the Social Order 1780–1830*. London: Blandford Press, 1969.

Harvey, A. D. *English Literature and the Great War with France: An Anthology and Commentary*. London: Nold Jonson, 1981.

Magnuson, Paul. *Reading Public Romanticism*. Princeton University Press, 1998.

Mendilow, Jonathan. *The Romantic Tradition in British Political Thought*. London: Croom Helm, 1986.

Paulson, Ronald. *Representations of Revolution (1789–1820)*. New Haven and London: Yale University Press, 1983.

Rajan, Tilottoma, and Julia M. Wright eds. *Romanticism, History, and the Possibilities of Genre: Reforming Literature, 1789–1837*. Cambridge University Press, 1998.

Sales, Roger. *English Literature in History 1780–1830: Pastoral and Politics.* London: Hutchinson, 1983.

Schenk, H. G. *The Mind of the European Romantics: An Essay in Cultural History.* 1966; reprinted Oxford University Press, 1979.

Williams, Raymond. *Culture and Society 1780–1950.* London: Chatto and Windus, 1958.

Woodring, Carl. *Politics in English Romantic Poetry.* Cambridge, Massachusetts: Harvard University Press, 1970.

## Publishing and the periodical press

Altick, Richard. *The English Common Reader: A Social History of the Mass Reading Public, 1800–1900.* University of Chicago Press, 1957.

Aspinall, Arthur. *Politics and the Press, 1780–1850.* 1949; reprinted, Brighton: Harvester, 1973.

Behrendt, Stephen C. ed. *Romanticism, Radicalism, and the Press.* Detroit: Wayne State University Press, 1997.

Clive, John. *Scotch Reviewers: The "Edinburgh Review," 1802–1815.* Cambridge, Massachusetts: Harvard University Press, 1957.

Cole, Richard Cargill. *Irish Booksellers and English Writers 1740–1800.* London: Mansell, 1986.

Erickson, Lee. *The Economy of Literary Form: English Literature and the Industrialization of Publishing, 1800–1850.* Baltimore: The Johns Hopkins University Press, 1996.

Fergus, Jan. *Provincial Readers in Eighteenth-Century England.* Oxford University Press, 2006.

Gilmartin, Kevin. *Print Politics: The Press and Radical Opposition in Early Nineteenth-Century England.* Cambridge University Press, 1996.

Hayden, John O. *The Romantic Reviewers, 1802–1824.* London: Routledge and Kegan Paul, 1969.

Hayden, John O. ed. *Romantic Bards and Scotch Reviewers: A Selected Edition.* Lincoln: University of Nebraska Press, 1971.

Houghton, Walter E. ed. *The Wellesley Index to Victorian Periodicals, 1824–1900.* University of Toronto Press, 1966–89 [contributors to *Edinburgh Review*].

Jackson, J. R. de J. *Annals of English Verse, 1770–1835: A Preliminary Survey of the Volumes Published.* New York: Garland, 1985.

  *Romantic Poetry by Women: A Bibliography, 1770–1835.* Oxford: Clarendon Press, 1993.

Johnson, C. R. *Provincial Poetry 1789–1839: British Verse Printed in the Provinces: The Romantic Background.* London: Jed Press, 1992.

Klancher, John P. *The Making of English Reading Audiences: 1790–1832.* Madison: University of Wisconsin Press, 1987.

Kuist, James M. *The Nichols File of the Gentleman's Magazine: Attributions of Authorship and Other Documentation.* Madison: University of Wisconsin Press, 1982.

Maxted, Ian. *The London Book Trades 1775–1800: A Preliminary Checklist of Members.* Folkstone: Dawson, 1977.

Mumby, Frank Arthur. "Part One: From the Earliest Times to 1870," in Frank Arthur Mumby and Ian Norrie, *Publishing and Bookselling*, 5th edn. London: Jonathan Cape, 1974, pp. 19–232.

Nangle, B. C. *The Gentleman's Magazine Biographical and Obituary Notices, 1781–1819: An Index*. New York: Garland, 1980.

    *The Monthly Review, Second Series, 1790–1818: Indexes of Contributors and Articles*. Oxford: Clarendon Press, 1955.

Parker, Mark. *Literary Magazines and British Romanticism, 1820–1834*. Cambridge University Press, 2000.

Reiman, Donald H. ed. *The Romantics Reviewed: Contemporary Reviews of English Romantic Writers*. 9 vols. New York: Garland, 1972.

Riga, Frank, and Claude A. Prance eds. *Index to the London Magazine*. New York: Garland, 1978.

Roper, Derek. *Reviewing before the "Edinburgh" 1788–1802*. London: Methuen, 1978.

Shine, H. and H. C. *The Quarterly Review under Gifford: Identification of Contributors*. Chapel Hill: University of North Carolina Press, 1949.

St. Clair, William. *The Reading Nation in the Romantic Period*. Cambridge University Press, 2004.

Strout, A. L. *A Bibliography of Articles in Blackwood's Magazine, 1817–1825*. Library Bulletin no. 5. Lubbock: Texas Technological College, 1959.

Todd, William B. *A Directory of Printers and Others in Allied Trades, London and Vicinity 1800–1840*. London: Printing Historical Society, 1972.

### Women writers

Adburgham, Alison. *Women in Print: Writing Women and Women's Magazines from the Restoration to the Accession of Victoria*. London: George Allen and Unwin, 1972.

Armstrong, Isobel, and Virginia Blain eds. *Women's Poetry in the Enlightenment: The Making of a Canon*. Houndsmills: Macmillan; New York: St. Martin's, 1999.

Armstrong, Nancy. *Desire and Domestic Fiction: A Political History of the Novel*. Oxford University Press, 1987.

Backscheider, Paula R. *Eighteenth-Century Women Poets and Their Poetry: Inventing Agency, Inventing Genre*. Baltimore: The Johns Hopkins University Press, 2005.

Barker-Benfield, G. J. *The Culture of Sensibility: Sex and Society in Eighteenth-Century Britain*. University of Chicago Press, 1992.

Behrendt, Stephen C. *British Women Poets and the Romantic Writing Community*. Baltimore: The Johns Hopkins University Press, 2008.

Blain, Virginia, Patricia Clements, and Isobel Grundy eds. *The Feminist Companion to Literature in English*. New Haven and London: Yale University Press, 1990.

Byrne, Paula. *Perdita: The Literary, Theatrical, Scandalous Life of Mary Robinson*. New York: Random House, 2004.

Craciun, Adriana. *British Women Writers and the French Revolution: Citizens of the World*. Houndsmills and New York: Palgrave, 2005.

    *Fatal Women of Romanticism*. Cambridge University Press, 2003

Demers, Patricia. *The World of Hannah More*. Lexington: University of Kentucky Press, 1996.

Doody, Margaret Anne. *Frances Burney: The Life in the Works*. New Brunswick: Rutgers University Press, 1988.

Feldman, Paula, and Theresa Kelley eds. *Romantic Women Writers: Voices and Countervoices*. Hanover: University Press of New England, 1995.

Ferguson, Moira. *Eighteenth-Century Women Poets: Nation, Class, and Gender*. Albany: State University of New York Press, 1995.

Fletcher, Loraine. *Charlotte Smith: A Critical Biography*. Houndsmills and New York: Palgrave, 1998.

Ford, Charles Howard. *Hannah More: A Critical Biography*. New York: Peter Lang, 1996.

Gilbert, Sandra M., and Susan Gubar. *The Madwoman in the Attic: The Woman Writer and the Nineteenth-Century Literary Imagination*. New Haven: Yale University Press, 1979.

Green, Katherine Sobba. *The Courtship Novel, 1740–1820: A Feminized Genre*. Lexington: University Press of Kentucky, 1991.

Homans, Margaret. *Bearing the Word: Language and Female Experience in Nineteenth-Century Women's Writing*. University of Chicago Press, 1986.

Jenkins, Annibel. *I'll Tell You What: The Life of Elizabeth Inchbald*. Lexington: University Press of Kentucky, 2003.

Kelly, Gary. *Women, Writing, and Revolution, 1790–1827*. Oxford: Clarendon Press, 1993.

Labbe, Jacqueline. *Charlotte Smith: Romanticism, Poetry, and the Culture of Gender*. Manchester University Press, 2003.

Landry, Donna. *The Muses of Resistance: Laboring-Class Women's Poetry in Britain, 1739–1796*. Cambridge University Press, 1990.

Linkin, Harriet, and Stephen C. Behrendt eds. *Romanticism and Women Poets: Opening the Doors of Reception*. Lexington: University of Kentucky Press, 1999.

McCarthy, William. *Anna Letitia Barbauld: Voice of the Enlightenment*. Baltimore: The Johns Hopkins University Press, 2008.

McGann, Jerome J. *The Poetics of Sensibility: A Revolution in Literary Style*. Oxford: Clarendon Press, 1996.

Mann, David, and Susan. *Women Playwrights in England, Ireland, and Scotland: 1660–1823*. Bloomington: Indiana University Press, 1996.

Mellor, Anne. *Mothers of the Nation: Women's Political Writing in England, 1780–1830*. Bloomington: Indiana University Press, 2000.

Mellor, Anne ed. *Romanticism and Feminism*. Bloomington: Indiana University Press, 1988.

Moers, Ellen. *Literary Women: The Great Writers*. New York: Doubleday, 1976.

Myers, Sylvia. *The Bluestocking Circle: Women, Friendship, and the Life of the Mind in Eighteenth-Century England*. Oxford University Press, 1990.

Perry, Ruth. *Novel Relations: The Transformation of Kinship in English Literature and Culture, 1748–1818*. Cambridge University Press, 2004.

Poovey, Mary. *The Proper Lady and the Woman Writer: Ideology as Style in the Works of Mary Wollstonecraft, Mary Shelley, and Jane Austen*. University of Chicago Press, 1984.

Rizzo, Betsy. *Companions Without Vows: Relationships among Eighteenth-Century British Women*. Athens: University of Georgia Press, 1994.

Ross, Marlon. *The Contours of Masculine Desire: Romanticism and the Rise of Women's Poetry*. Oxford University Press, 1989.

Schofield, Mary Anne, and Cecilia Macheski eds. *Fetter'd or Free? British Women Novelists, 1670–1815*. Athens and London: Ohio University Press, 1986.

Spacks, Patricia Meyer. *The Female Imagination*. New York: Knopf, 1975.

Spencer, Jane. *The Rise of the Woman Novelist*. Oxford: Basil Blackwell, 1986.

Staves, Susan. *Married Women's Separate Property in England, 1660–1833*. Cambridge, Massachusetts: Harvard University Press, 1990.

Taylor, Barbara. *Mary Wollstonecraft and the Feminist Imagination*. Cambridge University Press, 2003.

Todd, Janet. *The Sign of Angellica: Women, Writing and Fiction, 1660–1800*. New York: Columbia University Press, 1989.

Todd, Janet ed. *A Dictionary of British and American Women Writers, 1660–1800*. Totowa, New Jersey: Rowman and Allanheld, 1985.

*Dictionary of British Women Writers*. London: Routledge, 1989.

Wilson, Carol Shiner, and Joel Haeffner. *Re-Visioning Romanticism: British Women Writers, 1776–1837*. Philadelphia: University of Pennsylvania Press, 1994.

## Romantic fiction

Burgess, Miranda. *British Fiction and the Production of Social Order, 1740–1830*. Cambridge University Press, 2000.

Butler, Marilyn. *Jane Austen and the War of Ideas*. Oxford: Clarendon Press, 1975.

Copeland, Edward. *Women Writing about Money: Women's Fiction in England, 1790–1820*. Cambridge University Press, 1995.

Ferris, Ina. *The Romantic National Tale and the Question of Ireland*. Cambridge University Press, 2002.

Galperin William H. *The Historical Austen*. Philadelphia: University of Pennsylvania Press, 2003.

Garside, Peter. "The English Novel in the Romantic Era: Consolidation and Dispersal," in Garside *et al.*, *The English Novel 1770–1829*, 2000, vol. II, pp. 15–103.

Garside, Peter, James Raven and Rainer Schöwerling gen. eds., *The English Novel 1770–1829: A Bibliographical Survey of Prose Fiction Published in the British Isles*. 2 vols. Oxford University Press, 2000.

Greenfield, Susan. *Mothering Daughters: Novels and the Family Romance: Frances Burney to Jane Austen*. Detroit: Wayne State University Press, 2002.

Johnson, Claudia L. *Equivocal Beings: Politics, Gender, and Sentimentality in the 1790s: Wollstonecraft, Radcliffe, Burney, Austen*. University of Chicago Press, 1995.

*Jane Austen: Women, Politics, and the Novel*. University of Chicago Press, 1988.

Kelly, Gary. *English Fiction of the Romantic Period 1781–1830*. London and New York: Longman, 1989.

*The English Jacobin Novel 1780–1805*. Oxford: Clarendon Press, 1976.

Labbe, Jacqueline ed. *Charlotte Smith in British Romanticism*. London: Pickering & Chatto, 2008.

Markley, A. A. *Conversion and Reform in the British Novel in the 1790s.* New York: Palgrave, 2008.

Miller, D. A. *Jane Austen, or the Secret of Style.* Princeton University Press, 2003.

Newton, Judith. *Women, Power, and Subversion: Social Strategies in British Fiction 1778–1860.* Athens: University of Georgia Press, 1981.

Raven, James. "Historical Introduction: The Novel Comes of Age," in Garside *et al.*, *The English Novel 1770–1829,* 2000, vol. I, pp. 15–121.

Sedgwick, Eve Kosofsky. *The Coherence of Gothic Conventions.* London: Methuen, 1986.

Tomkins, J. M. S. *The Popular Novel in England, 1770–1800.* Lincoln: University of Nebraska Press, 1961.

Trumpener, Katie. *Bardic Nationalism: The Romantic Novel and the British Empire.* Princeton University Press, 1997.

Williams, Ioan ed. *Novel and Romance 1700–1800: A Documentary Record.* New York: Barnes and Noble, 1970.

Yeazell, Ruth Bernard. *Fictions of Modesty: Women and Courtship in the English Novel.* University of Chicago Press, 1984.

## Romantic poetry

Bate, Jonathan. *Shakespeare and the English Romantic Imagination.* Oxford: Clarendon Press, 1986.

Curran, Stuart. *Poetic Form and British Romanticism.* New York: Oxford University Press, 1986.

Harvey, A. D. *English Poetry in a Changing Society, 1780–1825.* London: Allison and Busby, 1980.

Jackson, J. R. de J. *Poetry of the Romantic Period.* London and Boston: Routledge and Kegan Paul, 1980.

Kucich, Greg. *Keats, Shelley and Romantic Spenserianism.* University Park: Pennsylvania State University Press, 1991.

Lipking, Lawrence. *The Ordering of the Arts in Eighteenth-Century England.* Princeton University Press, 1970.

Murphy, Peter. *Poetry as an Occupation and an Art in Britain, 1760–1830.* Cambridge University Press, 1993.

Rajan, Tilottama. *Dark Interpreter: The Discourse of Romanticism.* Ithaca: Cornell University Press, 1980.

Wittreich, Joseph. *Angel of Apocalypse: Blake's Idea of Milton.* Madison: University of Wisconsin Press, 1975.

Wolfson, Susan. *Formal Charges: The Shaping of Poetry in British Romanticism.* Stanford University Press, 1997.

## The culture of Romanticism

Altick, Richard. *The Shows of London.* Cambridge, Massachusetts: Harvard University Press, 1978.

Barrell, John. *The Dark Side of the Landscape: The Rural Poor in English Painting, 1730–1840.* Cambridge University Press, 1980.

Bindman, David. *The Shadow of the Guillotine: Britain and the French Revolution*. London: British Museum Publications, 1989.

Boime, Albert. *Art in an Age of Revolution 1750–1800*. University of Chicago Press, 1987.

Dobai, Johannes. *Die Kunstliteratur des Klassizismus und der Romantik in England*. Bern: Benteli, 1977, vol. III (1790–1840).

Eaves, Morris. *The Counter-Arts Conspiracy: Art and Industry in the Age of Blake*. Ithaca: Cornell University Press, 1992.

Heffernan, James A. W. *The Recreation of Landscape: A Study of Wordsworth, Coleridge, Constable, and Turner*. Hanover: University Press of New England, 1984.

   *Representing the French Revolution: Literature, Historiography, and Art*. Hanover: University Press of New England, 1992.

Kroeber, Karl. *British Romantic Art*. Berkeley, Los Angeles, London: University of California Press, 1986.

Kroeber, Karl, and William Walling eds. *Images of Romanticism: Verbal and Visual Affinities*. New Haven and London: Yale University Press, 1978.

Meisel, Martin. *Realizations: Narrative, Pictorial, and Theatrical Arts in Nineteenth-Century England*. Princeton University Press, 1983.

Paley, Morton D. *The Apocalyptic Sublime*. New Haven and London: Yale University Press, 1986.

   *Samuel Taylor Coleridge and the Fine Arts*. Oxford University Press, 2008.

Sha, Richard. *The Visual and Verbal Sketch in British Romanticism*. Philadelphia: University of Pennsylvania Press, 1998.

Wood, Gillen D'Arcy. *The Shock of the Real: Romanticism and Visual Culture, 1760–1860*. Houndsmills and New York: Palgrave, 2001.

Wood, Marcus. *Radical Satire and Print Culture, 1790–1822*. Oxford: Clarendon Press, 1994

# INDEX

# Cambridge Companions To ...

## AUTHORS

*Edward Albee* edited by Stephen J. Bottoms

*Margaret Atwood* edited by
Coral Ann Howells

*W. H. Auden* edited by Stan Smith

*Jane Austen* edited by Edward Copeland and
Juliet McMaster

*Beckett* edited by John Pilling

*Bede* edited by Scott DeGregorio

*Aphra Behn* edited by Derek Hughes and
Janet Todd

*Walter Benjamin* edited by David S. Ferris

*William Blake* edited by Morris Eaves

*Brecht* edited by Peter Thomson and
Glendyr Sacks (second edition)

*The Brontës* edited by Heather Glen

*Frances Burney* edited by Peter Sabor

*Byron* edited by Drummond Bone

*Albert Camus* edited by Edward J. Hughes

*Willa Cather* edited by Marilee Lindemann

*Cervantes* edited by Anthony J. Cascardi

*Chaucer* edited by Piero Boitani and
Jill Mann (second edition)

*Chekhov* edited by Vera Gottlieb and
Paul Allain

*Kate Chopin* edited by Janet Beer

*Caryl Churchill* edited by Elaine Aston and
Elin Diamond

*Coleridge* edited by Lucy Newlyn

*Wilkie Collins* edited by Jenny Bourne Taylor

*Joseph Conrad* edited by J. H. Stape

*Dante* edited by Rachel Jacoff
(second edition)

*Daniel Defoe* edited by John Richetti

*Don DeLillo* edited by John N. Duvall

*Charles Dickens* edited by John O. Jordan

*Emily Dickinson* edited by Wendy Martin

*John Donne* edited by Achsah Guibbory

*Dostoevskii* edited by W. J. Leatherbarrow

*Theodore Dreiser* edited by Leonard Cassuto
and Claire Virginia Eby

*John Dryden* edited by Steven N. Zwicker

*W. E. B. Du Bois* edited by Shamoon Zamir

*George Eliot* edited by George Levine

*T. S. Eliot* edited by A. David Moody

*Ralph Ellison* edited by Ross Posnock

*Ralph Waldo Emerson* edited by Joel Porte
and Saundra Morris

*William Faulkner* edited by
Philip M. Weinstein

*Henry Fielding* edited by Claude Rawson

*F. Scott Fitzgerald* edited by Ruth Prigozy

*Flaubert* edited by Timothy Unwin

*E. M. Forster* edited by David Bradshaw

*Benjamin Franklin* edited by Carla Mulford

*Brian Friel* edited by Anthony Roche

*Robert Frost* edited by Robert Faggen

*Elizabeth Gaskell* edited by Jill L. Matus

*Goethe* edited by Lesley Sharpe

*Günter Grass* edited by Stuart Taberner

*Thomas Hardy* edited by Dale Kramer

*David Hare* edited by Richard Boon

*Nathaniel Hawthorne* edited by
Richard Millington

*Seamus Heaney* edited by
Bernard O'Donoghue

*Ernest Hemingway* edited by
Scott Donaldson

*Homer* edited by Robert Fowler

*Horace* edited by Stephen Harrison

*Ibsen* edited by James McFarlane

*Henry James* edited by Jonathan Freedman

*Samuel Johnson* edited by Greg Clingham

*Ben Jonson* edited by Richard Harp and
Stanley Stewart

*James Joyce* edited by Derek Attridge
(second edition)

*Kafka* edited by Julian Preece

*Keats* edited by Susan J. Wolfson

*Lacan* edited by Jean-Michel Rabaté

*D. H. Lawrence* edited by Anne Fernihough

*Primo Levi* edited by Robert Gordon

*Lucretius* edited by Stuart Gillespie and
Philip Hardie

*David Mamet* edited by Christopher Bigsby

*Thomas Mann* edited by Ritchie Robertson

*Christopher Marlowe* edited by
Patrick Cheney

*Herman Melville* edited by Robert S. Levine

## TOPICS